"A tour de force of deep ethnography, nuanced reflexivity, and characteristic elegance. Alma Gottlieb has produced a sparkling text on an utterly neglected topic—the anthropology of infancy—that will challenge and change the way we think about culture and do ethnography."

CHARLES PIOT, *Duke University*

"*The Afterlife Is Where We Come From* is some of the finest anthropological work I have ever seen. The book is not just an analysis of Beng babyhood but a complete analysis of life as a Beng. Alma Gottlieb is able to tie together the slippery strands of ritual, ideology, daily practice, and expression to come up with a comprehensible look at Beng life. I found at times that I could not put this book down."

MEREDITH SMALL, *Cornell University*

"Welcome to the Beng world, where toddlers welcome strangers, and parents consult infants and diviners to better accommodate the desires and gifts that very young babies bring from their former lives in the afterworld. This delightful, insightful, and quite provocative book about very small people makes a very large contribution—an anthropology of infancy enables us to rethink nature and culture in new and important ways."

RAYNA RAPP, *New York University*

"This is a wonderful book—intelligent, clear, fascinating, humane, and often very moving. Any reader who cares about children will be caught up in the story of the Beng people and their babies. Like all the very best anthropology it makes us conscious simultaneously of the idiosyncrasies of our own techniques of child rearing and the universal human significance of the relations between babies and the people who take care of them. The book gives us a chance to discover and empathize with a very different, faraway world of mothers and babies, and at the same time makes us think about our own children in a new way."

ALISON GOPNIK, coauthor of *The Scientist in the Crib*

(continued on next page)

"*The Afterlife Is Where We Come From* is marvelously written. Gottlieb is able to contextualize Beng infancy in terms of specific issues arising out of the slender field of anthropology and infancy, while at the same time drawing attention to how infant research might proceed in the future. . . . Specialists in the study of infancy will find this book to be invaluable for its topical completeness and powerful methodology."

PHILLIP KILBRIDE, *Bryn Mawr College*

"With the publication of this astonishing book about reincarnation beliefs and infant development in West Africa, the study of the cultural psychology of childhood has come of age. . . . Read *The Afterlife Is Where We Come From* for an eye-opening interpretation of the local cultural meanings of developmental milestones, such as the transition from crawling to walking or the child's early articulation of intelligible speech. Read the book as a brilliant exposé of the dangers of presumptively universalizing culture-specific ideals for human development. Read it to deeply fathom why infant development is not, and perhaps ought not to be, the same wherever you go."

RICHARD SHWEDER, *University of Chicago*

The Afterlife Is Where We Come From

Alma Gottlieb

The Afterlife Is

Where We Come From

The Culture of Infancy
in West Africa

The
University
of Chicago
Press

*Chicago and
London*

Alma Gottlieb is professor of anthropology at the University of Illinois, Urbana-Champaign. She is author of *Under the Kapok Tree: Identity and Difference in Beng Thought* (1996) and coauthor of *Parallel Worlds: An Anthropologist and a Writer Encounter Africa* (1994, with Philip Graham), both published by the University of Chicago Press.

The University of Chicago Press, Chicago 60637
The University of Chicago Press, Ltd., London
© 2004 by Alma Gottlieb
All rights reserved. Published 2004
Printed in the United States of America

13 12 11 10 09 08   2 3 4

ISBN: 0-226-30501-5   (cloth)
ISBN: 0-226-30502-3   (paper)

Library of Congress Cataloging-in-Publication Data

Gottlieb, Alma.
    The afterlife is where we come from : the culture of infancy in West Africa / Alma Gottlieb.
        p.   cm.
    Includes bibliographical references and index.
    ISBN 0-226-30501-5 (cloth : alk. paper)—ISBN 0-226-30502-3 (pbk. : alk. paper)
    1. Beng (African people)—Social conditions. 2. Beng (African people)—Psychology. 3. Beng (African people)—Kinship. 4. Infants—Care—Côte d'Ivoire. 5. Infants—Côte d'Ivoire—Development. 6. Child rearing—Côte d'Ivoire. I. Title.

DT545.45.B45 G65 2004
306.874′089′9643—dc21

                                        2003011146

♾ The paper used in this publication meets the minimum requirements of the American National Standard for Information Sciences—Permanence of Paper for Printed Library Materials, ANSI Z39.48-1992.

For Philip, Nathaniel, and Hannah

A "natural" human being is . . . a contradiction in terms.

Robert Murphy, *The Body Silent*

CONTENTS

ix

Figures

Note: Color versions of the photographs here, as well as additional photographs, may be found at the Web site associated with this book, http://www.press.uchicago.edu/books/gottlieb.

Maps

One night while I was writing this book, my daughter Hannah, then nine months old, roused herself around midnight and stayed awake for two hours. She wasn't hungry, she didn't need a new diaper, she was too sleepy to play, she wasn't sick, and she clearly wanted to go back to sleep—yet every time she fell asleep in my husband's or my arms, she woke up a few minutes later, restless. Philip and I never did figure out what was in her mind or body that night that caused such anxiety in her exhausted parents. There are some mysteries that babies keep to themselves, forever leaving a question mark in those responsible for taking care of them. If attentive and loving parents are not always able to fathom the thoughts and desires of their own infants, with whom they often spend close to twenty-four hours a day, how can an outsider to the family—let alone an outsider to that family's society—expect to understand the feelings, experiences, musings of those small, preverbal people?

The act of imagining the perspective of any other human being—infant, child, or adult; Muslim, Catholic, or animist; female or male; gay or straight; queen or peasant—is always an exercise in hubris. Yet many people assume that with the right training and the right set of questions, we can find a means to achieve at least an intellectual understanding of, and perhaps even some emotional empathy for, another mode of living, another mode of perceiving, another mode of feeling. In that sense, the study of other people's lives is built not only on hubris but also on a fervent wish—the wish that such hubris is not entirely unjustified, that there will be some intellectual reward at the end of the scholarly day. At the same time, it must be acknowledged that at an existential level that wish is probably, at least in many cases, unrealizable.

In the early twenty-first century, the anthropological presumption of writing for an Other is under broad attack both within and beyond the discipline. Isn't the act of "imagining for" an Other—and a speechless Other at that—even more problematic? And yet it is just such an act of imagination that lies at the heart of cultural anthropology. Indeed, in an increasingly multicultural world with insistently heterogeneous populations banging up against one another, to refrain from trying to imagine the Other's perspective as proficiently, as engagingly as one can is a reckless and fearful proposition. To live in a world in which we have given up on the dream of understanding the motivations for behaviors, feelings, and opinions of other human beings or groups of human beings—whether each of those persons or groups comes from a different religious tradition, socioeconomic class, or language group from our own . . . or is our neighbor or child or spouse—this is a frightening thought. At an ideological level, such a world paves the way for war, with its assumption that the Other is epistemologically problematic and thus a legitimate candidate for annihilation.

Whatever else the underlying political and economic motivating factors, the major wars of the past century—the two world wars; the U.S. war in Vietnam; the Gulf War; the civil wars in Ireland, Cambodia, Rwanda, Somalia, Eastern Europe, and the Sudan; and the ongoing war in the Middle East—all have been premised on an intellectual assumption that another group of people lead lives of compromised legitimacy because of their Otherness. If anthropology has anything to offer the modern world, it is the insistence that the effort to understand the Other—any Other—is one worth making, even if that understanding can never be achieved with a level of completeness.

Like most cultural anthropologists, then, I affirm the fundamental humanness of my species-mates, and I crave an understanding of the ways of those humans that appear to be most different from my own. But how far can that argument, that craving, be pushed? I am the first to acknowledge that it was an act of presumption that brought me back to Bengland in the summer of 1993 to focus exclusively on a subject I had previously studied only intermittently—the lives of infants. That act of presumption suggested a wish and was motivated by a question; and of course that question led to many more, which led to many more.

From the time I began that project until I completed this manuscript, my major aim has been to challenge the assumption of an Everybaby that somehow exists outside of culture. Such an assumption implicitly underlies, for example, the two thousand or so parenting manuals now sold in bookstores and the myriad parenting advice columns dotting newspapers and magazines, so popular in many Western countries. In challenging the basic operating model behind the fact of such widely consumed folk models passing as neutral expertise, I hope to present an alternate model of a baby that is deeply constructed by culture.

Anthropologists have long promoted the notion that daily practices assumed by the members of one society to be natural may be surprisingly absent elsewhere, and that such practices, seemingly unnatural in the views of outsiders, make sense when viewed in the context of a variety of cultural factors whose meanings can be discerned only after systematic analysis of the local system of cultural logic. Some time ago, Clifford Geertz (1983) articulated this argument in relation to the notion of common sense, arguing that what is accepted as common sense is anything but common. Instead, common sense is a deeply culturally constructed artifice that is so convincingly structured as to appear transparent, self-evident. At one level, this book takes up that line of thinking, seeking to apply Geertz's insight to the seemingly commonsensical realm of infant care. Indeed, I interrogate a domain of human practice that perhaps more than any other exists in the realm of the routinely taken for granted even by anthropologists, accepted as somehow having a natural foundation beyond the reaches of culture. Yet as we will see in the chapters that follow, the everyday decisions that Beng mothers and other caretakers make concerning infants are anything but common when viewed from an outsider's perspective.

At another level, I hope in this work to further the general theoretical agenda outlined over a decade ago by Jerome Bruner, who urged psychologists to take seriously the "folk psychologies" that people in every society develop about how to behave and think in ways that appear to them normal and natural. In advocating that psychologists develop a healthy respect for and a desire to understand the meanings that people bring to their daily lives, Bruner was outlining an approach to "cultural psychology" that would aim "to put the psyche back into anthropology and culture back into psychology" (1990:351). In this book, I hope to bring such a perspective to the study of infants in one section of the West African rain forest.

As peasants do elsewhere, the Beng people of Côte d'Ivoire live double lives. Put crudely, they live lives of material poverty combined with spiritual and social wealth. An astonishing gap exists between the material deprivation that Beng people suffer in their moment-to-moment existence—an existence marked by a grueling work schedule for most people most of the year, fueled by an insufficient quantity of protein, vitamins, minerals, and often sheer calories—and their religion, which is rich enough for me to have written one previous book about it (Gottlieb 1996b) and coauthored a second one (Gottlieb and Graham 1994). As for their social ties, suffice it to say here that whenever we discussed the quality of daily life in the United States while in Bengland, my Beng friends always expressed sympathy for the level of loneliness that they perceived—often accurately—to characterize urban, postmodern lives. Here is an arena in which, for a change, African riches come out ahead of Western impoverishment.

The gulf between social and spiritual wealth and material poverty is difficult to reconcile. It threatens to leave an outsider alternating between envy and pity. Yet envy fosters a problematic essentialism hearkening back to a Rousseauian romanticizing model that is as unrealistic as any, while pity negates subjectivity and reduces creative humans to passive victims. In this work, I aim to steer clear of both these extremes by keeping firmly focused on the basic humanity of the subjects of this study. One of the ways I do this is by making comparisons from time to time between Beng infant-rearing practices and infant-rearing practices that are common in the United States. Such comparisons, of course, will remind the reader of the striking differences that mark contemporary North American and Beng child-rearing logics. By means of such stark comparisons, I argue that both systems are the result of cultural construction.

In these comparisons, I focus on a specific subgroup in the United States: those who consider themselves members of the middle class, who espouse at least a nominal connection to the Judeo-Christian heritage and are influenced (whether or not they articulate such an influence) by the major philosophical orientations of that religious tradition, and those whose ancestors hail predominantly from Europe. In my discussions throughout the book, I gloss this population as "middle-class Euro-Americans." Of course this group is itself heterogeneous, and particular subgroups and individual members of it undoubtedly diverge from the general trend I am outlining. Moreover, none of the three major defining criteria I have just listed is unproblematic or transparent. Socio-economic class is notoriously difficult to measure: crude economic parameters often conceal a great deal of cultural and other variation. The Judeo-Christian tradition is itself a rich and multistranded one, with sometimes notable divergences in beliefs and practices distinguishing denominations. And the European ancestry of Euro-Americans likewise conceals many significant differences in cultural practices, religious orientations, and historical experiences. Still, I am convinced that this not-fully-satisfying delineation of a cultural subgroup is nevertheless a heuristically useful one. Enough contemporary North Americans define their identities in relationship to all three of these factors that the subgroup exists at the level of self-reference as well as that of sociological observation.

In my comparative discussions, I have chosen to focus on this subgroup of North Americans in part because their child-rearing practices are documented more extensively than those of other subgroups in the United States. Moreover, their parenting strategies are at least discursively hegemonic: they dominate mass-media representations of family life in popular television, film, newspapers, and magazines, thereby often influencing the family structures and values of other subgroups. My own positioning as a native of this subculture gives me further access to relevant data—although I should note that in my own parenting practices, I frequently diverge from many of the values and practices I call middle-class Euro-American. As my case demonstrates, it is important to remember that some subgroups and individuals distance themselves from the general trends I will be outlining for middle-class Euro-Americans.

In the same way, some Beng mothers identify with particular infant-care practices I will be detailing more than others do. All Beng women would recognize these practices as normative, but depending both on personality and life history, on the one hand, and on their positioning vis-à-vis village and town and regarding the indigenous Beng religion and Islam or Christianity, on the other hand, the extent to which particular women actively embrace the specific parenting practices I document here is somewhat variable. I often discuss such variations in the text, inserting individual women's perspectives and perceptions whenever possible so as to deconstruct the generic category of "Beng mother" and allow multiple lives to illuminate, and sometimes complicate, my larger claims.

~

The title of this book speaks both respectfully and critically to a posthumous collection of essays by the noted psychoanalyst D. W. Winnicott, *Home Is Where We Start From* (1986), whose title was itself inspired by a line from T. S. Eliot's *Four Quartets.*

Summing up his life's work on infants, Winnicott laid out in clear terms his theoretical framework, in which he accorded mothers pride of place for forming the social and emotional template with which infants will grow up and with which they will live their lives as adults. It is an elegant work, and one that goes some distance toward making sense of life as lived in the middle-class, largely Euro-American nuclear families that constitute the common social building blocks of contemporary Western industrial societies. But Winnicott's framework, like all such constructions, is guilty of a certain amount of reductionism even in the cultural setting in which he applied it, let alone in other cultural settings where people have radically different understandings of the family and the cosmos. The Beng constitute one such setting, and my title offers a different vision of "where we start from." In this book, I endeavor to take a Beng infant's perspective and challenge the reader to imagine how life would be lived if each newborn were seen as emerging not from a womb or from an unproblematic "home," but from a culturally constructed space of prior history—in this case, an afterlife.

In the following pages, I examine a range of connections that discursively link Beng infants to the "other world." Beng infants' lives are not comprehensible without considering the role of the indigenous religion in shaping the minute-by-minute decisions caretakers make, and the actions they take, concerning the infants who are their charge. In focusing on infants' connections to the afterlife, I highlight, as Adeline Masquelier might term them, "imaginative categories of the cultural landscape" (Masquelier 2001:16) in order to understand the "processes of signification" that impart order and meaning to Beng life (Williams 1981:13).

In this book, I emphasize daily practices as well as cultural representations. In other words, I will focus both on the exotic and the mundane—and on their mutual engagement. In the language of theory, the conceptual framework I embrace aims to combine the insights of practice theory with the understandings of interpretive anthropology, all deployed with more than a sidelong glance from political economy. The work that follows explores the often vexing combination of local and global structures that interact to create meaning each time a Beng baby is born.

~

As I complete the writing of this book, the young nation of Côte d'Ivoire has tragically become embroiled in a civil war. Disturbing local reports indicate that Beng villagers are currently caught in the crossfire. The political fate of the Beng, along with that of their countrymates, is not yet clear; those of us who live outside the country but care deeply about its future log onto African news Web sites daily, searching for hopeful news.

Throughout my more than twenty-year engagement with the Beng, I have been awed by their capacity for religious tolerance. The extended coup attempt that began in September 2002 threatens to divide Muslims from Christians and animists in ways that the Beng previously have managed to resist. My fervent hope is that this increasing religious intolerance, which may be tapping into an increasingly globalized discourse of religious division, will continue to elude and repel the Beng. Concerning religious ecumenism as in so many other matters, the Beng have much to teach others.

ACKNOWLEDGMENTS

For many stimulating conversations over the years about the big issues—babies, parenting, human nature, culture, Africa—a hearty thanks to Liora Bresler, Jerome Bruner, Robbie Davis-Floyd, Judy DeLoache, Brenda Farnell, Gillian Feeley-Harnik, Pamela Feldman-Savelsberg, Philip Graham, Sharon Hutchinson, Harry Liebersohn, Jennifer Nourse, Charlie Piot, Carolyn Sargent, Dorothée Schneider, Paul Stoller, Charles Varela, and Paul Tiyambe Zeleza. Over the ten years I have spent working on this project, I have been blessed to receive provocative suggestions from many friends and colleagues, who have tried valiantly to nudge me along in certain directions after reading different portions of this manuscript. My enduring gratitude to Nancy Abelmann, Ann Anagnost, Edward Bruner, JoAnn D'Alisera, Judy DeLoache, Brenda Farnell, Robbie Davis-Floyd, Katherine Dettwyler, Shanshan Du, Deborah Durham, Eric Gable, Philip Graham, Sara Harkness, Dell Hymes, Alejandro Lugo, Michelle Johnson, Philip Kilbride, John McCall, Simon Ottenberg, Sarah Mangelsdorf, Jennifer Nourse, John Peel, Charlie Piot, Rayna Rapp, Denise Roth, Meredith Small, Carol Stack, Barbara Tedlock, Edith Turner, Thomas Weisner, Richard Werbner, Cindy Williams, and Stephen Wooten. A special thanks to Bertin Kouadio, to date my sole Beng reader, who continually offers his invaluable perspective.

During the long gestation of this book, I have also received inspired comments from distinguished colleagues and students attending my various talks. I am indebted both to the organizers for the invitations and to members of the audiences for their many stimulating questions and comments. If I have failed to take full advantage of all these comments, that is undoubtedly the result of my own stubbornness.

Researching this book has taken me into many intellectual fields. For help locating sources, heartfelt thanks to a host of superb detective-librarians worthy of Sherlock Holmes in several of my home university's many departmental libraries: Raeann Dossett, David Griffith, Andrea Johnson, Jenny Johnson, Al Kagan, Jo Kibbee, Priscilla McIntosh, Victoria Pifalo, Christopher J. Quinn, Sarah E. Reisinger, Mary Shultz, and Beth Woodard. For sharing relevant literature and expertise in their various fields, I am grateful to Scott Anderson, Renée Baillargeon, Clark Cunningham, Cindy Fischer, François Gasse, Janet Keller, Linda Klepinger, Steve Leigh, Tyrone Melvin, Daniel Picchietti, and Alex Winter-Nelson. For serving ably as research assistants at different stages, deep appreciation to Bertin Kouadio, Isidore Lobnibe, Steve Maas, and Nicole Tami.

More thanks still to Nathaniel Gottlieb-Graham, Brad Horn, and Barb McCall, computer whizzes extraordinaire, for saving me from many a computer nightmare of my own making; to Steve Holland for expert help with photos and maps; to F. K. Lehman and Nathaniel Gottlieb-Graham for expert help with tables and charts; to Sam Beshers for expert sleuthing with beetles; to Judy DeLoache for the most productive detour imaginable; to Monni Adams for extraordinarily faithful news updates from francophone Africa; to David Brent for patience and support for this manuscript; to Meg Cox for copyediting with style; to the Council for the Anthropology of Reproduction for existing; and to Tiehua Du, Beena Shankar, Josephine Yambi, and Paul Yang and his crew for help-with-style on the domestic front, freeing me from the classic women's tasks.

Segments of the preface appeared in different form in DeLoache and Gottlieb 2000. I first presented a portion of chapter 1 at the annual meeting of the American Anthropological Association in San Francisco in 1992; portions of the chapter were later published in different versions as Gottlieb 1995a and Gottlieb, Graham, and Gottlieb-Graham 1998. I presented earlier versions of chapter 2 as talks given to the departments of anthropology at Boston University, Cornell University, Northwestern University, and the University of Illinois at Urbana-Champaign and the Department of Women's Studies at the University of Alabama, as well as at the conference "Engaging Africa: A Symposium Exploring the Future of African Studies" at the Oregon Humanities Center of the University of Oregon in 2001 and at the annual meetings of the American Ethnological Society in Seattle in 1997 and the American Anthropological Association in Philadelphia in 1998; different versions of chapter 2 have appeared as Gottlieb 2000b, 2000c, and 2002b. Short portions of chapter 3 appeared in different form in Gottlieb 2000a.

Versions of chapter 4 were presented at the Twelfth Annual Satterthwaite Colloquium on African Religion and Ritual in Satterthwaite, U.K., in 1996 and the annual meeting of the African Studies Association in San Francisco in 1996, as well as at the departments of anthropology at Oxford University, Washington University, the University of Illinois at Urbana-Champaign, and the University of Washington, and at the Center for Advanced Study at the University of Illinois at Urbana-Champaign; a somewhat different version of chapter 4 appeared as Gottlieb 1998, and some material was published in very different form in Gottlieb 1995b, 2000a, and 2002a. Different versions of chapter 6 were presented at the joint Africanists Workshop/Human Development Workshop at the University of Chicago, and at the interdisciplinary Faculty Seminar on the Stranger and the brown bag series of the Center for African Studies, both at the University of Illinois at Urbana-Champaign. A version of chapter 9 was presented to the Department of Psychology at the University of Illinois at Urbana-Champaign. A short portion of chapter 10 was presented at the annual meetings of the African Studies Association in Chicago in 1998 and the American Ethnological Society in Toronto in 1998, as well as the Center for African Studies at the University of Illinois at Urbana-Champaign. A short portion of chapter 11 was presented at the annual meeting of the American Anthropological Association in New Orleans in 2002.

This book is based most directly on research I conducted in the summer of 1993. I express my enduring gratitude to the entities that supported that research: the National Endowment for the Humanities; the Wenner-Gren Foundation for Anthropological Research; and International Programs and Studies (which granted me a William and Flora Hewlett Faculty Award) and the Center for African Studies, both at the University of Illinois at Urbana-Champaign. My previous research among and writing about the Beng were supported by the Social Science Research Council, the American Association of University Women, the Woodrow Wilson Foundation (Women's Studies Program), and the United States Information Agency, to all of which I am grateful for having given me my start in all things African. The John Simon Guggenheim Memorial Foundation, the National Endowment for the Humanities, and the Center for Advanced Study at my university have provided the luxury of time off from teaching to research and write this book. To all three, I am more appreciative than I can say.

In the field, my greatest debt is to the many Beng babies and their caretakers—mothers, sisters, aunts, and others—who put up with my incessant questions with grace. For their enduring interest in this and other research in their villages, I owe a continuing debt, which I always strive in vain to repay, to my long-time Beng collaborators and friends, Amenan Véronique Akpoueh and Yacouba Kouadio Bah. During the summer of 1993, three other Beng assistants were of enormous help in this research: Bertin Kouakou Kouadio, Augustin Kouakou Yao and Dieudonné Kwame Kouassi. Other Beng friends who shared with me their wise understandings of Beng infant culture during the summer of 1993 include Kouakou Bah and the late Kouassi Kokora, as well as dozens of Beng women, young and old, whose struggles with motherhood in the face of grinding poverty I found humbling.

Finally, my immediate family continues to inspire me, each in inimitable

A NOTE ON PRONUNCIATION

Beng words are pronounced as they would be in English, with the following exceptions:

ε = short "e," as in b*e*t
ɔ = "aw," as in p*aw*
ŋ = "ng," as in ba*ng*
ʹ = high tone
ˋ = low tone
˜ = nasalized sound

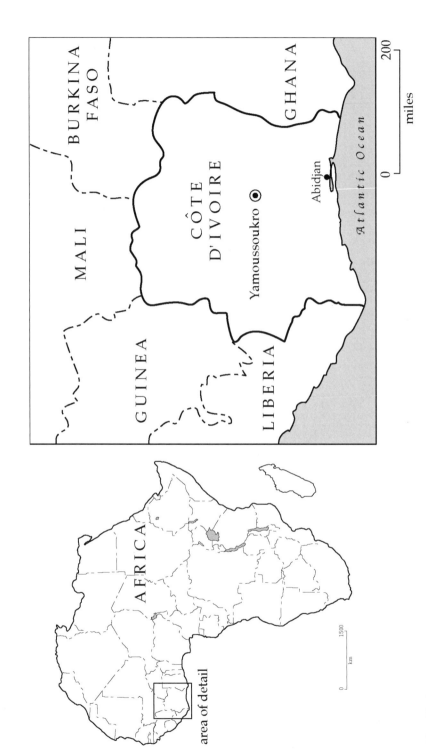

Côte d'Ivoire

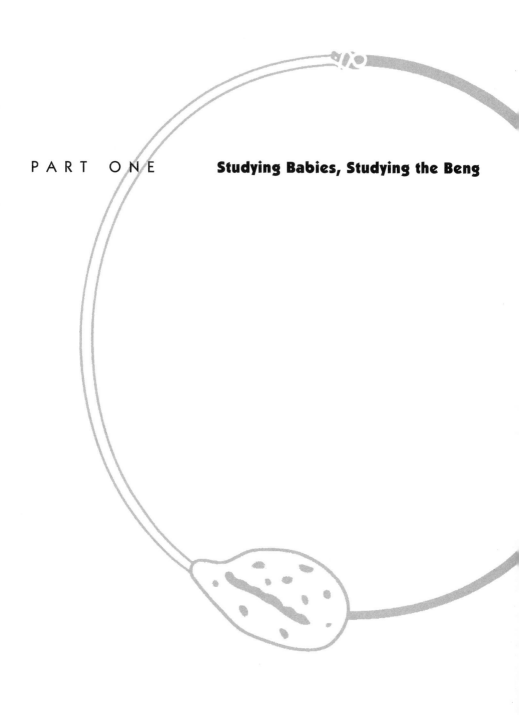

PART ONE   **Studying Babies, Studying the Beng**

CHAPTER ONE

Working with Infants

The Anthropologist as Fieldworker,
the Anthropologist as Mother

> There is no seeing from "nowhere in particular." . . .
> The agent of scholarship is a living person, not just a mind. . . .
> There is no way of understanding people except through one's
> own experience and power of imagination.
> KIRSTEN HASTRUP, "Anthropological Knowledge Incorporated"

Where should I best start a discussion of my fieldwork about, and with, Beng infants? Should it be by recounting the pleasures of my friendship with the delightful Sassandra, who was still nursing eagerly from his mother's breast when we began our relationship and was not quite nine months old when, to my great regret, I had to interrupt our camaraderie to return to another life? Or should I begin with tragedy, perhaps with the story of how I watched, and on occasion held, a dying Beng newborn as he stiffened his limbs and sharpened his screams with growing hysteria as tetanus overtook his tiny body? It would be humbling to inaugurate my discussion by relating how I begged the mother of a baby I was sure had meningitis to take the sick child down to the hospital, only to discover a few days later that the baby had recovered nicely with a treatment of far less costly herbal medicines acquired locally. Or should I begin more conventionally with the stories of the mothers of these babies, mothers who often confided their hopes and fears to me, a sometime stranger, sometime friend, sometime nurse, sometime baby-sitter, and always meddler? Perhaps I should choose the even more commonplace strategy of opening my tale by telling about training one of my research assistants to note each activity of a given baby as he followed a series of infants through their daily lives.

Every one of these constituted an important component of my experiences in the summer of 1993, when I devoted this segment of my ongoing work among the Beng community of Côte d'Ivoire, which began in 1979, to an intensive study of the lives of their babies. But none of them stands out as the single most important experience or definitive method. Most ethnographic fieldwork involves a multilayered tool kit and, equally importantly, a multilayered engagement with the emotions and textures of daily social encounters. This is perhaps even truer of work with infants because of the wiggly, unpredictable, and emotionally intense nature of the subjects. Our tiny informants have dramatic needs of their own; how we relate to them depends to a great extent on their momentary requirements. Holding them, treating their illnesses, listening to their babble and endeavoring to respond appropriately, playing with them, measuring their achievements, keeping track of their movements and moods, talking about them with those who know them best—all these can, and should, figure into how we approach infants' lives in a given hour. My approach to fieldwork with Beng babies was intentionally an intellectual and methodological grab bag. But the choices I made concerning how to pull together my particular grab bag began far earlier than the field experience itself.

In recent years, we have seen an epistemologically complex turn toward exploring various intersections between the personal and the professional. Beginning with a growing corpus of memoirs of the field experience, of which my own coauthored volume is but one of many, this trend permits us to recognize and try to account for the inextricable ways in which our so-called private lives conspire to shape our scholarly decisions and agendas—including the topics we choose to pursue, the field sites in which we come to feel at home, even the theoretical orientations we embrace.[1] In keeping with this scholarly move toward disclosure rather than concealment of how the work and nonwork aspects of our lives are mutually implicated—a move I heartily endorse—let me now acknowledge: I came to Beng babies through my own. Given the theoretical rationale for identifying such connections and the fact that so few anthropologists choose to focus their intellectual energies on infants, I start with a bit of autobiography so as to situate the current study of Beng babies in an ongoing life and career. Then I move on to enumerate my field methods.

The Anthropologist as Mother

As is the case with the vast majority of work in cultural anthropology, my previous field research among the Beng (conducted in 1979–1980 and 1985) overwhelmingly concerned the lives of adults (e.g., Gottlieb 1996b; Gottlieb and Graham 1994). Then, not long after my second field stay, I became a mother. The event changed my life—not just my family life but also my career. Being pregnant, undergoing childbirth, and embarking on the awesome project of raising a child raised for me countless questions, practical and emotional to be sure, but also intellectual. Entering this new stage of my own life cycle bestowed on me a double gift. Most important, of course, was the gift of a child. But along with that came a second gift, the gift of becoming an anthropologist of motherhood—and more generally, an anthropologist of parenthood, of caretaking, and of the object of all that affection and work, children themselves.

From the beginning, my first pregnancy and delivery were shaped decisively by what I had observed in Beng villages. Without romanticizing our Beng hosts, without ignoring the extraordinary hardships attendant on their grinding poverty, I still felt I had much to learn from many of their practices and the intellectual premises behind them. Having observed a regime of reproduction limned by contours radically different from those that surrounded me in the United States, it was easy to see the pregnancy and birthing practices of my countrymates as peculiar at best, and in some cases troubling.

For instance, while I was pregnant I became increasingly disturbed that in my native country adults, especially those who are not parents of young children, simply don't see children very often. I came to realize that although we lack the formal age grades for which many East African societies are known, American society segregates people by age quite systematically. Children typically inhabit different social spaces from those populated by adults. Moreover, youth are separated from each other by increments of merely a year beginning as early as one or two years old if they start at day care.

While pregnant, I began to notice small people in public places where I had previously overlooked them: restaurants, malls, waiting rooms. But their new visibility only confirmed what I'd already observed after our first return from Côte d'Ivoire: that even when older people and children occupy the same spaces in the United States, they rarely intermix. Instead, parents spend much public time disciplining their young sons and daughters to conform to adults' rules of politeness so they will be less conspicuous and will conform to the old Puritan adage, *Children should be seen and not heard.* "Don't shout!" "Don't run!" "Sit up straight!" were incantations I now heard regularly from exasperated mothers and fathers in civic spaces clearly never intended to accommodate the explosive energies and imaginations of children. Why were there no indoor playgrounds in shopping centers, post offices, airports, office buildings? I wondered. Why were children almost never invited to the workplace or to the adult parties we attended, whether gatherings with academic colleagues, artists' get-togethers, or fund-raising soirées for our favorite political candidates?

Pondering my upcoming delivery, I turned to my field notes. In Bengland I had encountered a set of childbirth practices that emphasized personal rather than technological connections.[2] My experiences attending and participating in Beng women's births constituted a reference point that shaped my subsequent consciousness of the event. With access to this alternative system of authoritative knowledge, as Brigitte Jordan (1997) would call it, the anthropologist in me was preshaping my perceptions of the moment when my own motherhood would come into being in a tangible way.

Having encountered home as the normal locale of birth in rural West Africa, I was tempted to follow the model of Beng village women and give birth to my child in my own house, and the more I considered the anthropological documentation of childbirth in other places, the more I thought there was much to recommend a home birth. I'd feel at ease in our bedroom and could assume any delivery position I found comfortable—maybe lean back into the comforting arms of a birthing companion as I'd seen my laboring Beng friend Amenan do. And I could avoid all those machines that measure a laboring woman's bodily events while ignoring her state of mind and heart (Davis-Floyd 1992; Jordan 1993). In short, I could relocate birth from a technological event defined by sickness and danger to an intensely emotional experience that might encompass anything from terror to joy.

Still, I was haunted by the story of my Beng friend Nguessan Kouakou. One day her husband came to fetch me while I was working in another village, imploring me to return immediately to drive Nguessan to the dispensary in town, almost an hour away, because she was having difficulty in her labor. Of course I agreed, and soon my husband, Philip, and I found ourselves racing down the gravelly road, Nguessan screaming her agony in the back seat. Perhaps the bumps in the road helped advance the baby down the birth canal, or perhaps the massaging that the midwife's assistant and I administered to Nguessan proved definitive. In any case, Nguessan delivered her baby soon after settling into the hospital bed. But the tiny infant emerged green and was not breathing. Only extraordinary efforts by the midwife's assistant revived the newborn.

At the time, I felt blessed to have been able to help in this event. But a few years later, Philip and I were devastated to learn that the little girl born after that fateful ride, frail ever since her traumatic birth, had died. Later, Nguessan herself, having no access to medical screening or transportation to town, died in another difficult labor.

Nguessan's tragedy warned me not to trivialize the dangers of childbirth. After reading up on further legal and practical complications of home births in the United States and the risks involved in transporting a laboring woman in distress to a hospital, Philip and I reluctantly decided to give birth in a hospital, while forging a commitment to recast the hospital's vision of birth to our own.[3] Having seen a very different system of birth in action in Bengland, we no longer accepted our culture's constructed knowledge as having a unique claim to authority. We hoped to convince the medical system operating in our local hospital to accommodate our model of birth.

When my labor began and I paced through our house and moaned loudly as the contractions intensified, I thought of my laboring Beng friend Amenan. Sitting on her dirt floor, leaning back slightly against her mother, legs outstretched, forehead sweating, she had said calmly to me in her fine French, *"Je souffre un peu"*—I'm suffering a little. Her stoicism shamed me. I thought too of Nguessan suffering in her bedroom; then of my friend Amenan's mother getting stuck in her labor for several hours before her sorcerer cousin, who had been bewitching her, was finally killed by a falling tree sent by an avenging Earth; then of Amenan herself almost dying during her delivery of her son Kouadio; and finally of Nguessan succumbing during her next delivery. Had my Beng friends ever lost hope, imagining they might never emerge from their ordeal? Or were they always confident that their bodies would cooperate, that the witches could be kept at bay, that a healthy baby would eventually be born?

The theme of my hospital stay became polite but firm rejection: No, I didn't want to be hooked up to machines, or take painkillers, or lie down in bed. My most serious resistance occurred when it was time to prepare for the delivery. The head nurse was adamant about resituating me in bed, but my midwife convinced another nurse to permit me to use the wooden birthing stool we had brought along. The head nurse panicked: it seemed the baby would be born onto the carpet, and what about all the germs? The idea was intolerable. I was too distracted to mention that during my Beng friend Amenan's delivery, not only was the baby born onto the floor, but it was a dirt floor at that.

~

After the birth, I craved company. Some of my friends called and said they would visit the next day or once we left the hospital or once we had "settled in." Depressed by these delayed offers, I thought back to my friend Amenan's birth. Only minutes after her tiny daughter had emerged into the world, Amenan was greeted by a line of dozens of villagers coming to congratulate her and give her small change as thanks for putting another child into the world (see chapter 6).

By contrast, on the assumption that fatal germs might threaten a new baby's life, my hospital displayed a sign that read "No Visitors while Baby in the Room." We had to make a choice: either we banish our child to the nursery or we quarantine ourselves from our close friends. After living among the Beng, I found this choice unacceptable. I had seen too many newborns, only minutes old, being passed from person to person to believe that healthy babies being held by healthy adults are endangered. We subverted the rule, finding hours when the nurses were too busy to notice our friends sneaking past the desk and creeping down the hall to our room.

Those who were already parents I bombarded with questions. In some I sensed impatience: surely my "mother's intuition" should tell me what to do when my new baby cried. But I had lived in Africa long enough to be convinced that even this sort of "common sense" is culturally constructed (Geertz 1983). The hundreds of parenting books lining bookstore shelves all seemed to dispense advice that was shaped by a cultural, not natural, script.[4] No, I did not put much stock in intuition when it came to raising our new child. Culture seemed to get in the way too much.

~

Our new son, Nathaniel, cried a lot. None of the advice offered by well-meaning nurses, doctors, friends, or neighbors helped. Struggling to manage the seemingly endless cascade of Nathaniel's tears, Philip and I cast about in our memories of Beng villages, crowded as they are with infants and young children. We wondered: Did Beng infants cry so much, and if so, what would a Beng mother do? Thinking back to the village life I knew, I imagined that a Beng mother of a crying baby might pack the infant onto her back to be carried around all day, tucked safely into a *pagne* cloth wrapped around her middle. Perhaps that was what Nathaniel wanted too. Philip and I decided to try it: we gathered tiny Nathaniel into a front pack and held him close to our chests. Immediately, he stopped bawling. As long as he stayed in there, he was content. And so it was that our new son virtually lived in his baby pack for the next three months. Beng mothers—at least those I was imagining from my removed position—had offered me good advice. As research by psychologists now confirms, most babies tend to be more content and to cry less the more they are carried.[5]

I suspected I had much more to learn from my old Beng neighbors and friends. During my previous field trips I had studied other aspects of Beng women's lives, especially their place and image in the indigenous Beng religion (Gottlieb 1988, 1990) and the level of autonomy available to them in their marriages (Gottlieb 1986a). Yet I was increasingly appalled to realize that I had largely neglected their lives as mothers. Undoubtedly my lack of direct experience on this front had crimped my ethnographic imagination, denying me meaningful questions to ask and precluding any understanding of which behaviors of Beng infants were problematic and which were normal in comparison to the behavior of infants in my own society. Moreover, for reasons I will enumerate in the next chapter, the discipline of anthropology had not encouraged me along these lines. After becoming a mother, I had come quickly to realize how overwhelming are the responsibilities of parent-hood even with one child, let alone six or more, as many women have throughout the "developing" world. Reflecting on this, I realized that I could not possibly begin to understand Beng women's lives without taking into account their experiences as mothers. At the same time, my initiation into motherhood opened up for me the universe of children's culture in my own society. Observing and participating in this world taught me many important lessons about my own community, while at the same time it suggested a vast new repertoire of issues to ponder concerning the world of Beng children. And so I began to imagine returning to Côte d'Ivoire to inaugurate a full-blown inquiry into Beng babies.

I combed my field notes to see what I had previously recorded about Beng childhood. With disappointment I realized that what scanty notes there were mostly catalogued rules, expectations, and beliefs, only rarely recording how actual people did or did not fulfill these. I began to fill dozens of index cards with questions that I had never thought to ask during my previous two trips. What is it like to be a Beng baby, painted twice a day with spectacular herbal paints and loaded down with beaded necklaces and waistbands to ward off diseases? How do infants develop their language? Do older people con-sciously try to teach them to speak, or do they just pick up the skills through listening to others talk? What do the games that adults and older siblings play with babies teach them about the world? Do Beng babies experience the stranger anxiety that so many middle-class, Euro-American babies exhibit toward the end of their first year? Do they develop the intense attachment to a single caretaker, usually a mother, that middle-class Euro-American ba-bies so often have? Does the Beng notion of reincarnation influence the way babies are treated? Do motor skills develop on the same schedule that they normatively do in middle-class, Euro-American infants?

With these and dozens of other questions that occurred to me daily as Philip and I changed Nathaniel's diapers (conjecturing how Beng mothers manage without them), tried to tempt a finicky Nathaniel to enjoy solid foods (wondering if Beng mothers had discovered tastier concoctions), and endeav-ored to train Nathaniel to fall asleep alone in his crib rather than attached to me or Philip in the front pack (speculating about whether Beng mothers ever bothered to teach their babies to achieve such independence), I formulated my next research project.

~

Meanwhile, our baby son grew from a colicky infant into a delightful young child. Soon after Nathaniel's sixth birthday, Philip and I decided that he was ready to be introduced to our African home.

Once in the village a scant week, Nathaniel plunged fearlessly into life in rural West Africa, finding social riches that he clearly thought more than made up for the technological lacks. In so doing, he taught me much about Beng society that had previously been invisible to me. In his own charming, child-like way, Nathaniel became my assistant (figure 1).[6]

From my earlier fieldwork, I had constructed an image of Beng society as thoroughly gerontocratic. Dan Sperber (1975) has wisely noted that in observing foreign cultures, anthropologists tend to be unconsciously drawn to that which is different from their own societies' practices, whereas they tend to gloss over, or even be unaware of, that which is similar. Accordingly, in Beng villages, I had doubtless paid attention to gerontocracy precisely be-cause the principle is so distinct from the way North American society is ar-ranged, with old people frequently cast aside like so much garbage, as a Tai-wanese graduate student had once put it after doing a depressing round of fieldwork in a nursing home in Champaign-Urbana (Hwei-Syin Lu, personal communication). At the same time, consistent with my focus on gerontoc-racy, during my previous field trips to Bengland I had ignored the existence of friendships across generations, as well as the respect that old people often pay children. Thanks to Nathaniel, I now began noticing regularly these pat-terns in Beng society that had previously been invisible to me.

It started when we remarked on all the attention the adults in our com-pound showered on Nathaniel. Initially I wrote that off to our son's status as the child of privileged parents—and, as I will discuss below, one accorded a locally venerable ancestral lineage at that. But soon I began noticing that many adults treated their own as well as others' children of all ages with a level of respect that I had not previously observed. They would quietly ask the children's opinions while seemingly issuing them orders. The single case of child abuse that I witnessed that summer was the subject of much continu-ing criticism by virtually all in the perpetrator's family.

Moreover, although Beng children display marked respect for their elders as long as they are near those elders, that summer I realized that I had not previously paid enough attention to how independent children are a good deal of the time. When they aren't required to work for their relatives, an obligation that varies quite a bit by season and labor schedule, they play in groups—sometimes small, sometimes large, often changing from moment to moment, and usually of mixed ages (figure 2). Even in a large village, the entire village is potentially children's play space. Indeed, during the day, Beng parents often have no idea where their children are, and unlike their Western, urbanized counterparts, they are not overly concerned on a minute-by-minute basis for their children's safety. I suggest that this is because the village,

1. Nathaniel joining in village life: catching a chicken for sacrifice. Photograph by Philip Graham.

2. Children of mixed ages often play together; these children range from about three to ten years old. Photograph by Philip Graham.

though by no means homogeneous or conflict-free, is nevertheless conceived as a moral community. Beng parents routinely assume that there will always be some adults, teenagers, or even other (barely) older boys and girls who can look out for their young children as they roam through the village.

After a few weeks back in Bengland, Philip and I found that we had adopted this assumption when we would realize to our amazement that we hadn't seen our own son in an hour or two. Nathaniel, who had previously been somewhat shy and clingy, quickly grew comfortable with the notion that the entire rather large village was his playground. Using impressive investigative skills, he devised a system to locate his parents when one or both of us had left the compound for an interview and, though he'd chosen to stay behind with his friends, he suddenly felt a need to see us. Like an accomplished !Kung hunter, he followed the distinctive tracks of our Eddie Bauer hiking boots on the dusty ground. Nathaniel and his friends soon turned this into a great detective game, romping through the village gleefully in search of those ground-level clues.

Being a good observer helped Nathaniel to remain confident that he could cope with unexpected developments. This is a skill I saw Beng parents value in their children. Not only do villagers take for granted that any adult, teenager, or older child will keep an eye on any young child within sight, they also assume that from the time children become competent walkers—usually between 1½ and 2½ years old—they are somewhat able to fend for themselves and to find their way back to their own compound (figure 3). Chantal, a feisty two-year-old in our compound, disappeared from sight many mornings only to emerge at noon for lunch and then again around 5:00 for dinner preparations. Though too young to report on her day's travels, others would chronicle them for us: she regularly roved to the farthest ends of this very large village and even deep into the forest to join her older siblings and cousins working and playing in the fields. With such early independence even toddlers are expected to be alert to dangerous wildlife such as snakes and scorpions, and they should be able to deal with them effectively—including locating and wielding a large machete. Toward the end of our stay that summer we realized how acclimated our own son had become to local habits and dangers when we saw little Nathaniel hacking away at unwanted grass in our compound with an adult's machete, almost as long as he was tall, that he had casually commandeered.

The independence of these Beng children diverged dramatically from that of the Euro-American middle-class children I had come to know firsthand through my own parenthood, subject as they were to constant parental worry. It echoed a pattern I was finding elaborated in my work with babies that

3. A girl of about 1½ years and her older brother, about four years old, walking across the village to buy fried snacks for themselves; their father is the diviner Kouakou Bah.

summer: Beng adults conceive of infants as people with their own sense of desire and their own memories. What middle-class Euro-American parents might term colic is perceived by Beng parents as a sign that the infant wants something. All relatives and neighbors therefore pay quite a lot of attention to even the youngest of babies, asking them directly what ails them when they fuss and imputing to them motives and wishes that Westerners would likely think could not be present in such small people.

I came to pay special attention to this aspect of interactions between infants and adults after observing the respect that adults accord older children—something I first noticed because of Nathaniel—and this new understanding of the Beng model of infant volition and desire shaped my fieldwork directly. In this way, and apart from his own conscious efforts to help me, Nathaniel became an inadvertent field assistant simply by his presence, pointing me to subtle timbres in relationships that challenged the monolithic conception of power relations that, I realized, I had previously held of Beng society.

Nathaniel also alerted me, if indirectly, to another layer of complexity in Beng society. My new understanding began along a most unlikely path of discovery. Shortly before we had left the United States, Nathaniel had become an enthusiastic whistler using an intriguing curled-tongue/through-the-teeth technique that he had invented; the result was a sharp blast that was far louder and shriller than an ordinary trill. Delighting in his new ability, Nathaniel had taken to whistling gaily whenever he was outdoors, engaging in a musical dialogue with any birds that might be perched in nearby trees.

I worried about the poor timing of Nathaniel's accomplishment. From my previous stays in West Africa, I knew that it is taboo for people to whistle while they are in a Beng village. Beng adults had explained this by reminding me that the *alufyɛ* spirits who are said to live in the forest communicate with one another by whistling. From this I inferred that if someone were to whistle in the village, it might create alarm that the *alufyɛ* spirits, who ought to remain in the forest, were now in the village, and this might well cause a dangerous panic. I knew that because the separation between people-in-the-village and spirits-in-the-forest is so basic to the Beng world, the punishment for violating the whistling taboo was a serious one.[7] Before leaving for the field, I dug out my field notes to refresh my memory and was horrified to read my record of a conversation with our friend Yacouba: "Anyone who whistles in the village will be punished as follows: an elder heats a raw egg on the fire until it is hot (though not cooked). He then shoves the whole egg up the person's rectum until it reaches his stomach. With this punishment, 'He'll never shit again. His intestines will rot by the next day.' If something drastic isn't done, he'll die." Before entering Bengland, Philip and I had warned Nathaniel that he might have to give up whistling for the next three months. His face fell. How could a six-year-old fully restrain his youthful exuberance?

When we arrived in Asagbe, one of the first questions I asked my friend Amenan was what the consequences would be if Nathaniel, with his childish energy, were to violate the whistling taboo. Happily Amenan reassured me that Beng adults do not deem it problematic for children to whistle in the village since "children don't know anything"—the taboo just applies to adults. Of course, I was relieved. At the same time, I was bothered by my friend's statement. The worldview behind the assertion that "children don't know anything" offended my own middle-class approach to child-rearing, which assumes that children craft a sophisticated knowledge base and that this is something to which good parents ought to pay attention.

Still, I reminded myself that I was in Bengland not to challenge but to learn. So I took note of the statement and tried to pursue its implications. To my surprise, these were far from consistent. As I will show in chapter 4, the very youngest of children—newborns—are attributed a tremendous degree of both personhood and knowledge by Beng adults and are seen as far indeed from Amenan's characterization that children "don't know anything." But as infants mature, the knowledge with which they come to this world from their previous existence in the "other world" is gradually stripped from them. They progressively become something approximating a tabula rasa, rather than starting out as one, as some Western folk models of childhood development and socialization suggest. It was Nathaniel's casual whistling that first clued me in to the complexities embodied in the composite relation to knowledge that Beng children are understood to occupy at different points in their childhood.

Methods

While motherhood partly shaped my field experience that summer, so too did scholarly theory. For reasons I will discuss in chapter 2, I was eager to devise ways to view and study infants as agents.

Formal Methods

One way to appreciate the texture of infants' lives and the fullness of their being is to construct broad biographies of a few babies. Here I was inspired by work by psychologists and psychoanalysts, from Shinn 1985 to Stern 1990, that focuses extensively on individual babies so as to avoid lumping infants together as an anonymous group, instead acknowledging their individual personhood. I did not intend to go so far as to construct a universalistic theory on the basis of intense observations of a few children, as Piaget did through observing his own children. Still, I was convinced that understanding the particular contours of a small number of infants would allow me to account for individuality and would complement my identification of broader norms and patterns.

To that end, in 1993 I followed around two babies—one boy and one girl—rather intensely much of the day, from early morning through evening, most every day. Sassandra was the infant grandson of our host Amenan. An early riser, Sassandra was often the first person I saw when I awoke in the morning, and I spent much of my day with him as well as his grandmother and I often took turns caring for him. Nathaniel joined in this pleasant task, taking on his first job of baby-sitting and developing his first baby friend (figure 4). (Two years later, it was in good part thanks to this friendship with baby Sassandra that Nathaniel would say he was able to instantly bond with his new baby sister, Hannah.)

That summer, an older baby claimed almost as much of my attention. This was Hallelujah, the year-old daughter of my assistant Dieudonné, who lived just next door to our courtyard. The families of the two babies were related matrilaterally, and there was constant coming and going between the two spaces, which in many ways seemed more like a single dispersed compound. Hallelujah, an early walker, navigated back and forth to peek at the ingredients first of one mortar in which enticing pounding was going on in one courtyard, then at those of another in the other courtyard, then back again. Most days, I spent several hours chatting, playing with, and observing Hallelujah. I also followed the lives of several other babies a bit less regularly.

In chronicling these babies' lives, one of my goals, as I will discuss at a more theoretical level in chapter 2, was to treat and view the babies as agents. If I had a sense of the personality of a given infant, I reasoned—of her daily habits and how these might be disrupted by unusual occurrences, of the events and interactions that frustrated her and those that delighted her—it would be easier for me to deploy that attractive notion of agency than if I merely confined my observations to abstract behaviors divorced from a given baby's personhood.

~

To complement my observations of infants, I conducted hundreds of interviews with mothers and other caretakers of infants. To help me make sense

4. Nathaniel playing
with baby Sassandra

of the information I was gathering through these many conversations, I relied in part on methods that Victor Turner (1973) enunciated long ago for the decoding of symbolic phenomena: exploration of informants' own "exegeses," identification of the "operational" meanings of symbols in particular ritual and social contexts, and provisional establishment of a model or grammar of "positional" meanings of such symbols in a wide variety of social contexts.

Although I began by directing these interviews fairly actively, I often relinquished control of the conversations' direction to my interlocutors. In telling about their relations with their children or young charges, people often spoke out of sequence, inserting tangents and asides that appeared irrelevant at the time but later proved revelatory. Sometimes I held a conversation with a single woman; other conversations were held with small groups that, more often than not, formed spontaneously—constituting something less formal than a prearranged focus group (Morgan 1988) but more directed than a random conversational grouping. Chatting with me and with one another about babies and the pleasures and challenges of raising them proved an agreeable diversion for many women and young girls while they shelled peanuts, hulled rice, washed laundry, pounded yams or corn, and nursed and played with their babies (or infant charges).

I also conducted many formal interviews and informal conversations with another group of adults who took a serious professional interest in infants: diviners. These specialists claim to understand the speech and desires of babies in ways that other Beng adults, even parents, cannot. Thus it was especially important to document their perspectives on Beng infants. To complement these interviews, I attended many divination sessions to which parents had brought their sick or crying babies for a diagnosis. Sometimes I just watched quietly; other times I chatted afterward with the parents or the diviner about the problem and the proffered solution. With one diviner in particular, Kouakou Bah, I formed a special friendship. A gentle, soft-spoken young man who commands a quiet authority, Kouakou Bah clearly fits the category "native philosopher" that Paul Radin long ago identified (1957). Reflectively inclined by nature, Kouakou Bah enjoyed the many long hours we talked about the nature of life and death, the invisible world of spirits, and the place of human infants in all these (figure 5).

At many of these interviews, I was accompanied by my host and fictive sister Amenan Véronique Akpoueh, my long-time friend and assistant and a bottomless fount of local wisdom (figure 6). Speaking mostly in Beng but sometimes in French, I took notes during all these conversations with mothers, baby-sitters, and diviners. I taped most of them as well. Two

5. The young diviner Kouakou Bah with his toddler daughter

6. Research team from summer 1993. *Back row (left to right):* Bertin, Augustin, Alma, Yacouba. *Middle row:* Amenan. *Front row:* Dieudonné. Photograph by Philip Graham.

Beng assistants, Bertin Kouakou Kouadio and Augustin Kouakou Yao, later worked at transcribing the taped interviews and translating them into French.[8]

Seated at a handmade wooden table on chairs that we'd commissioned from local carpenters, the two young men, sporting their impeccably ironed city clothes and crisp leather shoes, cut striking figures under a lush mango tree where they located their outdoor office. On occasion curious children would convince Bertin and Augustin to relinquish their earphones and share the infant babble that I often taped and, to everyone's great amusement, asked my assistants to transcribe. On these occasions, the onlookers made every effort to locate the baby who was chattering on the tape and would place the headphones on the tiny head so the infant might listen to her own babbling. Older children and adults alike took great pleasure in this activity and endeavored to make out Beng words mumbled in the chatter. *"Mye jɔɔlo, mye jɔɔlo!"* they exclaimed in excitement to the sometimes intrigued, sometimes perplexed infant—"That's you talking, that's you talking!" From such encounters I learned much about how seriously Beng adults take the vocalizations of infants, classifying them as legitimate speech.

~

In attempting to view babies as agents, I also borrowed a page from psychologists who specialize in child development, most of whom offer a model of subtle interaction between infants and others that is quite different from the tabula rasa model many cultural anthropologists seem to hold, if only unconsciously. From the developmental psychologists I learned to adapt sampling procedures that social scientists, including anthropologists and economists, had already developed for adults to the needs of infants. I chose to sample continuous portions of time—a method called continuous sampling, focal sampling, event sampling, or actual sampling—rather than sampling predetermined intervals of time as some researchers prefer to do. Continuous sampling represents far more accurately the duration of behaviors as they occur in people's daily experiences—especially the short-lived behaviors that characterize infants' lives and their relations to others (Mann, Have, Plunkett, and Meisels 1991). Thus I developed a continuous sampling chart that allowed me to keep track of a series of meaningful activities and emotional states of a given baby minute by minute, usually for 2¼ hours at a time. I recorded my observations on a grid.[9]

As I honed the chart to make it more nuanced, adding and subtracting behaviors to observe as they appeared more or less relevant to the lives of the infants around me, I also engaged a young Beng man in the village, Dieudonné Kwame Kouassi—father of our baby neighbor, Hallelujah—to supplement my observations and fill in the charts. Happily, his gender was not an obstacle to working with women. To the contrary, Dieudonné was widely admired by village women for being an unusually dedicated father of a year-old daughter, frequently carrying Hallelujah on his back, dressing her, and doing other caretaking activities with which Beng fathers of young children rarely occupy themselves (figures 7 and 8). Having been to school through the junior high school level, Dieudonné also had the literacy skills that the project required. His easygoing personality, gentle sense of humor, and ability to adapt to changing circumstances were valuable assets in undertaking the work I planned for him. And Dieudonné had his own ambitions: from his salary gained through our work together, he planned to start a village-based business to better support his growing family.

The very process of hiring Dieudonné proved the occasion for fieldwork.

7. Dieudonné observing a group of three babies playing; he records their movements on activity charts.

8. Dieudonné carrying his daughter, Hallelujah, on his back. Photograph by Philip Graham.

On our first day together I explained the goal of the infant time charts. One of the factors I especially wanted to observe was how many times in a given time period Beng infants are passed from one person to another. I explained to Dieudonné that I had informally noticed that Beng infants seem to be passed around quite a lot—far more than occurs in my own country, I told him, where in many middle-class families either a mother or a single baby-sitter takes care of a baby all day long. I wanted to use the time-sampling charts to determine, among other things, whether my informal impressions about Beng babies' multiple caretakers could be verified quantitatively.

My observations of Beng habits made sense to Dieudonné, but he was shocked when I compared them with the American custom of confining an infant to the care of a single individual. Indeed, it seemed impossible for him to imagine: once I mentioned it, he kept asking me every so often if I had been joking! To underscore how unlikely this model of child care would be in a Beng village, Dieudonné mentioned that his year-old daughter Hallelujah had recently gone off with a variety of people in the village for a full day, and he had remained totally ignorant of her whereabouts until six o'clock in the evening. Although that was an extreme example of the sort of pattern I'd remarked on informally, I came to see it as consistent with the general tendency for infants to lead active social lives—something the time charts Dieudonné and I recorded came to document quite persuasively (see chapter 6).

I also tried to take systematic note of motor development that summer. In the year preceding my research, I had studied the norms for motor development in middle-class, North American infants. Now I was curious to compare these with the development of Beng infants. To do so, I recorded the ages at which Beng infants were first able to sit up alone, to crawl, and to walk, taking notice of illnesses that might have delayed the onset of these skills. Some significant differences from Western norms echoed an earlier child development literature on "African precocity," while other differences diverged from that model. In every case, I tried to understand the development of motor skills as an achievement with cultural and not just biological implications (see chapter 9).

Observing the various activities, moods, and developmental stages of infants allowed me to gain some sense of their daily lives. But was it possible to communicate meaningfully with these tiny people in any way that an anthropologist would find respectable and reportable? I had spent years intensively studying the Beng language, and had even produced a dictionary (Gottlieb and Murphy 1995), so I would be able to converse in the language of the group whose lives and ideas I wanted to make sense of. Now my notion of a conversation clearly had to expand in order to accommodate the attempts at communication in which infants specialize.

One way in which I tried to learn directly the perspectives of the babies was to study what proved to be, in effect, the dialect of Beng infants, which was conducted in a register far different from the one on which I had previously concentrated. This time, the dialect was that of adornment. By focusing on the visual appearance of babies, I learned to read the "text" that was constituted by infants' necklaces, bracelets, anklets, and facial paint. When I studied the decorations bedecking a particular baby, I could discern quickly whether that small person had been to a diviner multiple times because of frequent crying or sickness that had been attributed to a troublesome memory from a previous life, and I could estimate the extent to which the baby's mother was dedicated to alleviating or financially able to alleviate her infant's current emotional and medical miseries. As we will see in chapter 4, Beng babies are said by adults to lead extraordinarily complex and deep emotional lives—lives drenched in the construction and suffering caused by memory. Identifying babies' bodily embellishments as the visual locus of these memories made an understanding of the mental and affective processes attributed to them by adults surprisingly accessible.

Of course, these understandings were mediated by the perceptions of adults, so the infants' adornments did not constitute data directly revealing the perceptions of the infants themselves. Yet this gap is true of adults as well, if in subtler ways. Personhood is always a cultural construction, most cultural anthropologists are now willing to acknowledge, a multiply mediated fabrication. Identity constitutes what others attribute to us as much as what we attribute to ourselves. Perhaps infants are not nearly as different from adults in this regard as we might think—though with them this phenomenon is far more obvious.

Finally, I also used visual methods quite extensively that summer. Over the course of three months, I shot dozens of rolls of film and filled four videocassettes. Through these images I tried to document the bodies of babies in their various guises, as well as the babies' moods and states.

Informal Methods

My research methods during summer 1993 included more informal and spontaneous strategies as well. Babies are insistently somatic creatures. It is impossible to establish any meaningful relationship with them, any understanding of their being, without seriously taking into account their bodily orientation to the world and without engaging that bodily presence directly. Thus, working ethnographically with infants means holding infants. During much of that summer, while I was talking about babies with adults I was also balancing a small child on one thigh and my notebook on the other. Indeed, of the seven hundred or so hours I passed with Beng infants over the summer, a large proportion were spent holding babies—which meant that I was the object of assorted leaks on a somewhat continual basis. Sometimes while I was holding infants I was also moving: I carried babies with me to and from the fields, walking on a narrow path behind a mother or baby-sitter, who was then freed to carry her machete and hoe or logs that she'd just chopped down or crops that she'd just harvested or water that she'd just pumped. I never got very good at the local style of carrying infants on my back in a *pagne* sling, but I did hold them Western style—over my shoulder or on my lap (figure 9)—and I had my share of getting peed on.

The classic ethnographic tactic of informal "hanging out" sometimes brought revelations; at other times it just helped me to fit in, to establish

9. Alma holding a sleeping baby on her lap while talking with the baby's mother. Photograph by Philip Graham.

myself as a decent fellow human person—a *son*—worthy of a conversation. My offers of baby-sitting/baby-holding/baby-carrying services were always appreciated by overworked mothers, who sometimes had to look after their infants while they were cooking, washing laundry, bathing, washing dishes, farming, chopping wood, heating water, and processing crops. This was especially the case for the two babies I followed extensively, Sassandra and Hallelujah, whose mothers otherwise depended on older siblings and cousins as baby-sitters every evening from around six to seven o'clock, when they needed to cook dinner. The classic hour of whining and whimpering for many families with babies the world over often proved a delightful time for me to join in my two favorite babies' developing babbled conversations, to watch the games that their older siblings and cousins played with them, or to carry them around while observing the intriguing activities of the many people starting to congregate in the two adjoining courtyards, which were filling rapidly with noise and energy.

The Anthropologist as Nurse

In addition to using anthropological methods, both formal and informal, for encountering infants in the context of guided research, I had many encounters with babies and their caretakers, especially their mothers, through a daily nursing clinic Philip and I offered. During our previous stays among the Beng, Philip and I had always sought to repay the hospitality and generosity of our hosts in ways we judged feasible and they found appropriate. In recent years, many cultural anthropologists have argued that we no longer have the luxury of remaining on the political and ethical sidelines of our field sites, especially when those sites are located in cultural spaces of dramatic economic and power inequities (e.g., Scheper-Hughes 1995)—all of which is too true of Beng villages. Anthropologists who subscribe to this position must search for appropriate means in a given cultural setting to becoming advocates, consultants, *compañeros*. In Beng villages, meeting people's medical needs and demands has always turned out to be the most compelling arena in which we can provide immediate, daily assistance.

The nearest dispensary to Bengland with minimally acceptable supplies and services is in the town of M'Bahiakro—a mere twenty-five miles or so away by road, but a world away in both culture and economy. As elsewhere in the non-Western world, because of the prohibitive cost of medicines and rural transportation, a problem sometimes compounded by cultural conservatism, sick people living in Beng villages rarely travel to town to visit the dispensary. When they do, tragically, it is often too late. Recently the government constructed a dispensary in one of the Beng villages. However, by all accounts it does not have much to offer. At best, nurses but no doctors are available, and only basic services and medicines are offered. This dispensary was closed entirely for the full three months of our 1993 stay.

Whenever we live among the Beng, then, Philip and I serve as best we can as village nurses. We spend a large proportion of my grant funds on such supplies as bandages, antibiotic creams and washes, malaria medicine, aspirin, and vitamins, and we offer basic nursing services daily (Gottlieb and Graham 1994). In 1993, this assistance was sought more frequently by more villagers than it had been during our previous stays. The reason was mostly economic. In the years just before 1993 a complex mix of international economic factors had caused Beng villagers to become both increasingly impoverished and increasingly ill (see chapter 11). That summer, day after day, mothers brought their sick children to Philip and me, hoping we would have the proper medicine to cure them. As they described the symptoms to us, we conversed. While Philip and I administered Baby Tylenol, a mother would explain that she had tried this and that herbal wash but that the child's fever had continued to rise.

As I examined a lump under the neck of one baby, my friend Amenan remarked, "He's sick too much—let's throw him away!" I looked askance at my friend—how could she be so callous? Then I did some quick genealogical calculations and realized that Amenan was the baby's mother's father's sister's daughter—a relationship that Beng kinship terminology classifies as that of a cross-cousin.[10] Among the Beng, all cross-cousins stand in joking relationships with one another. It was natural that Amenan should tease, mock, or insult the baby, sick as he was. And so it went.

But there were costs involved in running our nursing clinic. We now know that ethnographic fieldwork is far from a neutral activity conducted by an invisible observer working behind a one-way observing glass. Every role one plays during fieldwork makes friends of some and enemies of others. In our case, even dispensing Western medicines, while seemingly a benevolent act, had its drawbacks.

Most obviously, the medicines drew boundaries between the Beng and ourselves even as they attracted our neighbors to us—for the attraction was based on difference. We had access to a scarce resource—and the system of knowledge that produced it—a resource to which the Beng lacked, but desired, access. In that sense, each request for our medical services or supplies was also an acknowledgment of our strangeness. Our outsider status was itself built on differences of class constructed by accidents of history and biography that made all the difference. Moreover, as Marcel Mauss (1990) might put it, any act of charity is at once the bestowal of a gift and the creation of a debt that is never repayable. The asymmetry inherent in such relations becomes painfully marked at the moment of such exchanges.

Aside from the world economy and north/south inequalities undergirding such broader issues, consider the asymmetry from the perspective of the most powerless of our victims: the infant patients. One day, for example, our neighbor and otherwise friend year-old Hallelujah was brought to me by her mother, who sought medicine for a minor illness. I complied, but Hallelujah hated the syrup I offered, and she made every effort to spit it out. On her mother's urging, I restrained the baby while Hallelujah did battle with impressive energy. For several days afterwards, Hallelujah remained part furious with me, part terrified of me. On one occasion before she decided to forgive me, she ran to cling to her mother's long, wrap-around *pagne* skirt as soon as she saw me bring out my video camera—an object that had previously tickled her fancy. An older cousin, Esi, was amused by Hallelujah's fear. She teased her, calling her an *alufye* spirit. When I asked Esi about the connection, she explained that Hallelujah was short like such a spirit. But I doubted that Hallelujah appreciated the subtleties of the analogy. Instead, she prolonged her retreat into her mother's *pagne*.

Rapport with babies, I was discovering, is a fragile thing. After my betrayal of Hallelujah, when mothers brought their sick children to the nursing clinic, I asked them to administer dreaded syrups and other loathsome treatments to their children themselves, or, taking advantage of my husband's good nature, I asked Philip to take on the task. If I was to be the purveyor of the children's torture, at least the instruments of that torture didn't need to come from my own hands.

Not surprisingly, the nursing aspect of my field identity generally was appreciated more by adults than by infants and young children. Still, although adults were grateful, we were painfully aware that we could help only some individuals and not others, and that we certainly could not help the village as a whole. Our efforts, however well meant, were of the most transitory sort—quasi-ritualized encounters "for the nonce," as Barbara Myerhoff might have said (1992:131–33). Soon after we departed, whatever medical supplies we left behind would run out, and rural Beng people would have as little access to Western biomedical care as before we had arrived.[11]

The Anthropologist as Human

Fieldwork is a sometimes exhilarating, often perplexing, and always peculiar combination of head and heart. In many fieldwork projects, the heart component is evident enough to the researcher at the time of the research but becomes easily submerged in the writing that later chronicles the experience. One understandable reason for such a submersion is that the ostensible subject of the research is far enough removed from the heart part of the field-work that it seems distracting to discuss that part. That is not the case for this project.

Children, more than adults, live a life of the heart. Often the younger the child, the more this is the case. Of course, there are cognitive events that even the youngest of children are constantly mastering, but those events often take second seat to emotions.[12] We adults live emotionally rich lives as well, but most of us are better at concealing this aspect of ourselves for all but those with whom we are most intimate. Scholars are especially adept at this move, being meticulously trained into the tendency in graduate school. By contrast, children tend to be far less consciously aware of the adults' in-clination to conceal emotions, and they tend to express their emotions far more easily. Again, the younger the child, the more this tends to be true (figure 10).

The babies I worked with in Beng villages expressed their emotions readily, and my family found them irresistible. Indeed, because we were work-ing with infants, perhaps it was inevitable that there would be more than the usual moments of joy. Most groups take delight in their babies in one way or another, even if they become strict as the children start to grow older (e.g., Delaney 2000; Reese 2000). Proud parents often revel in showing off their babies even in a society such as that of the Beng, where direct compliments to a baby are considered dangerous to the infant's well-being (see chapter 10). There are moments when parental pride overtakes cultural taboo.

One day, for example, Dieudonné merrily wrapped a woman's scarf around his daughter Hallelujah's small head. As playful as her husband, Dieu-donné's wife immediately joined in and showed her husband how to tie the scarf in the style of an adult woman's turban. The image of baby Hallelujah sporting a grown woman's turban was so adorable, I immediately grabbed my camera and indulged my impulse to take a series of photos (figure 11). Her parents and I *kvelled*, Dieudonné and his wife glowing in the delights of parental pride and I, a parent myself, experiencing vicarious pleasure. Such moments allow me to forget momentarily the walls that culture so insidiously erects between us and to savor the joys, however temporary, of communitas.

At the same time, the poverty in which Beng families were living was even more heartbreaking for me to see that summer than it had been on previous visits to the area. This was partly because their poverty had, by objec-tive measures, increased (for a lengthier discussion of this, see chapter 11), but it was also because on this visit we had brought our son, and were seeing local living conditions through his eyes. While enjoying playing with his

10. A baby bawling his unhappiness when his "nephew" (mother's sister's daughter's son), baby Sassandra, shows too much curiosity about his bracelet; Sassandra seems surprised and confused

11. Dieudonné's wife proudly observing their toddler daughter, Hallelujah, wearing a women's style turban

village friends, Nathaniel managed not to focus on poverty much, but when he did, he was appalled, and he freely expressed his sense of outrage at the injustice he already, at six, perceived clearly.

~

This time around, I was much less hesitant than I had been during my previous field research to speak my mind and offer frank opinions about Beng life and customs. And I felt less compelled than on previous occasions to prove that I could "go native"; I no longer believed that I must do everything possible to fit in. Partly this was because I felt quite comfortable in the Beng world on this, my third field trip, and less conscious of being conspicuous. I had a network of adoptive kin, I spoke the language with relative ease, and my presence no longer produced obvious resistance or resentment. Moreover, returning as a mother meant I was accepted as someone who had finally, if belatedly, attained full adulthood. Given this, I often felt comfortable sharing my opinions and thoughts in an honest exchange with my friends and neighbors, especially when it came to child-rearing. Tapping into my own experience of motherhood, I not only listened to fellow mothers' stories but regularly shared with them my own, occasionally dispensing advice to them when it seemed welcome.

For example, one day my friend Amenan and I paid a postchildbirth call on our neighbor Moya, who had delivered a baby girl two days before. Moya's milk had come in and her breasts were full, but during the hour I spent with her, the newborn, though awake, didn't nurse at all. "She's just drinking water," Moya complained, "she can't suck yet." Moya seemed uncomfortable with her full breasts, unable as they were to release their milk, and she put the baby to her breast to see if the infant would latch on. But the tiny child didn't seem interested. "You see?" asked Moya, a bit plaintively.

Amenan spoke gently to the two-day-old: *"nyo mi,"* she urged the tiny girl—"drink the breast." But the little mouth didn't open with eagerness even when Amenan put the little one's face next to Moya's nipple. Having had my own share of breastfeeding troubles when Nathaniel was an infant, I was sympathetic. Before I could reflect on the ethics of interference, I found myself inspired by the vision of other Beng women helping their younger compatriots with nursing troubles and offered to reposition Moya's baby and breast so as to achieve a more comfortable fit. Gently, I moved Moya's breast ever so slightly and the baby ever so slightly until mouth and nipple were aligned. Then I pressed lightly above the nipple and lifted the breast softly from below, as I remembered doing dozens of time when my own baby son wouldn't latch on for any number of reasons. Moya was intrigued—she didn't know this trick, which I had learned from a book—and took over the positioning herself.

To her frustration, her first comment to me remained accurate. The baby hadn't learned to suck. I was disheartened that I wasn't able to help, but Moya seemed to appreciate my impulse. Our talk about her new motherhood continued easily, with Moya asking me as many questions about my experiences as I asked about hers.

My involvement in Beng society over the years has also meant that I have assimilated some views of the world from my adopted society. Sometimes when asked for advice by Beng women, I would, ironically, offer a suggestion that was "more Beng" than the advice a Beng person might provide. One day a Beng woman brought her three-month-old baby to the nursing clinic. The baby seemed healthy to me—no fever, the ears looked clear, and there were no other obvious symptoms of any illness I could identify—but the woman complained that the baby had been crying all day, a screaming, piercing cry. Lacking biomedical options given the information we had available, and not convinced that an expensive trip to the dispensary in town was warranted, I suggested going to the village diviner for a consultation. I had come to hold a great deal of respect for these professionals, and I valued the advice they dispensed. The woman seemed shocked at my proposal—undoubtedly she had expected a medicinal syrup, ointment, or other biomedical bromide, rather than a suggestion to evoke spirits. From her perspective, I had offered conceptual crossed wires. But with globalization comes a host of ironies— among them, unexpected shifts in knowledge systems.

I was not the only one in my family who eagerly tried Beng culture on for size. That summer Philip's father died back in the United States. Unable to return in time for the funeral, Philip mourned his father's passing through a series of Beng funeral rituals that were conducted in the village in his honor. Later he began writing a new novel inspired by the Beng conception of the afterlife (Graham n.d.). That summer, too, Nathaniel was given a Beng name, and not just any Beng name—"Denju," the name of a revered matriclan ancestor (Gottlieb, Graham, and Gottlieb-Graham 1998). In naming our son after his own matriclan's founder, the reigning Master of the Earth in the village, Kouassi Kokora, instructed us that once we returned to the United States and saw that all was well with our son, we should send money back to the village so he could sacrifice a sheep to the original Denju as thanks for protecting Nathaniel, his new American namesake and sociological heir. A few months after leaving Bengland, we found a means to send back money for the sacrifice. Living in West Africa has taught us to take no chances, to exclude no protective options out of ideological prejudice.

If my involvement in Beng society over the years has meant that I have become more willing to engage in two-way rather than one-way conversations, this lesson has not been risk-free. In 1993 my new willingness to share opinions sometimes meant disagreeing honestly with my Beng friends and informants. In the years since I was first trained in anthropology, I have come to acknowledge that my opinions about local practices are not irrelevant to my work, that depending on the context they can sometimes be expressed frankly without incurring damaging criticism and that they can even in some cases be an effective research tool. Likewise, as long as Nathaniel was not rude or offensive, I did not discourage him from expressing his opinions. One day he unwittingly tested the limits of my new, less timid approach to field-work.

No one in our compound seemed to like little Meda very much. He was frequently teased for being too small: although almost two years older than Nathaniel, he was noticeably shorter and thinner. Worse, some weeks his mother, Tahan, hit him and yelled loudly at him on a daily basis. Nathaniel had come to be friends with Meda (figure 12), and seeing Tahan abuse his

12. Meda picking up Nathaniel in a moment of friendship

13. Tahan in a tender moment with her baby son, Sassandra

playmate troubled Nathaniel greatly. One day Tahan slapped her son's face so hard that his mouth started to bleed. Upset at this, his first case of witnessing such a level of parental violence, Nathaniel boldly walked over to Tahan, tapped her on the shoulder, and rebuked her roundly in English. The language barrier proved quite permeable: Tahan understood her young critic's meaning easily. I felt divided. I agreed with Nathaniel's easy disapproval, but I selfishly worried about the effect such direct interference might have on the rapport with my neighbors that I had worked so hard to establish. Fortunately, I need not have worried. Tahan later joked about the incident to me, saying with an amused lilt in her voice, *"N'zri denju n mè!"*—Nathaniel hit me! Taking inspiration from my young son's courage, I decided to defend his position, and I took the opportunity to tell Tahan that in my country we don't let parents hit their children violently as she had done.

"Iiiiih?" she said inquiringly, but I couldn't really judge how moved she was by my point. I still feared for the future of Tahan's baby, Sassandra. So far she was a caring and kind mother to her youngest child (figure 13), but did his future hold regular beatings too? Later I recounted the incident to Tahan's mother, my dear friend Amenan. From across the courtyard, Tahan pretended not to listen. I expressed my dismay at Tahan's treatment of her son and mentioned that in the United States, the government might intervene and remove such an abused child from his mother's care and give him to another relative to be raised. I anticipated that my comment would provoke a reaction of outrage, but Amenan surprised me by saying quietly that the Beng have a similar practice themselves, albeit without government intervention. In fact, Tahan's first child, whom Tahan had also abused, had already been taken from her by the child's paternal grandmother, who was now raising her grandchild. Then Amenan glanced over at her daughter and said pointedly, "Did you hear that?" I was pleased that my friend agreed with my assessment that Tahan was acting abusively toward her son, and I did not regret having expressed my opinion.

I doubt that our exchange had any long-term effects on Tahan's mothering style. Yet neither did it ruin my fieldwork. We had at least engaged in a frank (if brief) conversation. And I didn't feel the need to interfere any more in her relationship with her infant son, knowing that Beng family networks would probably do so before long. At a broader level, I felt relieved to realize that the mainstream Beng definition of child abuse coincided on this score with my own culturally based model. But what if it had not? If what I considered child abuse was accepted as normal by the Beng community, would I have acted differently? Would I have risked my good graces in the village by endeavoring to convince Tahan to change her parenting style or by suggesting alternative child-care arrangements for poor Meda? Fortunately, I did not have to try out this more invasive scenario.

~

Living out the vaunted trope of the Glorious Return to the Field does not mean storybook acceptance, instant and full. Even in 1993 I occasionally experienced the same sort of rejection that we had encountered during our first months in Beng villages years before, when it seemed we would forever be unwelcome strangers (Gottlieb and Graham 1994). I recall especially the day when I visited four-day-old Kouakou. His umbilical cord stump had just fallen off, and his maternal grandmother was ritually marking the occasion by making special jewelry for him. Kouakou's mother had agreed that I could videotape the event. I arrived heavy with technology but light with excitement. My enthusiasm dampened quickly as the grandmother, who was starring in the ritual event, wagged her finger at me; she warned me that I'd better not videotape the ritual, and she threatened to withdraw from it if I did. My pride was hurt, and my heart sank—partly because of my disappointment that I wouldn't be able to record the event, but mostly because of the sting of the rejection. I started to pack up my equipment, hoping that the grandmother would let me remain as a fly on the wall, but to my surprise, the baby's mother was not willing to let her mother interfere. "If *you* don't want to talk into the camera," she rebuked her mother in a shockingly firm tone, "then you don't have to. But *we* can still talk to the camera, and the lady can still take the pictures." The other women in the room agreed, instructing the old woman to remain silent if she preferred, but warning her not to interrupt the proceedings.

How would I characterize such a scene and my role in it? Could I claim that in this small group I had "gained rapport"? It certainly didn't feel as if I had. Indeed, as I followed the insistent instructions of all but one of the women and continued filming the ritual, I felt more and more intrusive and wondered how I could justify my presence.

Other days, I brought my troubles upon myself out of simple ignorance. After working so long in Bengland and with Beng materials, I sometimes allowed myself the hubris of thinking myself an expert on Beng society, imagining that I knew all there is to know about the important subjects and that I was back in the field simply to fill in trivial gaps. This is a very dangerous attitude for an ethnographer to hold, and cruelly, it seems to come more easily the longer one works with a population—just when humbleness is most needed.

One day, I was chatting with Anie as he was taking care of his twin babies. As we were talking about the demands of parenting twins, I noticed that one of the children seemed quite a bit larger than the other and I made passing mention of it. Perhaps I hoped to hear whether there is a Beng theory of equal versus preferential treatment of twins, perhaps I wanted to see what Anie's explanation of the difference was, or perhaps it was simply an unthinking comment with no intellectual motivation whatever behind it. In any case, I immediately knew I should not have made the remark when a look of alarm crossed Anie's face and he studiously ignored my comment. Later, my friend Amenan explained that such an observation can provoke extreme jealousy in a smaller twin, who, in a fit of rage, might decide to return to *wrugbe*—that is, to die![13] Immediately I prayed that the twin baby wouldn't fall sick. I had plenty of failings as an ethnographer, but so far I had managed to avoid homicide in the field, and I cringed at the thought that I might have unwittingly committed infanticide. Thankfully, the smaller twin remained healthy as long as I stayed in Bengland that summer—my callous remark, made in ignorance, appeared to have done no harm. Nevertheless, it was a humbling reminder of how much I still had to learn of Beng ways. It also echoed a theme I was finding elsewhere that summer—that Beng babies are listened to, taken seriously, and imputed consciousness and understanding in ways that had previously been invisible to me.

~

Some days, playing ethnographer just seemed to take too much out of me. One day I found myself holding a baby who was screaming from the pain of tetanus. A few days later, the baby died (see chapter 10). This was the first child the baby's mother had lost, which meant that the funeral would be of a particular sort that the Beng call *fewa*. In *fewa,* the grieving parents undergo stringent rituals both to heal their loss, in a psychological sense, and to prevent future losses, in a magical sense. Perhaps to accentuate further the serious nature of the ritual and to heighten its efficacy, those who have not lost a child of their own are forbidden to attend most portions of the funeral. Everyone knew that Philip and I were fortunate enough not to have suffered the loss of a child, and so, as with others in our position, we would be banned from nearly all of the funeral. It was just as well. I didn't think I could be much of an ethnographer for this one: my heart just wasn't in dispassionately observing the behavior and charting the kin relations of the mourners.

Nine days later, a small boy with a haunted look was brought to me by his mother, who asked for medicines to cure her sick son. My attempts to counteract his malnutrition lasted two days; then the boy died. This time I was relieved when I heard that it would be a *fewa* funeral—I wouldn't have to attend most of this funeral either. Was I losing the stomach for fieldwork?

~

The human toll of poverty was not the only unsettling aspect of fieldwork that year. So was learning about the childhood and child-rearing experiences of my dear friend and assistant, Amenan, who claimed one day in a conversation with me that parents never like their oldest child. Skeptical, I teased her to produce the evidence. To my dismay, she cited her own case. As a baby, her oldest daughter—the same Tahan whom Nathaniel had recently upbraided for beating his buddy Meda—had cried and been sick a great deal. Tahan had also been very argumentative in her youth, Amenan added, and so she had spanked her oldest child quite a lot. Once, when Tahan was about ten years old, Amenan had spanked her daughter so hard that she later regretted it. To flee from her mother and her unpredictable rages, Amenan added with a nervous laugh, young Tahan had frequently gone to the fields with her maternal grandmother.

Hearing this shocking story, I immediately wondered if Amenan's abusive parenting might go some way toward explaining why now, as a mother, Tahan abused her own two oldest children. It seemed that Tahan had learned her violent parenting style from her own mother. This certainly echoed the tendency, now all too convincingly documented by psychologists, for abusive parents to produce abusive children (e.g., Barnett, Miller-Perrin, and Perrin 1997; Egeland 1993). Culture seemed irrelevant to this sad psychological pattern. The more I thought about Amenan's confession, the more depressed I became. I had held Amenan in such high esteem, written about her so admiringly. It had been painful to see Tahan beating her son, and now it was painful to realize that Amenan herself may be responsible for the abuse Tahan heaped on her own children. Could my friendship with Amenan continue unaltered after this revelation?

~

I experienced another disappointment that summer. As a parent, I began paying far more attention to the behavior of Beng parents toward their children than I had on previous visits, when I was still childless. One parental tactic I observed was that of frightening wayward children in order to convince them to obey. Often adults threatened children with an invented monster figure named Kotokoli or some other fearsome creature. If Philip and I were around, we were sometimes accorded the role of threatening monster. Adults sometimes warned young children that we would take their photos if the children didn't do whatever it was they were being asked to do. Other times, people would threaten disobedient children that Philip and I would punish them by giving them a shot!

Some adults encouraged toddlers to be afraid of Philip and me for another reason—our "white" skin echoed the imagined whiteness of the bush spirits the Beng call *alufye*. These spirits should remain in the forest, and the possibility of their presence in the village is a terrifying prospect. A child who claims to see one of the spirits is either severely rebuked for lying or is taken to a diviner for verification. If we were *alufye,* we were trouble. The association appalled us—confining Philip and me to a racial category and assimilating us to the colonialist role of frightening monster as well. After all our years of involvement in the Beng community, our adoption into kinship networks, and our efforts to learn the language and to help with medical crises, were we, after all, nothing but ordinary, colonialist, racist, *tubabu*—white people?

Were I to have confronted my friends with my disappointment, I suspect they would have been chagrined to learn that the practice had hurt us, and they would have ceased using us as a disciplinary tool for disobedient children. But I never had that conversation. I was reluctant to criticize my neighbors; perhaps I was embarrassed to confront the colonial legacy of racism that divided us, or perhaps I feared that even in the face of our discomfort they would continue the practice, revealing that our friendship was far less solid than I wanted to believe.

~

In short, conducting fieldwork among the Beng on infants and infant-rearing was intense and at times overwhelming, provoking a full range of emotions from the joyful to the tragic. I love babies; I chose the topic for my research in good part because of my personal attachment to the subject. But I do not want to romanticize my research. Even in the best of circumstances, raising children is a challenge that many parents the world over find alternately invigorating, delightful, frustrating, and perplexing. Beng mothers love their babies as much as I have loved my own; yet the contours their love has taken—its boundaries, its shape—look quite different from those mine has taken. For one thing, extreme poverty has made the challenges of rearing children one whose hardships are almost unimaginable for those who have never suffered the frustrations and humiliations of material deprivation, the resultant constant threat of sickness, and the all-too-frequent sorrow of holding a baby dying in their arms. And then there is the small matter of culture.

Is it possible for me, a woman of comfortable financial means, reared in a Jewish but largely secular family as an only child and trained with a formal education according me access to a variety of knowledge systems, to understand the perspectives and suffering of nonliterate women with a local, polytheistic tradition, who are living in extreme poverty and trying to rear six or more children without access to the resources that literacy and money offer? Yes and no. The methods of cultural anthropology developed over the past century have endeavored to provide us with both intellectual and methodological tools to bridge the formidable gaps that culture, economy, and history construct between groups of people. In the chapters that follow, my readers—who I hope will someday include many Beng people—must judge the extent to which these methods have done just that for the subject at hand.

~

In the chapter that follows, before plunging into the world of Beng babies, I try to answer a basic, conceptually orienting question: Why have we yet to develop a robust and influential anthropology of infancy?

CHAPTER TWO

Do Babies Have Culture?

Explorations in the Anthropology of Infancy

Where Have All the Babies Gone?

Whatever their parenting skills at home, most contemporary cultural anthropologists don't seem to think analytically about babies very much. Of course, this doesn't mean we don't like babies. But in our professional lives we have often ignored those small creatures, who just don't seem to hold out much scholarly promise as we have defined the ethnographic imagination. At a theoretical level, babies constitute for most of us a nonsubject, occupying negative space that is virtually impervious to the anthropological gaze.

The evidence for this claim is multiple. I have identified only two full-length ethnographies devoted to the infants of a single society (Hewlett 1991; LeVine et al. 1994). To date, no anthropological journal exists on infancy.[1] We have no professional society as a unit of the American Anthropological Association—or, to my knowledge, elsewhere—that is dedicated to the anthropological study of children, let alone infants. One rare anthropologist who has taught a course on infants reported that when her students undertook library research projects, they were frustrated by the scantiness of information on infants available through the Human Relations Area Files. The course itself was so novel for our discipline that the article describing it carried the proselytizing title, "The Benefits of Teaching a Course on Infancy" (Peters 1995).

Within anthropology the subject of infancy may carry too low a level of prestige to invite a lot of scholars to tackle it. As humans operating in our own culturally shaped environment—with the values of the academy and our particular niche in it—we researchers inevitably, if unconsciously, make decisions with a hierarchy of prestige in mind (Ortner and Whitehead 1981). One prominent colleague who conducts research on children's linguistic development confided to me that after several of her panels were scheduled at times when few conference-goers attend sessions at the annual meeting of the American Anthropological Association, she learned to conceal the fact that the subject of the proposed papers concerns young children. Instead, she now uses broad theoretical concepts for her paper and panel titles, alluding only indirectly, if at all, to the topic of children, and the panels are now scheduled at popular times. In crude ways such as this, conceptual gatekeeping may help replicate the relative invisibility of infants in the anthropological canon.

A related sign of the dearth of developed anthropological interest in young children concerns methodology. To my knowledge, there are only two field guides to conducting anthropologically oriented research with children, and both were developed for very specific kinds and contexts of research. One, which is now out of print, was assembled by the Harvard-based Whiting team to test specific hypotheses generated by the Whiting project some four decades ago (Whiting et al. 1963). A second, more recent collection of articles was developed specifically for researchers working with nongovernmental organizations (NGOs) and is available largely through the NGO that sponsored its publication (Boyden and Ennew 1997). As far as I know, no more general methodological work for conducting anthropological work with children of any age has since augmented these two. Clearly the field remains wide open.[2]

Although I focus here on cultural anthropology, it is worth noting that in the related field of biological anthropology there is a corresponding lack of scholarly consideration of infant and child anatomy, except for that of the fetal period. A short article by Stephen Jay Gould (1996) from the sister field of evolutionary biology is one of the few recent pieces to consider the subject (Stephen Leigh, personal communication). For their part, archaeologists have not contributed significant amounts of scholarship toward understanding the lives of infants and young children in the recent or distant past (Silverman 1998). One intriguing reason for archaeologists' neglect of children may be purely technical: because of lower density and mineral content, the bones of children under two years old may not be preserved as well as those of older children and adults (Guy, Masset, and Baud 1997; Klepinger 1997). Ingenious technological innovations are just now being developed to expand research capabilities in ways that will ultimately help us understand, for example, patterns of lactation and other aspects of nutrition in infants and toddlers in the early archaeological record (for a review, see Stuart-Macadam 1995).

Of the four subfields of anthropology, it is probably linguistic anthropology that has paid the most attention to children's worlds. Over the past two-plus decades, an exceptionally strong group of scholars has produced nuanced discussions of language socialization and language use in a variety of social settings.[3] Yet even within this subdiscipline, Goodwin (1997) recently pointed out how much still remains to be researched concerning the rich topic of children's language use. Moreover, of the work done to date, a far greater amount of comparative research has been conducted on toddlers and older children than on language use and development among infants. In any case, the work of most of these linguistic anthropologists remains, sadly, sidelined by mainstream cultural anthropology. As regards a developing anthropology of infancy, this intellectual neglect is especially lamentable because of the exceptionally rich contributions that linguistic anthropology stands to make.

In short, the field of anthropology in general, and cultural anthropology in particular, has paid scanty attention to young children (see van der Geest 1996). Moreover, the younger the child, the less attention has been paid. All this poses a stark contrast to our sister field of psychology. That discipline now boasts a voluminous canon on infants, including two journals devoted to infancy and many other journals on child development that routinely feature articles on infants. Correspondingly, the discipline hosts a biennial international conference on infant research and several other annual conferences on childhood research.[4] By these measures, anthropology lags sorely behind.

~

Despite the striking neglect of infants in mainstream cultural anthropology, young children have not been entirely ignored. I do not have space here for a thorough review of the research, so I mention only some highlights.[5] In the last century, scholars associated with the U.S.-based Culture and Personality school inaugurated by Margaret Mead undertook significant research projects on children. Indeed, as Scheper-Hughes (2001) recently pointed out, Mead was the first anthropologist to take children seriously as a subject of anthropological inquiry. In the United States, though not elsewhere, the perspective on children that was adopted in the work published by Mead and her associates was quite influential in mid-century (Langness 1975). The research of anthropologists Beatrice and John Whiting and of those who participated in the Whitings's ambitious "Children of Six Cultures" study (1975) continued this tradition.[6]

Yet even in these writings, infants receive far less attention than do older children. And critics have pointed out that the analytic model these scholars brought to the project is hampered by important theoretical limitations. For one thing, their writings typically overlook variations in time (historical change) and space (ethnicity/race, class, religion, and gender). Moreover, a Freudian perspective precluded the development of alternative interpretations that might be more appropriate in given cultural settings. As Mead (1963) herself acknowledged in her later years, unwarranted Eurocentric assumptions underlie the Freudian model, with its culture-blind insistence on a small number of factors, such as toilet training, that we now know are interpreted variably in diverse cultural settings (e.g., Wallace 1983:213–17). These shortcomings continue to apply to more recent psychoanalytically oriented research on infants and children, though these works are generally quite rich in data.[7] In any case, aside from the writings of adherents to the Culture and Personality school and a few other anthropologists that evidence a passing interest in the lives of children,[8] it can safely be asserted that children in general and infants in particular retained a low profile in mainstream cultural anthropology, especially outside the United States, in the mid-to-late twentieth century.

In the current era, some writings on child-rearing and the broader span of the life cycle from a non-Freudian perspective address the socialization of infants in a chapter or section on the topic.[9] Likewise, several works looking specifically at rituals pertaining to the life cycle include discussions of infancy and young childhood (e.g., La Fontaine 1985; Ottenberg 1989:3–32). A large number of general ethnographies contain chapters or sections devoted to the period of infancy or toddlerhood (e.g., James 1979; Seremetakis 1991). But insofar as such intriguing but brief discussions occur in the context of analyses of specific issues relevant to a given society rather than constituting a focus on children in and of themselves, they beg for the nuances that full-length studies might provide.

In addition to these works, there is a growing parallel literature treating a range of issues concerning women's reproductive lives. One group of scholars subtly explores the cultural production and imagining of the fetus and the ritual and symbolic foundations of procreation and birth more generally.[10] Another important group investigates the range of reproductive strategies and decisions available to women in a variety of contemporary cultural settings.[11] A closely related set of writings focuses on the experiences of women as midwives and birth attendants.[12] Together these varied works speak indirectly to the lives of infants, and they might be brought into play more directly as contributions to a developing anthropology of young children.

Other important parallel contributions are worth mentioning. In recent years an interesting literature on the anthropology of emotion has been developing (for a review, see Lutz and White 1986). Although this work has by and large neglected the domain of infancy, the high emotional involvement of infants suggests a rich vein for future research. Likewise, over the past two decades a rich literature has explored the notion that personhood is culturally constructed (e.g., Jackson and Karp 1990; Rosaldo 1984; Shweder and Bourne 1984). Although once again research with infants has not contributed significantly to this otherwise fertile body of work (for an exception, see Poole 1985), such research does stand to make important contributions in the future.

An eclectic group of writings has begun to address a variety of topics concerning, especially, older children's experiences (e.g., Reynolds 1996; Toren n.d.b), as well as adult-oriented perspectives on child-related issues, such as child care (e.g., Lamb, Sternberg, Hwang, and Broberg 1992;

Swadener, Kabiru, and Njenga et al. 2000), the early development of roles relating to gender and the state (Dragadze 1988), and the practice of adoption and fosterage (e.g., Anagnost 2000, n.d.; Bledsoe 1990, 1993, 1995; E. Goody 1982; for an early precursor, see Lambert 1964, 1970). At the theoretical level, there has recently been a small upsurge of writing on older children and youth undertaken from a political economy perspective.[13] Effects of the world economy are actively explored in these studies to situate the lives of children in a realistically globalized context. The daily world of labor, the tragedy of homelessness for "street children," and popular culture are all addressed.[14] As the impact of the global economy and global culture more generally is increasingly documented in seemingly remote places, the effort to include children in analyses that take into account international cultural and economic flows is welcome indeed.[15]

Illuminating though these recent works are, their contributions are circumscribed in two ways from the standpoint of a richly theorized anthropology of infancy. First, most of these writings also focus on older children rather than infants. Second, the political economy model itself has limits. Most notably, a sense of the indigenous perspective of children's experiences and how these fit in with other cultural features of the social landscape—including religion and other ideological structures—is often underdeveloped or absent in works espousing a political economy perspective. As with other ethnographies, finding a productive balance between the global and the local, the political and the cultural, and the social and the individual is proving a challenge in many of these writings. In short, in spite of promising developments, the ethnography of infants is, if you will, still in its infancy.

Yet in that scholarly infancy we have now become able to at least imagine the contours of a disciplinary toddlerhood. In recent years we have begun to see a small number of exemplary writings by North American scholars who either are trained in or have been influenced by anthropology and who are focusing extensively on the lives of infants and young children and their parents; some of these scholars are working in collaboration with scholars in other fields.[16] In Europe and Africa, a parallel development is occurring.[17] These authors are notable for the extent to which, from sophisticated perspectives, they identify cultural factors affecting infant and child development. Yet it is frustrating that these studies that privilege infants have been sidelined from mainstream conversations in cultural anthropology. Their authors rarely publish in anthropology journals, and they often present their findings at psychology or human development, rather than anthropology, conferences. And although a new body of interdisciplinary literature is now emerging on the cultural construction of childhood and youth and on children and youths' active negotiation of cultural life, infants occupy a marginal place even in much of that literature.

Interestingly, discussion of the social matrix of children's lives appears to be developing more rapidly in fields other than anthropology. Inspired by the pathbreaking work of Ariès (1962), history and sociology have become especially fertile ground for emerging discussions of children as culturally situated.[18] Indeed, considering the accumulating weight of this interdisciplinary work, two authors have recently suggested that "a new paradigm for the study of childhood is emerging" (James and Prout 1990:2).[19] Even though this work once again tends to underrepresent the experiences of infants in comparison with those of older children, the development is noteworthy. This increasing scholarly interest in children within a variety of disciplines is beginning to attract attention, especially in cultural psychology, indigenous psychology, and ethnopediatrics.[20] Together contemporary authors in anthropology and allied disciplines are signaling exciting paths down which a developing anthropology of infancy is heading.

~

Thus far I have rather uncritically deployed the categories of infant and infancy as though they are self-evident. Yet if cultural anthropology has taught us anything over the past century, it is that the most seemingly transparent of categories often turns out to be the most unexpectedly noncommensurable. Anthropologists, professional pests that we are, love to take on the obvious, shake it up and toss it around, then throw it back in a totally different form from the one in which it began. Consider the classic topic of kinship: we have long known that the person who is classified as a cousin in much of the West is considered a sibling in many non-Western societies. Similarly, a "week" may vary in traditional African societies from three to eight days (Zaslavsky 1973:64–65). Or the domain of activity that is easily defined as "politics" to, say, a Westerner may, throughout much of Africa, take on features that to the Westerner look suspiciously like "religion" (e.g., Arens and Karp 1989). Even mathematical operations are subject to surprising redefinition: what appears to be addition to a Westerner may be interpreted as subtraction among some indigenous Brazilian groups, and vice versa (Ferreira 1997). A century of destabilizing revelations such as these should alert us to the nontransparent nature of many seemingly transparent concepts. Why should the categories of infant and infancy be any less problematic?

Developmental psychologists routinely define infancy as the period encompassing birth to the onset of toddlerhood, which in conventional texts normatively begins at the age of two years. (For the sake of convenience, this is how I have been using the term thus far.) These texts specify that by the time healthy and developmentally normal children turn two, they can walk effectively without repeatedly falling and have begun to understand and respond to linguistic communication.

Yet this disciplinary estimate is not a biological certainty; rather, it is a cultural convention premised on the Western calendar—itself, of course, an eminently cultural construction (see Duncan 1998). The pinpointing of the second birthday as the end of infancy is also based on a cultural assumption that life stages ought to be defined by reference to absolute time spans rather than to, say, shifting activities (Evans-Pritchard 1940). Yet among young children, there is, of course, wide variation in verbal and motor abilities at two years (see Cole 1983). The indigenous understanding of a life stage will necessarily be rather different in societies that do not emphasize fixed calendrical points as determinative.

Indeed, many non-Western peoples take a more relative or contextual approach to locating the end of one stage and the beginning of the next. In these societies, adults identify the acquisition of a particular developmental skill—such as walking or talking—as paramount, no matter when it is mastered by a given child. For example, the Lahu people of southwest China assert that children inhabit the "red-and-naked" stage, which we might translate loosely as "infancy," until they can walk confidently and, more importantly, speak with some degree of self-expression. The Lahu acknowledge that the acquisition of these skills may occur at different times in different children, and they resist specifying the duration of the "red-and-naked" stage (Du 2002).[21]

Even when it is accepted that a relatively fixed age is a proper benchmark for the end of infancy, that age may be historically and cross-culturally variable. For example, the Puritans of colonial New England ended infancy firmly at one year, rather than at the two years of contemporary Western science. Devoutly Christian people who organized most of their lives around their religious faith, the Puritans asserted that at the end of the first year the malevolent entity they termed the devil begins to exert control. To counteract this nefarious influence, Puritan leaders urged parents to introduce strict discipline immediately following a child's first birthday (Reese 2000). Elsewhere, the period we might translate as infancy is prolonged significantly beyond the contemporary duration of two years. For example, the Ifaluk of Micronesia consider the demonstration of what developmental psychologists would call a moral sense to be the benchmark for ending infancy. But the Ifaluk maintain that young children remain mindless *(bush)* for their first five or six years; they begin to acquire intelligence *(repiy)* slowly at two or three years but do not fully attain a moral sense until they reach childhood *(sari)* at five or six years (Le 2000; Lutz 1988).

If the termination of infancy is variable cross-culturally, the same is true of its inception. Although birth may seem the commonsensical inauguration of this period, it is useful to bear in mind Geertz's perpetually challenging insight that what passes for common sense for some may be anything but that for others (1983). Thus some peoples locate the inception of infancy in the womb, while others delay it until some time after the birth. In the contemporary United States, of course, this is a topic of much public debate among (largely secular) "pro-choice" and (largely religious) "pro-life" activists (Ginsburg 1989; Morgan 1996; J. Taylor 1992).

If the dominant secular Western model suggests that infancy begins immediately after birth, people elsewhere suggest otherwise. For example, among some Melanesian peoples, the boundary between fetus-hood and infancy is not clear. Summarizing data from several Melanesian groups, Butt writes that an infant is seen "as an immature but complete person who was formed inside a woman. They are 'partial persons,' according to local ideologies, made complete by the social, ritual, and nurturing actions of others" (1998:21). Elsewhere the distinction is clearer but the transformation does not occur at birth. Some Muslim African peoples, for example, hold a naming ritual after the sixth day. Although it is not orthodox belief grounded in the Qur'an (Valerie Hoffman, personal communication, 25 August 1998), in these groups the newborn is not considered an infant at all before the ritual occurs. It is regarded as not having yet achieved any sense of personhood (see D'Alisera 1998; Johnson 2000a). Other groups delay the onset of infancy even longer. For example, the aboriginal Murngin people of Arnhem Land call newborns by the term that is used for the fetus. Only when the newborn begins to smile—typically at three to six weeks—is it called a child—and this stage lasts until the youngster is between nine and twelve years old (Hamilton 1981:17).

The Chewa, or Cewa, of Malawi extend the postuterine but pre-infant stage farther. According to my reading of Marwick 1968 (3–4) and Kaspin 1996 (572), the first three months beyond the womb constitute an in-between stage, the word for which might be inappropriate to translate as "infancy." During this period, the tiny creatures are seen as still "cold" and "wet," and thus both they and their parents are subject to ritual injunctions or taboos. Only at the end of the three-month period does the small being become what we might comfortably term an infant. This transformation occurs through deliberate cultural manipulation rather than any local notion of inevitable biological progression. After three months, Chewa parents traditionally had sexual intercourse while the soon-to-be infant lay on the wife's chest. The wife rubbed a combination of vaginal fluids and semen on the now-becoming-infant, thus inducting the little one into a dryer stage—what we might roughly term infancy. Elsewhere there is a more indeterminate conception of the onset of personhood. Among the Wari' of Brazil, for example, "personhood is acquired gradually, and it may be lost or attenuated under certain conditions," though in some sense it is initiated by the first act of breastfeeding (Conklin and Morgan 1996:658, 678).

Is a stage of infancy even present in all societies, or might a given society decline to single out the early months or years for special conceptual or ritual consideration, as appears to be the case in Arnhem Land? The relative dearth of knowledge about the lives, habits, and conceptions of infants cross-culturally makes it difficult to answer this and related questions with certitude. For, as I have suggested, although a good number of anthropologists have briefly mentioned assorted cultural habits concerning infants, few have taken infants themselves seriously as the proper subject of extended anthropological inquiry.

Through this canonical roundup my point is simple: by and large, anthropologists have not had much to say about the experiences of the youngest members of the societies they have studied. I now move to a more vexing but, to me, a more anthropologically interesting aspect of this subject—the qualitative rather than quantitative issue. Why is it that to date there has been no systematic, wide-ranging, and influential anthropology of infancy?

Why Have All the Babies Gone?

Six reasons can account for the relative tininess of the space that infants occupy in both the empirical world and the anthropological corpus.[22]

Remembering Childhood, Imagining Parenthood?

Personal experience may interfere at two levels with anthropological discussion of infants, causing a noticeable gap. First, although all adults were once infants, few, if any, of us remember any component of the experience. This lack of memory—save what parents and others implant after the fact—may disincline us toward considering an aspect of human experience that seems so remote from our individual perspective.[23]

Moreover, many cultural anthropologists are relatively young—often in their twenties—when they begin fieldwork, and they are not yet parents. Therefore, they may be unaware of the emotional, medical, pragmatic, and theoretical challenges that infants pose. This ignorance may make it unlikely that a cultural anthropologist will envision a study of infancy. Lack of direct experience on this front may mean that a researcher has no idea of the proper questions to ask—and may even have little notion of which sorts of infant behaviors are unusual and which are normal by the standards of the researcher's own society. When members of our ranks later become over-worked parents, not all of us have the luxury of pursuing additional post-doctoral fieldwork, whether concerning infants or anything else; the result is another missed opportunity for conducting research on infancy even if members of this group of older ethnographers has an interest in doing so.

Is parenthood necessarily a prerequisite for fieldwork on infants? One of the classic hallmarks of cultural anthropology is the study of "the other." Throughout the past century of research, cultural anthropologists steeped in the Judeo-Christian tradition have productively investigated the lives of Mus-lims, Hindus, Buddhists, and animists; middle-class and wealthy anthropolo-gists have investigated the lives of poor people; urban-based anthropologists have studied the lives of farmers, hunter-gatherers, and nomads; female an-thropologists have investigated the lives of men (though regrettably, not much of the reverse has occurred until recently); monogamously married an-thropologists have investigated the lives of polygynists; and so on. It is hard to imagine a more different Other to an adult than an infant, no matter what the cultural background of both. Extrapolating from the lesson of all this existing other-directed research, we might propose that parenthood need not be a prerequisite for studying children. Indeed, their outsider status could lend an analytical edge to nonparent anthropologists investigating children's lives. Yet this analytical edge has not often been sharpened.[24] Ironically, even anthropologists who are parents have rarely taken on the challenge of such a scholarly journey to life-cycle otherness despite our disciplinary mandate to travel down just such an intellectual road. Why should that be? Let us explore further factors.

The Missing Agency of Infants?

The younger the child, the more dependent she or he is on others for basic biological sustenance. By anthropological standards, babies simply look boring. They seem to be so much at the mercy of others that there doesn't appear to be any of that push and pull between two individuals, or between the individual and society at large, that makes for interesting scholarly consid-eration. At one level, infancy can be said to constitute a lens through which to understand critical cultural decisions and orientations. However productive this model might be, however, it necessarily, if implicitly, posits a passive baby-as-object rather than an active baby-as-subject. Babies seem as distant as possi-ble from the epicenters of power of a given society. After all, can babies set their own agendas?

Related to this general concern is the more specific fact that infants in most, if not all, societies are classified as minors. Unable to testify in court either for the defense or for the prosecution, they have no legal effect on others. Given the legalistic foundation of much of our discipline's British functionalist heritage—especially in Africa—the legacy of such a legally incon-sequential positioning of infants seems relevant even today and may uncon-sciously serve as another factor dooming babies to their ethnographic invisi-bility.

More generally, infants' opinions seem irrelevant in making life decisions about others. With a model that posits a passive baby-as-object rather than an active baby-as-subject, it is hard to imagine how infants might set their own agendas; a baby-as-object model does not seem to make for promising material from babies as informants.

And yet, as new parents in many societies know, passivity is far from a complete description of a newborn's life. Right from the start, infants demand to be accounted for, even though adults may not interpret those demands accurately. Indeed, parents—especially mothers—in most societies continu-ally rearrange their days and nights to accommodate the demands and moods of their newest child. Given this, a study of the lives of women that did not look carefully at the ways in which their babies' needs shape years, even de-cades, of their own lives would, in many societies, produce a hopelessly partial understanding of women's experiences. This is particularly the case for socie-ties that have high fertility rates and whose members generally lack access to reliable birth control methods. Of course, these are the societies that have until recently been the mainstay of anthropological research, yet as a disci-pline, we have not yet taken serious note of the implications of such high fertility rates for the texture of women's daily lives. This is related to our implicit ideology of infants as passive creatures.[25]

Is the model of babies as nothing more than passive recipients of others' care a universal one? Members of some societies may have ideas about infant volition and desire that are distinct from the model of infant passivity just outlined. For one thing, rather than producing cultural negligibility, the very dependence and seeming passivity of infants may signal semiotically significant cultural markers at the local level to which we ought to pay attention. Among Hausa living in Niger, for instance, it is said that most witches prefer infants as their victims precisely because of what they consider babies' passivity. Their assumption has a particular cultural foundation. Since infants do not yet know how to talk, Hausa adults maintain, they will not accuse witches of perpetrat-ing their evil against them; moreover, witchcraft attacks on infants may easily be masked as illnesses, since Hausa babies are sick so often. Here, infants' reputed dependence serves to orient an ideological system of evil and its cul-tural constitution in anthropologically interesting ways that can easily be grist for the analytic mill (Schmoll 1993:201).

Elsewhere, infants may be considered far more engaged social actors. In the course of my fieldwork among the Beng, I have observed how women make the preponderance of their day-to-day decisions in relation to infants. As with the Hausa case, this model is premised not just on a pragmatic foundation, but also on a deeply cultural one. As we shall see in chapter 4, Beng adults maintain that infants are reincarnations of ancestors, so for their first few years in this life, babies remember with longing their previous existence in the "afterlife." Given this ideological orientation, a major duty of Beng parents is to discern, via diviners, the desires that their infants retain from their previous incarnation, then to grant those desires. In this model, Beng infants are far from helpless creatures with no opinions and no impact on the world. For the Beng, as for many non-Western peoples, the complete dependence of infants that is widely if unconsciously assumed by Western-trained anthropologists is a nonissue. This perspective challenges our implicit ideology of the infant as a passive creature, an ideology that has foreclosed the possibility of privileging babies as legitimate sites, let alone active producers, of culture who are anchored in a moral landscape.

Yet one of our tasks as ethnographers is to pay attention to and interpret indigenous models. There is significant intellectual payoff to the realization of such a goal. For one thing, indigenous models may well challenge the ones we bring to the field, often unconsciously, and this itself is a theoretically ripe possibility (Rosaldo 1989). In seeking to understand the ways that babies might take an active role in negotiating culture, the anthropologist of infants is much like the parent. Endeavoring to learn a new language that has neither a ready-made dictionary nor a published grammar, the anthropologist of infancy searches out rules, patterns, and creative innovations that are undoubtedly present and can be examined—if only they can be unearthed, or as some developmental psychologists would say, mutually created (e.g., Lewis and Rosenblum 1974).

Babies and Women?

Infants in most societies spend much of their time attached to women—frequently, though not necessarily, their mothers[26]—and until the past two decades, women themselves were neglected as social subjects by many anthropologists. As Butt has observed, "The very young are aligned with women and essentially left out of descriptive data" (1998:11). Even many feminist scholars investigating the experiences of women have tended to privilege the easily studied—and theoretically safer—"public" domains of women's lives that most approximate men's public lives: women's involvements in the economy, in social networks, and in political structures. By contrast, the maternal work that women typically undertake around the world has long remained in the shadows, relegated to the so-called domestic sphere (Stack and Burton 1994). To the extent that anthropologists assume that infants belong to this theoretically inconsequential space, babies seem as distant as possible from the epicenters of power of a given society.

Even though in recent years scholars have begun to pay serious theoretical attention to women's reproductive lives, the products of all that reproduction—babies themselves—usually remain in the background. Why should this be so? The prevalent Western assumption of something we easily but imprecisely call maternal instinct is at the root of the answer.

In the Western academy, feminist theory has happily been at the forefront of a broad intellectual tendency to problematize aspects of gender that were previously taken for granted (e.g., MacCormack and Strathern 1980; Ortner 1989–1990; Rosaldo 1980). This scholarly move often takes the form of a challenge to the seemingly natural or biological basis of gender differences. In good part, the anthropological stance of cultural relativism has been an inspiration for this move, even if our discipline has not always been directly at the helm.

And yet the notion of a maternal instinct still appears to have staying power in its claims about women's nature. Whether in the context of a Jungian search for some archetypal maternal essence (e.g., Lowinsky 1992), or of a political search for viable world peace (e.g., philosopher Sara Ruddick's celebrated *Maternal Thinking* [1989]), many contemporary scholars, including feminists, have been reluctant to relinquish the seductive image of woman-as-nurturing-mother. Even some feminist anthropologists have independently endorsed the implicitly biological model of woman-as-nurturer (e.g., Rosaldo and Atkinson 1975). This is, of course, far more the case outside the academy than within it.

All too frequently, women-as-mothers are seen as somehow "naturally" playing their role. In this case, what is there of interest for the anthropologist studying cultural processes? Not much. If women somehow naturally know how to be mothers, it would follow that the babies they are mothering somehow naturally know how to be babies. In this case, there would likewise be precious little grist for the anthropologist's mill in the domain of infant experience.

But there are serious problems with the popular assumption of a maternal instinct.[27] First and most obviously, not all women intentionally become mothers. For those who deliberately eschew motherhood, how relevant is the postulated maternal instinct? In other words, if maternity is such a strong instinct, why would some women opt to avoid it, and how might individual women manage to overcome the presumed urge?[28] On a different note, what do we make of abusive mothers—women who behave violently or neglectfully toward their own children in ways that decidedly fall outside the scope of that hypothesized gentle instinct?[29]

Perhaps it will be suggested that the posited maternal impulse is lacking in these mothers as the result of some genetic anomaly. But this is an argument that would be difficult to support on philosophical as well as scientific grounds. Alternatively, one might propose that in some women the instinct is repressed by decisively distracting social and psychological factors complicating their lives. However, this is an equally problematic mode of argumentation that long ago proved disabling to much of Freud's work on supposedly universal psychological processes such as the Oedipus complex.

Then, too, how should we interpret the actions of men who behave in nurturing ways either toward their own children or toward other people? Are these men somehow women *manqué*? This is an absurd view that surely most (nurturing) men would reject out of hand. Alternatively, is men's nurturing behavior rooted in cultural or psychological patterns rather than in the biological urges that supposedly guide women's nurturing behavior? But if this is so, could one not make the same argument for women's nurturing behavior? It is significant that no one has seriously proposed the existence of a paternal instinct.

In short, considering the many critical flaws in the postulation of a maternal instinct, I suggest that the notion reveals far more of Western cultural preoccupations than of an actual biologically based imperative. Motherhood, like fatherhood, is an *achieved* cultural status—but one that is shaped by society so convincingly that its very essence, however variable cross-culturally, may well end up appearing natural, inevitable.

In recent years, some works have pointed the way toward a feminist analysis of motherhood as socially constructed. Oddly, while much of this work is perhaps inspired by anthropology, it does not come directly from the discipline. For instance, a provocative book by psychologist Diane Eyer (1992) demonstrates the vacuity of the notion of bonding between new mothers and their babies that was endorsed by a host of respectable scientists in the 1970s. Historians have also begun to document the social and political matrices within which motherhood—and its inverse, infertility—has been constructed over the past century, especially in Western nations,[30] and authors in a variety of related disciplines have joined in the growing scholarly conversation.[31] Happily, anthropologists have also begun to contribute to this now burgeoning field.[32]

Feminism has taught us that the neglect of women distorts our understanding of any society. So too the neglect of children, including infants, results in an extraordinarily partial view of that society. While a single ethnography inevitably offers only a partial view or analysis of a given society, some analyses are decidedly more partial than others. The failure to take seriously the lives of children as central components of the lives of women dooms us to a strikingly incomplete view.

Fortunately, feminist anthropologists have reoriented discussions of women's seemingly private involvements, including those in the arena commonly defined as domestic, and now view them as fully cultural and as having a direct impact on "public" events. At a theoretical level, the conceptual boundary between public and private, so long impermeable, is now being challenged, disturbing the definitions of categories that lie at the heart of much of our discipline (e.g., Comaroff 1987; Lugo and Maurer 2000; Rogers 1978). The anthropological study of babies ought to profit enormously from this theoretically productive shakeup.

Can Babies Communicate?

Most cultural anthropologists treasure the proposition that language signals the presence of culture. Indeed, this proposition still holds pride of place in many introductory textbooks in our discipline. But babies are—or at least appear to many adults to be—incapable of speaking. If infants cannot communicate their wishes and views in a way that anthropologists feel proficient in interpreting, how can we admit these small creatures into our cherished, charmed circle of culture? Even if we suppose that infants lead secretly cultural lives, how would an anthropologist go about understanding the world of these nonlinguistic humans?

At a methodological level, our field techniques typically require us to rely rather heavily on chats and interviews. But we won't get much of an answer when we ask a baby to explain, say, the meaning of a prayer, or what kind of dinner is appropriate to serve a boss, or why children are segregated by age in school. All this is beyond an interview with an infant. For babies can't speak—at least not in the language we are taught in fieldwork classes to use in interviews.

And yet the various noises that even young babies make, often dismissed as meaningless babble by Western observers, may be seen as meaningful in some places. Paying attention to the sounds that infants make, and if and how these are interpreted by those around them, should result in an intellectually productive inquiry.

Moreover, even if babies' babble is locally considered meaningless, the obstacle their lack of speech competence poses to achieving a sense of *verstehen* may not be as formidable as it appears. The impediments to attaining rapport even with adults are now well-known. Field memoirs abound demonstrating that complete empathy with and understanding of another human being—even one within one's own cultural tradition, however defined—is at best difficult, and perhaps impossible, to attain. Nevertheless, most cultural anthropologists would assert that the effort to reach some level of empathy for and understanding of a given group of others lies at the heart of the ethnographic enterprise. Accordingly, most of us seem to operate with the hope that a partial realization of this lofty but elusive goal is possible. The situation with infants may not be much different: it may be no more impossible to gain some level of rapport with a tiny nonspeaking person, and some level of understanding of his or her experiences, than it is to do so with a full-grown one.

However, to achieve rapport, we may need to rethink the theoretical agenda behind our assumptions. The common disciplinary insistence on verbal language and linguistic ability as an index of culture may fortuitously reflect a system of "folk knowledge" in some cultural traditions (e.g., Harris 1980:72–73), but scholarship is increasingly suggesting that insisting on linguistic competence as a sign of culture is by no means universal. Acknowledging that verbal communication is only one of several means of communication means rethinking the options available to us in our field methods. Students of language are now suggesting that the classic criterion for identifying something as a text—the presence of an alphabetic or ideographic system of writing—may be too narrow. Students of comparative hermeneutics have convincingly demonstrated how a variety of other communication systems— clothing and adornment, games, table manners, and so on—may be productively analyzed as semiotic texts.[33]

This expansion of the definition of text may be parallel to a current move , some archaeologists to question the history/prehistory divide, which also assumes the reification of the notion of text as a written document based on an alphabetic or ideographic system of writing (Pauketat 2001). Following this effort in several scholarly arenas to redefine the semantic field of the concept of text, I suggest that it likewise makes sense to consider infants' lives as texts to be read, though possibly with a new set of glasses.

We would need to inquire how local adults say their babies communicate—and to whom. During my fieldwork in Beng villages, adults told me that babies are driven to communicate, but that adults are too unenlightened to understand those attempts. Therefore, Beng parents are urged to consult diviners, who speak the language of babies through spirit intermediaries living in the "afterlife" from which infants are said to have just (partly) emerged. The babies enunciate their wishes, which diviners interpret to parents; in turn, the parents are obliged to fulfill these desires, often by adorning the babies with various items of jewelry (see chapter 4). Given such an ideology, the methodological imperative for me during fieldwork was to consult with diviners and attend their baby "séance" sessions as often as possible. Privileging communication with spirits via diviners is not something we are normally trained to undertake. Nevertheless, we owe it to our infant informants to follow wherever their culturally mediated attempts at communication lead us—whether that be to the spirit world, or to some other unexpected but culturally meaningful space.

Babies' more direct efforts to communicate are frequently accomplished by nonspeaking means: with nuanced or not-so-nuanced noises—gurgles, chortles, clucks, and screams; with facial expressions—smiles and grimaces, arched eyebrows and closed eyes; and, of course, with body language—waving hands, kicking legs, arched backs. Indeed, so much communication with babies is inevitably bodily rather than purely verbal. The theoretical impact of this difference is enormous.

Babies' Bodies, Babies' Leaks?

In recent years, cultural anthropologists have begun to question our emphasis on verbal communication in our work with adult humans to the exclusion of other forms of communication. If, as Kirsten Hastrup puts it bluntly, "Knowledge is profoundly embodied" (1994:236), we are just beginning to take note of that fact by redesigning our field methods. Marcel Mauss outlined a theoretically viable basis for an anthropology of the body well over half a century ago (Mauss 1973), but we are just beginning to take his agenda seriously enough to reimagine the discipline's theories and methods.[34]

Our disciplinary definition of language is now broadening to include nonverbal modes of communication—a move that at least some anthropologists have recently argued elegantly is long overdue. A new generation of scholars in anthropology and allied fields has urged us to seek data in modes of sensory communication beyond verbal language.[35] Local interpretations of how infants communicate may lead us far afield from our verbal models. Studying infants should enable us to take seriously the theoretical imperative to somatize our methods that these studies are now urging.

~

For what they lack in verbal skills, babies make up in somatic communications. Infants are messy, and the younger they are, the messier they are. They spend much of their time engaging in bodily processes rather than intellectual pursuits. Many of those processes involve the expulsion of products that are devalued in Western society (see Bakhtin 1968)—tears, urine, feces, spit-up. As intellectuals, anthropologists are not trained to view such messy matter as appropriate sites for scholarly research, despite Mary Douglas's long-fertile model for analyzing leaks and other "matter out of place" (1966).

Yet elsewhere babies' leaks may be culturally significant. How various leaks are dealt with and by whom is indeed a cultural issue, but not one I have seen properly theorized, apart from the predictably restrictive Freudian model of defecation. A more cultural model would be necessary to analyze, for example, the Senufo understanding (in northern Côte d'Ivoire and southern Burkina Faso) of urine as a gift from an infant, a means by which the baby establishes a relationship with whoever is holding him or her (Lamissa Bangali, personal communication). The bodily based model of communication embodied in this understanding challenges the prevalent Western models for establishing social relationships, which emphasize verbal interchange. Shifting the theoretical axis from the vocal cords to the urinary tract—or, for that matter, to some other body part—would unsettle our language-based model of communication at the same time that it may violate our notions of bodily pollution.

Another aspect of babies' bodies that can reveal culturally rich data is motor development—long seen by psychologists as only slightly variable in healthy babies. For example, describing how Baganda adults in Uganda systematically sit one-to-three-month-olds on their laps and prop up three-to-four-month-olds on mats to train them to sit independently and smile, Janet and Philip Kilbride (1975) noted that healthy Baganda infants typically sit independently by the age of four months—a third of a lifetime earlier than most infants from Euro-American middle-class families sit. The reason is eminently cultural: sitting up and smiling allows infants to communicate with those around them, and this skill is considered to be a valuable asset in the insistently face-to-face Baganda kingdom. These data provocatively suggest that the standard Western benchmark for healthy babies—sitting independently at six months—is as much a cultural as a biological statement.

Other aspects of motor development may be deliberately *delayed* for culturally relevant reasons. For example, as we will see in chapter 9, Beng parents traditionally prevent their infants from walking before one year of age for reasons they articulate according to a cultural script. Reclaiming the realm of motor development, which anthropologists' have largely left to the developmental psychologists as though such development is wholly biologically determined, may yield surprises of interest to members of both disciplines.

～

An equally promising line of research concerns an activity that babies do quite a lot of: sleeping. Recently, sleep has been the subject of research that suggests it as a superb locus of cultural attention. Anthropologists have been collecting material for some time indicating that co-sleeping—usually, but not always, with the mother—is prevalent for infants and young children other than those living in industrialized societies.[36] This common pattern appears to present certain significant biological advantages for survival,[37] yet noticeable variations suggest strong cultural foundations as well.

An ethnography of slumbering babies might ask: Do infants sleep with someone (with whom?) or alone? Do babies sleep upright or horizontally, stretched out as on a Native North American cradle board or curled up as in a Native Central American hammock? How much time are they sleeping in a quiet place versus a noisy place? For how long do they sleep without waking—during the day and at night? And how do local ideologies concerning babies' sleep needs interact with all these local practices—in other words, what cultural sense do such patterns make? Paying attention to the cultural shaping of somatic practices such as sleep may entail adapting time-sampling methods that are well developed for the study of adult lives (see Gross 1984). Investigations of such questions may ultimately provide us with a rich sense of both the breadth of and the limits to variation in infants' sleeping experiences (see chapter 7). In turn, such data should speak to broader issues concerning the interface between biology and culture.

Answers to these questions may reveal significant variations not only interculturally but intraculturally as well. Even among babies of the same age in the same region, significant differences may be accounted for by such factors as family structure, income level, and religious orientation. To psychologists, such studies may demonstrate that developmentalists must be wary of making cross-cultural generalizations about infant development and behavior on the basis of culturally limited studies. To anthropologists, they may demonstrate that the bodies of babies are significant markers pointing to critical cultural values; from a theoretical standpoint they may further strengthen the case for the power of culture to shape human experience—even when it comes to the seemingly impregnable bastion of biological development.

With the employment of a combination of methods developed in relation to these considerations, the experiences of infants themselves should become at least partly accessible to the gaze of outside observers. Indeed, the very definition of *experience* may change if we agree to expand the corpus of communication channels to include both the spiritual and the bodily—in the case at hand, "to identify the existential conditions which constitute the experiential world of Beng babies" (John McCall, personal communication; cf. Bruner and Turner 1986).

Are Babies Rational? Are They Human?

Finally, bodily events have long been assumed by Westerners to represent our closest ties to a biological nature; hence they have been taken as more resistant to cultural influence than are other aspects of our lives (cf. Butt 1998: 17–23, 101–28, and passim). We might take the following opening passage of a scholarly article as representative of mainstream Western views: "An infant's behavior is the ultimate expression of its biological functioning. At the time of birth, the infant is closest to its biological heritage, and thus the neonatal period can be considered the most appropriate time for exploring its biological programming for survival" (Thoman 1980:243). No wonder that babies, with their overwhelming involvement in the body, get defined as precultural—as what I have come to think of as a "biobundle."

Nowadays, however, such biologically influenced processes as sexuality, breast-feeding, menstruation, and eating have been identified as appropriate subjects for the cultural anthropological gaze.[38] Indeed, the notion of the senses and the body in general as culturally constructed is now a serious proposition. In keeping with these theoretical shifts, I suggest that it is time for the somatic statements of infants to be taken seriously by our discipline. Is the prevalent Western model of infant-as-biobundle really applicable universally? The Beng vision of infants as recent, reincarnated exiles from another world suggests otherwise. While they are seemingly helpless and all body, in the Beng model of the life cycle infants lead a rich inner life. Our own, often unconscious, assumptions about infants may prevent us from seeing such alien ideologies simply because we do not bother to interrogate the world of babies. For if Westerners define rational processes by reference to intellectual capacities—the ability to communicate via speech, to construct complex social ties and institutions, to organize our surroundings, to plan for the future—where does that leave the infant, who instead appears to specialize in the more creaturely processes of eating, sleeping, and eliminating?

Moreover, babies cry a lot. To the extent that they spend time in other than biological pursuits, that time seems more often dedicated to emotional states, and often unhappy ones at that, than to intellectual activities. We are trained to deal with informants who may be difficult, but they should at least respond reasonably to us without throwing tantrums. Babies may find this disciplinary expectation an impossible challenge.

Recently Emily Martin (1999) pointed out the extent to which anthropologists privilege rational systems of thought over other modes of experiencing life. Martin's insight might be applied to the case of infants. Whatever logic babies may exhibit, it appears remarkably distant from the standards of rationality enunciated by over two thousand years of formal Western thought.

With that intellectually problematic profile, any inclination toward serious anthropological study of such creatures is understandably low (Peters 1995:14). Indeed, insofar as rationality has been taken in the European tradition as the hallmark of humanity itself at least since the so-called Enlightenment, the apparent absence of rationality on the part of infants puts them at risk of having a problematic fit with the very category of "human." Let us consider this unsettling passage from the acclaimed novel A *High Wind in Jamaica*, by British author Richard Hughes:[39]

> Babies of course are not human—they are animals, and have a very ancient and ramified culture, as cats have, and fishes, and even snakes: the same in kind as these, but much more complicated and vivid, since babies are, after all, one of the most developed species of the lower vertebrates. . . .
>
> Babies have minds which work in terms and categories of their own which cannot be translated into the terms and categories of the human mind.
>
> It is true they look human—but not so human, to be quite fair, as monkeys.
>
> Subconsciously, too, every one recognizes they are animals—why else do people always laugh when a baby does some action resembling the human, as they would at a praying mantis? If the baby was only a less-developed man, there would be nothing funny in it, surely. . . .
>
> One can no more think like a baby, in the smallest respect, than one can think like a bee. (Hughes 1999:158–59)

To be sure, Hughes's unnamed narrator exudes a deeply bleak, if ironic, vision to which few of his readers would fully subscribe. Still, one cannot help but wonder if Hughes's cynical interpretation is only a witty exaggeration of a basic view commonly held by Westerners.

Toward an Anthropology of Infants (and Their Caretakers)

Can infants, with all their attributed conceptual liabilities and somatic messinesses, contribute to social theory? I suggest that they can, and moreover that excluding them from the possibility carries significant intellectual risks. Current directions in social science have taught us that the questions we ask inevitably inform the answers we discover. Could it be that if we start to ask new questions—indeed, any questions at all—of infants and those who spend time with them, we might begin to imagine the contours of new knowledge that such questions will generate? A full-blown anthropology of infancy might well create the possibility of significant epistemological shifts.

For the moment, I suggest that two big-picture issues might be productively illuminated. The first concerns relations between structure and agency. Ironically, the tendency for anthropologists to emphasize individual agency has intensified at the same time that the discipline has embraced a discussion of historical and global processes that can easily overpower individual agency at the analytic level (Marcus and Fischer 1986). Thus in recent years we have seen a spate of biographies and autobiographies of individuals and families;[40] accounts of social life coauthored with informants and local scholars;[41] and reflexive, theoretical, and programmatic calls for privileging the voices of our informants.[42] At the same time, we see analyses of social life that are grounded in the effects of a historicized and globalized political economy.[43] The divergent directions of these two bodies of literature is a peculiar feature of the scholarly landscape of the past two decades. Can an anthropology of infants and infancy avoid crashing into either the Scylla of pure structure on one shore or the Charybdis of pure agency on the other?

It might be tempting at a methodological level to allow others to speak for infants entirely—to allow an anthropology of *infants* to become an anthropology of *infancy* as seen by others. This would assume that infants are completely vulnerable to structures imagined by adults, incapable of asserting any subjectivity. Yet it would be desirable to attempt to eschew this if an anthropology of infancy is to include not only a consideration of others' perspectives of infants, but equally importantly, an anthropology of infants themselves—premised on the notion that infants may themselves be social actors (Morton 1996), albeit ones who may utilize exotic modes of communication.

I have already hinted at some methodological shifts that a fully developed anthropology of infants might necessitate—including becoming attuned to somatic modes of communication and to local theories of infant communication, as well as acknowledging that infants, like adults, are part of a cybernetic system in which identity is defined as constitutive of society (e.g., Derné 1992; Shweder and Bourne 1984). In some ways, the anthropological effort to find an appropriate middle ground between agency and structure is related to our disciplinary attempt to forge a suitably independent identity from psychology on the one hand, with its tendency to hypostatize agency while ignoring structure (until the recent "cultural psychology" movement and, to some extent, the development of the subfield of social psychology), and from sociology on the other hand, with its opposite tendency of hypostatizing structure while ignoring agency (at least until recent attempts by some theorists, such as Giddens 1984; and Varela and Harré 1996).

Infants might provide us with a median course to chart between the shores of structure and agency precisely insofar as they embody an extreme test case. In the common Western view, infants appear to be the most dependent of creatures, exhibiting the least initiative of any humans. If elsewhere infants are held responsible for their actions even in the context of dependence on others, that would be a significant check in the agency column. I have hinted at such a scenario on the basis of my own fieldwork, and there are signs from other societies that the Beng model of infancy may be replicated, with local variations, fairly broadly outside the Western world (see chapter 4). Indeed, some developmental psychologists and psychoanalysts (e.g., Fogel 1993; Stern 1985) now embrace a model of infant behavior that is more interactive, accommodating infants' social lives and acknowledging agency even during the earliest days of extrauterine human life, than the dominant model constructed by earlier researchers. If even infants actively shape the lives of those around them, contributing to the constitution of their social worlds, surely there is a lesson to aid us analysts in understanding social life in general.

Yet investigation of the ways in which infants are enmeshed in the lives of their relatives (see Harkness and Super 1996; LeVine, Miller, and West 1988) and in broader institutions, both local and global, should provide a significant check in the structure column. As Christina Toren suggests, "one cannot understand what children are doing unless one understands the conditions produced by adults with which children have inevitably to come to grips" (1999:29). If we pay sufficient attention to indigenous ideologies regarding infants as well as to their day-to-day lives, infants may steer us toward the balanced assessment of structure and agency that so many of us crave.

An adequate cross-cultural assessment of infants may also help us to overcome our assumptions about the nature of nature and the nature of culture. For many centuries before the invention of anthropology as an academic discipline, Westerners debated the role of culture in shaping human behavior.[44] Is some, most, or all of what we humans do forged by immutable biological structures rooted in genetic configurations that we are only beginning to chart? Or is human behavior shaped by flexible cultural structures that are far more variable than biologistic models suggest? If the often appealing compromise position—*Stop, it's both!*—wins out, what proportion of human behavior is each contribution responsible for, and how would we calculate this?

Westerners tend to assume that the younger the child, the more dependent the child is on biology, and the more biologically oriented are the decisions of the child's caretakers. Yet developmental norms have been constructed on the overwhelming basis of Euro-American, middle-class children's growth, leaving the majority of the world's children unstudied and the so-called norms vulnerable to recasting. For example, we have seen that the age at which infants sit independently is variable to some extent, signaling that the timing of this motor achievement is more flexible than heretofore considered. On the other hand, four months seems to be the earliest that this ability can be mastered. If we can document upper and lower ends of the spectrum for the normal achievement of such early motor tasks, we will be in a better position to assess the role of cultural practices in accelerating or delaying their mastery.

The same may apply to social development. For example, developmental psychologists have long posited that separation anxiety is a universal stage of infants from about seven to twelve months of age. Beng infants occasionally exhibit this behavior at precisely the same stage in their first year that Western infants do. But as we will see in chapter 6, in Beng infants it is rare and is actively disapproved of, perhaps because extended families allow for highly flexible caretaking arrangements for a given infant from day to day. Here the interaction of biological timetable and cultural practices appears delicate but critical.

As these examples suggest, once we begin to study systematically the lives of infants and young children in other cultural settings, we should be able to transcend polemics and assess more realistically the relative contributions of culture and biology to cognitive, emotional, social, and even motor development at the earliest stages of postuterine life. Thus an anthropology of infants (and their caretakers) should contribute to enduring social and philosophical debates about the role of nurture in shaping human lives. As has been noted before (e.g., Lallemand and LeMoal 1981), children have long figured actively in such conversations, but more as ideological than as ethnographic markers. A fieldwork-informed ethnography of infants may contribute significantly to this ongoing conversation.

Let us turn, then, to our ethnographic case—the Beng of Côte d'Ivoire.

CHAPTER THREE

The Beng World

The Beng are one of those doubly peripheral peoples whose lives are doubly ignored by those in power. They are a relatively obscure minority group living on the economic and political fringes of a small, debt-ridden nation that itself exists on the economic and political fringes of the global economy and that is currently embroiled in civil war.[1] In this chapter I provide a brief overview of Beng history and society so as to situate my study of infants' lives in a meaningful context. I aim to offer a balanced portrait of both visible and invisible forces that shape Beng villagers' daily decisions concerning their young children.[2]

The Beng as an Isolated Minority?

Currently, the Beng make up one of the smallest of approximately sixty ethnic groups that occupy the West African nation of Côte d'Ivoire (see map below). In the nation at large, several other groups, including the Baule, Bété, Jula, and Senufo, tend to dominate the ethnic landscape. Since the death in 1993 of the nation's long-ruling founder and president, Félix Houphouët-Boigny, a series of power shifts has reconstituted the country's ethnic politics. Those classified as southerners are now pitted bitterly against those classified as northerners, with two additional binary pairs—native-born versus immigrant and Christian versus Muslim—partly overlapping the first dyad. Until the current civil war, the Beng were generally invisible in such contests.

One reason for the relative invisibility of the Beng is geographic. Depending on whose perspective one adopts, the homeland of the Beng is situated on the northern edge of the forest zone or on the southern edge of the savanna zone. Thus the area falls squarely between the two major geographic regions that are now symbolically configured as the humid/Christian/native-born south and the dry/Muslim/immigrant north. Escalating tension between these increasingly polarized groups recently developed into an unresolved coup attempt, and there is no end in sight to the ensuing civil war. Caught between the largely northern Muslims and largely southern Christians and "animists," the Beng region was recently identified as a convenient site for a rebel stronghold. Until the current insurrection, however, living in a betwixt-and-between geocultural space has ensured that the Beng were thoroughly ignored in national discourse.

Another factor contributing to their relative invisibility is demographic:

Ethnic/Linguistic map of Côte d'Ivoire. Drawn by Steve Holland.

with a population of only approximately twelve thousand in a nation of over 14.5 million (UNICEF 2000), the Beng constitute a minor presence in simple population terms. This basic fact has political ramifications. They pose no significant political threat as they do not constitute a voting bloc of import to those in power—or, for that matter, a potential site of resistance or uprising. Of course, to pose a political threat, a group needs access to structures of power. As an economically and politically disadvantaged minority, the Beng lack systematic access to most decision-making channels at the national level.[3] And as we shall explore in chapter 11, the relatively low level of literacy and school involvement further guarantees the general removal from the corridors of power.

The Beng are also relatively invisible on the national scene because of their language, which is most closely related to the languages of several other very small minority populations, especially the Mwan and Wan, who live far to the west. The Beng are surrounded by much larger groups of neighbors who speak languages that are unrelated to theirs. To the north they are bordered by the Jimini (= Djimini, a subgroup of the Senufo); to the south and west, by the Baule (= Baoulé); and to the east, by the Ando (= Ano or Anno, related closely to the Baule). In order to converse with all who are not Beng—including neighbors who are members of these groups, traders who come into their villages, and people they encounter when they travel to distant towns and cities—the vast majority of Beng people become at least bilingual early in their childhood, and many become multilingual.

Although it is common for West Africans to be at least bilingual (Williamson 1997:175), the minority status of the Beng gives their particular linguistic prowess a certain inevitability that is shaped by political and economic obscurity. By contrast, it is quite rare for members of other linguistic groups in the country to learn the Beng language. Even ethnic immigrants who have lived for many years in Beng villages often know barely more than a smattering of passing greeting formulas in Beng, opting instead to converse with their Beng neighbors (and even their Beng affines) in one of the country's more widely spoken languages, such as Jula or Baule. This asymmetry in the contours of bilingualism indexes a hierarchical prestige system in which the Beng language occupies a very low position.

Yet another reason for the relatively low profile of the Beng in the nation's ethnic politics relates to religious history. The Beng consider themselves pacifists insofar as it is taboo to the Earth spirits they worship to commit homicide with physical weapons.[4] Their religion dictates that anyone who violates this taboo will die quickly unless a full year of ritual treatment is inaugurated immediately after the act. Even this may fail to save the murderer, or though it may save the person's life, the assassin may soon go mad. The single Beng veteran from World War II whom I knew to be living in a Beng village was widely considered to suffer from periodic bouts of insanity as a result of his wartime experience.

Given the taboo against murder, the Beng reaction to military aggression has typically been to retreat. Living partly in and partly on the edge of the tropical rain forest, the Beng have availed themselves of their intimate knowledge of that forest to flee into the deep woods when under threat of attack. Villagers who have not attended Western schools claim to have no knowledge of the Atlantic slave trade. Contemporary Beng who have been educated about that abysmal epoch of African history speculate that their ancestors must have lived (or retreated?) so deep in the rain forest that they never encountered (or they avoided?) the slave traders' nets. Likewise, retreat was apparently their reaction to Almami Samori Touré (ca. 1830–1900), the Muslim Jula invader from Guinea who conducted a jihad-style rampage through this portion of West Africa to build a Muslim empire during the second half of the nineteenth century and was stopped only by the simultaneous French invasion of the region. According to my Beng consultants, Samori never succeeded in conquering the Beng, who apparently prayed to the Earth for salvation and hid out quite effectively in the forest during Samori's local sorties.[5] Most recently, according to local reports, some Beng villagers have utilized the same strategy, fleeing deep into the rain forest to avoid the depredations of rebellious soldiers occupying the Beng region during the developing civil war.

Of course, the Beng were not so successful in hiding from the colonizing French, who effectively invaded and occupied their region in the 1890s. As with other peasant populations of Africa, the Beng suffered greatly under European colonialism. Through the first half of the twentieth century, the French compelled Beng farmers to perform forced labor to build roads. As a mode of paying taxes to support the colonial regime, the Beng had to devote much time to planting new crops, especially coffee, cocoa, and new varieties of rice and cotton, to be sold to the French for minimal, and sometimes no, recompense. Although the Beng resented their subjugation as bitterly as any, unlike members of the many African groups that did not espouse pacifism the Beng never took up arms against their conquerors.[6]

The pacifism of the Beng has gone hand in hand with a tendency to resist cultural conquest. After independence, the Beng again tried to keep a low profile vis-à-vis the new government. For example, until the early nineties, most parents resisted sending their children to government-run schools. Nowadays some young parents are rejecting this conservatism of their elders, and a growing proportion of Beng children are being sent to elementary school for at least a few years. However, the dropout rate at the elementary school level remains quite high (see chapter 11). Even today many village dwellers feel a deep need to maintain a certain distance from modernity, which—with its origins in the Europe that conquered them—many Beng people still distrust greatly.

Despite this tendency toward military and, to some extent, cultural independence, the Beng have by no means lived in total seclusion. It is true that, unlike many groups in West Africa, they have not ventured far from their homeland as long-distance traders. However, before the colonial era, they did sell goods and produce to Jula long-distance traders who came regularly to their villages, and they walked to distant villages of other ethnic groups to trade such items as well. Although the Beng have taboos against potting, weaving, and metalwork, they became regionally renowned for other products, including bark cloth and indigenous cotton, as well as kola nuts. They traded kola nuts for cowry shells with long-distance Jula traders, who brought the nuts back north to Muslim populations living in the drier regions of the West African Sudan, where kola trees cannot be grown. Precolonially the kola nut, which has a noticeable caffeine content, was used as a stimulant and energy source as well as an ingredient in a variety of social and ritual encounters in many parts of West and North Africa.[7] Additionally, Beng men traded bark cloth and homespun cotton with Jimini neighbors for other goods in kind, especially ceramic pots and woven cotton *pagnes,* and they also sold their goods to itinerant Jula traders.[8] This local engagement with a variety of ethnic neighbors suggests a consideration of the cultural space that the Beng occupy in the regional imagination.

Most members of surrounding groups consider the Beng to be the autochthonous population of the region. Their history is by no means completely understood. Linguistic evidence points to the current nation of Mali as a starting point because their language, a member of the southern Mande group, is distantly related to the northern Mande languages now spoken in Mali.[9] However, linguists estimate that the two language groups split apart over two millennia ago, and virtually no Beng people living today acknowledge an origin in Mali. It is probable that the Beng have a complex migration history for the period following this early separation from a proto-Mande group (Gottlieb 1996b:4–8). In any case, their neighbors consider them the longest-settled group in the region. This accords them a certain culturally privileged position vis-à-vis the residents of villages that surround them.

This privileged position also comes from their cultural practices, especially those rooted in their religion. Let us explore briefly the cultural universe of the Beng.

Contemporary Society

Both within the region and to some extent beyond it, when they are recognized as a group at all, the Beng are known for a fierce commitment to their traditional religion and for the powerful efficacy of that religion.[10] The Beng world is populated not only by beings who are visible to the human eye but also by forces that are invisible to humans. Although a gulf is said to separate humans from the world of the spirits, the lives of spirits reportedly parallel the lives of humans in uncanny ways. Moreover, the existence of animal sacrifices implies a certain continuity between the human and animal worlds. This conceptual continuity is a hallmark of Beng ecothought.

The Beng recognize several types of spirits that are somewhat related yet also distinct. One group, called *wru* (souls), exists as ancestors in the afterlife (*wrugbe*, literally "soul village"). These figure prominently in the lives of the living and especially in infants, as we will see. A second major group exists as miscellaneous spirits living in the bush, with two distinct subgroups: *gaŋwróŋ* and *alufye*. The latter are pygmy-sized spirits—some say powerful beings rather than spirits—living on the border between the village and the forest. The third group of spirits *(bɔŋzɔ)* is directly associated with the Earth.[11] They congregate around certain spots, especially where there is a hill and an adjacent small pool of water, which is considered an especially hospitable setting for these spirits. People put shrines at such places, and indigenous priests come once every six days to make offerings at the shrines.

Each village is affiliated with a specific Earth (in some cases, two or even three Earths). Each of these Earths has a proper name that, while known to most adults, is considered too powerful to utter in normal discourse,[12] and each is considered to have precise contours localized in a particular spot. Villagers generally make offerings to the spirits connected with the Earth that is associated with their village, though on occasion they travel to other villages to make offerings to other spirits that a diviner has told them are responsible for their well-being. The religious tradition of the Beng emphasizes the offering of prayers and sacrifices to all three of these groups of spirits but especially to the *wru* and the *bɔŋzɔ*.

The Beng also name a deity called *eci*, which I translate loosely as "sky/god." As in many African religious systems, this deity is rather remote and, though evoked frequently in casual speech, is never the direct object of sacrifice.[13] Rather, the terrestrial orientation of the Beng places far more emphasis on the spirits of the Earth.

Indigenous religious practitioners are of two sorts: diviners *(srandiŋ)* and Masters of the Earth *(ba gbali)*. Diviners, who may be male or female, use a variety of techniques (including "reading" the patterns of cowry shells thrown on a mat, or made by kaolin mixed with water when swirled around in a brass bowl) in order to communicate with invisible bush spirits; the diviners then interpret the spirits' communications to concerned clients.[14] One of the commonest causes for villagers, especially mothers, to consult diviners, Masters of the Earth, or both is to discover the reason or cure for their own or their children's illnesses. Frequently, adult patients and mothers of sick children first consult a diviner—in good part because a diviner's services often cost less than do those of a Master of the Earth. The diviner may offer a simple herbal remedy or may prescribe a sacrifice to a particular spirit or spirits—affiliated with the bush, the Earth, or the land of the ancestors. Sacrifices are carried out by a Master of the Earth, who is almost always male. Masters of the Earth worship the Earth spirits once every six days, according to the six-day Beng calendar, by offering prayers and animal sacrifices on behalf of individuals or, occasionally, groups. Those who request sacrifices seek protection against evils such as witchcraft, desire relief from afflictions that are deemed to have a spiritual cause, want to give thanks for past wishes granted or good luck experienced, or wish to make atonement for sins committed.

The Beng are not the only people who consider the spirits they propitiate to be powerful. Their spirits have earned a widespread reputation throughout many parts of the nation. Not only their neighbors of other ethnic groups, but also some who live much farther away are afraid of the Beng because of their reputed access to these powerful spirits. On the weekly day of rest dedicated to religious practice, one commonly sees non-Beng visitors lined up to consult with a local diviner, or to ask a local Master of the Earth to offer sacrifices to the local Earth spirits on their behalf. I have even heard of police officers from as far away as Abidjan coming to Beng villages to use the services of such religious specialists. A non-Beng hotel manager living in a distant city once told me that if he were ever traveling through the Beng region and saw a Beng person looking for a ride, he would always stop to pick up the hitch-hiker, for fear of instant revenge—via witchcraft—were he to drive by without stopping.

Industrial visitors to—and sojourners through—the Beng region indeed encounter such spiritual disasters from time to time. On one occasion during the rainy season, two molasses trucks on the way to Abidjan became mired in the mud ditch on the side of a dirt road leading through the Beng region. Effort after effort failed to free the stuck trucks—until the non-Beng, Muslim drivers agreed to offer a chicken sacrifice to the local hill spirits, which were reputedly offended by the noise and weight of the vehicles. Soon after the chicken was offered, a rescue truck arrived and pulled the molasses trucks back onto the road (Gottlieb and Graham 1994:204–208). A somewhat similar, if darker, incident involved loggers. Some years ago, several lumberjacks were severely injured or killed by the trees they were endeavoring to fell. Their surviving colleagues interpreted the tragedy as the act of spirits dwelling in the trees, which were reportedly angered because the loggers were chopping down their forest abodes without offering them propitiatory sacrifices in advance. Apparently, the loggers are now fearful of the local forest spirits, and some refuse missions in the region.

Those who visit or even just pass through the area thus often experience firsthand what they consider to be the force of the Beng spirits, and they bring stories of their frightening adventures back to the cities. To the extent that they are known at all, then, in the nation's cultural imaginary the Beng continue to occupy a somewhat respected, somewhat feared place. While modernity makes its seemingly resolute march forward, the fiercely held religious traditions of the Beng serve as a potent counterweight to the apparent inevitability of social change.

Until very recently, most Beng villagers have maintained an active commitment to the religious practices I have summarized. However, in the past few decades an increasing number of Beng have become attracted to Islam, and some have endorsed Christianity—a development that began later in Bengland than in many other regions of Africa. There is now a mosque in one village (Bongalo), and most other villages have a significant minority of Muslims. Moreover, in the mid-twentieth century, a smaller number of Beng endorsed Catholicism, and one village (Asagbe) now has a church. In addition, a German Protestant missionary couple lived in one Beng village for much of the 1980s and attracted some followers, although by local accounts they failed to make many converts.

Some villagers who have become devout Christians or Muslims now explicitly reject the Beng pantheon for a monotheistic god, and they consider themselves exempt from the religious obligations I have discussed. Yet this discursive rejection is often not rigid: many of the new "converts" continue to maintain some level of engagement with indigenous religious practices. For example, if prayers to the Muslim or Christian god do not bring relief to a sick or unlucky Muslim or Christian, consultations with a diviner—perhaps by a concerned "animist" relative on behalf of the afflicted—are not unknown. If a sacrifice to a spirit is called for, the patient may find ways to explain the act as compatible with the tenets of Christianity or Islam. In short, as with many Africans (Gottlieb n.d.a), most Beng who have adopted one of the "world" religions see different faiths as complementary rather than competing, and most continue to practice at least an attenuated version of their local religious tradition while simultaneously endorsing the major precepts of a new religion. Only a much smaller number have definitively converted in the usual sense of the term.

~

Most villagers also continue to reproduce the long-standing Beng family structure. Many extended households consist of a man, his wife or wives, all their unmarried daughters, all their sons, and their married sons' wives and children. Until the 1960s, such extended families typically lived together under the single thatched roof of a large, round house. In the 1960s the government bulldozed all these houses and required that all newly constructed dwellings be smaller, square houses with tin roofs (Gottlieb 1996b:135–36). Yet extended families have often remained residentially intact, with components of this large group inhabiting small buildings that are adjacent to one another and surround an open courtyard.

A dual descent system of clans crosscuts these households, with each individual holding life membership in both a matriclan and a patriclan (Gottlieb 1996b:46–71). Until recently, virtually every woman's first marriage was arranged according to a complex set of rules regarding cousins and structural duplication of alliances (Gottlieb 1996b:72–97). Even now, the first marriage of many women is arranged, although some women manage to rebel against the system (Gottlieb and Graham 1994).

The matriclans divide up all known space in the culturally meaningful world. Each village is split into neighborhoods *(tuwa)*, each of which is affiliated with and named for a single matriclan. The publicly acknowledged space of each matriclan extends into the adjacent forest, dividing the entire forested region of Bengland into sociologically significant segments. Villagers cut and routinely maintain named paths that crisscross the forest and lead both from village to fields and between villages.

Complicating matters, patriclans segment social space in both village and forest along a second axis. In the village, within each matrilaterally constituted neighborhood, the courtyards house patrilaterally constituted extended families, which farm together as well as live together. Thus within each matrilaterally constituted region in the forest, men establish fields by reference to paternal ties: a man and his sons farm pie-shaped wedges grouped in a full circle (*peŋ)*.[15]

Matriclans and patriclans thus combine to thoroughly classify all local space of both village and forest. The cognitive and emotional effect of all this cultural classification is to make the forest—particularly the surrounding rain forest, which houses dangerous flora and fauna and, it is said, dangerous spirits—not just a source of known risk and fear but also a site of culturally meaningful space that is in some ways structurally equivalent to the village.

The villages themselves are grouped into two political regions, which the Beng call Forest *(kleŋ)* and Savanna *(bao)*, and are roughly correlated with the two ecozones for which they are named. A king-and-queen pair, who stand in a symbolic sibling relationship to each other, rules each region. This ruling pair is considered responsible for all that occurs in its region. Although the queen is viewed as essential for the smooth running of the polity, people hold the king more directly responsible for day-to-day events. When a king ascends to the throne, he ritually weeps for the weight of the responsibility he now carries.

The kingdom is envisioned as a moral community. Each act of immorality—in particular, each act of witchcraft—is considered an affront to the community that the king must endeavor to counteract. Every night, when everyone else is asleep, the king is said to use his own powers of witchcraft to do battle with the realm's resident witches. If he wins, another life is saved; if he loses, there is another death in the village.[16]

The vast majority of Beng people still live in relatively small, rural villages of the sort described above, and theirs is a mixed economy of farming and hunting and gathering. Some twenty-odd villages call themselves Beng.[17] In these villages, virtually every mother is also a full-time farmer. Women and men both work hard—sometimes separately, sometimes together—to produce the varied foodstuffs that make up the diet, including yams (the main starch staple), rice, corn, manioc, and peanuts, as well as a variety of fruits and vegetables. But it is women who primarily control the day-to-day decisions about who eats what.

During some seasons men work hard at farming—especially clearing land of trees for new planting, making mounds in which to plant new yams, and spending long hours in the village making cords from lianas to use for trailing the shoots of new yam plants upward for sunlight. However, most men readily acknowledge that women work even harder than they do. Women are full-time farmers year-round. In addition to gathering wild forest products and occasionally hunting small game, they burn the underbrush before planting and then plant and weed fields and harvest rice, corn, and a large variety of vegetables, with some men helping on occasion. Moreover, women do all of the cooking and laundry, much of the house maintenance (though men do some tasks), and much of the child care, especially of the youngest children.

Women and girls often appear to feel solidarity among one another because of their shared knowledge of their difficult work burden. Once I asked my friend Amenan why men have an open-air structure *(tumgbo)* for chatting among themselves while women lack such a culturally approved space for socializing. Amenan laughed uneasily and explained that women have too much work to do—unlike men, who have time to just sit and chat. Some men listening nearby chuckled guiltily their assent.

Whether or not they attend primary school, young children are also educated in local farming techniques. Children as young as two to three years old help in various agricultural tasks to the best of their ability, starting with

14. A toddler learning how to pound food in a small mortar after watching her mother do so for months

15. A girl of about five years old carrying yams on her head back to the village after helping her mother in the fields

jumping up and down and shouting to serve as human scarecrows in the fields. Adults regularly send boys and girls throughout the village as messengers. Young girls learn very early—from when they are just beginning to walk—to help their mothers with cooking (figure 14), washing laundry, and carrying head loads (figure 15).

In precolonial times, men hunted regularly, catching such forest game as several varieties of duiker, antelope, and monkey, as well as rarer species such as wild boar and porcupine. The growth of a cash economy, with its more labor-intensive farming techniques based around monoculture, has reduced the time available for nocturnal hunting expeditions, and the price of bullets is also now too expensive for many men. As a result, the amount of available animal protein has declined since the colonial period (see chapter 11). When they have the time, women, men, and children continue to collect wild plants, especially berries, and leaves of certain trees such as the kapok and iroko, as well as snails and other small forest creatures.

As with farmers everywhere, the Beng view themselves as vulnerable to the vagaries of weather, the predations of animals, and a variety of other "natural" dangers. Yet in accord with their basic view that there is an intimate relation between the visible and invisible worlds, the Beng see weather as socially and spiritually derived. What Westerners might term natural disasters are seen as anything but that by Beng farmers. Take the following entry from my 1993 field notes:

> *24 July 1993*
> There is a drought currently in the region, and recently some men from Tolegbe came to Asagbe to offer prayers and a sacrifice to the Krileŋ shrine, for rain. But right after they arrived, the chief of Asagbe died, and they weren't allowed to proceed with the sacrifice—you can't do this during a funeral. The village is therefore waiting for the funeral to end, so that the men can do the sacrifice. But meanwhile, another old man in Asagbe is very sick and may die soon—and then the men from Tolegbe STILL won't be able to do the sacrifice until THAT funeral is ended. As a result, everyone is very worried.

Among the Beng, rain is seen as subject to manipulation by people's religious practices. Yet in this model, the religious practices themselves are believed to be regulated by other sociological and spiritual rules, so that prayers and sacrifices may only be offered at culturally appropriate times. Farmers thus see themselves both as efficacious actors able to cause changes in the weather patterns that determine success or failure in their fields, and as vulnerable victims constrained by local proscriptions on effective measures to protect their crops.

~

The period since 1960, when Côte d'Ivoire achieved independence from France, has presented formidable hardships to African peasant populations such as the Beng. For example, prices paid to rural Ivoirian villagers for these crops (until recently, by government agents) have fallen precipitously since the 1980s. This is in part because of falling prices of commodities such as coffee and cocoa on the world market, but also because of the government's extravagant spending on projects of dubious utility. The reduction in prices for their cash crops has meant a seriously diminished cash base for Beng farmers. As a result, in the 1990s some severely impoverished families reverted to a virtual subsistence economy (see chapter 11).

The implications of this declining economy for children's lives are drastic.[18] Nowadays, many Beng parents cannot afford relatively inexpensive luxuries that are considered necessities in the "developed" world. Many parents would like to send at least some of their children to school, but they are unable to afford all the ancillary expenses associated with the nominally free school system (see chapter 11). Many cannot afford childhood inoculations, which the government makes available at minimal cost via roving teams of nurses. Moreover, when they or their children fall ill, few parents can afford the relatively expensive bus trip to the nearest town (M'Bahiakro) to consult a Western-trained doctor. Even if they can manage a trip to town, and even though the doctor's services are government-provided and thus free to patients, they can rarely afford the expensive medicines the doctor is likely to prescribe for them to buy at the local pharmacy. Indeed, nowadays some villagers cannot even afford to consult local Beng healers, whose fees are relatively modest (usually 50–100 CFA) even by the standards of the local economy.[19] Also, as a result of the decline in available food in general and protein sources in particular, more children are sick more often, and because of the unavailability of cash, fewer sick children are treated properly. The current civil war is seriously exacerbating all of these problems. Undoubtedly, more Beng children are dying now than were even in the 1990s.

~

In the pages that follow, as in all my published writings to date, the scope of my claims ends at the boundaries of Beng villages, where I have concentrated my research. My informal observations among the still relatively small group of Beng families now living in towns and cities would suggest a fair amount of continuity in infant care practices with the practices reported in this work. This accords with the findings of a new generation of scholars who have argued that the rural/urban divide in Africa may be far more porous than was previously assumed and may in some ways be more productively thought of as a continuum than a divide. Exciting studies of urban migration within Africa as well as of the contemporary urban African diaspora in Europe and the United States show an often provocative combination of predictable ruptures and surprising continuities between "traditional" rural practices and new urban lives.[20]

My somewhat informal observations suggest that the current group of Beng migrants now living in towns and cities shows such a combination, with more continuities than ruptures in many cases. Nevertheless, among urban Beng families, infant care practices seem to vary depending on a host of factors, especially the mother's education level, whether she has married a Beng man, and whether she is surrounded by Beng neighbors. Further field research is required to determine to what extent, and in what ways, this small but growing group of Beng families now living in cities in Côte d'Ivoire and elsewhere replicate or challenge the models I explore in this work.

In the following chapters, I will have far less to say about fathers than about mothers for the simple reason that far fewer Beng fathers than mothers are significantly involved in the day-to-day care of their infants. Most Beng fathers take great pleasure in their babies. But unlike mothers, they rarely feed them, bathe them (twice daily), give them enemas (twice daily), apply jewelry or paint to their bodies (twice daily), clothe them (two to three times daily), or carry them on their backs (for many hours each day). Fathers do enjoy playing with their infants for short intervals so long as the babies are not fussing.

As infants turn to toddlers, this child-care pattern changes dramatically where boys are concerned. Many fathers take care of their young sons for much of the day soon after the little boys can walk well, usually by the time they are two or three years old. When they are very small, toddlers ride on the handlebars of their fathers' bicycles. Later, they walk on their own to their fathers' farms or, if their fathers have enough cash, they ride their own bikes. In the fields, little boys learn from their fathers how to do men's agricultural work.

Different persons in Beng villages offer decidedly different perspectives on child rearing. In the chapters that follow, I endeavor to discuss a range of individuals' perspectives when possible. However, in the next six chapters I especially emphasize the spiritual foundations of child-rearing decisions, both because these provide a distinctive shape to Beng infant care and because they are emphasized by many Beng themselves as determinative of their child-rearing decisions. This is not to say that the Beng live in a timeless spiritual reality unchanged by historical circumstances. At the same time that a rich conceptual model gives meaning to the Beng configuration of the life cycle, poverty shapes and crimps the specific ways in which that spiritually oriented child-rearing agenda can be implemented.

Of course, poverty itself is overdetermined by a multitude of confounding factors resulting from the combined legacies of colonial and postcolonial regimes. In chapters 4 through 9, I discuss the effects of poverty as they become relevant. In the final two chapters, the issue takes center stage: there I directly explore the intersection of religion and political economy as I examine the effects of several key factors—including colonialism, out-migration, the nation's declining health care system, and changes in agriculture, schooling, and the world economy—on the project of rearing children in Beng villages.

Let us begin by exploring the religious underpinnings to Beng child rearing.

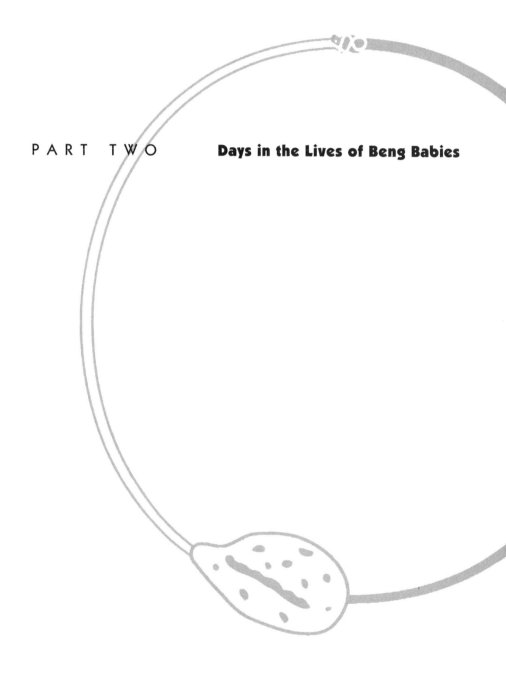

PART TWO   **Days in the Lives of Beng Babies**

CHAPTER FOUR

Spiritual Beng Babies
Reflections on Cowry Shells, Coins, and Colic

The Spiritual Nature of Beng Infants

Most secular, Western folk models of child development imply a mute and uncomprehending newborn arriving for the first time in the world of humans from a restricted uterine life of minimal stimulation and no social interaction. Before that, the underlying biological model further implies, the fetus was a mere zygote of a few cells, and before those cells were joined, it had no existence whatsoever. Hence the average Western caretaker of an infant, whether the mother or anyone else, usually attends to the bodily needs of the young tot with great care but pays far less attention to social concerns, and virtually none to spiritual ones.[1] The Beng view of fetal development is quite different. Beng adults maintain that infants lead profoundly spiritual lives. In fact, the younger they are, the more thoroughly spiritual their existence is said to be. To understand this indigenous conception of infants' spirituality, we must investigate the Beng understanding of life before the womb.

In Beng villages, each baby is said to be a reincarnation of someone who has died. By itself this ideology is by no means rare in Africa, and it is also well-known in South Asia and native North America.[2] But we anthropologists have rarely asked what the implications of this common ideology may be for how infants and young children are cared for. Given the many reasons for our disciplinary reluctance to engage with infants, this is not surprising. Following the general pattern, anthropological explorations of religion have tended to focus on the lives, experiences, and viewpoints of adults. The great canonical works on religion have scarcely a word to say about how religion might affect children's lives. Most recent social scientists continue to assume the irrelevance of early childhood to spirituality and vice versa. The one significant exception to this tendency is the discussion of teenagers and younger children in the context of organized initiation rituals (Ottenberg 1989; Richards 1956; Turner 1967). Otherwise, silence reigns concerning the religious and ritual experiences of minors. If this is true of young children, it is even more so of infants, with only rare exceptions (see, for example, Leis 1982).

We begin our exploration of infant care practices with an investigation into the conceptual framework that, I suggest, gives the Beng child-rearing agenda meaning.

The Afterlife Is Where We Come From

In the Beng world, infants are believed to emerge not from a void before gaining life inside a woman's womb, but from a rich, social existence in a place that adults call *wrugbe*. How do the Beng conceive of this culturally imagined space that is so critical to their understanding of the human life cycle? Several Beng adults explained that *wrugbe* is dispersed among invisible neighborhoods in major cities in Africa and Europe (although everyone who told me about this named a different city). Given the rural nature of traditional Beng society, the imputed urban nature of *wrugbe* implies an other world that is truly Other. Considering the relatively short time the Beng have been engaged with the globalized, urban world, this presumably recent innovation in the indigenous cosmology is significant, revealing at once a creative effort to incorporate modernity into the framework of tradition and an effort to distance the other world as dramatically as possible from this one.

The literal meaning of *wrugbe* is "spirit village" or "spirit town." The most obvious English translation is "the afterlife," the place to which the *wru*, or spirit, of a person travels once that person's body dies and the *nenen*, or soul, transforms into a *wru*.[3] In the Beng view, infants have very recently been living an invisible existence in this other space.

The doctrine of reincarnation is based on a cyclical trajectory with no beginning and no end, and death as another kind of life. With this orientation, one's sense of time must sit on a different axis from the one on which sits the common Western sense of time, with its discrete, unilinear notions of past, present, and future (Duncan 1998). With a model of reincarnation comes the idea that what existed in the past actively persists into the present through the regular insertion of ancestors into the daily lives of the living. As Gillian Feeley-Harnik writes of the Sakalava of northwestern Madagascar: "There is no separate land of the ancestors. The ancestors exist among the living. Or rather, it would be more accurate to say that people live among ancestors. . . . To be is to live with ancestors. To live elsewhere is to be 'lost' *(very)*, cut off from one's kin, tantamount to being enslaved" (1991:125). In such a conception, both the present and the future are actively shaped by what happened in the past. Moreover, in the Beng model, all infants and young children, as well as adult diviners, tack back and forth between past and present by traveling—one might even say commuting—to *wrugbe*. The three dimensions of time, so discrete in formal Western thought, have far more intimate relations in this model (Fernandez 1986:169n7).

My understanding of the contours of *wrugbe* has been gained through a series of conversations over the years with many Beng people, especially religious specialists, both Masters of the Earth and diviners. During my last visit, the diviner Kouakou Bah regularly shared with me his exceptional knowledge of *wrugbe*. Still in his late twenties, Kouakou Bah had already built up a large following because of his reputation for speaking the truth on the basis of his early training as a diviner. Here is how Kouakou Bah explained his understanding of the temporal and, we might say, demographic dimensions of *wrugbe*: "Every day, there are deaths and births. The number of people living here and in *wrugbe* keeps going up and down. You know who you're replacing from *wrugbe* if someone dies on the same day that you're born. Otherwise, if no one dies on the day you're born, you don't know whom you're replacing."

Two issues emerge from Kouakou Bah's statement that bear discussion. The first is that of personal identity. In the Beng model, everyone is considered to be a reincarnation of an ancestor, and some people know whose prior identity has returned in them. Although there is no general set of terms to distinguish those who know from those who do not know their prior identities, an individual whose previous identity is known may be treated in particular ways according to the ancestor's personality and life circumstances.

Kouakou Bah's statement also carries intriguing demographic implications that we might be tempted to put in economistic terms. That is, the indigenous conception of demography in which each human life given from *wrugbe* must be counterbalanced by one taken back to *wrugbe* might be recast as a zero-sum understanding of human life. But does this necessarily imply an empirically stable population, with births and deaths continually balanced? This would hardly be possible at any given moment, as the number of births and deaths vary according to a complex set of factors that are surely impossible to equalize. What is significant for our purposes is that the idea of reincarnation-as-demographic-balance operates at the ideological level regardless of actual demographic fluctuations.[4]

This possible lack of fit between ideology and praxis, as we might put it, is mirrored at another level. Once someone dies, the *neneŋ*, or soul, is transformed into a *wru*, or spirit. Yet when that person is reincarnated as someone else, the *wru* nevertheless continues to exist as an ancestor. The ideology posits a dual, rather than an either/or, existence. Unlike the classical Aristotelian framework, which demands that an identity be either one thing or another but not both simultaneously, the Beng view allows that a being may exist simultaneously at two very different levels of reality—the one visible and earthly, the other invisible and ghostly.[5]

The boundary between *wrugbe* and this life is held to be permeable in another way. Although *wrugbe* is said to be located in distant countries or metropolises where the lifestyle of the living residents is quite different from that of rural Beng villagers, Beng adults do not perceive *wrugbe* as unreachable. Indeed, I was told of several living adults who had managed to travel invisibly to *wrugbe* in their dreams in order to converse with ancestors, and had then returned easily to tell the tale. When I expressed amazement—perhaps influenced unconsciously by the classical Greek conception of the afterlife, with its formidable Cerberus guarding the river Hades—my interlocutor assured me that anyone could converse with an ancestor and that the dreamtime journey to *wrugbe* is not dangerous.

Reciprocally, the *wrus* of Beng ancestors are said to traverse back and forth between *wrugbe* and this life on a daily basis. As we have seen (chapter 3), before local officials of the Ivoirian government ordered all thatch-roofed houses to be destroyed in the late 1960s, the Beng lived in large, round dwellings that accommodated an extended family, which was meant to include not only the living but also the dead. Every night someone in the household would put out a small bowl of food for the ancestors of the family, and the last person to retire would close the door, locking in the living and the dead to sleep together. In the morning the first person to open the door released the *wrus,* who traveled back to *wrugbe* for the day—only to return again at night for their dinner and sleeping spot once again.[6] Nowadays, although the destruction of the large, round houses has caused some significant shifts in daily life, the ancestors continue to maintain a significant presence in the villages. The living nourish the dead at all times of day and night: before taking the first sip of any drink (water, palm wine, beer, soda), adults spill a few drops on the ground for the ancestors to drink. In this and other ways, the notion of the interlinking of past, present, and future through reincarnation continues to be rendered relevant to daily life in a regular, if invisible, traffic between the dead and the living.

This reincarnation ideology does not exist only at the conceptual, invisible level. In the twenty-first century, after some two decades during which "practice anthropology" gained an almost hegemonic position in social scientific analyses (Ortner 1984), it would be naive to repeat the mistakes of mid-twentieth-century anthropologists such as Marcel Griaule and his associates, who focused on a seductively rich ideology to the exclusion of its implications for daily life. In the remainder of this chapter, then, I explore the relationship between praxis and ideology in the context of Beng life. Considering the model of a regular traffic between *wrugbe* and this life, and considering Beng adults' assertion that infants have just emerged from *wrugbe*, what ramifications does the Beng ideology of reincarnation have for the day-to-day experiences of actual babies and those who take care of them?

The Spiritual Lives of Beng Infants

The Umbilical Cord: Lifeline to *Wrugbe*

According to Beng adults, until the umbilical cord stump falls off, a newborn is not considered to have emerged from *wrugbe* at all, so the tiny creature is not yet classified as a person *(sòŋ)*. If the newborn dies during those first few days, there is no funeral. The event is not announced publicly, for the infant's passing is conceived not as a death, but as a return in bodily form to the space the infant was still psychically and fully inhabiting.

Beng women told me that the umbilical stump usually drops off on the third or fourth day. This is indeed the case for the Beng newborns I have observed during my fieldwork. Assuming my Beng informants' comments are accurate and my own observations representative, the Beng pattern is somewhat accelerated compared to other regions of the "developing" world, and significantly accelerated compared to the industrialized world.[7] How can we account for this relatively rapid biological development on the part of Beng newborns?

Medical researchers have observed that "age at cord separation has been shown to be associated with the agent used for umbilical cord care" (Novack, Mueller, and Ochs 1988:220, citing Arad, Eyal, and Fainmesser 1981). Beng women apply an herbal mixture (which may include salt) to a newborn's umbilical stump to dry it out quickly and enable it to wither and drop off. The practice may indeed shorten the number of days before the stump separates. This biological event occasions a spiritual one: the infant can now begin the critical journey from *wrugbe* to this life. As long as the umbilical cord stump remains attached to the newborn, the little one is said to remain wholly in *wrugbe*—and thus all too susceptible to the temptation to return bodily. Drying out the umbilical cord stump quickly, then, is a critical bioritual act that, it is believed, helps the newborn to leave *wrugbe* in much the same way a birth attendant helps an infant to leave the birth canal.

Given these culturally vital implications of umbilical cord care, Beng women take their responsibility seriously. When I asked how many times the herbal mixture is applied to a newborn's umbilical cord stump, I was skeptical when I heard from several women that it is applied constantly, but my own subsequent observations confirmed their claim. Next to every newborn sits an older woman, usually the baby's maternal grandmother, who dabs a tiny bit of an herbal mixture on the dangling cord every few minutes.

The day that a baby's umbilical cord stump falls off is a momentous one, for the newborn is considered to have just begun to emerge from *wrugbe*. Both to mark the beginning of this passage, and to inaugurate it more actively, the infant's mother and some of her female relatives conduct two or three bodily rituals of transformation on the tiny new person.[8] First, they administer an enema to the baby (called *gbelɛ fālɛ*—"splitting the anus").[9] A mother knows that this medical treatment will cause pain to her infant, and the child's tears and cries of protest are expected. Yet women looked at me with incredulity when I inquired whether they might have pity on their newborns and delay the ritual for some time. Clearly, this is not an option.

A mother is taught how to administer an enema to her first baby by a female elder who has been bathing the baby four times a day since the birth. The mother learns to use the leaves of a plant called the *kprɔkprɔ láná* crushed together with a single chili pepper and some warm water. After the initial treatment, the mother will give such an enema to her baby twice a day, in the morning and at night. Older children often take regular enemas as well, and many adults give themselves enemas on a regular basis. Thus the baby starts to be "toilet trained" from the first week of life, and a series of "civilizing" processes has been inaugurated that marks the baby's entry into "this life."[10]

Typically a few hours after the first enema, the newborn is the subject of a second major ritual.[11] The maternal grandmother or another older woman makes a necklace *(dē)* from a savanna grass of the same name (see figure 16). This necklace will be worn night and day by the infant to encourage general health and growth until it eventually tears and falls off. At that point, depending on the baby's age and the mother's industry, it may or may not be replaced. The ritual to attach the first necklace is held in a secluded and dimly lit space—inside the bedroom of the infant's mother—and with a solemn tone. After this first necklace is applied, the mother or grandmother is permitted to add items of more complex jewelry with beads, shells, and other ornaments.

For an infant girl, a third ritual manipulation of the body occurs on the day the umbilical cord stump falls off: her ears are pierced. Now she is authorized to enter into the gendered space of feminine beautification.

The Call of *Wrugbe*

As soon as the umbilical stump drops off, the baby is said to start the spiritual journey of emerging from *wrugbe*. The process of moving from one sociospiritual space to another is believed to be long and difficult, and it takes several years to complete.[12] Here is an excerpt from a conversation I had with Kouakou Bah on the subject:

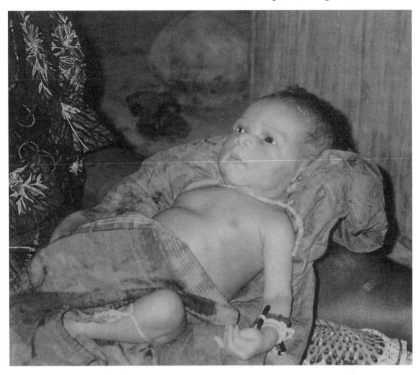

16. A newborn wearing a necklace and kneeband of *dɛ̃* grass and the first bracelets put on right after the grass cords were tied on

> *Kouakou Bah:* At some point, children leave *wrugbe* for good and decide to stay in this life.
>
> *Alma:* How do you know when this has happened?
>
> *Kouakou Bah:* When children can speak their dreams, or understand [a drastic situation, such as] that their mother or father has died, then you know that they've totally come out of *wrugbe.*
>
> *Alma:* When does that happen?
>
> *Kouakou Bah:* By seven years old, for sure! At three years old, they're still in-between: partly in *wrugbe,* and partly in this life. They see what happens in this life, but they don't understand it.

Infants and young children remain vulnerable to returning to *wrugbe* for several reasons. One is that certain spirits of the bush may find them attractive, as babies and toddlers still retain an other-world identity to which the spirits can relate. Certain signs may make children especially attractive to the spirits. For example, bush spirits are said to prefer the color red. If they see children wearing red, they are tempted to kidnap the children and bring them back to the land of spirits. To protect infants and young children from being snatched away by spirits, caretakers often avoid dressing their babies and toddlers in red clothes. But once in a while, they forget this culturally approved advice. Let us consider this case:

> "Bɔŋzɔ Kofi" ("Spirit Kofi"), who is now about four years old, was originally named Kofi Denis Komena. This is how he got his current name: One day when he was going to the fields with his grandmother, Kofi wore red underpants. In the fields, he went to sleep. His grandmother went to throw some garbage away, and when she returned, the boy was gone. The grandmother screamed for him and went all around to the nearby fields, but he was really gone. She returned to the village and failed to find the boy there. The chief of the village instructed all the people of the village to look for him both there and in the forest; he said that no one was allowed to sleep until the child was found.
>
> A diviner, Ajua, was consulted, and she said that a female spirit had taken the boy. The spirit had only one child and wanted a second child. The spirit had seen Kofi, had liked him (presumably because of his red underpants), and had taken him. However, her spirit husband told her to return Kofi to the people because the child wasn't eating and might die of hunger. If he died, the people would be upset and realize that it was the spirits who had killed the boy, and then they would no longer plant their fields in that area of the forest. In that case, how would the spirits eat?[13] The next day, the spirit husband threatened to kill his wife unless she returned the child.
>
> Meanwhile the diviner, Ajua, said that the afflicted family must sacrifice a guinea hen to the female spirit, who would then return the boy. To do so, the family must put a piece of black string on the live bird's foot and leave the bird at a certain spot. The hen would replace the child, and the spirit would return the boy. This sacrifice was soon done, and a woman who went to the fields saw Kofi standing all alone, a bit dazed, and hungry. The female spirit had taken the boy's red underpants (which she liked), and in return she'd given him two duiker horns with a cowry shell on each, and four beads, all strung on a black and white string that had been put around the child's waist in the place of his red underpants. Ajua instructed the boy's family to guard these objects always. Now that Kofi is too big to wear them, his parents keep them hanging on the wall inside their house.

Children's vulnerability to spirit kidnapping remains even past toddlerhood. I recorded cases of older children being kidnapped as well, although they are rarer than kidnappings of infants and toddlers. Very small children are considered to be the most vulnerable because of their close ties to the land of the spirits.

Another reason for children returning to the land of spirits concerns their own consciousness. During the liminal time of early childhood, as we might term it, the consciousness of the baby or toddler is sometimes in *wrugbe* and sometimes in this life. In the Beng view, parents ought to do all they can to make this life comfortable and attractive for their infant, to ensure that the child is not tempted to return to *wrugbe*. For help with the child's bodily needs, a mother regularly consults her own mother, her grandmother, and any other experienced mothers around her. But sometimes infants appear miserable for no obvious reason. In this case, the Beng say the baby is endeavoring to communicate a spiritual need. Such an infant is probably homesick for *wrugbe*. This is where diviners enter the picture, for these specialists are seen as intermediaries between the living and the ancestors, as well as between the living and the bush spirits.

Given the culturally valued space occupied by diviners, mothers ought to consult them regularly during the first years of their children's existence, even if the children are not sick. My research assistant Bertin Kouadio told me that in the "old days" mothers automatically consulted a diviner almost immediately after the birth of each of their babies. This statement may well index a goal that was not always realized. For one thing, diviners charge money for their services, even if the fee is modest by local standards.[14] As elsewhere, some mothers are more devoted to their children than others; some are more concerned about avoiding future complications; some are more willing to spend scarce resources to gather items that are judged culturally necessary for their children's well-being; and some simply have more available cash. Still, the practice outlined by Bertin represents an operative ideal that is clearly consistent with the Beng ideology of the life course.

Almost invariably, when diviners are consulted by parents—usually the mother—the specialists recommend that the new mother give a cowry shell to her baby. Bertin put it this way:

> All babies must be given a cowry shell as a first gift when the baby is born, because the cowry was important as currency for the ancestors—it was the second most important thing after gold. The newborn had contact with the ancestors before birth, and the cowry shell reminds the baby of the previous life in *wrugbe*.
>
> Nowadays not all women contact a diviner immediately after the birth; they may wait for a day when the baby is in distress. Other mothers may give a cowry shell to the baby as a personal gift, though they weren't told to do so by a diviner.

Another Beng friend added this commentary: "Infants like money because they had money when they were living in *wrugbe*. In coming to this world, they all choose what they want. This could be *wali pu* [lit. "white money"— French coins from the colonial era], or jewelry [usually cowry shells]—whatever is like what they had in *wrugbe*."

As with the *dɛ̃*, an infant may wear the cowry shell or coin as an item of jewelry, usually a bracelet. Diviners may recommend a single shell or coin, or they might suggest a number of cowries strung close together on a bracelet (see figure 17) or two or three coins strung on a cotton thread.[15] The mother may leave the jewelry on the baby continually, washing it carefully during the baths she gives her child (chapter 5), or she may put the bracelet or necklace on the infant on particular days according to the spiritual calendar.

At the psychological level, the diviner is communicating to the parents the message that the infant needs to be valued more and needs to wear a visible sign of this valuing. Western-trained child psychologists would probably applaud this practice, as it encourages parents of a small creature who cries regularly to devote themselves to the needs of the often stressed and stress-inducing newborn (see Lewis and Rosenblum 1974). At the level of local belief, a diviner's instructions to parents to buy jewelry for their crying child may serve to remind them that although the infant seems helpless and unable to communicate, the little one was recently living a full life elsewhere and thus needs to be respected as a fellow person rather than viewed as a suffering, wordless creature. "I miss my other home," a Beng baby might be trying to communicate while crying wordlessly, "please give me something to remind me of home."

17. Sunu wearing cowry shell and "Sunu" bracelets (see also the caption to figure 22)

I discovered another connection between *wrugbe* and currency one day after asking an innocent question. My friend Amenan and I were visiting with the mother of a two-day-old baby, and I noticed that the newborn's hands were clenched into tight fists—a tendency I had never regarded as significant but that suddenly seemed potentially interesting. Knowing that Beng adults attribute culturally meaningful reasons to seemingly innocuous behaviors, I asked Amenan, "Why does the baby make a fist?" Amenan answered, "Elders say when it's like this, babies have something in their hand." My curiosity piqued, I inquired, "What kind of thing?" I was amazed when Amenan easily replied, "Some gold." Here we see the Beng insistence that babies retain their memories of life in *wrugbe* carried to a more empirical level: even their basic somatic habits are said to be shaped by the contours of the afterlife.

The fact of reincarnation may prove critical in the life of a given newborn in yet another way. It may be apparent as early as childbirth whose *wrugbe* ancestor the newborn embodies. If a woman in labor is having trouble delivering even after receiving the usual herbal treatments (Gottlieb 2000a:67), a diviner may be consulted to discover if there is a spiritual reason for the difficulty. One cause that is sometimes cited relates to *wrugbe:* it may be said that the baby is refusing to emerge from the womb because no one is calling the baby by the right name—the name to which the baby responds from life in *wrugbe.* In one case I heard about, a diviner who was consulted to discover why a woman was having a very difficult childbirth said that spirits had named the baby Mo Jaa, and she was waiting to hear her name before coming out. As soon as the women in the room called, "Mo Jaa, come out quickly!" the baby emerged from the birth canal right away.

～

There are other routes to discovering the afterlife identity of a new child. For example, as I noted earlier, if someone in the family dies on the day a baby is born, this is taken as a sign of instant reincarnation (*e ta, e nu*: "s/he came, s/he returned"). Alternatively, a name that is shared, seemingly by coincidence, between infant and ancestor may indicate a reincarnation. One nine-month-old girl I knew had a series of names: Amélie Ndri Ajua Kla. Most villagers called her "mama," or grandma. This is because the baby was said to be the reincarnation of her father's mother, Ajua Kla Bande, with whom she had two names in common ("Kla," an ancient family name, and "Ajua," a day name for girls born on a Tuesday).[16] Hence she was spoken to and about as if she were that ancestor.

But the former identity of most babies is not revealed immediately after the birth. When I asked the mother of a newborn if she knew which ancestor had returned through her baby, a mutual friend answered, "It isn't time since he just came to life. It's by the behavior that we can find out which ancestor has returned." Later a baby's afterlife identity may make itself known through misery. The diviner may pronounce that the infant is unhappy with his or her name and prefers another one. The new name is usually given to commemorate the baby's *wrugbe* identity, which the baby is said to remember and to miss.

Alternatively, a baby can be renamed for a spirit rather than an ancestor. For example, a baby named Kouassi cried day and night when he was a month old. In despair, his mother consulted Kouakou Bah, who said that Kouassi was crying for two reasons. First, Kouassi "wanted" two bracelets on his left hand, one with cowry shells, the other of *ŋà ti* (silver). Second, he had been misnamed; his real name—which he apparently remembered from *wrugbe* and now missed—was "Anie," after a local sacred pool of water that was said to hold resident spirits. After hearing Kouakou Bah's pronouncement, the baby's mother found the required bracelets, and the baby's family began calling the infant "Anie." According to reports, after these two changes, Anie stopped crying.

Bearing an ancestral identity can have ramifications for a baby's life far beyond naming. It can organize the manner in which the infant is treated in many other contexts. For example, a baby who is born following the deaths of two siblings in the family is inevitably called "Sunu" (for a girl) or "Wamyā" (for a boy). The infant is seen as the reincarnation of one of the two deceased siblings. Like all Beng children who die, the dead siblings will have been buried in a muddy patch behind the home. Because Sunus and Wamyās remember their recent resting place, as babies and toddlers they are said to like mud, so their mothers may pat mud over their small bodies.

The reincarnated identities of Wamyās and Sunus may have consequences for their personality development well beyond infancy. As older children and adults, it is said, they are prone to depression and they can predict someone else's demise. When a Wamyā or Sunu appears depressed or acts aggressively without obvious cause, people worry that someone is about to die. For instance, one day a nine-year-old Sunu spent the entire afternoon hitting her older sister for no apparent reason. Family members and neighbors worried aloud that it was a bad omen. The next morning, two deaths were announced in the village. On hearing the news, the girl's mother and aunts proclaimed, "So that's why she was hitting her older sister yesterday!" The deaths confirmed for them the ability of this Sunu—and that of all Sunus—to foretell death.

A funeral reminds Sunus and Wamyās of the deaths of their infant siblings and former selves; hence they are always among the saddest mourners. To commemorate this, all Sunus and Wamyās—both female and male, from infants to very old people—wear a special necklace or bracelet made with scorpion tails during any funeral they attend (see figure 17). One Beng friend told me that considering their propensity for depression, it would be terrible for a Sunu and a Wamyã to marry. On days they are both sad, they would be unable to take care of their children: a mourning or depressed Sunu may fail to nurse her infant, and both parents might refuse to work in the fields.

People named Sunu or Wamyã are generally said to have a "difficult personality" *(sie grégré)*. Their parents may find validation of this psychological diagnosis through divination. Sometimes the divination reveals an unexpected Sunu or Wamyã identity brought to this world from the afterlife. For instance, Au told me that when she was pregnant with her son, her uncle consulted a diviner, who predicted that his niece would have a child who would be very difficult, prone to crying a lot. However, Au was told that she shouldn't become too upset or angry about this child's behavior or the baby would leave the family and return to *wrugbe*—in other words, die.

Au assumed that this prediction applied to the baby she was carrying, but he turned out to be easygoing. During her next pregnancy, she thought back to the diviner's prediction, but this child too turned out to be relatively unflappable, as was her next. It was only with her last child that the prediction was finally validated: her daughter Jeanne turned out to be a *"wrugbe* Sunu" who indeed exhibited a difficult personality. The diagnosis was made by an old woman related patrilaterally to Au. During a village funeral, this elder had a dream that Jeanne had been a Sunu while living in *wrugbe*. Word circulated, and soon relatives and neighbors classified Jeanne as a Sunu. Because she was a *wrugbe* Sunu, they thought, Jeanne would have an even more difficult personality than an ordinary Sunu would.

Not surprisingly, this foretelling proved accurate. When she was just starting to walk, Jeanne wanted to stay on her mother's back all day while Au worked in the fields. If Au put her down, Jeanne stamped right in front of her mother wherever she was walking, or she dared Au to cut her with a machete, then had a temper tantrum when her mother failed to comply. Jeanne's older sister Afwe had been designated as her baby-sitter *(leŋ kũli)*, and it was Afwe's primary job was to carry her younger sister; but Jeanne frequently hit Afwe while being carried on her back, and Afwe wasn't always able—or willing—to carry Jeanne.

As she grew older, Jeanne's difficult personality remained. She frightened other children in the neighborhood and provoked disputes and physical fights. One day I videotaped about half an hour of a temper tantrum Jeanne threw in two adjoining courtyards. Enraged at a perceived slight, she toppled furniture and hurled pails around her—behavior that would be quite unheard-of for someone without the spiritual profile that Jeanne possesses.

It is clear that Jeanne has internalized her identity as a *wrugbe* Sunu. This should not be surprising. Because she often hears others discuss the difficult personality that is assumed to accompany a *wrugbe* Sunu identity, Jeanne is surely aware of the expectation that she act "difficult." As psychologists might say, the labeling has been successful (Rosenthal and Jacobson 1968).

Let us consider another case: I noticed that a young woman named Amwe was wearing the distinctive bracelet that normally only people named Sunu or Wamyā wear. Amwe explained that she was not a real Sunu, but a *wrugbe* Sunu. She said that she had cried quite a lot when she was a baby, and her mother had gone to consult a diviner. The diviner had pronounced that little Amwe had been named Sunu while she was living in *wrugbe*. Because she was a *wrugbe* Sunu, the diviner explained, the baby should wear a Sunu bracelet to remind her of her *wrugbe* identity. This would calm her and stop her from crying. Amwe's mother obliged and bought her daughter the bracelet, and Amwe indeed stopped crying. To this day, Amwe continues to wear the Sunu bracelet, acknowledging her former identity in *wrugbe*.

Not only do the Beng believe that children continue after birth to retain a memory of the previous life in *wrugbe*, but it is said that they retain their parents from *wrugbe*, who continue to look out for their baby even after the infant has begun to leave the afterlife. In some instances, this can cause conflict with the parents of this life. A child's *wrugbe* parents will be displeased if they judge that the child's parents of this life are mistreating the baby, either through abuse or neglect. The mother may not be breast-feeding her infant often enough, or may not be offering enough solid foods to an older infant. She may leave her baby to cry, may wait before taking her sick baby to a diviner or a healer, or may use poverty as an excuse to avoid buying the items or conducting the sacrifices that a diviner declares necessary to the baby's spiritual well-being. Any of these can have dire consequences: the *wrugbe* parents may decide to snatch the infant back to the other life, where they will raise the child temporarily as they wait for a more suitable couple to emerge as better this-life parents for their *wrugbe* baby.

Related to this is another infant care practice. If a baby cries or fusses for no apparent reason, the mother or other caretaker's first reaction is generally to apologize directly to the baby, saying, *"je a dīe"* ("I'm sorry"—lit., "Pass by it"), before doing anything else to console the baby. A more elaborate method to cheer up an unhappy child is to sing a particular song and move the baby gently to dance to the tune; this practice is referred to as *yeka yu*, or *gbekalɛ* (to apologize) (for more on this, see chapter 11). Why should caretakers apologize to an unhappy infant they are endeavoring to comfort? I suggest that this practice indexes the model of an infant as a complete person fully equipped with desire and memory. Only such an intellectually developed person would understand the meaning of an apology enough to be moved by it.

The Spiritual Vulnerability of Beng Babies

At the same time that their *wrugbe* ties enrich their intellectual capacities, the spiritual connections of infants produce a notable vulnerability against which their mothers should be constantly vigilant. All infants are imperiled by a variety of diseases and conditions whose nature and origins the Beng judge to be spiritual, though their effects are decidedly physical. Their recent exit from *wrugbe* gives Beng infants an insufficient hold on life in this world and makes them an easy target for witches and other spiritual forces that can readily overpower the fragile beings. As Victor Turner might have put it, babies are liminal creatures living "betwixt and between" two worlds; as such, they are seen as only weakly attached to each world while they slowly make the transition from one to the other. Beng women warn that indifference to this vulnerability of babies can easily result in an infant's death—an all-too-common occurrence in Beng villages. In this way, indigenous religious beliefs intersect with poverty, explaining the appallingly high mortality rate for infants and young children that looms large in the consciousness of every Beng mother I know. In chapters 10 and 11, I discuss the larger political and economic factors that conspire to produce Beng infants' deaths; here I focus on women's own perspectives.

Faced with the possibility of their babies dying, Beng women see themselves and their infants as at once victims and agents. Infants—and, by extension, their mothers—are victims of the spiritual conditions whose symptoms take the shape of diseases caused by poverty; yet mothers are agents insofar as they believe they have a culturally meaningful toolkit at their disposal with which to protect their babies against these conditions and their symptoms—especially if they work in tandem with diviners. Beng women are, of course, realistic about the limits of their methods, and they recognize that these toolkits are all too far from perfect. Let us investigate a few specific culturally shaped dangers to which babies are seen as vulnerable because they are tied directly to the infants' recent emergence from *wrugbe*.

All infants, and especially newborns whose umbilical stumps have not yet fallen off, are said to be susceptible to the dangerous—and often lethal—effects of having contact with the corpse of a human or an animal, and especially of smelling the odor of the rotting cadaver.[17] While everyone is seen as somewhat vulnerable to the ill effects of proximity to a human corpse, young children are considered especially vulnerable, and fetuses the most vulnerable of all. Hence it is taboo for a pregnant woman to approach the cadaver room during a funeral, and most pregnant women won't approach any part of a funeral. To protect against the danger of contact with a corpse or its odor, once they bathe a newborn baby, many mothers pat the face and body with crushed leaves from two related lianas *(kɔkɔwɛ banɛŋ* and *kɔkɔwɛ pléplé banɛŋ)*. They do so whether or not there is currently a corpse nearby—the routineness of the application has a just-in-case rationale.

Even mothers of infants and children as old as eleven or twelve years rarely attend funerals. I attended the village funeral of a Ghanaian woman with my friend Amenan, who, because she was married to a Ghanaian man, was obliged to pay her respects to a countrywoman of her husband. But when we reached the outside of the corpse room, Amenan declined to enter it with me: her nine-year-old daughter was nearby, and she feared that the girl would follow her into the cadaver room and be caught by the disease "corpse."

If they must attend a funeral because the deceased was a close relative, mothers take comprehensive ritual measures to protect their children. They might attach a lemon to each child's wrist, or tuck leaves from the lemon tree or the *nonu pléplé* plant into their children's clothes. My inference is that the odor of the protective plants is meant to envelop the young children and thereby protect them from being encased by the dangerous smell of the rotting corpse.[18]

The symbolic logic of cadaver avoidance seems relatively clear. Having only recently emerged from the world of the "dead" themselves, infants, and to a lesser extent young children, can easily return to that world. Their own souls might be "caught" by the souls—or smell—of the dead animals or people and taken back to *wrugbe*. Alternatively a human or animal corpse might remind infants of their recent home in *wrugbe;* so reminded, babies might decide to return there. In the latter case, a cruel inversion of the *wrugbe* connection would be at work, with the soul that is newly arriving in *wrugbe* returning with a soul that had only recently left it. And of course, let us not forget the likely connection between the corpse and the infant: if the cadaver belonged to an old person, as is often the case, the special tie between the very young and the very old is again at work, but now for a grim purpose.

Another funeral I attended brought out a different danger to which infants and young children are said to be especially susceptible. Toward the end of my fieldwork in the village of Asagbe in the summer of 1993, the aged male village chief died. While I was in the courtyard with other mourners, a huge tree in the courtyard keeled over for no obvious reason, barely missing a young grandson of the chief, who was standing nearby. A diviner was soon consulted to explain this extraordinary occurrence. The diviner pronounced that the tree had been sent by the chief's *wru*. Though already far away in *wrugbe,* the dead chief's soul was angry with his family, because no one had taken proper care of him during the long illness that preceded his demise: indeed, no one had even fed him regularly.[19] Now in death, he chose as the target of his attempted revenge an especially defenseless individual who was himself not far removed in time from *wrugbe:* a young child.

Adults perceive infants and young children to be open to the vengeance of not only angry ancestors but also beleaguered spirits *(bɔŋzɔ).* Because most spirits are not associated with particular families or clans, infants are considered vulnerable to any *bɔŋzɔ.* One infant of about nine months was brought to me by his mother with a case of what I judged to be meningitis. His mother was happy for the ten days worth of ampicillin pills I gave her as a cure, seeing no conflict with the spiritual cause of the disease that she invoked. The condition, she explained, was brought on her infant son as revenge by *alufyɛ samɛ* spirits, which forbid village women to dump their cooking fire ashes in a pile on their territory. Apparently some widows had violated this taboo, and the resident spirits had become angry upon seeing the pile of ashes.[20] As punishment, the spirits "threw" meningitis at the village to afflict whatever vulnerable person happened to be passing nearby at the moment the disease landed. The victim turned out to be the infant boy I was now treating.

In addition to ancestors and pygmy forest spirits, infants are also subject to the wrath of the Earth itself *(ba),* whose spirit messengers *(bɔŋzɔ)* may convey punishment to infants when adults have violated the Earth's taboos or when the Earth has been invoked as a curse *(ba tõ).* One night two grown sisters had a bitter argument: the one who normally cooked dinner for the family was too tired to do so, because of her advanced pregnancy, and her younger sister refused to take over for her when asked by their mother. The first sister became angry, and the second sister, a hothead by temperament, cursed the first, invoking spirits of the Earth. The next morning their mother explained to me that the younger sister would have to sacrifice an animal to the Earth by way of apology if the curse was to be revoked, and she was terrified that her hotheaded daughter would refuse to go through with it. In this case, the Earth's curse would be forcibly carried out, and she worried that this would endanger the pregnancy of her oldest daughter, who might have difficulties during her impending delivery, and whose life and that of the baby she was carrying might be imperiled.

Such scenarios to explain various forms of fetal distress during labor, which share a reliance on underlying reference to spirits' dissatisfactions, are by no means uncommon. Another example of endangerment by the Earth involves infant rather than fetal mortality. I was chatting with an aging friend of mine about her life, and she lamented all the children she had lost: seven out of twelve, she calculated painfully for me, with most dying as infants. Later a mutual friend explained that at least some of the children had most likely died as the Earth's punishment of the mother. When a young woman marries for the first time, she must confess the names of any lovers she had before the marriage; if she conceals one or more names, the Earth is displeased and later kills some of her children, usually as infants. Apparently this had been the case with my aging friend—or so the village gossips had it. Once again, infants proved vulnerable to the avenging Earth and its spirits; returning to the *wrugbe* they had inhabited only recently, they left their mothers to grieve.

Memory and Wrugbe

The Beng model of reincarnation embedded in the foregoing discussion offers a strong case for the social construction of memory. Psychologists tell us that memory is integral to the construction of desire in the present moment as well as to the forging of plans for the future. In recent years, medical documentation of the debilitating paths of Alzheimer's disease has shown us poignantly how devastating the effects of severe memory loss can be to the operation of personhood in aging adults.[21]

At the same time, a popular Western folk view is that the younger the infant, the less developed the memory function. Child-rearing books published in the United States and other industrialized countries frequently remind parents of this, often advising them that it is possible to take advantage of a young child's lack of memory. Parents are instructed that they can distract an infant or even a toddler quite easily from something they don't want the child to have or to do, for the child, lacking memory, will easily forget the desire once a new temptation has appeared. Does a young toddler see a cookie she wants on the counter, but it's too close to dinner? Just offer an orange instead, child-care guide and advice column writers suggest, then surreptitiously put the cookie back in the cabinet. All will be forgotten—out of sight, out of mind.[22]

Once again, we are reminded of the reasons infants are excluded from anthropological study. For if, in the common Western opinion, infants have little or no memory, how can they participate in the vaunted cultural processes that are the sina qua non of anthropological inquiry? The inclusion of infants in the Western category of "culture" is a problematic proposition for many reasons; their reputed lack of memory is just one more.

It is true that in recent years developmental psychologists have begun to devise ingenious experiments that demonstrate that infants remember more than most adults have realized. However, these experimental scientists are also demonstrating the limits of infants' memory: the memory documented in these experimental studies with infants is still quite modest compared to the far more extensive memory documented for older children and adults.[23] In any case, professional research has probably not changed the widespread popular image held by most Western adults—that infants more or less lack memory. By contrast, in the Beng world adults consider memory to be a highly relevant aspect—perhaps even the center—of an infant's life. For Beng adults tell us that, far from having no memories, or at best a few short-term memories, infants have a surplus of long-lasting and persistent memories, and hence a surplus of desire based on them. This contrast between common Western and Beng beliefs about infant memory suggests that assumptions concerning who has memory, how much, and why are strongly shaped by cultural models and expectations. For some time now anthropologists have been suggesting that the workings of our memories—the thoughts that seem to be at the heart of our most intimate, private experiences—are shaped in surprising ways by cultural factors that are often invisible to us. Typically, though, this insight is applied only to the lives of adults. The Beng model of infancy corroborates anthropological studies of adults' memories as something socially as much as psychologically constructed, making a compelling case that what passes as memory is itself a local construction.[24]

Wondering what sort of ramifications infants' imputed memories of their life in *wrugbe* have for their daily care, I once asked the young diviner Koua-kou Bah to describe a good parent. He answered without hesitation:

> You should go to a diviner to find out what the baby wants, then go and buy that thing for the child. It's the child's *wrugbe* relatives—usually one of the baby's *wrugbe* parents—who has told the baby to cry, to say what the baby wants. Or sometimes it may be a spirit who's told this to the baby. Infants choose these desires to copy the objects they liked back in *wrugbe*—usually jewelry, money, or cowries. In any case, once the parents of this life discover the baby's desires, they should do all they can to indulge them.

From Kouakou Bah's statement we learn that the baby has desires but is unsure how to communicate them directly. We also learn that *wrugbe* parents continue to take an active role in their infant even after the child has begun to enter this life, to the point of instructing the baby to cry to make a particular desire known. Through the infant, the *wrugbe* parents indirectly communicate to and instruct their counterparts in this life.

Of course there was something a bit self-serving about Kouakou Bah's answer. In his view, a "good enough parent," as D. W. Winnicott would call her (e.g., 1987), is one who gives the diviner regular business. Kouakou Bah's economic motives for encouraging clients to consult him and his colleagues notwithstanding, how does a diviner manage to communicate with his infant clients? Are babies as mute and uncomprehending as they appear?

The Language of Wrugbe

One day I was playing This Little Piggy with the toes of Amenan's then six-month-old daughter, Amwe. As the last little piggy went home, I laughed aloud at myself, acknowledging that baby Amwe couldn't possibly understand the words of the ditty, all the more because they were in English. To my amazement, Amenan objected strongly to my remark, which she took as an insult to babies. In fact, she insisted that Amwe understood perfectly well all that I was singing. When I asked skeptically, "You think so?" Amenan explained her answer by invoking the linguistic situation of *wrugbe*. Unlike in this world, she pointed out, in the afterlife different ethnic groups do not live apart from one another. Rather, in *wrugbe* members of all the world's ethnic groups live together harmoniously. Associated with this ethnic mixture is a striking degree of linguistic ecumenism: when the residents of *wrugbe* speak to each other in their own languages, everyone understands; they have full mutual comprehension.[25]

Beng newborns are thus believed to still be partly inhabiting an afterlife where everyone understands every language. This adds new complexity to the purported memory and knowledge base of infants. It means that in the Beng view newborns—and, to a diminishing extent, older infants and toddlers— have full comprehension not only of the Beng language, but of every language spoken in the world.

Even more complexity is added by the related ideology that Beng infants leave their previous existence behind only gradually. Thus although newborns are said to understand all languages spoken by humans, they come to specialize in what will much later become their "native" language by slowly losing their ability to understand other languages. As we have seen, emerging from *wrugbe* is a protracted process that takes several years. Until it is complete, children are said to continue to understand the many languages that are spoken in *wrugbe,* though with only sporadic and diminishing comprehension, gradually giving up their knowledge of languages other than the one spoken around and to them daily.

Developmental psychologists often write about language acquisition as if the very concept itself were transparent, self-evident. Yet as with other notions, the term belies a vast burden of cultural baggage that may not be easily transported across social borders. The common scholarly model of language acquisition implies a tabula rasa: a newborn arrives for the first time in the world of humans with no linguistic system intact. It is true that a more biologically oriented model of language development influenced by Noam Chomsky vigorously disputes this implication, arguing instead that human language capability is essentially given by virtue of species evolution and has little to do with either personal or cultural effort. Nevertheless, it is the presuppositions of the behaviorist and social interactionist groups of scholars that tend to be adopted, even exaggerated, in many widely read guides to child care that discuss language acquisition in a way that implies a prenatal linguistic blank slate.[26] The immensely popular British child-care author Penelope Leach writes unequivocally, "At the beginning a new infant has no language other than crying" (1983:62). For the many middle-class Western parents who eagerly read passages such as this in parenting guides, young infants simply lack linguistic abilities. They start out in a prelinguistic phase and only slowly develop the ability to engage intelligently with language.

The Beng model poses a stark contrast to both the innatist model and the behaviorist model proposed by the two extreme camps of scholars.[27] In the Beng view, language is neither a biological given nor the product of interaction with living adults. Rather than being either nonlingual or naturally inclined toward language, infants are believed to be multilingual. The widely used concept of language acquisition is thus inappropriate in the Beng context, for in the Beng model infants are doing the opposite of acquiring new languages. It is thought that they are slowly shedding their understanding of numerous languages in order to strip away excess linguistic baggage, as we might put it, and leave room just for the language or languages that will be most appropriate for this life. In the Beng context, the process Westerners call language acquisition might be better conceived as one of language choice through loss.

How does this conceptual orientation manifest itself in daily praxis? In Beng villages, both the babbling of babies and speech addressed directly to infants are valued and strongly encouraged. Because Beng babies are said to have a passive understanding of all languages spoken to them, adults consider it appropriate to make use of that comprehension. Thus older people address speech directly to even newborns, often continually. In my hundreds of hours of observing babies with their mothers and other caretakers, rarely did five minutes go by when someone was not speaking directly to an awake infant.[28]

After being impressed by all the verbal attention paid to babies, one day I asked Kouassi Kokora, a Master of the Earth, "Do all mothers talk to their infants?" He responded emphatically, "Most mothers do!" Kouassi Kokora continued, "When her baby cries, a mother says, '*ye ta! pɔlɛ mi mãɛ̀? je a dĩe!*'" (Shush! What's the matter? I'm sorry!). I saw Kouassi Kokora's claim confirmed myriad times, often word for word. If a baby keeps crying, the caretaker may continue with a series of diagnostic questions addressed directly to the infant: "*yi mlu mi delò? yi mi delò? mi nɔ mi seēlò? mi mi sɔɲni batù?*" (Are you thirsty? Are you hungry? Do you have a stomach ache? Do you have a fever?) and so on.

Consider the following scene. A new mother I was visiting was holding her four-day-old daughter on her lap. The woman sat with her legs out-stretched, leaning over the baby a bit while chatting with me and two other friends. In between talking to us, she spoke to her baby regularly. At one point, her tiny daughter's eyes were open wide, and the new mother asked her child tenderly, "*myé blicalò?*" (Are you looking around?).

I saw linguistic encounters such as this replicated by virtually every mother and caretaker whom I visited during my research. On offering her baby her breast, a mother often instructs her infant, "*nyo mi!*" (Nurse!). After the breast-feeding session, many mothers of infants, including newborns, question the little one, "*mí kanà?*" (Are you full?). This linguistic attention extends to nonsomatic contexts. For instance, a newborn is introduced to each visitor by being asked, "*dɛ kána? mí dò?*" (Who's this? Do you know?) (figure 18).

While I was not systematically studying the speech registers people used when they were addressing infants, I observed that adults and older children alike tended to simplify and slow their speech when conversing with babies. According to extensive research, this tactic is also very common among middle-class, Euro-American caretakers. Developmental psychologists hy-pothesize that these linguistic shifts make speech patterns more "user-friendly" for the babies.[29]

If Beng adults believe that Beng infants are capable of understanding language because of their previous life in *wrugbe*, what of the babies' verbaliz-ing abilities? Beng infants' babble is routinely remarked upon, delighted in, and encouraged as protolinguistic—not only by Beng mothers, but by sib-lings, grandparents, other relatives, neighbors, indeed anyone who observes it. Let us consider the day Tahan was observing her son Sassandra, then seven months old, as he looked with interest at two nearby pigs who were grunting. When the pigs quieted, Sassandra made noises that Tahan interpreted as an imitation of the animals. She clapped her hands with pleasure and exclaimed, "*ja, e za dō!*" Literally, this meant, "So, he understands things!"; figuratively, it meant, "So, he's smart!" attesting to a perceived connection between speech and intelligence even in a young infant.

18. Amenan points to me (about to take their picture) while asking her infant daughter, Esi, "Who's this? Do you know?"

Adults also take an active role in teaching their infants to speak the Beng language by engaging in a formal routine of speaking for their infants. In this discursive routine an adult asks a question directly of an infant, and another adult—the mother or whoever is currently minding the baby—answers for the child in the first person as if she were the baby, in effect prompting the child with lines the infant will presumably repeat months later when capable of such speech. A visitor may directly ask the baby her name. In response, whoever is primarily tending to the baby at the moment will hold up the infant and, much as a puppeteer might speak through a puppet, answer in the first person as if she were the child: "My name is So-and-So." This practice is so deeply entrenched that adults sometimes apologize if they fail to engage in it.

One day an infant of about seven months was seated on a mat on the ground without anyone obviously serving as a caretaker. Philip arrived and, following Beng etiquette, he asked the baby how he was, but no one responded. When an unrelated woman in the courtyard—the only adult nearby—realized that no one had answered for the baby, she immediately provided the first-person response, *"ǹǹ, n kenè"* (Yes, I'm fine), and apologized for not having answered sooner. As this reveals, adults consider it critical to encourage (as psychologists would say) or to acknowledge (as Beng would say) the active verbalizing abilities of infants.

It is important to note here that it is not universal behavior for older people to encourage babies' babblings or to address them with a high level of speech. Psycholinguists and sociolinguists have shown that the amount of speech adults and older children address directly to infants is quite variable even intraculturally—let alone cross-culturally.[30] Indeed, in some societies infants' babble is fully ignored and adults address their speech only rarely to babies. Both these strategies of downplaying babies' language are well documented for Samoa, for example (though Samoan adults start speaking to infants when the latter begin to crawl), as well as for the Kaluli of New Guinea (Ochs and Schieffelin 1984). The Ifaluk of Micronesia take this pattern to an extreme: adults see all children under the age of six years as incapable of learning and thus never address language to them directly (Lutz 1988).

Still, we must acknowledge that the Beng are hardly unique in valuing the babble of infants, nor in addressing them directly and frequently. Both of these patterns of encouraging infant speech are very well established among middle-class, Western families, to mention just one familiar example (Ochs and Schieffelin 1984). Yet although the pattern is common, the local cultural systems that give it meaning are variable. The same behavior may make sense for different reasons in different contexts (Geertz 1973b). The active level of verbal interaction that Beng adults have with babies is consistent with the local ideology of the afterlife. As recent exiles from *wrugbe*, Beng infants are said to be capable of understanding any speech that is addressed to them. Behavior thus replicates ideology in a directly observable way.[31]

On the other hand, the babble of Beng infants is not always rewarded. Beng adults train even babies not to interrupt adults' speech because children are expected to show deference to their elders. But whereas adults in some other societies assume that infants do not make worthy conversational partners and hence are not worth training in this respect (Ochs and Schieffelin 1984), the Beng attitude is quite different. Because they are believed to be equipped to understand language, even the youngest infants are viewed as eminently trainable in adult norms of politeness.

My friend Amenan and I were once talking with some neighbors in her courtyard. Nearby, six-month-old Sassandra sat on a mat on the ground, making what I considered adorable baby noises. But the noises were so cute—and loud—that they proved distracting, and we adults in the courtyard were unable to continue our conversation. Amenan told her young grandson solemnly, *"mi jolɛ twaa!"* ("Stop your speaking!"), as she might gently rebuke an older child. She was taking infant babble seriously enough to treat it as she would the language of older children, subject to the same sociolinguistic norms of politeness. When Beng adults confirm the linguistic abilities of even the youngest of children in ways such as this, they affirm the continuing connection of infants to the linguistically complex world of *wrugbe*, from which they have emerged only recently and partially.

~

Despite Beng adults' positive and encouraging overall attitude toward the speech of their babies, the verbalizing abilities of Beng infants are said by adults to be in some respects problematic. For Beng adults acknowledge that, sadly, although infants are indeed able to express their desires and thoughts, most adults and older children are not capable of understanding the youngest children's utterances. The diviner Kouakou Bah explained to me that when babies cry, they are speaking the language of *wrugbe*. Babies may also communicate their wishes by failing to defecate or to nurse. However, none of these means of communication is readily understandable to the baby's parents, who emerged from that other life too long ago to remember its language. Thus parents of an obviously unhappy baby will typically take their child to a specialist who serves as an intermediary between the land of the currently living and the land of the previously living—a diviner. This intermediary serves as a translator, listening to the baby's "speech" and translating it to the bewildered parents.

The diviners themselves use the services of intermediaries: the spirits *(bɔŋzɔ)* who speak both the language of the other world and that of this world. The infant announces—albeit ineffectively—his or her desires to the parents of this life, via crying or digestive upsets. Eager to soothe their child, the parents consult a diviner, who summons the spirits or *wrugbe* parents, who then speak *for* the baby after speaking *with* the infant. Finally, the diviner conveys the baby's desires to the bewildered parents of this life. In this way, the *wrugbe* identity of the infant is maintained in this world, and through a series of intermediaries, the infant manages to communicate complex desires, rooted in memory, to the parents of this life.

Conclusion

In this chapter we have seen how infants occupy a liminal cultural space. Because babies have barely emerged from *wrugbe* and at the same time have barely entered into this life, their consciousness is believed to be oriented sometimes toward this life, sometimes toward the afterlife. This intellectual orientation produces a range of behaviors in mothers and other caretakers and goes a long way toward accounting for how babies are cared for in daily life. Ideology thus provides a blueprint—a "model for"—behavior by adults, while praxis, for its part, creates a "model of" ideology (Geertz 1973a).

Infants are accorded a high level of agency in this indigenous model— an agency that is seen not only as biological but also as intellectual, as Beng babies are attributed a high level of consciousness that is believed to require decoding by an elite group of adults with special translation skills. Beng ideas about infant care thus provide an alternative to dominant Western models of childhood and child rearing. At the same time, they challenge anthropologists to take seriously both the domain of religion in understanding infancy and the domain of infancy in understanding religion.

In this chapter I have focused on the nexus between two domains of inquiry that anthropologists have long regarded as discrete: the seemingly commonsensical or natural domain of infant care, and the more exalted domain of religion. In the Beng world, religion, that bastion of adult contemplation worthy of the great philosophers and social theorists, turns out to be critical to, and critically defining of, the lives of the tiniest humans. As an intellectual and moral anchor, Beng religion organizes much of daily life. At the same time, more secular or pragmatic factors relating to colonial history, political ecology, and other realities exert their own force in shaping life experience. Now that we have explored the nature of the young child in the Beng imaginary, we move on in the next chapters to consider a range of quotidian infant care practices that intersect with this ideological orientation in varying ways. In chapter 5, we investigate how this ideology and other, more pragmatic imperatives combine to shape the lives of Beng infants during their first and last hours of wakefulness every day.

CHAPTER FIVE

Soiled Beng Babies

Morning Bath, Evening Bath, and Cosmic Dirt

Amenan and I are gossiping about the madwoman, Amwe, who lives next door. I've often seen Amwe mumbling to herself, walking around her compound in the nude after bathing; once she even left the village at night to walk twenty-five miles to town in search of her brother, who she knew was living in some distant city. Amwe's madness has never been in question to anyone in the village, so I'm surprised one day when Amenan asserts quite vigorously that her neighbor is a fine mother to her children. Throwing cultural relativity to the wind and inserting my own ideas of good mothering into the conversation, I protest (a bit mischievously, I admit), "How could a madwoman be a good mother? It's impossible!" Having been goaded by me, Amenan easily defends her statement: "Amwe feeds her children enough food, and when they were babies she bathed them twice a day. That's enough." Amenan leaves the rest of her meaning implicit: enough to make Amwe a good mother.

Is that all it takes to be a good mother in Bengland? Especially striking to a Western observer—at least, to this Western observer—is that Amenan considered bathing one's infants twice daily to be as important as feeding them. I had long observed Beng mothers bathing their babies outside in their courtyards regularly in the morning and evening. Some baths were enforced even on mornings and evenings that were so chilly from the rains or the cool Harmattan wind blowing down from the Sahara in December that the babies shivered and cried. Surely it was not cruelty that compelled a Beng mother to subject her infant to such an unpleasant experience. But the cultural logic had so far managed to escape me. Now Amenan's comment impelled me to inquire further. What motivated Beng mothers to be so relentless about bathing their babies outdoors every day, twice a day, no matter what the weather?[1]

It is true that Beng families, like others in tropical environments, live virtually all their waking hours outdoors, much of them in the fields or forest, and that by the end of the day bodies typically become dirty. But one fact is clear to any reader who has ever taken care of a baby. Infants who are not yet at the crawling stage, which typically begins somewhere between six and nine months, generally remain quite clean—at least in an empirical sense—

for days on end. As my own mother protested when she thought I was bathing her two-month-old grandson Nathaniel too often, "Where does he go to get dirty?" Considering simply the demands of hygiene or health, to the Western observer there doesn't seem to be any compelling—that is, biomedical—reason to bathe precrawling babies daily, let alone twice daily. Infants who are crawling or starting to walk can be filthy by sundown but if they have been bathed late in the evening before being put to bed (as Beng infants are), they generally awaken clean. Why, then, another bath immediately upon rising? And why devote a good hour or more to a long and complex bathing routine each time the overworked Beng mother embarks on it? For the typical Beng bath begins with an enema, includes a good scrubbing of both body and jewelry, and often concludes with the application of body lotion and of facial and body paints.

As Mary Douglas (1966) has shown so convincingly, dirt is not always just dirt. It carries with it an enormous burden of social and symbolic connotations that make of it as fertile a field for anthropological inquiry as the more classic subjects of kinship, economy, or political structure. In Beng baths we are confronted with an ideology that places dirt as a symbolic marker at the metaphoric forefront in indigenous views of the body. Let us inquire, then: When a Beng mother bathes her young children every day, twice a day, what is the nature of the dirt that she is endeavoring to wash off? And why must she do it so relentlessly—morning and evening, day in and day out—until the child is old enough to bathe independently? In the Beng view, *can* all dirt be washed off, and if so, with what? Or is removing dirt—whether empirical or invisible—the only goal of the long bath routine?

Let us observe a typical bathing session before inquiring into the meanings of all this activity—mostly from the perspective of Beng adults, but also, when possible to envisage it, from the perspective of the infants themselves.

～

While living in Beng villages over the course of twenty months, I have observed over a thousand baby baths. I highlight a fairly representative bath that Tahan gave to six-month-old Sassandra. As with the vast majority of Beng mothers and babies whose washing routines I have observed, both Tahan and Sassandra are developmentally normal; as with some but not all such duos, both are as healthy as they can be in an impoverished village in the tropics—give or take the stomach parasites inhabiting Tahan from time to time, the cough and respiratory tract infections frequently troubling Sassandra, the unexplained low-grade fever that Tahan detects when patting Sassandra's warm stomach today, or the bout of malaria occasionally overtaking either one.

The Bath Routine

Tahan awakes with the roosters at five in the morning. Baby Sassandra is still sleeping, and Tahan takes advantage of the opportunity to rekindle the hearth fire in the courtyard to heat water for her family's morning baths. When the water is hot, Tahan washes herself in the shared bathhouse that is one of several buildings in the courtyard. Then she walks to the forest edge to gather some leaves, which she will use in purging and bathing her son. Tahan peeks in on her child—the little one is still sleeping, and Tahan decides to cross over to the other side of the village to draw the day's water from the well.

Walking back along the narrow path, Tahan balances the heavy basin of water carefully on her head. When she arrives at her compound, she takes note of Sassandra, now awake and whining quietly in his maternal grandmother's arms. His grandmother asks Sassandra, "*mi dá má lò?*"—Where's your mother? Sassandra looks around until he catches sight of Mama and then cries harder. Perhaps he is thinking, in his own baby way, *I'm hungry, and here's the woman with the breastwater, so why aren't I drinking?* But it's not yet time to nurse. First Tahan must unload the water she is carrying on her head. With the help of a grown sister, Tahan carefully tips over the heavy basin balanced on her head, directing the gushing water into an enormous ceramic water jar inside her kitchen. Then she takes Sassandra from his grandmother, loosens the cloth *pagne* that's wrapped around her waist, and uses it to tie Sassandra snugly onto her back. Before the baby can enjoy the morning's first milk, he must undergo an enema and receive a bath and an application of lotion. Then his mother will apply medicinal paints to his face and body and dress him. It's a bit too much to suffer, and Sassandra whimpers as he's slung onto his mother's back rather than onto her lap to nurse. But he's seen all this before— at six months, he's had over 180 mornings like this one. He hushes and peeks around his mother's shoulder, wide-eyed as the woman-with-the-breastwater starts preparing the enema and bath.

With Sassandra strapped on her back, Tahan walks into her bedroom and emerges with an empty pink plastic pail and a blue plastic basket filled with Sassandra's bathing supplies. She brings the basket over to a flat stone slab that's resting nearby on the ground. Then she unties a knot that she has twisted from the corners of her *pagne* skirt at the waist. Such a tiny pocket often holds a woman's treasures—beads, coins, folded bills. This particular sac conceals some crumpled leaves that Tahan collected yesterday in the forest. Tahan reaches for a large, smooth rock that sits next to the flat stone slab and, using the rock as a rolling pin, mashes the herbs into a paste (figure 19). Then she gets a rubber bulb-style syringe from the plastic basket and sucks

19. Tahan bends down to crush medicinal leaves into a paste to give as an enema to baby Sassandra, who is still on her back.

up the herbal mixture, adding a little water to make it into a liquid. Sassandra peers with interest over his mother's shoulder at all this activity. Ever since his third day in this world, when his umbilical cord fell off, Sassandra has been receiving enemas with such concoctions twice a day, every day. Does he have a pretty good idea of what's to come? His grandmother doesn't think so. She claims her grandson is seeing all this as if for the first time. Perhaps she's right—there's no comment from him yet.

Meanwhile Sassandra's mother takes the pink plastic pail over to the huge, rusted rain barrel that stands under the eaves of her tin roof and dips the pail into the barrel to fill it halfway with cool water. Then she carries the pail to the large iron pot of bubbling water perched over the crackling fire in the center of the courtyard. Her baby son still centered firmly on her back, Tahan bends over to tilt the heavy pot, carefully pouring some boiling water into the pail. Next she retrieves a large enamel basin that's standing against the wall of her house and sets it down on the ground in the courtyard.[2]

Tahan crosses the compound to bring over her pail of bath supplies and a low wooden stool. Finally she loosens her baby-carrying *pagne* and swings Sassandra around to the side, releasing the naked baby from his snug wrapper. Sassandra expectantly eyes the breast that's hidden cruelly behind his mother's *pagne*. But as she sits down on the stool, instead of laying Sassandra face up on her lap to nurse, Tahan lays him face down across her knees and reaches for the bulb syringe.

It's 6:30 A.M. Tahan has been up for an hour and a half, and Sassandra has been up for over half an hour. Both are hungry. Until now, Sassandra has been quietly observing all that his mother has been doing. Now he squirms and starts to fuss, perhaps thinking, *What, we have to do an enema and a bath first? I know that's what we did yesterday, but I was hoping things could be different today. Don't you know I'M HUNGRY? I want to nurse NOW!* Tahan takes no note of her son's mild protest. She begins to scrub his smooth skin with her nylon washing net, which she has dipped into the warm herbal water in the pail. In the midst of scrubbing, she reaches for the bulb syringe and inserts it into the little one's anus. Immediately the baby squirms and whimpers—he seems resigned to his fate, yet not so docile that he doesn't wage a slight protest. Sassandra's intestines oblige his mother. Tahan continues to wash him, splashing herb water gently over her infant, who continues to defecate into the basin below while whining ever so slightly, perhaps thinking—as his grandmother interprets his whimper for my benefit—*I'm looking for a breast!*

With Sassandra's intestines now emptied, Tahan finishes scrubbing her son's skin, then attends to the low fever she detects. She takes some tomato plant leaves that she picked yesterday in the fields and lays them on the burning embers of the hearth fire nearby. After a few moments the leaves wilt, and Tahan rubs them between the palms of her hands to extract their juice, which she pats all over Sassandra's warm skin.

Having cleansed every inch of Sassandra's body, Tahan must now do likewise with the many items of jewelry the baby is wearing: bracelets, anklets, waist bands, necklaces. There are a bracelet on his left wrist with four white beads dangling down from the string, another bracelet on his left wrist made from his mother's hair, a strand of tiny black beads circling each ankle to darken Sassandra's light skin, a waist belt of alternating black and white beads to prevent him from developing the intestinal worm the Beng call *kanima*, another waist belt made of a black cord and a white cord knotted together, cotton cords tied around his ankles, and a silver bracelet on his right hand that Tahan bought her son after a diviner pronounced that Sassandra wanted the bracelet.

Tahan takes her bar of soap and carefully wipes each of these strands and bands, bead by bead, until she is satisfied that the jewelry is spanking clean. Then Tahan squeezes the moisture out of the necklaces, pulling them firmly with a towel to dry them while explaining to me, "*ma a baŋi yi bɔ a lo*"— I'm taking the water out of his cords. *Now are we done? Now can I nurse?*

Sassandra seems to be thinking as he fusses just a bit more insistently. As if reading her baby's mind, Tahan at last directs her breast toward Sassandra's mouth and addresses her son: *"Mmmm, nya ca, nyo mi"*—Okay, look at this, go ahead and nurse.

All the medicinal and ritual requirements having been attended to, a pair of tasks remains: Tahan must make her infant's skin beautiful, and she must protect him against a few other conditions by applying medicinal paints to various body parts. These are as important a part of the routine as the bath itself. As it happens, Tahan has had some success selling couscous in the Sunday market this month, so she has been able to buy some shea butter *(nyoro)* to add to her basket of bath supplies. Still seated in front of the bath water, she dips a finger in the shea butter she has packed into a tiny, spherical gourd and, as Sassandra nurses happily, she starts to rub the oily lotion over the baby's body. Tahan applies factory-made eyeliner around her son's eyes to protect against eye diseases, then she warms a few medicinal leaves over the fire, squeezes out their juice, and with her fingernail uses them to paint green lines on his forehead to make him grow (figure 20). Finally, she chews a bright magenta kola nut, spits out the orange juice onto her palm, dips her right index finger into the instant palette, and presses an orange circle onto the still-soft fontanel spot of her child's head (figure 21).[3] Sassandra's skin glows, showing off the squeaky-clean beads, bangles, and shells and the bright face paints to great advantage.

~

The routine has taken over an hour. Through it all, Tahan's face has been impassive. She has not scolded her son for fussing—her infant's mild protest is nothing she need react to—but neither has she played with Sassandra. No rubber ducks, plastic fish, squirt guns, or bubble bath to entertain this baby; Tahan simply got down to the business of scrubbing. As with other Beng mothers, Tahan has been engaging in this routine every day, twice a day, ever since Sassandra's umbilical stump fell off—and many more times than that with the two children who preceded Sassandra. It is a routine Tahan knows well, and one that she believes important.

One time I described typical middle-class, American-style bath toys to Tahan—spouting whales, colored-foam sticky letters, vinyl bath books, plastic interlocking hoses and funnels, and all manner of other washing wonders that a casual walk up the bath aisle at a Toys R Us store might reveal. Hearing about such frivolities, all a frowning Tahan could blurt out was *"Yi! Yi! Yi!"* in a combination of critique and rising astonishment.

Why should a baby's bath be such serious business for a Beng mother? Let us begin with the spiritual dimensions of Beng "dirt," investigating how

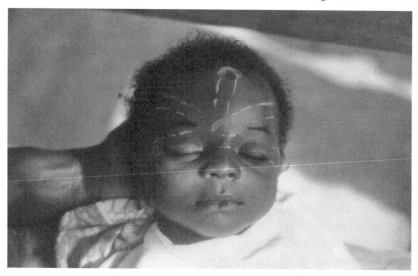

20. Baby René's forehead has been lovingly painted by his mother with medicinal herbs applied in radiating lines expanding outward to metonymically promote growth in the baby.

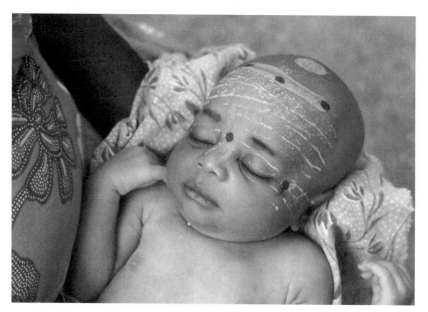

21. This baby wears bright kola "paint" as a large dot on her fontanel spot to keep open the "head road" that is said to run down to the throat, permitting an infant to swallow easily.

these are both activated in and constitutive of the various stages of the infant's twice-daily bathing routine. We will go on to trace the medical dangers that bathing, enemas, and the post-bath applications of jewelry and body paint are said to prevent or treat. Finally we will consider the economic, aesthetic, and sociological aspects of the entire bathing procedure.

Understanding Beng Babies' Baths

In the United States, when middle-class parents bathe their infants, they typically rely on two prime washing ingredients: warm water and commercially manufactured soap (and sometimes shampoo). Together, these substances are meant to wash off any bodily fluids or visible dirt that may be clinging to the baby. Like their American counterparts, Beng mothers always use one of these ingredients, warm water, and if they can afford it, they often use the second, commercially made soap. However, they frequently add a quite different third ingredient to their washing repertoire: herbal decoctions made from the leaves of particular plants. Almost all of these herbal washes are intended to prevent disease or to cure an illness that is said to have "caught" the baby.

In the Beng world, many dangers are said to threaten the spiritual and medical health of infants, and the younger the infant, the more vulnerable the baby is thought to be to these dangers. Through the bath routine, Beng mothers take measures to prevent such diseases from catching their babies in the first place. If a disease does overtake an infant, a first-choice therapy, especially if the disease has spiritual origins, is to wash the baby with a specific herbal wash in addition to—or, more likely, instead of—commercial soap.

To create such a medicinal wash, a mother must use special equipment. Rather than using the plastic pail of ordinary bathing water, she must pour the medicinal water into a dried, hollowed-out calabash, probably one she has grown herself. In addition, rather than employing the sort of modern washcloth that most Beng use nowadays for scrubbing themselves—one made from the shredded fibers of a plant or manufactured from nylon string and bought in a local market—the mother must employ a traditional bark cloth washcloth, which men make from the bark of the zɔ tree in a very labor-intensive process. The explicit insistence in these practices on actively resisting modernity and its technological offerings is striking (Gottlieb 1996b: chapter 6).

Attending to the demanding bathing regimen in all its stages and details, including correctly identifying the disease afflicting a sick baby and the appropriate herbal washes to cure the infant, is generally a woman's responsibility. However, if a man suspects that his wife is not properly fulfilling these duties—if their baby is frequently falling ill or is not recovering from a sickness—

the father may become involved as well. In one case I knew of, a new mother was sleeping in her mother's house, as is frequently the practice until the child begins to walk. After a few months the baby fell ill, and the child's father suspected that his wife was not properly treating the condition with judicious application of herbal washes. He informed his wife that he wished her to resume sleeping in his house in another section of the village (though not to resume their sexual relationship, as this would be a violation of Beng postpartum rules). This way, he reasoned, he could ensure that his wife was washing their infant son with the proper medicines.

On the other hand, women retain a near monopoly on knowledge concerning the elaborate jewelry their babies wear. When I first asked men about the various items of baby jewelry, even those adorning their own infants, most responded either that the beads were just for decoration, or that they had some sort of medical value but they really didn't know what. When I probed for further insights, the men inevitably shrugged and suggested I ask their wives. "It's *leŋ za*," they explained—women's affair.

What initially appeared to me as a sea of dazzling beads, shells, and cords of uncertain meaning gradually became meaningful as I began to document the biography of a cord, the symbolic associations of a knot, the name of a bead. Order slowly replaced chaos, and a visual grammar began to shape in my mind. I came to understand that jewelry comes in three forms. The first kind of jewelry is held to be mystically powerful *(grégré)* for the combating of spiritually derived diseases; the second is believed to have medical efficacy for combating diseases that do not appear to be the result of mystical or spiritual intervention; and the third is said to have no practical or magical efficacy whatsoever—it is placed on the baby merely because of its aesthetic value.

Virtually all Beng babies—male and female, newborn and crawling, healthy and sick, village dwelling and (usually) city dwelling—wear at least a few items of jewelry; some wear so many necklaces, bracelets, anklets, knee bands, and waist bands that an outside observer might well wonder how the weighed-down infant ever manages to crawl (figure 22). As a Westerner attuned to safety issues emphasized in child-care classes, I asked a Beng mother early in my research whether the necklaces did not put her baby at risk for suffocation. My friend just laughed. Clearly this was not a culturally meaningful line of questioning. Far from being considered a health risk, these necklaces and other items of jewelry are seen as *minimizing* medical risks to the infant who wears them. We are reminded of Mary Douglas's perspective on danger and compelled to acknowledge that risk is as much a matter of cultural perception as it is a pharmacological or physical reality (Douglas 1966, 1970, 1992: 3–121; Douglas and Wildavsky 1982). As Irene Rizzini and Andrew Dawes challenge us succinctly, "even in the case of 'risk factors' one can ask—a risk for what?" (2001:316).[4]

In the Beng case, reducing infants' medical risk requires extensive knowledge of the techniques of bodily adornment. These techniques include keeping the baby's beads and cords clean during the bath. The mother of an infant must also attend to the state of each cord. Once the cord begins to unravel and is in danger of losing its beads, the mother removes the beads from the string and immediately reties the frayed cord onto the infant. She then gives the beads to whoever first made the jewelry—often her mother or perhaps an aunt, cousin, or friend—and the jeweler soon returns the beads, now strung onto a new cord.[5] During the baby's next bath, the mother ties the newly beaded cord onto the baby right next to the old, frayed string; only when this new fiber is firmly tied on does she cut off the tattered and beadless old cord. At no moment is the baby left unprotected by at least an incomplete necklace.

Beng women say it is critical to take this restringing procedure seriously, for prematurely removing the old cord before replacing it with a new one will leave the baby at risk. If there is a chance that this might occur, a woman will refrain from putting necklaces on her baby altogether. To highlight the importance of this practice, Amenan once told me that she wanted to send

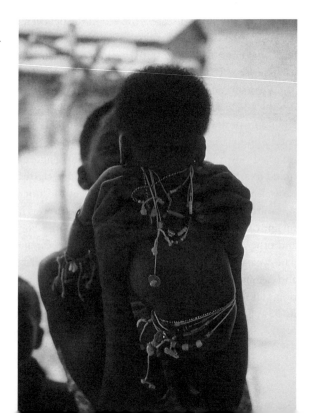

22. This infant, Sunu, wears abundant jewelry. Most of the necklaces, bracelets, and waist bands are medicinal, but some are merely decorative. Sunu was often in poor health and her previous two siblings died before she was born. Her mother worried for her health and tried to take every precaution. Years later, as a teenager, Sunu died from an allergic reaction to a bee sting.

some necklaces to her sister Aia, who was living in Abidjan, when she had a baby, but Amenan knew that Aia, who had lived in the city for many years, did not know the proper procedure for replacing an old cord, so she decided against sending any jewelry.[6]

Stringing also requires specialized knowledge of knotting, for on some baby jewelry the knots are as important as the beads. Although no Beng woman ever offered this interpretation, the knots appear to symbolically tie up whatever disease the jewelry is meant to protect against, so as to prevent the illness from infecting the baby.

The particular items of jewelry worn by a given baby may vary considerably. Partly the choice of jewelry reflects the knowledge base of the baby's mother, who typically learns such esoteric information from her own mother, another female relative or affine, or a neighbor. The beads constitute a veritable doctor's bag of preventive objects. All the items of jewelry are named, as are the individual beads, though few women know the names of all the beads.[7] Practical and financial considerations also determine which items of jewelry an individual baby wears. Some beads are more expensive than others, and some are harder to come across in the markets than others. Any medicinal jewelry may have several variations on the aesthetic theme, reflecting both the mother's artistic palette and her pocketbook.

How much faith do Beng mothers put in these items of jewelry? One way to answer this question is to ask how they might interpret an apparent failure of a necklace or bracelet to protect a baby. Amenan recounted just such a case from her child-rearing history. She confided that her daughter had worn a *gbre baŋ* to protect her from the disease "dirt" (*gbre*), but nevertheless the baby had come down with the disease. I asked Amenan what accounted for the failure. She was quick to blame herself rather than the jewelry. Thus, in the face of an apparent therapeutic failure, Amenan—like most people in most societies—found cognitive means to retain her faith in the medical system on which she routinely relies.

Spiritual Aspects of Dirt: Risks from *Wrugbe* and Beyond

As we have seen, Beng newborns are said to arrive in this life after residing in another world. Their transition from the one space to the other is a delicate one, their hold on their new life precarious. As Victor Turner has shown (1967, 1969), liminal states such as this one classically produce special symbolism, special states of being, special emotional contours. In the Beng case, this applies to infants' perceived medical vulnerability.

Babies' vulnerability is especially evident right after birth. Because the newborn is just beginning to leave the previous existence in *wrugbe*, it is crucial to wash off as much of *wrugbe*—and the principle of death—as possible.

Until the umbilical stump drops off, the baby must be washed four times a day. The inaugural bath of the newborn baby is especially critical. First, the female head of the mother's matriclan washes the newborn's skin thoroughly, preferably with traditional black soap *(zamla ti)* that only female elders know how to make. This soap is used on only two ritual occasions: to wash a newborn and to wash a corpse. These two opposite categories of person are intimately connected, as they are both making a passage from one life to another—in the case of the cadaver, leaving this life for *wrugbe;* in the case of the newborn, leaving *wrugbe* for this life. The specially formulated soap seems a powerful ritual ingredient to facilitate both these transitions.

Once the newborn's body has been washed thoroughly with *zamla ti,* the female matriclan head washes out the newborn's mouth with lemon juice and strings a whole lemon onto a cord, which is secured around the infant's tiny wrist. Until the stump of the umbilical cord falls off, the baby's mother continues to wash out her newborn's mouth with half of a newly cut lemon four times a day, with each bath.

What makes the lemon appropriate for this ritual task? A Turnerian "positional" analysis of other ritual uses of the fruit can lead us to relevant clues (Turner 1973). The lemon is also used in the ritual paraphernalia of funerals: as soon as someone dies, the corpse is washed with leaves from the lemon tree. In addition, a mourner may wear a lemon bracelet (just like a newborn's) to a funeral, and ritual attendants of the cadaver may burn leaves from the lemon tree in the room sheltering the corpse in order to dissipate the odor. No doubt because of its pungent scent, the lemon is thus used to protect against the contagious stench of death at a funeral (see Crocker 1985), where, the Beng assert, a cadaver may infect mourners with the disease "corpse" *(galɛ)* before the cadaver is buried.[8]

Considering this funereal set of uses for the lemon, it becomes clear that newborns form a pair with the newly dead. In the case of both newborn and cadaver, the soul *(wru)* is in the precarious state of passing across the life/death divide. If a female elder does not wash the newborn's skin thoroughly, preferably with *zamla ti,* then wash out the newborn's mouth with a lemon, it is said, the newborn will quickly return to *wrugbe.*[9]

Significantly, lemons are used only for medicinal and hygienic purposes, but never for culinary purposes.[10] Indeed, most Beng adults find the idea of cooking with lemons disgusting.

Once the umbilical cord stump falls off her newborn, a mother may rub *nonu pléplé* leaves onto the spot after each bath. These pungent-smelling leaves are also utilized at funerals, where they are meant to chase away the odor—and essence—of death and its potential contagion. Thus it makes sense to use these leaves after the umbilical cord stump falls off, since this event is taken by Beng adults as the first sign that the newborn has begun to leave the world of the dead in nonbodily form and to enter the world of the living. Applying *nonu pléplé* leaves should hasten that long spiritual journey.

Yet until the process of entering this world is completed once and for all, the little one remains vulnerable to a host of dangers. It is precisely to minimize the risks from these culturally shaped dangers that Beng women direct their attention during the time they spend twice daily bathing each of their infants. Here we are back in Mary Douglas territory, where a firmly cultural notion of risk is shaped by the local imaginary. Let us try to understand from the Beng perspective, then, exactly what is being washed off when a mother devotes such serious, concentrated, and lengthy attention to all this scouring.

Like parents the world over, Beng women scrub babies to wash off dirt. A single Beng word refers to all forms of dirt *(gbre)*, but in Beng thought, dirt comes in two varieties. There is the visible dirt that rinses off into wash water, but there is also an invisible form of dirt that the Beng say is more potent than visible grime, and therefore more threatening to an infant's well-being. Moreover, there are other, nonempirical dangers that Beng mothers fear will afflict an infant's body. All these types of dirt and other risks, both visible and invisible, can ideally be prevented—or, failing that, washed away or treated—through the bathing routine. Let us explore these dangers, beginning with the local understanding of dirt itself and moving to other symbolically potent dangers, all of which are considered to be preventable by means of the bodily practices addressed in the bathing routine.

Sexy "Dirt." The Beng word for *dirty* is *gbregbre* (n., *gbre*). The term covers a broad semantic field. In fact, as in the colloquial English usage of *dirty books* or *talking dirty,* where dirt is seen as a metaphor for sex, the Beng word *gbre* can also refer to sex. The Beng see the symbolic dirt from sex in a particular context as especially dangerous to infants during the period when they are nursing and before they can walk. Any adult—male or female—who fails to bathe early in the morning after having had sex the previous night is said to be dirty *(gbregbre).*[11] All adults are required to bathe every morning in case they had sexual relations the night before. Here we can talk about a veritable habitus that is inscribed on the body from birth. For adults say that the best way to train people to get into the morning bath habit that will be so critical to maintaining symbolic purity during their adult lives is to start them on the routine immediately after birth. The repercussions of not following this regime are drastic: infants who are not bathed twice daily are expected to come down with the disease "dirt" *(gbre).*

Adults are expected to maintain the twice-daily bathing routine without error. Nevertheless, the Beng are realistic: they recognize that humans are a frail lot, subject to laziness, even moral decrepitude. Not everyone can be counted on to follow the rules, and sometimes dirt will make its way to places it ought not be. In the case of sex, the assignation of dirt is clearly, as Mary Douglas would say, a symbolic classification of "matter out of place"—and out of time as well, since the scent and invisible but symbolically potent marker of sex are being inappropriately brought into the village during the day, when they should be confined to the house at night. The person who violates the hygiene rule is considered to be in a temporary state of contagion that will end once the person bathes. This state is said to be dangerous— symbolically polluting, to use the language of Mary Douglas—to infants who are still breast-feeding and not yet walking. If a sexually dirty person touches someone else's infant even briefly, the sexual dirt that is soiling the person's body is said to catch the infant. No amount of bathing with mere soap and water can wash off this type of dirt, which will cause the baby to fall ill with a "dirt cough" *(gbre drɔ)*.[12]

A related source of sexual dirt afflicting an infant can be the baby's mother herself. Although she must maintain a celibate state until her child is weaned and begins to walk, a breast-feeding mother's genitals are considered potentially polluting to her infant if she does not wash her own underwear twice a day.[13]

A more specialized sort of sexually produced dirt is likewise said to pose a medical threat to infants via spiritual contagion. Women who were not virgins at the time they became engaged to be married are said to be dirty *(gbregbre)* for the rest of their lives.[14] No amount of twice-daily bathing can wash this type of dirt from the unfortunate woman. If she touches someone else's infant even briefly, the dirt that soils her body permanently is said to catch the infant, producing in the baby that same dirt cough *(gbre drɔ)*.[15]

To prevent the disease "dirt" from catching their babies, many mothers adorn their infants with a *gbre baŋ*, which can take many shapes. One variation is a bracelet made exclusively from the mother's hair twisted into a bracelet for the left hand, as Sassandra wore while being bathed by Tahan.[16] If, despite the mother's best efforts, a baby develops symptoms of the disease "dirt," the mother can endeavor to cure her child through the bathing routine by "washing off" the affliction with leaves from the *vowlo* liana. When combined with water, these leaves are quite slippery. A metonymic logic appears to be relevant: the slippery herbal treatment allows the disease to glide easily off the baby. The disease called dirt is considered so lethal that the mother may wash her baby five or six times a day with the herbal wash. Moreover, because the medicine itself may be polluted by contact with the baby's skin, each time the mother of an afflicted infant washes her baby, she must spill out the leaves and collect a fresh batch in the forest for the next bath. On these days, the mother is occupied with nothing but curing her child and has no time to work in her fields at all.

Sexual dirt is not the only symbolically constituted danger that, according to Beng adults, threatens the well-being of their infants. Other cosmologically meaningful dangers lurk in the words babies hear, the ground beneath, the cadavers of bodies nearby, and the sky above. Fortunately, all of these can be addressed through the bathing routine.

"Mouth." The disease "mouth" *(ye)* is named metonymically after the direct source of a compliment. "My what a big baby!" "How plump he is!" "Look at how she's grown!"—these are compliments that warm the hearts of most middle-class, Euro-American mothers. In Bengland, such remarks would never be appreciated by the mother of a baby—in fact, they would be perceived as potentially lethal, and the person uttering them would be considered either a fool or, worse, a witch.[17] The words are said to produce the opposite situation of their apparent meaning: they reportedly cause the baby to stop growing and to lose weight. The force of speech is paramount here (Tambiah 1968)—words are seen as being constitutive, not just reflective, of reality. To be sure, the means of the words' efficacy are acknowledged as mystical, but the effect is conceived of as nonetheless real.

To prevent the disease "mouth" from catching them, many babies wear a *ye baŋ,* or "mouth cord." Some mothers are so concerned about this illness that they put two or more such bracelets on their baby's wrist. One ten-day-old I observed wore four different mouth bracelets on his left hand and two more on his right.[18] His mother carefully scrubbed all six bracelets twice daily during the bath to maintain their freshness and efficacy.

"Dew." A third source of symbolically constituted danger to babies that may be addressed through the bathing routine is dew. While English recognizes only a single substance called dew, Beng women told me that there are two types—*plíŋ* and *dɔndɔ (or drɔdrɔ)*—which are distinguished by the height at which they are found. The first term refers to dew that is situated at a relatively low level—for example, resting on leaves of plants that are found along a forest path. Because it is down low, this type of dew can readily touch people. The second type is situated too high up to contact most people—for example, on rooftops. Beng adults say that in both cases the substance itself is generally auspicious and that it is good for dew to touch adults *(o géŋ)* because it "gives you a hot body." However, the opposite is true for babies,

who are seen as neither old nor strong enough to handle the perceived hot strength of dew and thus are considered vulnerable to its effects. If a baby is touched by either form of dew—more likely the low form, of course *(plíŋ)*—the result is a fever that, if left untreated, can be fatal.

Many babies wear a *dɔndɔ baŋ* ("dew cord") to prevent the disease dew *(dɔndɔ)* from catching them. The dew cords I have observed can take the form of a necklace (figure 23) or can adorn the leg. The simple dew cords worn by one newborn girl were just cotton string with knots worn around each ankle. A far more elaborate design adorned my friend Marthe's baby: a cord ran up the baby's shin, connecting on top to a cord just under the knee and below to another cord around the ankle (figure 24); the same design graced both the baby's legs except for a change in one bead. Such dew cords are carefully washed twice daily during the baby's bath.

"Corpse." Having close contact with a corpse *(galɛ)* is said to be extremely dangerous for an infant.[19] If an infant approaches a corpse, the child will be caught by the disease that is named metonymically for its source—*galɛ.* The logic seems rooted in the notion that the infant emerged only recently from the world of the dead. Contact with the previous life via a corpse may induce the newborn, whose memories of that life are still vivid, to return.

If a baby contracts the disease *galɛ,* or "corpse," the mother of the sick child collects curative herbs according to symbolically elaborated codes. If her child is a boy, she finds a girl's or woman's tomb and gathers any plants growing there; conversely, for a sick girl, the father does the same at any boy's or man's grave. Here, the opposition of gender serves to cure the disease, while the homeopathic principle of "like cures like" that is the foundation of biomedical vaccinations is also operative.[20] The mother may apply the gathered herbs as a bath wash or as face paint.

If a baby or older child tragically suffers the loss of a parent, the child is in acute danger of being tempted to return to *wrugbe,* and a special effort is made to wash the odor of *wrugbe* from the little one's body. Lemon leaves are mixed with clay and smeared over the child's body; the process is reminiscent of the thorough mouth washing with a lemon that marked the child's birth.

"Full Moon," "New Moon," and "Bird." Additional symbolically constituted risks to babies come from the sky. Beng adults say that the bright light of a full moon *(kpandri mɔ bli)* is dangerous to an infant. If a baby is caught by the light of a full moon, the little one's stomach will become quite round and swollen—metonymically resembling, perhaps, the roundness of the full

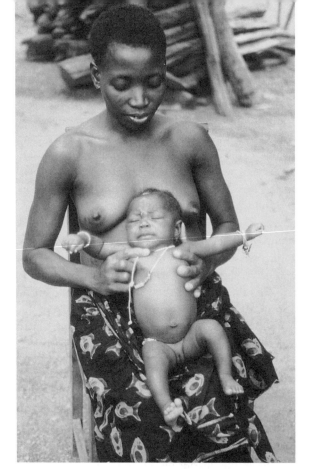

23. This baby wears a "dew necklace." The baby died a few years later. Her mother, Nguessan Kouakou, later died in childbirth.

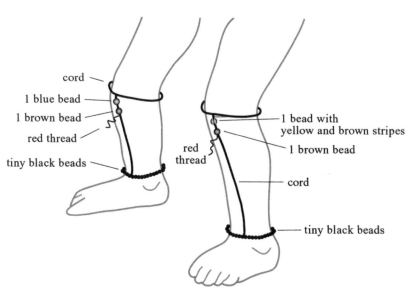

cord

1 blue bead

1 brown bead

red thread

tiny black beads

1 bead with yellow and brown stripes

1 brown bead

red thread

cord

tiny black beads

24. Design of "dew cord" for Marthe's infant

moon itself. This interpretation is not as farfetched as it might appear, for one of the Beng names for a full moon is *e le à krúkrú,* which means "it is very round" (lit., "it is round-round")—much like the swollen stomach of an infant, which is feared and treated as a harmful medical condition. At the opposite point on the lunar cycle, the darkness of a new moon is also considered perilous to babies. To protect against these lunar phases, many mothers paint a sliver of a crescent in black charcoal on the forehead of their babies on a new-moon night, or a full white circle on a full-moon night.[21]

Associated with the darkness of a new moon is a type of bird deemed dangerous to young children. The Beng classify as "rotten birds" *(sieŋ vɔŋni)* those birds of prey, including owls and vultures, that fly on moonless nights. If such a bird passes over a baby who happens to be outside at the time, it is said, the bird will catch *(kū)* the baby with the sickness that is named, simply, bird. In its worst form, the symptoms of the disease are drastic: the baby's neck is said to break and bend backward, and the eyes become white. To protect against this risk, some mothers tie a "bird cord" *(siéŋ báŋ)* of alternating black and white beads—mimicking the extreme dark and light of the two opposite points on the lunar cycle?—around the baby's waist (figure 25).

Why should both full and absent moonlight be considered dangerous to an infant? The moon in general is seen as a powerful force. Beng women have noticed that they often begin their menstrual periods at one of three points in the lunar cycle (the new moon, the quarter moon, or the full moon) and are at a frustrating loss to explain this convergence. The mystical power of the moon is more explicitly acknowledged in another arena: men who wish to become great hunters may purchase a certain medicinal amulet from a neighboring ethnic group (the Jimini), but if they want the amulet to work, they must never hear the normal Beng word for moon *(mɔ)* spoken aloud by others. Instead, people must be careful to use a metonymic circumlocution (*lɔlɔ,* meaning "high") when discussing lunar affairs with such great hunters. Not only are adults responsible for maintaining the practice, they must train their children to say *lɔlɔ* when speaking about the moon in the presence of reputed hunters. In short, the moon is an entity with acknowledged mystic power, and its perceived danger to infants is part of a broader intellectual complex.

These lunar phases and the disease called bird are linked by a single article of preventive jewelry that, from the perspective of symbolic analysis, is one of the more interesting such items. The *kpandri/mɔ bli* cord is worn to prevent a baby from being caught by both bird *(sieŋ)* and full moon *(mɔ bli).* Visually mirroring the opposite points in the lunar cycle, the bird cord consists of a

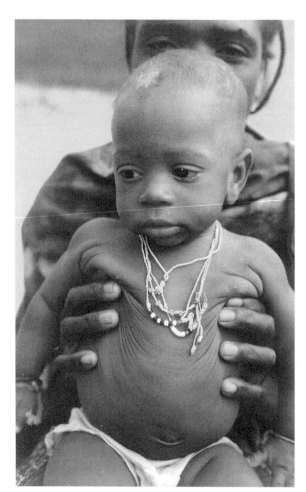

25. Marthe's son, baby Kouakou, wears several items of jewelry: a "bird cord" *(siéŋbáŋ)* with black and white beads to protect against the harmful influence of nocturnal birds of prey, a "dirt cord" *(gbri báŋ)* of yellow and red striped beads to protect against sexual dirt, and a necklace of a white bead with a blue dot to help him gain head control by strengthening his neck muscles.

26. Design of *"kpandri/mɔ bli"* cord to protect baby against the dangers of a full moon's brightness and a new moon's darkness, including the birds of prey that fly on new moon nights

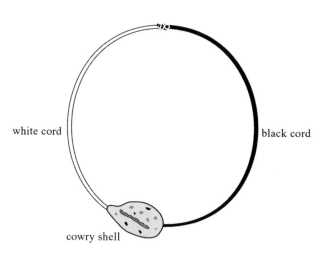

white cord

black cord

cowry shell

black cord and a white cord knotted together, with a cowry shell knotted between them at one of the places where the two cords meet (figure 26). The cowry shell is an item of great symbolic and economic value in Beng history and culture. Perhaps its symbolically constituted power acts here to tie up the two medical dangers attached to it via the black and white cords.

~

What do these mystically activated conditions have in common, and why should they, as a group, be considered especially threatening to infants? Although Lévy-Bruhl might have relegated them to the incomprehensible category of mystical participation (1985), we can detect a certain logical consistency behind their constitution. All are conditions of extremes—of boundaries being either marked or, worse, inappropriately crossed. The full moon and new moon occur at opposite points on the lunar cycle. "Rotten birds" flying on moonless nights likewise represent the termination point of the lunar cycle as the Beng perceive it, and they also represent the unacceptable schedule of daytime creatures that cross over into night. A corpse occupies one end of the earthly part of the life cycle and is about to enter into another world. Dew appears at the two terminal points of the day, predawn and postdusk. And "sexy dirt" marks the person who transgresses any of several culturally constituted boundaries regarding the locally appropriate time and space for sex.

Logical though it may be, this set of relationships raises a further question: Why are infants but not older children or adults seen as vulnerable to these dangers? Perhaps because inappropriately crossing boundaries in any of the ways just enumerated might remind infants of the cosmic boundary they themselves are said to have just passed—and across which they are thought still to be frequently passing. According to this line of thought, adults might see the transgressive crossing of symbolically constituted boundaries as potentially inducing babies to cross their own boundary once again in the wrong direction—this time irrevocably, leaving this life for good to remain in the other world.

Toilet Training. Beyond addressing diseases, the twice-daily bathing routine also assists with digestive regulation. The cultural logic to this aspect of the bathing regimen has a surprisingly spiritual referent. As we have seen, a mother begins to regulate her infant's bowels beginning a few days after birth into this life, administering an enema twice a day before and during each bath. This unfailing practice is in part explained by Beng cultural perceptions of feces: they say that feces are "bad" *(à gɛŋɛ),* with all the moral connotations that the Beng term carries with it.

The mystical potency of feces is evident in a related taboo: young children must never defecate underneath a kola tree. If a toddler should violate the taboo, whoever is with the child must clean up the mess immediately. If she neglects to do this, the results are tragic: when one of the kola nuts from the tree falls onto the feces underneath, it is said, the child who defecated there will die immediately. In this case, feces themselves are seen as intimately connected with the life force of the child in such a way as to make the child critically vulnerable. A mystical connection links children and kola nuts via the mediating force of human feces.

Why is this true of the kola tree and not any other? The kola is a highly significant tree in Beng economic history. In precolonial times, its nut constituted a source of wealth for the Beng, and today the Beng classify kola trees as one of only three types of tree that they consider valuable *(trowe)*.[22] As a ritual marker of the central role that it played in the precolonial Beng economy, the kola tree is the object of many taboos *(sō pɔ)*, such as one dictating that, on pain of automatic death, a man's shadow must never fall across the spot at which he will be planting a new kola tree. Here again, the tree has a mystical connection with humans. The Beng taboo against children defecating beneath a kola tree thus partakes of a broader spiritual tie between kola tree and personhood, in this case via the agency of feces, themselves a symbolically potent product.

Given these multiply resonant meanings of feces, a Beng mother's imperative to toilet train her child from birth makes cultural sense. Not only is she regulating her infant's digestive system, she is also teaching her baby that feces must be contained for mystical as well as pragmatic reasons.[23]

Medicinal Properties of Bathing Practices

So far we have explored aspects of the bath routine that concern spiritual or mystical forces and dangers. These are the threats that Beng mothers rate as the most severe to their infants' well-being. But mothers also recognize threats with purely medical origins, or at least with origins that remain otherwise unknown to them. Although they do not invoke a complex etiology to explain the appearance of these miscellaneous ailments and conditions, mothers nevertheless endeavor actively to protect their babies against these dangers through the bath routine too.

~

In addition to its spiritual foundations, the administration of enemas from the first week of life after birth is also seen as having positive consequences for the child's lifelong health. Most obviously, the enema produces intestinal control in the infant. The treatment causes the baby to be regular, defecating on a predictable schedule. The twice-daily enemas also train the young child for regular use of enemas later. Irrespective of the contents of and reason for a particular enema, the procedure itself should habituate an infant to a bodily practice that will remain important for the rest of his or her life.

Many medicines are also administered rectally. When children and adults become afflicted by various diseases, herbal enemas are often the remedy of choice. Diseases for which medicinal enemas are offered as treatment range from the spiritually difficult disease of corpse *(gale)* to a variety of intestinal troubles. Some enemas are given proactively to prevent or produce certain future medical conditions or states. Each purgative cure has its own herbal recipe; some involve symbolic principles as well. For example, to induce a baby to crawl, a mother can locate a left-handed person who then finds any shrub growing on a mound. The person uproots the plant and gives it to the baby's mother, who crushes it well with chili pepper and uses it as an enema for her infant. Both left-handed people and hills are considered to contain mystical powers, though in opposite directions—inauspicious and auspicious, respectively. Perhaps their combined powers are seen as having an effect on accelerating a baby's motor development.

Some jewelry is also believed to prevent medical symptoms that have no specific spiritual foundations. For example, a necklace of seven small white beads and one larger brown bead, or a variation on this theme, is said to ensure that an infant's neck will "stand up straight" (so the baby will be able to hold her head up by herself) (see figure 25 above); certain anklets *(gā diŋ baŋ)* are worn to promote general growth; and a grass necklace cord with one small black bead, one large black bead, and one dried *zyewlɛ* fruit strung on it is said to prevent a baby from catching the head cold that is caused by the ripening fruits of the *saŋlumɛ* tree. This specialized medical knowledge is valued by women and men alike, even though women maintain a near monopoly over it. Never in Bengland have I heard of anyone disparaging the practice of bejeweling babies to protect them from illness, and never have I seen a baby devoid of such jewelry. The jewelry is considered as necessary to an infant's general health as breast milk.

After washing these and other items of jewelry on her child twice every day, a mother usually applies paint to the infant's face or body. When freshly applied twice a day, certain facial and body paints are said to prevent diseases that are believed to have purely biomedical origins, without suspicion of witches or spirits. The particular paints that a baby wears vary from mother to mother. Often this depends on what a woman has learned from her own mother or grandmother, with matrilines of medical knowledge operating in the family.

Some preventive or remedial medicines are more common than others. One popular treatment is applied to the face. If a baby begins to lose weight rather than gain it, an attentive mother may pat a mixture that she makes from the roots of a certain plant over the baby; or, as Tahan did, she may paint green horizontal lines on the upper eyelids and vertical or horizontal lines along the baby's forehead with paint that she makes from the crushed leaves of a certain plant. These radiating lines are said to promote growth in an infant who is not gaining weight normally (see figure 20 above). Here we are talking about a visual efficacy, with aesthetic metonymy serving as magical force: the lines expand outward, just as the baby's body ought to be expanding.

An especially striking medicinal paint is the bright orange dot that many infants wear on their forehead or fontanel spot (see figure 21 above). Beng mothers say that the soft fontanel spot on top of newborns' heads is the end point of a "head road" (or path) *(ŋru zrɛ)* that runs down to the throat. Women explain that when this road remains open, the infant can nurse and eat properly, but if the path is blocked, the throat becomes closed off and the infant can no longer nurse or eat well and may develop a fever or a cough. In this case, the fontanel spot itself may shake or vibrate slightly *(a ŋru zrɛ o tutu)*.[24] The orange dot, made from saliva mixed with the juice of the symbolically powerful "red" kola nut and applied twice daily after the bath, is meant to ensure that the head road remains open. By the time the child starts to walk, the road is said to have closed up, and the infant is no longer considered to be at risk, hence a mother no longer paints the orange spot on top of her baby's head.[25]

Another kola product may adorn the head for a different purpose. If her baby cries excessively for no apparent reason, a mother can paint a white line down the infant's scalp after each bath. The white line is made from the juice of a white kola nut mixed with saliva. As with the red kola, the mother chews a bit of the nut, then spits out her white saliva onto her finger. Here, the economically valuable kola nut lends its symbolic worth in another medical arena.

Another visually arresting medicine found on babies addresses a particular type of head cold that, Beng mothers observe, plagues children at the same time each year, with runny nose and fever as the classic signs. There is a certain tree, the *saŋlumɛ yíri*, whose fruits, which are judged too hard to be edible, start to ripen toward the end of the second rainy season (in late September or early October). Beng mothers believe that the ripening of these fruits brings on the children's head colds. To cure the symptoms, a mother can formulate a medicinal paint that involves—ironically—the actual *saŋlumɛ* tree. She crushes some of the implicated fruits and adds the juice of a white kola nut. She then rubs this colored mixture on the afflicted baby's body, or if she has a more developed aesthetic sense, she can put the mixture on her index and middle fingers and use them as paintbrushes to apply double lines of the medical mixture all over what are considered the important parts of the baby's body, including the joints and limbs, either horizontally or vertically, in keeping with the lines of the body.

A simpler but equally striking cure involves using a red powder called *siiŋ* to treat a baby's eye ache (conjunctivitis, or pinkeye). The mother cuts a small piece of *siiŋ* wood and wets the end to obtain a red dye. She smears the red dye above the eyes all the way to the ears, producing a dramatic visual effect. Once again, we notice the homeopathic principle we have found elsewhere: like cures like—the mother uses a red dye to cure a baby of a disease that produces a reddened eye.

Yet another cure with striking symbolic associations concerns a fever that Beng mothers say develops when a baby cuts a new tooth.[26] One cure for such a fever requires the mother to gather a few *lati* leaves, warm them on the fire, extract their juices, and combine the juices with a small amount of cooled ashes from a fire; the mother then pats this mixture over the infant's body. Although no Beng woman ever explained it to me this way, a symbolic logic seems to be at work here once again. Ashes represent the cooling down of a heated fire; the principle indicates a metonymically linked wish that the infant's hot body will likewise cool down.[27]

All the medicines discuss in this section harness visual imagery or symbolically resonant principles to prevent or cure diseases that threaten a baby's health. In the next section I turn to a set of related factors that complicate these somatic treatments in intellectually productive ways. The aesthetic aspects of the bathing routine and sociological and economic factors related to it are important even though they are often less discursively emphasized by Beng women themselves.

Aesthetic, Sociological, and Economic Factors

The majority of the face and body paints that mothers apply to their infants are intended as medicine rather than decoration. Only a few items are intended as decoration alone, including commercial women's cosmetics such as eyebrow pencil and eyeliner (figure 27). Nevertheless, it is difficult to draw a rigid boundary between the two categories of health producing and aesthetically pleasing, for the Beng see the two as related. In recent years, Africanist art historians have suggested that the notion of art as a separate category may be inappropriate in many traditional African societies (e.g., Vogel 1980). On Beng babies' bodies one can detect this lesson quite aptly.

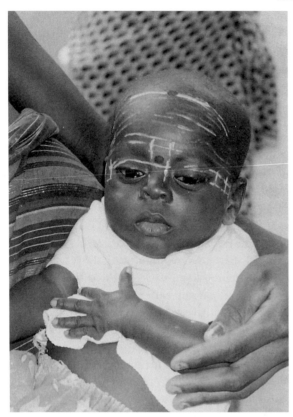

27. This baby boy wears thick eyebrow pencil and eyeliner for beauty, in addition to the medicinal paints lining his forehead.

For example, one Beng mother emphasized to me that the red *siíŋ* line she drew above her infant's eyes was primarily there for the sake of beauty, but she acknowledged that it had medicinal properties as well. Likewise, white paint used on a baby's skin has multiple meanings. When it is made from kaolin—the whitish, crumbly clay that the Beng term *sepɛ*—the paint is thought to convey spiritually purifying qualities. It also has purely medicinal uses. A mother may pat a mixture of water and crumbled *sepɛ* over the body of her infant for the general health of the baby's skin. Ironically, a mother may use the same mixture for a purely aesthetic purpose, to darken light patches on the baby's skin, especially in the skin folds, which often are lighter colored than other parts of the skin.[28]

~

How do these preventive and medicinal paints look on a given baby when applied by a particular mother? Let us look in on my friend MoKla as she goes about readying her newborn son Mauricey for the day.[29]

Early in the morning, after washing Mauricey, MoKla spends about half an hour putting medicinal paints on her son. First, she mixes the colors of her plant-based pigments to achieve the right tone and consistency. To achieve a bright orange, she bites off a piece of a white kola nut and chews on it long enough to mix it with her saliva and produce a good quantity of juice. This she dribbles out in a slow, even stream onto a flat stone. She puts down the stone and lets the pale yellow juice turn thicker and darker over the next few minutes until it is a thick, bright orange dye. While it is thickening, she rubs karity butter on her infant son's body and pats commercial *eau de cologne* all over his skin and hair. Then she crushes a few pieces of crumbly whitish *sɛpɛ* clay, rubs the palm of her hand on a special *sɛpɛ* stone, adds a drop of water, and rubs the mixture on her palm again. She then presses her palm all over the baby's body—chest, legs, arms, back—as well as on his forehead. In this way, her palm has served as both palette and applicator.

Next, MoKla dabs a bit of the bright orange kola paste on her right index finger. With her left thumbnail she traces two thin, vertical lines along the fingerprint. With this finger she then makes lines across the baby's forehead, careful to align each set of lines on one side with the corresponding set on the other. Her finger thus serves as a delicate paintbrush. She continues by painting orange kola dots all over little Mauricey's body. Next come black dots between the orange lines on the baby's forehead, to contrast with them. For this MoKla takes a small piece of charcoal for the new-moon night—it would be the juice of a white kola nut for a full-moon night—and rubs it on the other side of the kola stone. She dabs a drop of water on the charcoal and mixes the two together with her finger, then dabs the black paint between the orange lines adorning Mauricey's forehead: one drop at either end of each pair of lines, and another drop in the middle. Finally, MoKla pats some talcum powder over her son's chest and cheeks, especially where there are pimples. He is now ready for the day (figure 28).

Can there be any doubt that MoKla is an artist? It is true that she lacks paintbrush and canvas. But we might conceive differently of her tools, and her baby serves as her canvas.

~

If the beautification of their babies is an expressive statement made by Beng mothers, it also has an instrumental motive. In many West African societies, visual beauty in general, and bodily beauty in particular, is conceived as illustrative of inner moral strength. Here we are far from the common American expressions with their roots in the Puritan tradition: "Beauty is as beauty does," or "Beauty is only skin deep." Rather, inner and outer beauty are often seen as mirrors of one another in many parts of West and Central Africa (Ben-Amos 1995; Hallen 2000; Thompson 1968). In some girls' initiation rituals,

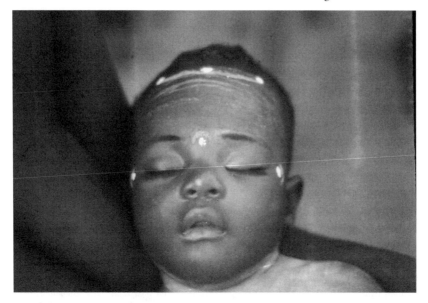

28. Mauricey after a long bath routine by his mother, MoKla, wearing bright orange lines from the juice of a red kola nut and bright white dots made from the juice of a white kola nut, to protect against the brightness of a full moon

much is made of the beautification of the initiates, with efforts to make the skin lustrous and the face and hair attractive in order to reflect inner beauty (Boone 1986). The common West African use of the mirror in rituals points to the extent to which bodily beauty is symbolically valued throughout the region (Fernandez 1986). This regional ideology is instantiated in Beng babies. If they are spectacularly embellished and beautified, babies attract notice. It is here that the expressive and the instrumental fold into each other. For in Beng women's eyes, a beautiful baby can be the ticket to a new mother's peace of mind. In extreme cases, the infant can even be the determining factor in whether the entire family has enough to eat . . . or starves. Let me explain.

For the first two or three months after the birth, a new mother ideally relaxes while her own mother and other female relatives pamper her. In those early months, her main job is to breast-feed and bathe her new baby. Female elders recommend that new mothers stay at home a full three months to recuperate fully from the delivery. Nowadays, though, women often rush back to their farms after only two months (see chapter 11). Their female elders may caution them: "Start slowly—at first only one or two half-days a week in your fields, then three or four half-days. If you start back working full-time too early, you won't recover properly from the delivery."

Whenever the new mother returns to farm work, her days will be much easier if she finds herself a *lɛŋ kūli*—a baby carrier—to care for her baby when she is busy. While the mother is working, the baby-sitter can take care of the infant in the fields, and the mother will only need to stop working every so often to nurse. A mother can ask an older daughter, a younger sister, or a niece to serve as her *lɛŋ kūli*. If they can spare the time, most girls or young women are delighted to serve in this way; however, a mother of a new baby may not be able to locate an available girl. Given the vagaries of demography, her own family may include only boys or just one girl; or her sisters and nieces may all be too young or too old. Alternatively, her young siblings or cousins may be off in the city going to school or helping an aunt (see chapter 11); or they may be sickly or weak (see chapter 10). If a mother of a new baby finds herself in such a situation, she can try to find a *lɛŋ kūli* outside her family, among other households in her village.

To interest such a person in carrying her baby every day to the fields, she should make sure that the child looks beautiful. After the morning bath, she should make her infant's face paints attractive. For example, she should draw the green medicine lines across the little forehead and down the baby's nose as straight as possible, and she should chew a kola nut a good long time before spitting out the juice to make sure it's a bright orange for the dot over her baby's fontanel. In addition to the medicinal jewelry that her mother has given her or that a diviner has prescribed, she can add a few other items for beauty— perhaps a belt of shiny green beads or an anklet of bells. Finally, she can rub shea butter all over the baby's skin after the bath. The skin will glow, showing off the infant's beads, shells, and bright face paints to great advantage.

The expressive and the instrumental thus are deeply intertwined. If a baby is irresistibly beautiful, someone will be eager to carry the little one for a few hours, and the mother can get her work done. If she is lucky, maybe the day's baby-sitter will agree to serve as a regular *lɛŋ kūli*. If the girl does a good job, after a few months the baby's mother may buy her a pair of earrings at the market. At the end of a year, she may buy her baby-sitter a dress if she has the financial means. Then the mother will be optimistic that the girl will be happy to continue serving as her child's *lɛŋ kūli* for another year. And she may be optimistic as well that her own agricultural work can continue uninter-rupted; as long as the rains come and no disasters intrude, she will be able to continue to feed her family.

Conversely, the worst-case scenario can spell disaster. If a mother is un-able to find either a regular *lɛŋ kūli* or several part-time *lɛŋ kūli* and she has three children to care for full-time—let us say a new baby, a two-year-old and a four-year-old (a family pattern that is common in Beng villages)—then what started out as the blessing of high fertility and good health might quickly turn into a curse. Unable to hold several full-time jobs at once—taking proper care of three young children, farming her fields, and doing all the cooking, cleaning, laundry, firewood gathering, and water carrying for her growing family—she may have to neglect at least one of her tasks. If she neglects her children, they will likely fall ill, have accidents, or become troublesome. If they do fall ill, she may be so overworked that she ignores the symptoms as long as she can—possibly until it is too late. By contrast, if she neglects her farming to take care of an ailing child, she risks starving her family. Alternatively, if she neglects cooking, cleaning, and laundry, neighbors and relatives may chastise her and gossip about her, and her husband may abuse her. Without extra child-care help there is no good solution.

In short, having a regular *leŋ kūli*—or a pool of several potential *leŋ kūli* to draw from—is not a luxury but a necessity for most Beng mothers of babies, especially those who already have one or two young children in their charge. Taking extra time twice a day to beautify her baby is not just a routine that the mother of an infant does for aesthetic pleasure. It *is* that, but it also has serious medical, social, and economic consequences for the baby, for herself, and for the others in a woman's family. The painted and bejeweled Beng baby is an overdetermined bundle radiating out life and implications for a large set of others.

The early toilet training of Beng infants also has important economic implications. Throughout the last century, the optimal age recommended by Western child development "experts" for toilet training children has increased. In the contemporary United States, pediatricians now recommend that parents err on the side of toilet training a child later rather than earlier. Some now suggest that not even all three-year-olds will be toilet trained and that this is nothing that should worry a parent.[30] Beng mothers could not disagree more. Why is it so important that toilet training be accomplished so early in a Beng baby's life?

As with the application of jewelry and paint, the Beng enema is a multileveled performance, with multiple goals and multiple effects. Most obviously, of course, it serves the pragmatic aim of regulating the infant's bowels. Technological considerations are one factor. Like people in the rest of the "Third World," villagers in Côte d'Ivoire do not have access to any sort of disposable diapers. Although they might construct reusable diapers from available cloth, they do not do so. Partly this may be a way to save both labor and money. Women wash all their family's laundry by hand, and adding an infant's cloth diapers—typically ten to fifteen each day for a young infant—would add enormously to her work burden. It would also prove an economic strain, as she would have to buy much more soap—an expensive item for most women in Beng villages.

Aside from these practical matters, we must also consider a symbolic factor. As we have seen, in Beng thought feces are classified as morally bad *(à gene)*, and they should be cleaned immediately from babies. If an infant defecates on someone, the responsible adult always apologizes in embarrassment. The last thing a mother wants is for her baby to defecate on someone who might be doing a favor for her—especially a *lɛŋ kūli*. A beautiful baby will remain beautiful in the eyes of the *lɛŋ kūli* as long as the baby does not defecate on the baby-sitter. If the infant does, it is unlikely that the girl will remain as *lɛŋ kūli* for long. Every Beng mother thus makes great efforts to toilet train her baby from birth so as to attract a possible *lɛŋ kūli* who can be recruited to the job without fear of being soiled. The goal is for the infant to defecate only once or twice a day, during bath time, so as never to dirty anyone between baths, especially while being carried. By two to four months—the time Beng mothers typically return to working in their fields and thus have need of a *lɛŋ kūli*—most healthy Beng infants have more or less reached the goal of defecating only during bath time, according to my Beng women friends and my own observations.

If a mother were to fail to properly toilet train her infant—something that was unheard-of among the women I asked—she would hypothetically be at risk of not attracting a *lɛŋ kūli*, with all the grave dangers attendant on that unhappy state. But that scenario was not easily imagined by the Beng mothers who spoke to me about this subject. Once again, we are in overdetermined territory, with toilet training accomplishing at once medical, aesthetic, economic, and sociological goals.

Conclusion

Tiny as it is, the body of a Beng baby occupies ample social and conceptual space in the Beng landscape. Twice every day, every baby's body is scrubbed, pumped, painted, medicated, bejeweled, and often oiled. All this somatic activity must make a continuing statement to the baby, as it must make a continuing statement to those who observe, talk to, hold, play with, think about carrying, and do carry the infant. Certainly the baby himself comes to experience his body as something to be paid a great deal of attention by those around him, especially his mother. As an infant's sense of self is formed, his experience of his own frequently fussed-over body must shape that sense in vivid, deep, and permanent ways.

To others, the baby's body conveys a great deal of locally meaningful information. At a crude level, the baby's beauty—or lack thereof—is a direct gauge of her mother's attentiveness. The degree of beauty also either increases or decreases the likelihood of finding a regular baby carrier. The infant's body represents a crossroads of intellectual, symbolic, and spiritual concerns on the one axis, and aesthetic, pragmatic, economic, and sociological concerns on the other axis. All of these zones work in tandem to make of the tiny body an instantiation of a complex genealogy of interests.

~

Consideration of somatically oriented means to attract a baby carrier and the labor burdens of women that guide a mother to devote a great deal of time to beautifying her baby leads us to think about the baby's experience of being held and cared for by a series of baby carriers and caretakers. This, in turn, brings us to an exploration of sociability in the overall life of the Beng infant. To this set of issues we turn in the next chapter.

CHAPTER SIX

Sociable Beng Babies

Mothers, Other Caretakers, and "Strangers" in a Moral Universe

> The infant self is dialogical and . . . is experienced primarily in
> the realm of participatory . . . rather than imaginative cognition.
>
> ALAN FOGEL, *Developing through Relationships:*
> *Origins of Communication, Self, and Culture*

Unlike the situation of most middle-class, Euro-American babies, in the day-to-day lives of Beng infants, toys and other objects are far less a source for pleasure and discovery than are people (Bornstein, Toda, Asuma, Tamis-LeMonda, and Ogino 1990). Once, in the course of conducting a study of perception and cognition with Beng infants (DeLoache, Pierroutsakos, Uttal, Rosengren, and Gottlieb 1998), I left both a book and a video camera within reach of the babies in my study. Both were unfamiliar objects that I expected to elicit much curiosity and exploration on the part of the children. But the babies saved their excitement for the older children and women who had gathered around to watch the scene. The exotic objects paled in interest by comparison to the exciting presence of people—even, in this case, very familiar people.

As this scene suggests, Beng babies seem to rate their relations with both older children and adults quite highly. What produces this apparent preference? For one thing, the waking—and even sleeping—hours of Beng infants are marked by a high level of active social interaction with a large number of people. Young children learn to feel physically and emotionally comfortable with a wide array of relatives and neighbors, many of whom serve as (often impromptu) caretakers; they also learn to feel comfortable with strangers.

I begin this chapter by exploring the multiple social ties Beng infants forge with a large range of familiar others, highlighting specific infant care practices that promote a large number of social relationships and meaningful attachments to a wide variety of people, including both relatives and unrelated neighbors. I then go on to investigate the striking case of "strangers" who form part of the social universe of village-dwelling Beng babies. I begin that section with a brief comparative discussion of the stranger in Beng and Western settings. I then explore how the general image of the stranger shapes the ways in which Beng parents and other caretakers teach their babies to react to strangers. All of this forms part of a broader argument: that a major goal of the Beng child-rearing agenda is to teach the value of sociability. Guiding infants to value social ties even to strangers is a dramatic component of this wider strategy.[1]

Multiple Caretakers

A small but growing literature is now exploring the multiple options for caretaking of infants that exist in numerous societies. It is increasingly clear that the model of a mother being the exclusive or even major caretaker of her own young children—the normative model in the American public imagination, which is still enacted in at least some middle-class American families (see Richman, Miller, and Solomon 1988)—is of decreasing relevance even in middle-class, Euro-American society (Harkness and Super 1992). It is far less relevant in other American subgroups, as well as in many other societies (Weisner and Gallimore 1977). From Pygmies in Central Africa (e.g., Hewlett 1991; Tronick, Morelli, and Winn 1987) and peasants in Cameroon (Nsamenang 1992), to rural farmers in the highlands of Ecuador (Stansbury, Leonard, and Dewalt 2000) and small-town residents in central Italy (New 1988), data are accumulating that, globally and historically, the relatively recent Euro-American model of mother as sole caretaker may be something of a statistical anomaly. The Beng pattern of caretaking fits in with a growing awareness among scholars that in many societies, the care of infants is more a collective than an individual (mother's) responsibility.[2]

Somewhere between two and four months of age a relatively healthy Beng baby starts to range out from the household fairly regularly. It is then that the mother, if she has recovered normally from the delivery, starts returning to work in the fields. At first the new mother may work on her farm for just an hour or two, and maybe for just one or two days per week. However, by three to four months postpartum at the latest, she will generally be back at her agricultural labor full-time. What of the baby? The little one spends much of the day in a vertical position on someone's back, often napping. Sometimes this back belongs to the baby's mother, but undertaking very demanding physical labor with a baby attached to her back is not considered optimal for a new mother's own health, and Beng women recognize that it can also seriously reduce their work productivity. For these reasons, a mother often tries to find a regular baby-sitter, or *leŋ kŭli*, for her infant. This is especially important if a woman has other young children she is taking care of, or if her fields are far from the village and she would have to walk long distances carrying her baby on her back at the same time that she carries a load of crops, farm tools, cooking pots, or firewood on her head. A *leŋ kūli* can help out by holding the baby while the mother walks to and from the fields balancing her heavy head load.

A lucky new mother will be able to commandeer the baby-carrying services of a relative. If she has a much younger sister living nearby, a newly delivered mother frequently requests her own sibling's services soon after childbirth. Otherwise, she may wait until the baby can sit up on her own, at around four months of age, to start looking for child-care help. Either way, a girl between the ages of seven and fourteen is ideal: old enough to have the strength to carry an infant but not so old that she is working full-time in her own field. If a potential *leŋ kūli* has several unmarried sisters and brothers who can help their parents in their family fields, the girl's mother can easily spare her daughter from the farm, and the girl agrees to serve as a *leŋ kūli*.

My friend Amenan explained to me that women usually choose girls rather than boys for baby-sitters because boys generally accompany their fathers to work in the fields, but if a competent boy is available, he will not be overlooked as a baby-sitter (figure 29). In seeking a baby-sitter, mothers try to find someone with a "good character" *(sie geŋ)*. In some cases the baby grows quite attached to a young caretaker. In later years, the older child may point to a now grown woman and reminisce warmly, "She was my *leŋ kūli*."

Nevertheless, not all baby-sitters can work full-time. For one thing, the younger the child caretaker, the more likely that she will tire quickly, and the baby will not last long on her youthful baby-sitter's aching back (figure 30). Older baby carriers have their own reasons to put down their charge after some time (figure 31). In particular, adult women and even teenagers have their own fields to farm, and perhaps their own children to raise. The babies themselves may fuss in ways that adults interpret as a request for a change of carrier. Recalling the high degree of both cognition and volition attributed to infants because they have so recently lived in *wrugbe*, this attribution makes cultural sense. The net result of this array of mitigating factors is that many babies do not spend all of their days attached to the back of a single person, whether their mother or a single baby-sitter. Rather, they tend to be passed quite often from one back to another on any given day (figure 32).

Recognizing this likelihood, many Beng mothers of infants try to create a reliable network of several potential *leŋ kūli* who can care for their infants intermittently while they do their farming and other work. As we have seen, one reason mothers typically spend an hour or so every morning grooming their babies is to make the children as physically attractive as possible in order to attract a wide pool of potential baby holders. In effect, the routine is de-

29. *(Upper left)* A boy is chosen as a baby-sitter for baby Sassandra for this day in the fields.

30. *(Upper right)* This young girl needs help from an older girl to wrap her baby charge securely onto her back.

31. Ti, a single woman, enjoys baby-sitting both because of her bubbly personality and because she has more time than do most adult women to help others with child care.

32. Ajua, about eleven years old, is about to return this cranky baby to her mother after the little girl awoke from a brief nap on Ajua's back.

signed to seduce potential baby-sitters into offering their caretaking services to the adorable baby.

Typically, a baby will not spend more than an hour or two with a given person. A quantitative study that I conducted confirms this.[3] In the study, the most common length of time that infants remained with a given caretaker was a mere five minutes. The next most common duration for remaining with a single caretaker was ten minutes. After that, the next three most common durations were fifteen, twenty, and twenty-five minutes, respectively (the latter two times were tied for fourth place) (see figure 33). During the forty-one 2¼-hour sessions we observed, the babies were engaged with an average of 2.2 people, but in many cases they were engaged with three to four people, and in two cases they were engaged with five or six people (see figure 34).

My more informal observations suggested that given frequent changes of caretaker, it was not rare for a mother to be unaware of where her baby was, and in whose care, at some points in a typical day. A mother may hand her baby to her first-morning baby holder knowing that the latter is likely to pass the baby to another person if she herself becomes tired or if the baby fusses or if another person requests the child. By the time the infant is brought back to the mother to breast-feed—depending on the child's age, this might be up to a few hours later—the little one may have been passed around to several people as caretakers. The mother may not even hear the full list of who was taking care of her child during this period.

In analyzing somewhat similar infant care practices among some Italian families, Rebecca New cautions that "high social density does not always translate into attention for an infant" (1988:56). However, in the Beng case (as in the Italian case explored by New), the two are often correlated. That is, the quality of Beng caretaking is as intense as its quantity is dense. When Beng adults and older children are around infants, it is common for them to engage actively with the babies. Traditionally, infants enjoyed any number of body-oriented games and songs (figure 35) (but see chapter 11 for recent changes). There is much face-to-face engagement (figure 36), and there are frequent changes of the faces in the baby's line of vision. Babies often play with one another and with toddlers in their family or in neighboring compounds, with a high degree of social stimulation for much of the day (figure 37).

Babies also change position frequently. Adults and older children may place infants in moving positions in which they gain a great deal of physical as well as social stimulation—such as being enthusiastically dragged about for a rough ride in an old box by an older sibling (figure 38), or sitting on the handlebars of a bicycle for a playful ride around the courtyard with a favorite uncle (figure 39). With this abundance of impromptu caretakers and adults and older children actively playing with and talking to them, Beng babies learn early to value sociability.

The contrast with common middle-class, Euro-American child-rearing patterns is notable. In a study of middle-class families with infants conducted in Boston, researchers Richman, Miller, and Solomon found that "many of the U.S. infants' activities are separate from those of other family members, and their opportunities for participating in social interaction are reduced" (1988:72). In these American families, the goal of promoting independence seems often to supersede a desire to promote abundant, continuing social stimulation. Beng babies lead quite different lives.

In Beng villages, the phenomenon of being passed about among a large and fluctuating group of caretakers takes on new dimensions after infancy.

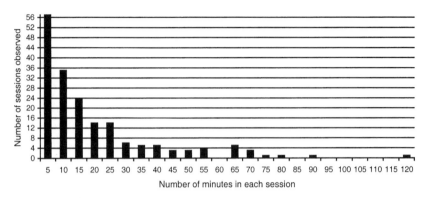

33. Number of minutes spent with a given caretaker

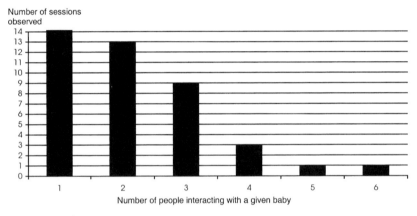

34. Number of people with whom babies interacted during forty-one 2¼-hour periods of observation

35. An older brother playing a body game with his baby sister

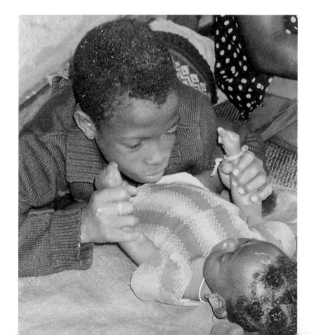

36. Moya enjoying playing with her paternal half-sister, baby Sunu, the daughter of her mother's co-wife. Photograph by Philip Graham.

37. These eight babies and toddlers are closely related and live in adjoining compounds; they play together regularly. Photograph by Philip Graham.

38. Sassandra enjoying
a ride around the
courtyard in a large
cardboard box pulled
by his elder brother,
Meda

39. Sassandra enjoying
a ride around the
courtyard on the back
of his maternal great-
uncle Baa's bicycle

My notebooks are replete with examples of the casual movements of toddlers as adults care for them in rotation. To provide the flavor of such practices I quote from three typical entries from my field notes regarding a single child, not-quite-three-year-old Chantal and her mother, M'Akwe:

13 July 1993

Today M'Akwe brought Chantal along with her to the fields. But when she got to her sister Véronique's fields, she left Chantal with her brother's son, Alphonse Koua-kou, to serve as the girl's *leŋ kūli* for the day. Alphonse was weeding the fields of his father's sister Véronique. For her part, M'Akwe was going to work in a field that's very far away, helping her cross-cousin Akissi harvest rice. Chantal could not walk the long distance to the fields, nor would M'Akwe want to carry her all that way. It would be even more difficult for M'Akwe to carry Chantal back to the village while also carrying a heavy load of rice on her head.

Chantal spent the morning contentedly grilling forest snails and playing around her various older relatives working in her aunt's fields. But at noon, when two of her aunts and I mentioned that we were getting ready to return to the village, Chantal decided to come along. At not-quite-three, she had already learned that she might join any number of caretaking groups, and when there were reasonable alternatives, the adults in her life generally allowed Chantal to choose her preferred option at any given moment.

8 August 1993

This morning, M'Akwe went off to Manigbe to work in the fields with a friend from the village. The friend has parents living in Manigbe, and it's their fields that M'Akwe will be weeding with her friend. Because she'll be too busy working, she left Chantal in Asagbe for the day. [Chantal moved casually between many caretakers during the course of the day.]

9 August 1993

Today, M'Akwe went to the fields and left Chantal behind in the village. She is left in the care of whoever is in the courtyard. [Once again, Chantal moved casually among many caretakers during the course of the day.]

~

Cultural models shape perceptions of risk; this simple but potent claim illuminates much about the movements of Beng children. Whereas in the middle-class sector of postindustrialized nations, casual comings and goings of young children are themselves frequently taken as risk factors to which those in positions of authority are meant to pay attention, in Beng villages the opposite is the case. Here, the casual comings and goings of even very young children are meant to convey to the children—and are taken by the society at large as providing—a feeling of safety, not risk. Indeed, they should have the effect of socializing young children to feel comfortable with most transfers of care-taking responsibility over them.

Thus, in Beng villages adults view children's lives as normatively some-what peripatetic, and they do not consider this a risk for healthy emotional development. Instead, providing multiple caretakers from among the available pool of relatives and neighbors is a way to teach infants and toddlers to be comfortable with a wide range of people. Mothers take this overall child-rearing strategy farther in teaching their children to feel comfortable not only with a broad array of relatives and neighbors, but even with strangers.

Strangers in a Beng Land

In the West, strangers have had a vexed profile for some time. In an existential sense, as articulated in moving ways by Albert Camus (1946), strangers challenge the community that many postmodern people, largely ur-ban dwellers, crave—and for which we may nostalgically long, though per-haps with a false nostalgia.[4] In English, the term *stranger* itself has decidedly sinister connotations. Strangers are dangerous. They represent a potential threat to our safety and the safety, especially, of children—*our* children. Most middle-class Euro-American adults in particular actively socialize children to feel fear at the sight, and even the thought, of strangers.[5]

For example, the federally funded initiative D.A.R.E., which is adminis-tered by local police departments around the United States, takes as its first goal the socialization of kindergartners into wariness of strangers. Police offi-cers enter kindergarten classrooms and instruct five-year-olds to shun strang-ers who might abduct them for unspeakable purposes. "Don't talk to strang-ers," "Don't get into a car with a stranger," "Don't take candy from a stranger," "Don't open the door for a stranger"—these lessons become man-tras that we hope our young children will memorize and internalize for their own protection.

Significantly, D.A.R.E. is conceived of first and foremost as an antidrug campaign.[6] Thus, in quite explicit ways for older students, the category of stranger is metonymically linked with illegal drug use and drug trafficking, which constitute an undisputed site of evil in the contemporary public imagi-nation. Through initiatives such as D.A.R.E. in the United States and other postindustrialized and urbanized societies, and through the daily, more infor-mal teachings of parents and other adults, strangers have come to represent the epitome of the demonized Other.[7]

Following Mary Douglas once again, I suggest that the ways in which members of a society conceive of dangers—as located internally or externally, for example, or as sited in tangible or invisible loci—says much about how they imagine the notion of community and how they imagine their ideal model for relations among neighbors. This constellation of ideas may connect with social networks and the culturally sanctioned model of social ties in subtle yet significant ways. Thus I believe it is not coincidental that the generalized fear of the stranger-as-dangerous-other occurs in contemporary societies in which the bonds of family are themselves often strikingly attenuated. Although some families endeavor to maintain active extended family ties, in the United States in particular the achievement of this goal becomes ever more elusive as work demands and ambitions separate families, spreading them across the country and even around the globe at the same time that effective birth control techniques produce ever smaller families. In some cases, as Sarah Mangelsdorf has pointed out, children even perceive certain family members as strangers if they encounter them only occasionally (personal communication, 16 July 2001).

What effect do these socio-geo-demographic changes have on the consciousness of children? Child development researchers working largely in Western and Westernized countries have noted that infants and young children in these nations tend to establish a relatively small number of emotionally intense relationships, or attachments, generally to those in their nuclear families, and especially to their mothers. Accordingly, the bulk of the voluminous "attachment" literature in the field of psychology still remains decidedly matricentric. As Ann Easterbrooks and Wendy Goldberg have written: "Freud's . . . proposition that the infant-mother relationship was 'the prototype of all later love relationships' is of great importance to attachment theory and probably is responsible for the tendency to examine infants' relationships with their mothers to the exclusion of all other relationships" (1990:225).

Although the first generation of attachment researchers in developmental psychology took this striking pattern as a biologically based model with presumably universal relevance (e.g., Ainsworth, Blehar, Waters, and Wall 1978; Bowlby 1969, 1973, 1980), a more recent generation of researchers, who are sensitive to cross-cultural differences in infant behavior, has acknowledged that the pattern may be a primarily Western one resulting from a particular configuration of social, historical, and political structures not replicated elsewhere.[8] In observing that most psychologists researching child care tend to overemphasize the role of mothers, developmental psychologist Michael Lamb comments that this emphasis is unwarranted because in most societies and for most of history other than the recent epoch in the West, many people beyond mothers have tended to care for infants (1999:39–40). In accord with a growing awareness of this prior disciplinary bias, some contemporary developmental psychologists and other scholars are now endeavoring to forge a culturally nuanced model of emotional attachment by expanding the focus of their research to include infants' emotional attachments to fathers, day care teachers, and other adults.[9] In this section I aim to contribute to this stimulating and growing literature.[10]

Unlike many middle-class Euro-Americans, Beng adults do not socialize their youngest children to fear strangers with the goal of defining the very category of stranger as socially, symbolically, and legally threatening. Instead, Beng adults train children to view strangers as friendly, not dangerous.

Strangers in Beng Infants' Lives

Before we look at child-rearing strategies with regard to strangers, let us ask a basic demographic question: How common is it for a Beng child to encounter a true stranger—one who was previously altogether unknown, rather than merely encountered rarely? The Western stereotype of the insulated rural community must give way here to a more nuanced and internationalized model. As we will see in chapter 11, Beng villages are as "remotely global" (Piot 1999) as most villages in late-twentieth- and early-twenty-first-century Africa.

The appearance of isolation given by dirt roads and the absence of electricity and running water is only part of the story—a story that is defined more by contemporary political and economic neglect than by essential lack of connection to the wider world. The lack of material resources is counteracted by the regular presence of visitors from afar, many of whom approach the village for the first time and speak no Beng. There are the loggers who come to chop down trees in the forest; the road maintenance men who come to smooth out the dirt road after hard rains; the Coca-Cola dealers who make deliveries from their trucks; the affluent middlemen who come to buy peanuts, coffee, or rice according to the season; the itinerant traders who come hawking the traysful of wares on their heads after walking all the way from Ghana or even Nigeria; the traveling diviners selling exotic spiritual connections to the other world; the educated healers in city clothes hawking products that they claim can cure everything from the common cold to impotence, and on and on. Although the ratio of strangers to known people is undoubtedly lower in African villages than in cities, it is higher than the stereotype of the "rural Third World village" might predict.[11]

In the Beng case, I suggest, it is not the quantitative presence of strangers that matters; rather, it is the quality of how strangers are interpreted that is of interest. Let us explore, then, the local meanings of the concept of the stranger. The Beng term that most easily approximates *stranger—tiniŋ*— spans a strikingly different semantic field from that which the corresponding term occupies in most urban, postindustrialized societies. By Beng definition, a *tiniŋ* is intrinsically neither morally good nor morally bad, neither threatening nor protecting.[12] However, far more often than not, *tiniŋ* are seen in a positive light. To refer to most *tiniŋ* who enter a Beng village, "visitor" or "guest" would be a better English translation than "stranger." Yet in some contexts, the English "stranger," with its typically negative connotations, does fit well. For it is true that some *tiniŋ* do in the end turn out to be unwelcome, occasionally even threatening. Such is the case for the guest who overstays her welcome or turns out to be a witch or humiliates the host with superior powers of magic, all of which I have seen occur from time to time in Beng villages. Nevertheless, on initial encounters, the *tiniŋ* is routinely accorded the benefit of the doubt. To make an analogy with the U.S. legal system, strangers are generally assumed innocent unless and until proven guilty.

A *tiniŋ* is immediately incorporated into the local social universe as soon as someone encounters the visitor. Even before entering a new village, a *tiniŋ* usually makes an effort to contact a resident of that village so as to forge a social link ahead of time. The designated host then welcomes the stranger into the village and introduce him or her to others in the village as *n tiniŋ*, "my stranger"—or perhaps we should say "my guest" because in most social situations, such strangers transform into guests quite rapidly. This is the sociological lesson implied by the fact that in the Beng language, a single word covers both concepts, concepts that are clearly distinguished in Indo-European languages.[13] Indeed, signaling the ambidextrous nature of the Beng term *tiniŋ*, those Beng who speak French use the term *étranger(e)* to translate *tiniŋ* when one might expect the friendlier term *invité(e)* (guest) to be used instead.

That *tiniŋ* occupy a categorically valued social space in Beng thought is revealed in architectural practice. When building a new house, a homeowner often incorporates one log of a particular tree somewhere in the construction. In the Beng language, the formal name of this tree is *gaŋwróŋ*, but people also refer to it as the *tiniŋ yrí*, or "stranger/visitor/guest tree." The reason is that this arboreal species is said to house benevolent spirits *(bɔŋzɔ)* that, when incorporated into a house frame, will attract numerous strangers, or guests, to the home. Considering the spiritual connection attributed to the *gaŋwróŋ*, rural Beng women are careful never to chop down these trees as firewood. If someone were to violate this practice, it is said that the spirits resident in the tree would be angered and would punish the offending woman by never allowing *tiniŋ* to visit her home. This would be considered a curse.

In most ordinary social situations, once a person has been placed in the "stranger" category, unspoken rules of politeness demand the abolition of the potential threat embodied by the "stranger" rubric as quickly as possible. This observation accords with the perspective advocated by some developmental psychologists, such as K. Alison Clarke-Stewart, who has urged her colleagues studying the extent of wariness or fear of strangers in young children to be mindful of the nature of a particular stranger and how the stranger presents himself or herself to a particular child on a particular occasion (1978).

Following Clarke-Stewart and others, I try to delineate the contextual nature of "the stranger" as presented in a variety of real-world settings in Beng villages. Accordingly, I suggest that in many contexts in Beng life, a stranger, in the Western understanding of the term, is typically transformed into something else almost as soon as his or her stranger status has been announced. At the point of being introduced and greeted, the newcomer enters into the moral community of those whom she or he has just approached. The geographic space that the stranger and the village residents share has become a social space, and the possibility of further social interaction is now publicly imagined.[14] Of course, a member of a moral community is the antithesis of a stranger, as Westerners understand the term. Thus the potential danger that strangers may represent is almost instantly neutralized in Beng villages. People are not continually made anxious by the fear of strangers precisely because in most situations, strangers don't remain strangers for more than a few moments.[15]

As psychologists might describe the scene, Beng hosts welcoming strangers exhibit a range of behaviors that "destrangerize" the visitor. For example, they use a formulaic welcoming greeting that is repeated in all such encounters, putting a familiar linguistic frame around the unfamiliar.[16] In the course of this greeting sequence, adults may initiate eye contact (if the stranger and host are of the same gender and approximate age) and will usually shake hands, and the host inevitably offers the visitor both a chair and a drink of water. Beng infants witness such ritualistic behaviors regularly. Their predictability may incline infants to interpret encounters with strangers in a manner that reduces or obviates any anxiety that a newcomer might otherwise produce. Observing that adults in the compound are exhibiting friendly and familiar behavior toward a visitor should key a young child into the friendly status of the guest—as psychologists have noted occurs in Western experimental situations (e.g., Clarke-Stewart 1978:115–19).

If Beng villagers attempt to familiarize the stranger, many middle-class Euro-Americans often attempt to do the opposite: to estrange the familiar. Consider the following commentary by a legal scholar examining the American legal basis for absolving people of responsibility to rescue minors over whom they have no legal authority:

One judge explained it this way: "I see my neighbor's two-year-old babe in danger-ous proximity to the machinery of his windmill in his yard and easily might, but do not, rescue him. I am not liable in damages to the child for his injuries . . . because the child and I are strangers, and I am under no legal duty to protect him." The judge wrote that in 1897—over one hundred years ago. And it's still true today.[17]

A similar situation in a Beng village would be evaluated quite differently. There, villagers would condemn anyone who did *not* attempt to rescue a young child—or anyone else—who was obviously in grave danger, regardless of their relationship or nonrelationship to the person at risk. In Bengland, people witnessing a dangerous situation—whether they are close kin, neigh-bors, or even strangers—are considered morally bound to attempt a rescue. Unlike in the American juridical context, the notion of stranger here constricts to the irrelevant.

In Beng villages, an extreme version of the tendency to incorporate strangers into the moral universe involves traditional widowhood practices. In earlier times, a married Beng man or woman whose spouse died was re-quired to observe four weeks of prescribed mourning restrictions. After the month was over, the bereaved ended most ritual restrictions and returned to working in the fields. However, she or he was not free to remarry or have an affair until a final ritual act was performed: the widow or widower was obliged to have sex with a stranger *(tiniŋ)*, someone previously unknown to the mourner. The stranger might be a Beng person from another village, or might be a member of another ethnic group entirely. If a new widow or widower ignored this ritual injunction and married or had an affair with someone who was *not* a stranger, it was said that the unfortunate new spouse or lover would soon die, and there were no cures or rituals available to reverse this fate. This striking practice is no doubt overdetermined and subject to several explana-tions, but my point here is that the stranger in this instance was incorporated into the most intimate of acts and was dramatically sought to enter the social universe precisely because of his or her stranger status.

~

How are Beng children taught a worldview in which strangers do not remain strange for very long? A variety of culturally mandated infant care practices teach even very young babies to welcome people who are unfamiliar. Let us begin at the beginning, in the very first moments of life in this world, when the infant is said to have commenced the first stages of leaving the previous life of *wrugbe* behind and is starting to enter, however tentatively, this life.

The first image the newborn sees is the several people, typically all women, in the birthing room.[18] Aside from the mother, a healthy, alert baby usually sees or hears a grandmother, often an aunt, and perhaps one or two other female kin.[19] Of course, at this early stage, the newborn knows nothing about kinship and is unable to distinguish between kin and non-kin, stranger and nonstranger. But very soon the baby will learn that the faces and voices of those first unfamiliar people in the birthing room show up regularly, and they will begin to seem familiar.

The newborn's social circle widens dramatically almost immediately following the birth. As soon as a healthy infant emerges from the mother's womb and is taken to be washed by one of the older women present, someone else from the mother's family walks around the village as a messenger, announcing the baby's arrival to members of every village household. On hearing the news, people flock to the courtyard to welcome the fresh arrival to the village and to this life. Within about an hour, a long line forms outside the door of the birthing room. One by one, men and women approach the doorway and address the new mother with a formulaic exchange:

> *Visitor: ná ka kwàu.* (Mother, good afternoon.)
> *Mother: àúúúŋ, mú wiyau.* (Good afternoon.)
> *Visitor: àúŋ. ka n gbà pɔ?* (Mm-hmm—what have you given me?)
> *Mother: lɛŋè* [or] *gɔŋè.* (A girl [or] A boy.)
> *Visitor: kà núwaliaà.* (Thank you.)
> (The visitor may then toss small change to the mother.)
> *Mother: àúŋ.* (Mm-hmm.)

This exchange is repeated over and over as a representative of, ideally, each household arrives to congratulate the new mother. Every village birth I observed or heard about was followed by such a large-scale ritual greeting.

As this stream of visitors welcome the new infant, the mother is lying on mats on the floor with her baby, keeping warm next to a fire. One of the older attendants, typically her own mother, takes over care of the newborn. One of this woman's major responsibilities is to make sure that the infant stays awake to see the visitors and realize how welcome she or he is to this new life. Depending on the size of the village, the line of guests may take up to an hour or more to complete the greeting series. In this way, within the first few hours of life outside the womb, the newborn is taught his or her first lesson: to be human is to engage sociably with a large number of new people. The fact that they are generally smiling and making eye contact, and often physical contact as well, with the newborn may serve at a very early stage to teach the small person that for strangers, the "default setting," as it were, is friendliness. Many, though not all, of the newborn's welcoming line of visitors will turn out to be kin. But kin or not, all visitors are equally gladly received by the baby's mother and those attending her.

Of course, Western-trained psychologists would point out that a new-born is not capable of remembering this point. Yet the general lesson concerning the positive value of a wide range of social contacts, including with strangers, will remain well past the completion of the ritual welcoming line. Indeed, a wide variety of practices will instill the same point on a continual basis throughout the coming months and years. Once the brain has developed further, the growing child will indeed internalize the lesson.

Over the first few weeks following the birth, and depending on the size of the village, the new baby will receive dozens, perhaps hundreds more visits. Some will be from the same people who appeared in that initial welcoming line, and some will be from other residents in the village or residents of different villages. The guests will typically enter the room in which mother and newborn are resting and will remain to visit for anywhere from a few minutes to an hour or two. As host, the new mother should allow each visitor to connect actively with the newborn.

The newborn is given early instructions in greeting that will become very important later in life (Gottlieb and Graham 1994) when the mother or another caretaker speaks for the baby in encounters with the guest (see chapter 4). Through this linguistic practice, an infant begins in the first days after birth to learn the value of engaging in social encounters. The typical such encounter involves direct eye contact between the baby and whoever is speaking for him or her. According to developmental psychologists, this is a critical feature for inclining young children to engage in friendly social encounters (e.g., Clarke-Stewart 1978:121–27).

In order to participate actively in such social engagements, a Beng baby is frequently introduced to visitors not only visually and verbally but also somatically: normally, someone who travels from another village to visit a new baby should immediately be handed the child to hold. The guest may decline the chance to hold the baby, but it is generally considered important to make the offer, whether that person is a relative or a stranger.

For the first few months after a birth, relatives will flock to see the new arrival. In order for the infant to meet all the relatives, it is considered preferable for the baby to be awake so the baby and visitor can be introduced. The mother or an attending kinswoman (usually her own mother) will address the baby directly, introducing him or her to this person-who-is-at-first-a-*tiniŋ*. The caretaker first points to the guest and then turns to the infant, asking the child directly, "Who's that?" (*dé kánà?*). If the question is greeted with silence, the caretaker may repeat the question. Depending on the little one's age, the baby may answer with a noise such as "Mm" or "Eh." The caretaker may interpret this as the correct answer and, pleased, may then say, "Yes, that's your cross-cousin" *(ah-heh, mi pɛnaɛ)* or "Yes, that's your little mother" *(ah-heh, mi da krɔɛ)*, thereby placing the guest in a meaningful social universe.[20] If the baby is too young to respond with a noncommittal noise that would be interpreted as an intelligent response, the caretaker just instructs the child gently with the same lesson without pretending to confirm the baby's prior knowledge. In either case, after such a formal introduction, the visitor can now have a face-to-face conversation with the little one.

Of course, such an exchange is problematic if—as happens often in the lives of infants—the baby happens to be sleeping when a guest arrives. Yet this obstacle is not considered insurmountable: it is common to awaken the little one, especially for high-status guests and relatives visiting from afar. This courtesy is sometimes extended to important relatives from within the village as well, especially in larger villages where babies might not see all their relatives on a given day because of the distance from one end of the village to the other. In the case of such guests, if a Beng mother or caretaker did not at least offer to awaken and hand over her infant, my Beng friends imagined, she would surely be criticized for being selfish—unwilling to allow her new child to be collectively claimed by the village and the Beng area beyond.[21] When I raised the possibility, my consultants could hardly imagine a mother or caretaker failing to wake the baby in a situation like this.

Beng villagers extend the principle behind this practice in a dramatic way. They maintain that, in theory, any young child is eligible to be adopted by anyone else in the village. In practice, this option is typically exercised by close female relatives, especially sisters, or cousins who call themselves sisters. Nevertheless, the option of adopting any fellow villager's baby exists at the level of local thought, emphasizing the extent to which the bonds of community define many visitors to the household as friendly to the utmost degree.[22]

The contrast with models of the appropriate level of social involvement for newborns common in many middle-class, Euro-American households is stark. In the United States, many middle-class parents are instructed by others around them, including not only their friends and relatives, but also professionals such as pediatricians, pediatric nurses, and trained advice columnists, that they should minimize—rather than maximize—social contacts for the newborn and young infant. For example, a recent "Baby Health and Safety" column in the popular magazine *Parents* was subtitled "Limit Visitors to Keep Baby Healthy." Here the first-time parent eager for authoritative advice could read:

> It's natural to want to show off your newborn to family and friends. But since even
> a simple illness is much more worrisome in a young baby than in an older one, try

to limit her contact with others—and thus her exposure to bacteria and viruses—for the first four to six weeks, says Thom M. Pantino, M.D., a pediatric urgent-care physician at Egleston Children's Health Care System, in Atlanta. "There's no harm in stopping by the office or your neighbor's with the baby," says Pantino. "Just don't stay more than an hour or so, or expose her to lots of people."[23]

A Beng mother would, at best, be perplexed by this advice, accustomed as she is to being urged to share her baby with as many people as possible from the earliest moments following the birth. Some Beng women might consider the American pediatrician's advice selfish, cruel, or even mad.[24]

In Beng villages, the somatic lessons of sociality extend from holding the baby to breast-feeding. For in the Beng setting, breast-feeding is a social act that potentially extends beyond the classic duo of lactating mother and child: a biological mother is only one of many potential breast-feeders who may nurse a young infant. A casual attitude toward wet nursing as an improvisatory feeding strategy produces the possibility that Beng babies experience the breast as a site not just of nourishment but also of sociability (see Kitzinger 1995:390). We will explore some detailed examples of this pattern in chapter 8. For now, let us look at the broader and longer-term implications of the patterns of early infant care that we have so far explored.

Stranger Anxiety?

In the United States today, many middle-class mothers who read popular child development books and articles recognize that the onset of stranger anxiety sometime toward the end of the first year of life is somewhat expectable, if not necessarily desirable. We can take this question-and-answer column by pediatrician William Sears, from the popular magazine *Parents*, as typical of this abundant literature:

Soothing Stranger Anxiety

Q: How long does stranger anxiety typically last? Our 21-month-old daughter gets upset around unfamiliar people. How can we make her more comfortable meeting strangers?

A: Stranger anxiety usually begins at around 8 months, and can intensify when a child is 1 to 2 years of age, when she becomes more discerning about who gets close to her. It commonly subsides by the age of 3. Rest assured that this behavior isn't a reflection on parenting skills or an indication that a baby is insecure. In fact, some of the most emotionally secure children go through many months of this common phase before they become comfortable meeting new people.[25]

Popular pediatrician-authors such as Sears take their cue from research conducted by developmental psychologists demonstrating that older infants' and young toddlers' fear or wariness of strangers, although not universal, is frequently considered normal. As one influential developmental psychologist specializing in this issue has recently written (without, unfortunately, specifying the cultural or class backgrounds of the infants about whom he is writing): "It is clear that negative stranger reactions are common in infancy" (Sroufe 1996:111).

The normalization of stranger anxiety is especially characteristic of work by psychologists espousing psychoanalytic, cognitive, and evolutionary models of child development, though it is implicit in other theoretical models of child development as well (for an intelligent review of the relevant literature, see Thompson and Limber 1990). Some professional research at least implicitly challenges the universality of the stage of stranger anxiety stage insofar as its authors argue that the context of particular stranger-infant interactions determines much of a given infant's reaction to a given stranger (e.g., Décarie et al. 1974; Mangelsdorf 1992; Rheingold and Eckerman 1973). Clarke-Stewart wrote early on that "fear of strangers is neither as predictable nor as universal at any one age as once was thought" (1978:111). Notwithstanding such important caveats in the professional literature, popular opinion nowadays among the Euro-American middle-class tends to valorize the normalcy of stranger anxiety.

Considering Beng child-rearing practices that actively promote multiple social interactions, what about the fear of strangers on the part of the Beng infant? Is there a place for the concept of stranger anxiety as a normal stage of development in Beng understandings of young childhood?

The Beng language indeed includes a term that might be translated loosely as "stranger anxiety." In describing some babies, Beng mothers use the word *gbanε*. When discussing the topic, women explained that these babies "do not go to people" *(ŋà ta soŋ klε)*. As with their Western counterparts, Beng infants who are classified by their mothers as *gbanε* are subject to noticeable wariness of strangers, and they exhibit a strong preference for their mothers over all others. And like their Western counterparts, these infants tend to begin exhibiting these qualities sometime during the second half of their first year. Nevertheless, there are significant differences concealed behind these similarities between Western and Beng patterns of stranger anxiety. To understand these differences, we must explore the meanings Beng adults attribute to babies who exhibit anxiety around strangers and are thus considered *gbanε*.

From the perspective of Beng mothers, there are two significant features—one quantitative, the other qualitative—that are notable about children who are classified as *gbanε*. First, unlike their Western counterparts, Beng mothers maintain that the appearance of any level of stranger anxiety at all is rare. Accordingly, very few Beng babies are classified as *gbanε*. In a large Beng village (population ca. 1,500) with a large number of infants with whom I interacted daily, only one infant was identified to me as *gbanε*. Although there may well have been a few others whom I did not have occasion to observe, they were certainly not abundant.

Second, children who are classified as *gbanε*, even mildly so, are considered by the Beng to be "difficult" (*ŋo sie grégré*—"their character is difficult") and are frequently criticized and derided. Indeed, Beng mothers and others actively socialize their babies to discourage this type of behavior. Mothers of *gbanε* children view themselves as unfortunate for having to deal with what they consider an excessive attachment to them. How will they get their work done? The mother of the *gbanε* child will have to keep the baby with her at all times, and for a full-time farmer this is quite physically demanding. An excessively *gbanε* baby can threaten the mother's ability to complete all the labor, both agricultural and domestic, that is required for her to run and feed a large household. In the worst-case scenario, a *gbanε* baby who hinders her mother's work efforts significantly may even put at risk the food supply of her household, thereby compromising the health of her siblings and others in the compound.[26]

For these reasons, a Beng baby who exhibits even the mildest form of stranger anxiety or wariness toward strangers is judged at best a nuisance, and at worst a failure. That is, some babies who would be categorized as emotionally healthy by psychologists would be categorized by Beng mothers as *gbanε* and emotionally unhealthy as well as socially problematic.[27]

~

So far I have focused on mothers rather than fathers. What about Beng fathers? Do they play a significant role in the early months of child-rearing? Most fathers have little to no involvement in the minute-by-minute routine care of their infants—bathing, feeding, carrying, cleaning—though there are some exceptions. However, their emotional involvement is variable. Some fathers obviously enjoy spending quite a bit of time playing with their babies, and mothers generally encourage such involvement. Indeed, Amenan once pointed out to me that some babies obviously prefer their fathers to their mothers (a situation described by the Beng phrase, *ó salε a mã̀*—"s/he sticks to him/her"). She cited the following case:

> Kouassi . . . was more attached to his father, Kofi, than he was to his mother . . . from even before he could sit up! Kofi often took Kouassi with him to the fields,

from the time that Kofi started crawling—Kofi carried Kouassi on his back while ped-
aling his bike!—unless he had too much to carry on his bike. On those days, he left
Kouassi in the village. Then, Kouassi cried and tried to follow him! When he was
two years old, someone often had to go and catch him in the forest, where he'd followed his father—up to five times a day! Kofi himself wanted to bring Kouassi with
him because he loves all his children very much.

After hearing about this case, I asked Amenan if a mother might be jealous or saddened to see her young child preferring her husband over herself.
She was amused by my question and answered unhesitatingly, "If a child
prefers the father over the mother, this is very good for the mother: she can
get more work done!" I then asked Amenan why a particular child might
prefer the father to the mother. For a change, my friend didn't have
much of an opinion other than to rule out several possible scenarios that
I queried her about: "It's not necessarily because the father has a better
personality than the mother. . . . Girls *or* boys might prefer the father
over the mother. It depends on the personality, not the gender, of the
child." Amenan added that a very young child generally reacts differently to
both parents in ways that advantage the father: "If the child stays with the
father, the child won't bother the father [when he's working] as much as
s/he would bother the mother [when she's working]—because the father
doesn't have breasts! The child knows s/he can't get milk, so s/he eats and
then naps nicely!"

As I have indicated, a panoply of Beng parenting practices discourage a
baby's formation of an intense "monogamous" relation with the mother.
What are the circumstances, then, that might produce the relatively unusual
gbanε baby who, unlike most of his or her peers, does not "go to people,"
including strangers?

Let us investigate the biography of one such baby I identified, a boy I
will call Kwame. At the time I came to know him, Kwame was nine months
old. In Euro-American babies, this is a classic age for the onset of stranger
anxiety, and in Kwame's case, the stage had set in with a vengeance. I first
noticed it in relation to my own interactions with him. Unlike other Beng
babies with whom I interacted, every time Kwame saw me, he crawled anxiously to his mother and stayed firmly in her lap or otherwise clung to her
pagne. Once, I left for a few minutes and returned to the courtyard to see
Kwame exhibiting a rare curiosity in playing with an exotic object—the external microphone of my tape recorder, which I had left on the ground. I decided
to seize the opportunity and use the object to see how anxious my presence
made him: I moved the microphone nearer to me, just out of his reach. Now

that I was back, Kwame refused to continue indulging his curiosity of a moment before: he remained steadfastly attached to his mother's *pagne*, clinging anxiously to her in my presence.

How do we explain Kwame's behavior, which contrasts so significantly with the behavior that most Beng babies exhibit and that all Beng mothers expect of their infants? Kwame's biography was marked by rather special circumstances. As a teenager, his mother—let us call her Au—had a boyfriend, but her father arranged for her to become the second wife of a distant cousin from another village, in accord with the complex rules for arranged marriage that dominate the unions of many Beng villagers even today (Gottlieb 1986a). Au was deeply unhappy over her forced engagement and made strenuous efforts to resist it. In the end she relented, but her year-long series of rebellions had exacted a toll on her family, whose habits of disputes and alcohol consumption on the part of several members became elevated from what had already been a high level.

Soon after she finally settled in with her arranged-marriage husband, Au gave birth, but the infant died. A second baby died as well. A third infant survived, but while still young, this girl was sent off to join her mother's younger sister, who was working on a plantation in the south of the country. Kwame—the fourth child—was thus the only living child who was currently residing with his mother.

Under these circumstances, one might expect that Au herself would have reasons to become more intensely attached to Kwame than most Beng mothers would. She had only one child with her, having lost two to the cruelty of death and a third to being foster-raised, and she remained unhappily married as a second wife far from her natal village and her natal (and somewhat dysfunctional) family, from whom in any case she remained somewhat estranged. If a mother in these circumstances might be tempted to overinvest in her infant son—to adapt the language of Western popular psychology to local standards—it becomes reasonable to expect that in turn, the baby might reciprocally overinvest in his mother, becoming (in the Beng view) excessively attached to his mother and wary of strangers. In short, examining the contours of Kwame's case may help us to understand what sort of relatively unusual social universe may produce stranger anxiety in a society whose members routinely—and fairly successfully—discourage its onset in most babies.

~

In contrast to Kwame, most babies who are classified by the Beng as not *gban£* are, other factors being equal, far more independent. They are also far more appreciated by their mothers. In explaining to me that none of her children had ever exhibited signs of being *gban£*, one mother told me proudly, *"ŋo ta sɔŋ klɛ—ŋà gbànɛ"* ("they go to people, they don't cling/stay attached [to me]").

Most Beng babies seem equally comfortable and happy with their mothers and a variety of others, often including strangers. In Beng villages, I watched infants daily being passed from person to person—sometimes to people with whom they were quite familiar, at other times to people who were new to them: *tiniŋ* (including myself). In almost all instances, the babies I observed went willingly to their new temporary caretakers, and it was rare for them to cry or otherwise express regret, fear, anxiety, or anger when their mothers disappeared from view. (As in many other rural non-Western communities, Beng babies are never left alone.)[28]

Later, when they were reunited with their mother, the babies might smile with mild pleasure at the sight of her—especially if they were hungry and hadn't been able to breast-feed while under their baby-sitter's care. But that pleasure was fairly quiet, and it almost never involved obvious relief from anxiety at being left in another's care. Indeed, separating from the mother to be given to someone else—whether or not that someone else is known to the baby—is expected *not* to induce anxiety but rather should be perceived as a routine event that happens without stress many times over in a typical Beng baby's day. Accordingly, in the Beng view, a mother's return should not normally be the occasion for major rejoicing.[29] I suggest that the tendency for the vast majority of Beng babies and young toddlers to exhibit little or no anxiety around strangers is due to a dual child-rearing agenda: Beng mothers' efforts train their infants to be minimally attached to them, and their complementary effort to provide abundant social networks, multiple reliable caretakers, and a high comfort level with strangers.

We have already considered a variety of methods Beng mothers have developed to decrease the chance that their children will become singularly attached to them. These include relinquishing a monopolistic hold on breast-feeding and relinquishing a monopolistic hold on caretaking in general. Now let us consider a particularly arresting technique that some mothers employ specifically to ensure that their infants do not become *gbanɛ*. I reproduce part of a conversation I had with Amenan:

Alma: When do we know that a child is *gbanɛ?*

Amenan: Five to seven months, but never before five months.

Alma: Why in this age range, five to seven months?

Amenan: S/he knows her/his mother already. It's naughty children who do that.

Alma: Do people say those children are naughty?

Amenan: They have a bad character *(sie voŋni)*, they don't go to people. . . .

Alma: Is it possible to know in advance which will be *gbane*? Is there a sign?

Amenan: Those who will become like that look at their mother [a lot].

Alma: When can a child notice the mother?

Amenan: When s/he is one month old.

Alma: Maybe because the mother is doing something intriguing?

Amenan: Me, when [my] babies look in my eyes I blow in their face. This way they don't become *gbane*. . . . If you get used to a child, you can't work. There are times to work. You can't if you have a child you like [too much]. You should give him to somebody else. It's not good to like the child too much.

In her own parenting efforts, Amenan deliberately endeavored to reduce her children's emotional attachment to her, using such direct and self-conscious methods as trying to break her infant's gaze at herself. Although not all Beng mothers resort to such a dramatic strategy, Amenan is not alone in her use of this technique. And other Beng women who do not use the technique themselves do not disapprove of it. In Amenan's statement we see encapsulated an extreme version of a child-rearing agenda that is vastly different from that which is common in many middle-class, Euro-American households today.

Strangers and Older Children

As Beng babies grow into young children, they tend to exhibit in delightful ways the understanding they acquired as infants: that strangers are rarely threatening. The perceived benevolence of strangers is evident in one game that children play. There is an insect in the Beng region, the *tiniŋ kaka,* whose name translates as "stranger insect." This is a large, flying insect, probably a beetle (Samuel Besheers, personal communication, 25 July 2001), that makes a loud buzzing sound. Normally these insects are not present in the villages, but on occasion they show up unexpectedly, usually in groups. Children become very excited at the appearance of these noisily buzzing, sometimes wildly flying bugs. As soon as the insects appear, the children rummage around for a piece of string or a strip of liana maybe two to three feet long. Then they run through the courtyard gaily to catch one of the unlucky insects. When they have done so, they tie the insect to the string or liana and swing it around their heads as the victim protests with its loud buzz and the children chant gleefully, *tiniŋ kaka! tiniŋ kaka!*—Stranger insect! Stranger insect! (Gottlieb and Graham 1994:300–301).

The children then start looking around the courtyard, and, according to their claims, just then a real *tiniŋ*—an unexpected guest, visitor, or stranger—inevitably shows up. Many times after the insect games that I observed, large groups of *tiniŋ* did soon arrive for an unanticipated event, especially a funeral of someone who had died suddenly. Adults in the courtyard smiled, and if a visiting anthropologist happened to be present, they explained with smug satisfaction that their worldview had just been vindicated: "See? The *tiniŋ kaka* was an omen—*tiniŋ* really have come!"

Although funerals, of course, produce grief for those in mourning, the village at large may take on a festive atmosphere; the greater the age of the person who died, the more this is the case. If the deceased was quite aged, the atmosphere becomes genuinely carnivalesque (Gottlieb 1992; Gottlieb and Graham 1994). Dances are held; everyone dresses in their finest clothes, with colorful, matching outfits for both men and women; food is cooked in abundance; youth may mock the deceased in an elaborate charade and march around shouting teasing, bawdy insults to each other; distant relatives and friends show up to catch up on gossip; new babies are shown off; and chickens are stolen by funeral guests from other villages as part of a structural joking relationship with members of the host village. The sudden arrival of the *tiniŋ kaka*, then, frequently signals the arrival of a large group of human *tiniŋ*, which in turn—especially for children—signals the arrival of fun. We are a long way here from the dominant vision of the stranger-as-menacing-other that prevails in so many contemporary urban societies.

Interpreting Strangers and Sociability in Beng Villages

Beyond indigenous values regarding child care itself, what might account for the distinctive pattern of child-care practices and behaviors that we have traced in this chapter? Cultural anthropologists are often cautious about posing causal scenarios, aware that social life is generally far too complex, too messy, too overdetermined to be explained by a single factor. At the same time, as social scientists we cannot entirely abjure the effort to explain. What follows, then, is discussion of a tentative set of three factors—concerning religion, political economy, and history—that together may go some way toward accounting for the child-care patterns and behaviors we have observed for the Beng. I do not claim that these three factors add up to a complete explanation, but I suggest that they are significant components of an explanation.

First, the pattern of welcoming strangers into their midst and the associated habit of encouraging the creation of a broad variety of social ties and emotional attachments accords well with Beng religious ideology. As we have seen, Beng adults maintain that babies come to this life after a previous existence in *wrugbe*. The birth of a baby, then, is seen as the occasion to receive not a strange new creature but rather someone who has already been here before and then left, who is now returning as the reincarnated ancestor. The ideology of reincarnation provides a template for welcoming the young stranger as a friendly guest with social ties to the community. In turn, the active welcoming of the baby-as-stranger into the village echoes the formal structures for welcoming adult guests to the village.

The pattern of encouraging children to form multiple emotional attachments with a variety of people—young and old, male and female, related and unrelated, familiar and even strange—from the earliest days of infancy also works well with the demands of women's labor. As has long been documented for much of rural Africa (e.g., Boserup 1970; Bryceson 1995; Coquery-Vidrovitch 1997:9–20), Beng women's lives are circumscribed by enormous labor demands. Most obviously, all women are full-time farmers. In addition, Beng women have sole responsibility for chopping firewood and hauling it from the forest; fetching water for the household water supply; hand-washing the laundry for a large family; and doing the vast majority of food preparation for that family, including pounding, cooking, and dishwashing—much of this while pregnant or breast-feeding. It is hard to imagine a woman performing all these tasks continually on her own, day in and day out, without relief, while competently taking full-time care of several small children—including, frequently, a baby and a toddler.

In order to keep her household running and her share of the family's food supply coming in, virtually every mother must arrange for either a single regular baby-sitter or a network of potential baby carriers who will provide dependable child care. The typical Beng mother's habit of encouraging an infant to accept strangers and to forge satisfying emotional attachments to many people—and of discouraging the infant from forming an especially strong and singular emotional attachment to her—thus makes pragmatic sense as it is situated in the universe of women's labor.

Finally, there is the obvious question of history. In what sort of historical circumstances would the embracing of strangers be a reasonable strategy? Here we are awash in a sea of irony. For at least the brief period for which there is some documented history—barely more than a century—the Beng have apparently been a relatively remote and insulated group. It is true that they are surrounded by neighbors speaking languages that belong to different language families, but the Beng have endeavored to maintain some distance from these neighbors. Their distinctive ritual practices have given the Beng a somewhat formidable reputation regionally for wielding spiritual powers, and the fact that Beng adults are usually noticeably shorter than the adults of most other Ivoirian populations lends them a distinctive physiological profile. Moreover, in earlier times of military threat, the Beng have reacted by retreating into the forest to maintain a stance of passive resistance, and it is only recently that Beng villagers have begun to convert to Christianity and Islam.

At the same time, this apparent isolationism belies a deep social, linguistic, and economic engagement with the neighboring world and beyond. As we saw in chapter 3, the precolonial Beng economy included a long-distance trade in kola nuts with Jula traders and in other goods with Baule, Ando, and Jimini neighbors. To enable them to engage in these transactions, most Beng were and still are multilingual. Thus, despite living deep in the rain forest and having a distinctive physiology, a reputation for mystically powerful ritual practices, and an aversion for military engagement, the precolonial Beng were intricately engaged in regional and long-distance networks in both economic and other forms of commerce. In such a setting, perceiving strangers as unwelcome could well have disrupted crucial economic links in potentially disastrous ways. By contrast, welcoming those strangers who appeared in the villages—and training their children to do so from the earliest days *ex utero*—made supreme economic and political sense.

From the perspective of an infant, especially in the early weeks and months after birth, many people appear strange. It is ironic that Beng infants probably encounter far more people who are strange to them than do Euro-American, middle-class infants, who are typically far more protected from social encounters in general. Thus, although in a Beng village there are far fewer people whom adults would consider strangers than there are in an urban Western community, Beng infants' experience of interacting with people unfamiliar to them is probably far richer than the corresponding experience of their Western counterparts.

Nowadays, economic routes to a wider world are even more open than in earlier times. Many Beng farmers sell crops to non-Beng middlemen who come to the villages from Abidjan to buy the fruits of their harvest. Other Beng farmers travel to nearby towns or distant cities to sell their agricultural wares at a greater profit. Still other Beng villagers are hiring themselves out as laborers on distant commercial plantations run by members of other ethnic groups, and some are migrating to the cities to seek their fortune (see chapter 11). In all cases, engaging productively with strangers continues to be critical to their survival.

The set of caretaking practices that I have described in this chapter speak to numerous issues that are relevant to Beng village life in several diverse arenas. In the next chapter, we explore how the effort to make sociability a prime value in the lives of Beng babies continues even into the experience of sleep.

CHAPTER SEVEN

Sleepy Beng Babies

Short Naps, Bumpy Naps, Nursing Nights

Many contemporary middle-class Euro-American parents of infants cling to three sleep-related goals. First, they hope their baby will begin to take a small number of long naps at predictable times during the day, and for predictable lengths of time, as early as possible (New and Richman 1996:395–96). Depending on the infant's age, the baby should ideally take from one to three naps daily, each lasting at least one hour and preferably two or three hours. Myriad parenting books, magazine articles, and online chat sites urge parents to try to shape their babies' expectations to this routine. As one such article proclaims in its title, this popular literature assumes optimistically that it is possible to "teach . . . good sleep habits" (Salmon 1996). The latest edition of Dr. Spock's best-selling child-care guide explains: "Each baby develops a personal pattern of wakefulness and tends to be awake at the same time every day. Toward the end of the first year, most babies are down to two naps a day; and between one year and a year-and-a-half, they will probably give up one of these" (Spock and Parker 1998:99).

Second, most middle-class Euro-American parents hope that their infant will sleep at night for progressively longer intervals without waking and wanting milk. Eventually—and preferably as early as possible—the baby will sleep continuously through the night (Richman, Miller, and Solomon 1988:71; Super and Harkness 1982). According to the pediatrician author of one popular sleep advice manual, currently in its twenty-fifth paperback printing, "It is in your child's best interests to have uninterrupted sleep" (Ferber 1985: 36). Reflecting this widely accepted assumption, U.S.-based online parenting chat sites are replete with desperate (mostly North American) parents begging one another for advice on how to achieve this often elusive goal.[1]

Third, most middle-class Euro-American parents hope their baby will learn to sleep alone both during the day and at night as early as possible—at least in a separate bed, and preferably in a separate room. Here, the basic value of promoting independence—that most American of notions—is explicit (Richman, Miller, and Solomon 1988:68). Confirming this widespread association, the widely read pediatrician Richard Ferber states bluntly, "Bedtime means separation. . . . People sleep better alone in bed. . . . Sleeping alone is an important part of [your child's] learning to be able to separate from you without anxiety and to see himself as an independent individual. This process is important to his early psychological development" (Ferber 1985:37, 39).

In recent years, scientific research has questioned the advisability of infants sleeping alone due to the risk of SIDS, among other medical concerns (e.g., McKenna 2000). Although this research has been reported in the popular media, it does not seem to have changed dominant sleeping patterns in middle-class American families with babies. The values underlying the common practice of infants sleeping alone trump such medical research. Indeed, although, to the great frustration of their parents, many babies do not accommodate the above-stated set of three early parental wishes regularly, if ever, the parents of such culturally troublesome babies often persist in assuming that their children are the unfortunate exceptions to a widespread pattern that is based on biological givens. These three commonly held goals for children's sleep are unquestioningly accepted by so many middle-class Euro-American parents, and they are confirmed so regularly by the vast majority of "experts" whom the typical parent from this subculture might consult, that the goals themselves probably appear to be natural to those who espouse them.[2] After all, wouldn't everyone support such ideals?

In Beng villages the typical mother endorses none of these goals. If the first objective—predictable naps—were considered at all, it would be judged unachievable and hence irrelevant. Mothers would enjoy it if their babies reached the second aim—sleeping through the night—but most Beng mothers do not dwell on the thought; nor do they do anything to actualize the goal, probably for reasons related to the next ideal. Beng mothers would consider the third goal—for the infant to sleep alone—downright cruel.

In recent years some scholars have begun to explore the ways in which sleep is a cultural construction as much as it is a biological experience (e.g., Crawford 1994; Morelli, Rogoff, Oppenheim, and Goldsmith 1992; Super and Harkness 1982). In keeping with this current interest, in this chapter I aim to limn the contours of sleeping Beng babies as a way to forge an understanding of the cultural context of sleep. Reaching an understanding of sleep practices that will seem alien to most middle-class Euro-Americans may throw the cultural construction of their own sleep patterns into sharper relief.

What are the culturally meaningful lessons that a Beng infant learns during all those sleeping hours? The answers to this seemingly absurd question may provide surprises.

Daytime Naps

Alma: So how many naps a day does your baby take these days?
Au: [Laughs.] I have no idea!

Alma: Well, how about an estimate?

Au: Oh, some days it might be one or two, other days it might be five or six. Every day is different! [Laughs.]

Alma: Really! And how long do the naps last, usually?

Au: [Laughs.] I don't know! Some days they're long, other days they're short.

Alma: Is that a problem—that you never know when the baby will nap?

Au: [Looking confused.] No—that's what babies are like!

This conversation is typical of many others that I have had with Beng mothers. The basic theme that emerged from my effort to find regularity in Beng babies' naps is that more often than not, there is none. Of equal importance, this absence of predictability is not a matter of concern to anyone—certainly not to mothers or, apparently, to babies. The common view held by Beng adults is that babies sleep when and where they want to sleep, and there is nothing more to be said about the matter.

To confirm the shared impression that Beng babies' naps are both sporadic in timing and significantly variable in length, I conducted a series of quantitative studies of Beng infants' daytime activities. Over the course of summer 1993, my research assistant and I systematically observed twenty-nine babies between the ages of under one month and twenty-four months, for forty-eight separate periods usually lasting 2¼ hours each.[3] In this study, my assistant or I recorded at five-minute intervals the state of each baby and every activity in which the baby engaged during the period of observation. We used a time/activity chart that I prepared after testing and refining a preliminary version. In all cases, my assistant and I tried to be as unobtrusive as possible. We followed a given baby along whatever path the caretaker happened to be pursuing, engaging minimally with the child when the baby showed curiosity but otherwise remaining as detached as an observer, whether native or guest, can be in a Beng village. The results of this formal study confirmed the claims made by my female informants, as well as the impressions I had gathered from my informal observations. We will begin with the duration of Beng babies' daytime naps.

In our study of napping Beng babies, we recorded thirty-six naps during our periods of observation. Of these, a very large majority—72 percent—lasted thirty minutes or less. Another 22 percent of the naps observed lasted between thirty-five and sixty minutes; only 6 percent lasted between sixty-five and ninety minutes. The average duration of the thirty-six naps was approximately only twenty minutes (figure 40).[4] Even more striking, the most frequent duration of the naps we observed was a miniscule five minutes for naps on a flat surface (the ground or a floor) and ten minutes for naps on someone's back. All of these figures are very far from the one-to-three-hour

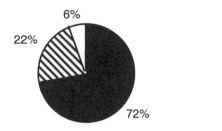

40. Length of observed naps (in minutes)

crib nap that so many middle-class Euro-American mothers expect of their young babies, preferably twice a day.

What accounts for this napping pattern of Beng babies and the stark contrast it poses with the Euro-American ideal (if not reality) of infant naps? There are several layers of explanation. Following Victor Turner's model for the interpretation of rich cultural data (1973), we will examine indigenous exegeses, relevant though unstated ideologies, and patterns of correlated factors that became clear to me as an outside observer, although they may remain unnoticed by most insiders. I begin with the indigenous perspective.

In the conversation reproduced above, Au maintained that it is not in the nature of babies to sleep at predictable times or for predictable durations. This is a widespread perception on the part of Beng mothers. I believe it is relevant in both cultural and psychological ways. If mothers do not expect their babies to sleep at predictable times or for predictable durations, the mothers will do nothing to try to bring about such an eventuality. Even if infants, individually and collectively, are prone to certain somewhat predictable biological sleep rhythms—something that many popular child-care authors assert but that, to my knowledge, scientists have not yet documented definitively—such rhythms would no doubt be influenced by environmental conditions and external stimuli, both crude and subtle. Even the pediatrician author Richard Ferber, an advocate of strict sleep schedules who makes frequent reference to biological factors shaping sleep, acknowledges: "Your own expectations can have a very strong influence on how your child's sleep pattern develops from the day you bring him home from the hospital" (Ferber 1985:17).

Acting from their own sense of the variability of babies' sleep patterns, Beng mothers do not "put their babies down" (as Euro-American mothers would say) at approximately the same time each day for a nap, and they do not encourage a waking baby to go back to sleep if "nap time isn't over yet," so Beng babies do not perceive that taking a regularly timed nap for a regular duration is a good thing to do, or even a possible way to orient their lives. They take matters into their own bodies and simply doze off whenever it feels right—depending on a thousand new variables that change each day. In turn, this behavior confirms their mothers' expectations that "babies don't sleep at the same time each day, or for the same amount of time."

Although I put great stock by the Beng explanation simply because it is the indigenous one, I complement it with some other factors I have identified as an observer. The first is at the level of ideology. As we have seen, Beng infants are considered by adults to be living part of the time in the spirit world from which they came, and the younger the baby the more time the infant is believed to spend in that world. Because babies are beings from another level of existence, it seems appropriate that they should propose their own agendas and determine their own activities—including their own sleeping and waking schedules. Indeed, insofar as babies, especially young ones, are to some extent considered spirits themselves with their own spirit-based agendas that they bring to this life, in the Beng view it would be an act of hubris on the part of a parent to try to influence an infant's basic biological timetable. The fact that Beng mothers are traditionally expected to regularly consult diviners about their young children's states and desires implies that it is considered more important to seek means to interpret and fulfill babies' wishes than to dictate to infants what those desires should be. Beng mothers' attitude that babies ought to, and do, set their own waking and sleeping schedules accords with this view of the human life cycle in general, and of infant volition and consciousness in particular.

A further explanation for the unpredictability of Beng babies' naps lies in three factors that I have observed as relevant, although no villagers made the connections I am suggesting. The first concerns where and how Beng infants sleep during the daytime.

From a Westerner's perspective, perhaps the most notable aspect of napping Beng babies is the position in which they often sleep during the daytime. Unlike Euro-American babies, who usually nap lying down on a flat surface, generally some form of bed,[5] Beng babies spend much of their nap time sleeping in a vertical position. This is an image that can be observed in any Beng village on any day of the week and at any time of day (figure 41). To determine the extent of the phenomenon, I conducted a more formal, quantitative, study of napping babies.

Once again, I refer to the activity charts that my research assistant, Dieudonné, and I compiled. In these tables, I note a number of telling facts. In well over half the nap times we observed, the baby was sleeping in a vertical position. Specifically, for the 875 total hours of daytime naps that we documented, in almost 60 percent of the sleep time the babies were sleeping in a vertical position. In only slightly over a third of the observed sleep time were babies sleeping in a horizontal position (on a mat or some cloths lain on the ground outside in the courtyard or inside the house). In the remaining sleeping time the babies were napping curled up in someone's lap (see figures 42 and 43).[6]

The position of the infant—vertical, horizontal, or curled up—is not the only notable aspect of these facts. Another significant consideration is whether babies were sleeping attached to another person or independently (unconnected to anyone). Nearly two-thirds of the observed nap time was spent joined to someone (whether the baby slept vertically on a back or curled up on a lap). In only slightly more than one-third of observed nap time were babies not attached to another person while sleeping (see figure 44).[7] This contrasts starkly with the common Euro-American pattern.

A further notable aspect of infants' daytime naps concerns their locale. In the study, almost 90 percent of the time, slumbering babies were outside (either on a mat on the ground, attached to someone's back, or curled up on someone's lap). Only slightly more than 10 percent of the time were they

41. Baby sleeping in a (more or less) vertical position while tied to the back of a girl who is carrying her around the village

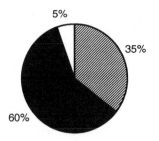

5%

35%

60%

Baby sleeping horizontally, not attached to anyone, on ground/bed outside or inside

Baby sleeping vertically, on someone's back

Baby sleeping curled up, on someone's lap

42. Physical positions of napping babies

43. Baby Esi sleeping comfortably in her mother, Amenan's, lap in 1980

inside a house, stretched out on cloths spread on the floor (figure 45).[8] The difference in these locales is significant. In Beng villages, life outside is frequently filled with people, with lively comings and goings especially on rest days but even, to a lesser extent, on work days. By contrast, the interior of a Beng house is generally dark, quiet, and devoid of people. Indeed, it should be avoided during the daytime unless a specific activity requires being inside (see Gottlieb and Graham 1994). Adults who regularly spend much time inside their houses during daylight hours are considered either to be witches or mad. Although this classification does not apply to napping babies, there is a general sense that because the interior is not an appropriate place for adults to pass long stretches of time during the day, neither is it for babies.[9] By contrast, napping outside keeps infants in the midst of the village's social whirl—something to be desired.

When babies were sleeping horizontally on mats or cloths, whether inside or outside, it was rare that they had fallen asleep in that position. Usually they had started out in the lap or on the back of someone who had put them down on the mat after some time asleep. As for the vertically positioned nappers, they were all attached to someone's back—that of their mother or another relative who might or might not be a regular *lɛŋ kūli*. When thus bundled up, the babies were almost always on the move. That is, not only were they oriented vertically, but they were constantly shifting position depending on the movement, direction, and activity of the person to whose back they were connected.

The paired moving bodies (Farnell 1999) of baby and baby carrier are reflected in Beng terminology: the Beng term that I have loosely translated as baby-sitter, *lɛŋ kūli*, means, literally, "baby carrier." The role is aptly named, as the primary responsibility of the *lɛŋ kūli* is indeed to carry the

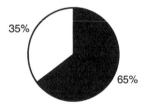

35%   65%

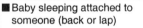
■ Baby sleeping attached to someone (back or lap)
□ Baby sleeping not attached to anyone

44. Social positions of napping babies

11.4%   88.6%

■ Baby sleeping in relatively noisy company of others (attached to someone, or near others)
□ Baby sleeping in very quiet place (inside), not in company of others

45. Noise/quiet levels around napping babies

46. A baby sleeping soundly on the moving back of his mother as she washes laundry

baby—whether the infant is awake or asleep. The contrast with the English term baby-sitter is notable. In the contemporary United States a baby-sitter does indeed spend a good amount of time sitting—on the floor playing with the baby or in a chair while the baby naps in a separate space. The Beng and English terms accurately represent complex bundles of cultural practices that differ greatly.

In Bengland, babies apparently come to expect verticality and movement as modal napping circumstances (figure 46). One toddler confirmed this quite directly. At a little over two years old, Chantal was especially articulate. One morning I went along to the fields with Chantal and her mother, my friend M'Akwe. At noon, we all decided to return to the village for lunch. On the way, Chantal announced, "Little Mama"—her maternal aunt—"will carry me on her back later while I take a nap in the afternoon." Young as she was, Chantal clearly understood in ways she could already articulate that for Beng babies and toddlers, napping is, often as not, an activity demanding a close physical connection with an older, moving person.

~

In Beng villages, a sleeping and moving baby occupies an advantaged position. Developmental psychologists have documented that repetitive motions tend both to lull a wakeful baby to sleep and to encourage a sleeping baby to remain asleep. In industrialized nations, parents have discovered technological iterations of this lesson. Many desperate parents with cars have spent hours driving babies on aimless rides through the countryside—knowing that the moment the car stopped, the baby would awaken. Beng mothers and *leŋ kūli* sometimes put their understanding of this principle to work without elaborate technological apparatus. They may take a long walk with a baby strapped to their back (say, to a faraway field or to another village to go visiting), knowing that they are giving the baby a good nap. Or a Beng mother or baby-sitter may keep her baby charge on her back while she does all manner of work, ranging from washing dishes or laundry (see figure 46 above), to pounding corn in a mortar (figure 47), to carrying logs for firewood (figure 48). When the baby is attached to a working woman whose position is constantly changing, the baby may fade in and out of sleep, depending on the interruptions to the rhythm of the carrier's movements.

Still, if the baby is sleeping for a long time, the baby's carrier at some point may want or need to put the infant down. If the baby carrier happens to be a young child herself, this may be a physical necessity. To an urban, Western observer such as myself, one of the salient aspects of Beng babies' lives is that they spend a fair amount of time being cared for by children rather than by adults. The children, mostly girls, who carry babies may be teenagers, but they can also be as young as six or seven years old.

A six- or seven-year-old child may tire quickly when carrying a little one on her back, especially if she is carrying an older baby or toddler—whose weight, if she is thin and the baby is chubby, may well approach her own. Her muscles are not fully developed, and she may have neither the strength nor the stamina to carry such a heavy bundle for any appreciable length of time. The result is that the younger the child carrying a baby, and the older or heavier the infant, the more likely it is that the *leŋ kūli* will put the heavy baby down to relieve herself of her burden. And once the sleeping baby is put down, the chances are fairly high that the nap will end abruptly. In my observations of Beng village life, I have seen countless instances of young girls carrying babies on their backs for a very short period of time; after five or ten minutes of the baby sleeping, the *leŋ kūli* puts the sleeping baby down on a mat—only for the baby to awaken immediately.[10]

Even a healthy adult may tire of carrying an infant for a long period, and other reasons aside from weariness may compel the baby chauffeur to unload her cargo. It may be her own bath time, or time to bathe the baby; she may

47. A baby sleeping soundly on the back of the mother, who is pounding corn in her mortar

48. Sassandra sleeping soundly on his grandmother Amenan's back while she carries a heavy log back to the village after chopping down a tree in the forest for firewood

have to go to the bathroom; or she may simply have run out of places to walk to, so she puts the baby down so she can sit down—or lie down for a nap, especially if she's an exhausted mother of a newborn. In short, the variable spacing and duration of Beng babies' naps is partly attributable to physical changes in their moving beds—at some point those beds must stop moving. Beng women are quite firm in their observations of what generally happens at this point. When a sleeping baby is removed from a baby carrier's back, women say with a resigned air, most babies immediately wake up. Even if they do not awake right away, they rarely continue napping for more than another five or ten minutes. Consider this narrative:

A young woman, Amwe, is sitting at a village-wide meeting holding fourteen-month-old Hallelujah in her lap. (The two are distantly related—Amwe and Hallelujah's father are members of the same matriclan.) Hallelujah is drowsy—it's 11:30 in the morning, and she hasn't had a nap yet. Soon she drifts off in Amwe's lap. After twenty minutes, another girl from the baby's father's matriclan, Ajua, who is about twelve years old, wanders over and gently picks up sleeping Hallelujah from Amwe's lap. Ajua puts the drooping baby on her back and tucks her in tightly with a *pagne* to keep her from slipping down. Then she takes Hallelujah over to her compound and lays her down on a mat for the little girl to continue her nap.

Ten minutes later, Ajua returns to the village meeting carrying Hallelujah—who is now wide awake. Once put down on the mat, the baby didn't last ten minutes asleep.

My impression from observing village life on a continual basis has been that babies' naps generally last longer if the babies are on someone's back than if they are lying either on the ground or on someone's lap. This impression was mildly confirmed in my formal study: the commonest nap duration for back-sleeping babies was ten minutes, and the commonest nap duration for horizontally sleeping and lap-sleeping babies was only five minutes. In other words, even though most naps were very short by contemporary middle-class Euro-American standards, being attached to a (usually moving) back meant staying asleep a bit longer.

Even so, knowing that a baby who has been sleeping on someone's back or in someone's lap may well awaken if transferred to a mat to sleep on the hard, flat ground does not always discourage a baby carrier from putting down a baby. The notion of the sacred nap that must never be interrupted—so common in middle-class Euro-American families—is rarely operative here. The beautifully lettered or hand-crocheted door signs that proclaim to visitors "Quiet! Baby sleeping!" would never find ready customers in Beng villages.[11] If a Beng infant's nap stops because of an interruption, this is rarely considered an unfortunate occurrence. If the mother or caretaker gives the baby's waking any thought, she generally judges that the little one will find another time to sleep. There is little regret or annoyance that the nap was prematurely shortened according to some abstract timetable. This is not to say that Beng mothers constantly make an effort to awaken sleeping babies or that they fail to take pains to soothe a grumpy baby who was abruptly awakened or that they never make an effort to allow a napping baby to keep sleeping. Rather, it is to say that the value of an infant's nap is contextually determined. Among the Beng, many factors are routinely judged more important than a sleeping baby's nap continuing uninterrupted, and some occasions demand that napping Beng babies be deliberately awakened. I discovered this in the course of my own relationships with Beng infants. As I discussed in chapter 1, during fieldwork my husband, Philip, and I regularly treated sick infants to the extent that our knowledge and resources allowed us to. Often the babies were asleep when the mothers presented them to us. If we were able to diagnose the illness and could provide appropriate medication, we asked the mother to come back for the medicine when the baby was awake. But the mother invariably balked and immediately awakened the baby, insisting that we administer the medicine right away to the now-bawling infant.

The same thing happened when I presented baby clothes as gifts to new mothers. Inevitably the mother opted to try out the new outfit on the infant right away. If the little one happened to be sleeping, the nap didn't last long as the mother moved arms and legs this way and that to put on the new outfit until the jostled baby awoke, tired and grouchy. The cries of such an irritated baby were judged a small price to pay for the child to gain the advantage of a relationship with a benefactor of clothes or medicine. And as we saw in chapter 6, another occasion especially demands the waking of a sleeping infant: when certain guests arrive from elsewhere to see a baby, especially a newborn.

In keeping with this flexibility in nap time, Beng mothers of infants often do not keep careful track of the naps their babies have taken on a given day or how long a given nap has lasted. In fact, the mothers may be more concerned to ensure that they take a nap themselves, especially if the baby has kept them up much of the night crying for some reason. One day, for example, I found Tahan sleeping on a mat outside in her courtyard, under the granary. Next to her lay six-month-old Sassandra, wide awake (figure 49). He looked around contentedly from his sleeping mother to the varied activities of others in his courtyard, but he never did join his mother in sleep. Later that day I checked in on Sassandra: by 5:00 P.M. he still had had no nap all afternoon, but Tahan didn't seem much concerned about it—she was simply happy to have gotten a nap herself. If Sassandra didn't take one, that was no problem for his mother.

In sum, Beng babies' naps reveal a fundamental principle at work that poses a strong contrast to the beliefs that underlie the napping practices of many middle-class Euro-American babies. With the latter group of infants, sleep is an activity that is frequently regulated according to two primary convictions: that sleep is important as an abstract biological necessity, and that pursuing that activity in solitude, at regular hours, and for regular durations is equally important. For Beng infants, by contrast, the importance of sleep as an abstract biological necessity is not really at issue. Rather, as with the famous Nuer sense of time documented long ago by E. E. Evans-Pritchard

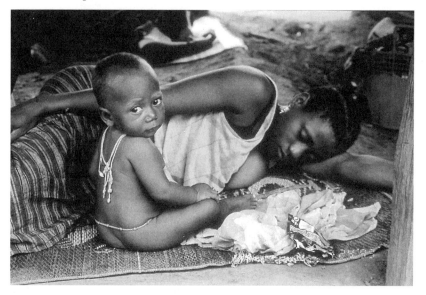

49. Sassandra sitting contentedly awake next to his mother, Tahan, while she takes an afternoon nap

(1940:94–138), what is important is that sleep activity be subject to a set of relativistic rules of engagement appropriate to social life in the Beng world. It would be considered far worse for a Beng baby to nap at the sociologically wrong time (such as when a relative is visiting from afar) than for that baby to go for a long period, perhaps even an entire day, with no nap whatsoever.

In the view of Beng adults, babies will always find time to sleep when they need to. It is not important to maintain a regular schedule for infants' naps or to ensure that the naps are of even duration from day to day. Instead, what is critical is that babies nap regularly in the company of, and often physically attached to, others. Equally critical is that they *not* nap when certain people are present—people with whom they should be developing social relationships. In short, in the Beng world, napping is an eminently social activity. Naps represent an opportunity for mothers and other caretakers to socialize babies into the life they will be leading—a life that is marked by a certain amount of unpredictability; an intense, lively, and extensive network of relatives and neighbors; and a never-ending series of social engagements.

Nighttime Sleep

In the United States, perhaps one of the most cherished goals of middle-class Euro-American parents is to "get the baby down" at a regular hour each night. The child should then remain soundly asleep—without waking to drink milk or for any other reason—at least until dawn and, preferably, later in the morning. North American popular parenting culture is pervaded by these goals. One online pediatrician claims that "every parent wants their child to go to bed by themselves and sleep through the night" and that "by the age of three months, 90% of babies are sleeping through the night."[12] In families that adopt these ideals, getting the baby to sleep for the night indeed means, literally, putting the baby down—generally into a crib, bassinet, or cradle, but, in any case, in a horizontal position. At this point, the mother is free to do what she wants or needs to do for an hour or two in the evening before her own exhaustion sets in.

Beng mothers do not view their babies' nighttime sleep in this way. First, they do not distinguish so starkly between daytime sleep and nighttime sleep that they aim to "get the baby down" at night at a particular time. Second, the initial stage of putting a baby to sleep at night does not involve moving the baby to a separate space from the mother or to a horizontal space. Third, Beng mothers do not expect that the child will remain asleep until the morning.

Let us imagine the scene in a Beng village between the hours of 7:00 and 9:30 P.M.—hours when most adults are still awake but darkness has set in. In Beng villages, life is generally lived outdoors during all waking hours—including the evening and early nighttime hours (Gottlieb and Graham 1994). Once the sun sets—between about 6:00 P.M. in December and about 6:40 P.M. in July—people start illuminating the night by lighting kerosene lanterns.[13] The light is enough to cast a soft glow for a short distance. After sunset, one sees adults, adolescents, and even young children moving about quietly, kerosene lamp in hand, visiting from compound to compound. Circles of light surround these moving figures, with darkness spanning the distance between them. Contained within the illuminated circles are babies tucked securely into *pagnes* tied to their mothers' backs. The babies have been purged, bathed, medicated, painted, and oiled in the long routine we explored in chapter 5. In a sense, as Euro-Americans would put it, they are "down for the night." However, unlike their Euro-American counterparts, these babies are in moving beds attached to their mothers. Moreover, there is no expectation that they will remain in their initial sleeping position, or even asleep, for the rest of the night.

A little while after the babies have fallen asleep on someone's back (usually their mother's) shortly after sundown, their older siblings start to get sleepy. The younger the children, the sooner they fade. As sleepiness sets in, toddlers lie down on mats on the ground of a courtyard—usually, but not always, their own. An older sibling or cousin may soon join them, and then another, until five or six children are sleeping in the courtyard. Mothers might not set down their sleeping babies at this time, though. Consider the scene in figure 50:

> At 8:45 P.M., Sassandra is asleep on his mother's lap. At 9:05, Tahan gets up and gives Sassandra to her husband to hold for a minute. She goes inside and returns with a *pagne*. She puts sleeping Sassandra on her back and tucks him into the *pagne*. Then she eases herself down sideways on a Western chair, positioning herself so as to allow the curled-up bundle that is Sassandra to continue sleeping on her back as she sits on her chair.
>
> Tahan doesn't look too comfortable like this, and I ask her, "Why don't you put Sassandra down on a mat to sleep next to the other children?"
>
> "He'd wake up as soon as I put him down!" Tahan answers.

In this case, Tahan indulges her son's interest in sleeping, as there are no intervening distractions to compel her to put him down. It is late evening. The family has been fed, the dishes are washed, it is a quiet time for chatting with relatives and neighbors, and Sassandra is clearly tired. Keeping her young

50. Sassandra sleeping all tucked into a cloth on his mother Tahan's back in the late evening while his mother chats in the courtyard with her family before going inside for the night

child on her back will likely afford her a peaceful half-hour or so before the two of them lie down together for the night.

At some point, when the mother herself is ready to retire—usually around 9:00 or 9:30 P.M. unless there is a special nighttime activity such as a dance, funeral, or wedding occurring in the village—she says good night to everyone in her courtyard (or whatever courtyard she has been visiting) and goes inside her bedroom.[14] If she has other young children who have fallen asleep outside in the courtyard, someone from the household—she herself or her husband or any of a number of available grandparents, aunts, uncles, or cousins—start to bundle up the littlest sleepers and take them inside the house. Older children are urged to stand up and walk inside on their own, even if they wake up grumbling about the interruption—keeping the sleeping children asleep is not considered a major priority. Inside the house, the youngest children are deposited on the ground or bed next to where the mother herself will sleep. Usually, this slumbering entourage includes girls and boys up to the age of preadolescence or early adolescence.[15]

Ready to retire for the night, the mother carefully unties the *pagne* that is keeping her baby safe and puts the baby down on the ground or bed; then she lies down next to her child. If the baby awakes, the mother immediately offers a breast. Then they both (probably) drift off to sleep. Some nights, the baby will sleep for a few hours, then wake up crying and possibly hungry, and the mother will sleepily slip her breast into the baby's mouth. Those nights, the baby will nurse happily and quietly maybe once or twice, then fall back asleep, letting the mother drift back to her dreams too. On other nights, the baby may repeat this routine quite a few times. But few breast-feeding mothers were able to recollect to me how many times their infants had breast-fed the night before—since they weren't sure they were always awake for the event.

On still other nights, the baby may not be satisfied by simply nursing and once sated may proceed to cry inconsolably. Let us consider this narrative:

Afwe: My baby cries all the time. He's especially bad in the evening, especially while the family is eating, and it lasts until he goes to sleep at night. He does sleep at night, though he wakes [often] to nurse. Then he wakes up for good at the first cock's crow—around 4 A.M.! He naps in the morning, but not so easily any more, since he's a bit older now. . . . In the afternoon, he doesn't really nap at all, unless he's carried on someone's back. Then, he naps a bit, but not for too long—and he awakes as soon as he's put down!

Alma: Are you worried about him?

Afwe: I'm not worried about the fact that he doesn't sleep much at all, because he's healthy. Indeed, he can chat nicely!

I was immediately sympathetic to my interlocutor's story, recalling similar sleepless nights that Philip and I had spent with baby Nathaniel crying inconsolably for hours on end his first months. I thought back to the never-ending series of questions we had asked our pediatrician and his nurse those early months, struggling to understand why our son could not keep the regular, calm hours that we thought most babies surely keep. Was it colic? Was it something my husband and I were unknowingly doing wrong? If only we could name the disturbance, give it an etiology, we felt sure we could cope with it more effectively.

Remembering my own attempts to understand the causes of unpredictable and inexplicable baby suffering we lamely term colic, I returned to the conversation with Afwe and tried to commiserate. Curious to see if Afwe had any better explanations of her child's misery than I had had of my child's, I asked Afwe what was wrong with her baby that would result in such disruptive nights. She looked perplexed and said simply, *"pɔtɔpɔ!"*—Nothing! Then I asked Afwe if her other children had been such bad sleepers as infants.

Afwe: Kouakou, the oldest, also never slept, and he also cried a lot as a baby. I carried him around on my back in the middle of the night for a few hours every night, from the time he was two months old until he was over five months old!

Alma: What was the matter with him?

Afwe: Nothing!

Again, I was encountering the perspective held by many Beng mothers that it is in babies' nature to be unpredictable. Otherwise unexplained misery needed no explanation.

~

Restless nights, nursing nights, wakeful nights, crying nights—none of these is terribly pleasant to a Beng mother, of course. But neither are they considered extraordinary, something beyond what one might expect of living with a baby. After all, in the view of Beng adults, infants are still living most of the time in the other world. Who knows what babies are thinking and experiencing, what makes them cry suddenly for a reason that even an attentive mother might not understand? Beng mothers acknowledge that the unpredictable moods of a baby may well have a foundation. But that foundation belongs to another world. If a baby's erratic behavior becomes truly disruptive or worrisome, a mother can always take him to a diviner to discover the underlying cause. Otherwise, she will just try to make him feel comfortable, luring the little one day by day into this life by carrying him, breast-feeding him, and lying next to him as much as possible.

Conclusion

Five years after my 1993 research, I was shopping one day for a new bed for my then three-year-old daughter, Hannah, in a children's furniture store in the United States. Browsing among the rows of cribs and cradles, I came across an ingenious new item: a "Bedside Co-Sleeper," a small bed that attaches to the parents' bed frame and in which a young infant can sleep. I asked the shop owner about the product. He was oddly embarrassed and explained that he'd meant to send back the sample, as he didn't intend to sell the item any more. Surprised, I asked the reason.

"People are too afraid of sleeping next to their babies," he explained. "They're afraid they'll roll over and crush them."

Although not all American parents have this attitude, the view that my local shop owner reported to me is indicative of great reluctance on the part of many middle-class Euro-American parents to sleep with their babies (see DeLoache and Gottlieb 2000; Shweder, Jensen, and Goldstein 1995; Small 1998). In one study, only 3 percent of this population reported sleeping with their infants (Litt 1981). Most parents in this subculture are uncomfortable with the practice for a variety of reasons. These include a fear of crushing the baby and a sense of shame concerning the possibility that their child might see or hear their acts of sex. In some of these parents there may also be a conviction—whether fully conscious or not—that learning early to sleep solo produces strongly independent people who will later do well in a fiercely competitive world.[16]

Things could not be more different in Beng villages. There, the notion of an infant sleeping for any appreciable length of time in a separate space unconnected to another human being is very far not only from the norm but also from the ideal, while the practice of a baby sleeping attached to the back of a moving body (or sometimes curled up into the lap of a seated body) during the day, and cuddled into a sleeping mother at night, is the norm and, at least for night sleeping, is heartily endorsed as the ideal. The different infant sleep practices in the two societies are both overdetermined and multiply consequential. Significant ideological and sociological factors combine to make these practices reasonable in their local settings.

Ideologically the Beng practice makes particularly good sense. Because Beng adults believe that newborns exist most of the time in the other world and are in need of being lured into this life, it is logical that parents and others should be as close as possible to babies, so as to convince them—largely through warm bodily practices—that this world is inviting and hospitable, a world for which it is worth separating from the other world. Sociologically, Beng sleep patterns are also appropriate to the Beng world because they teach early on the lesson that the most important thing about being alive is retaining and promoting firm social ties with a wide variety of people—especially one's closest relatives, but many others as well, with flexibility to transfer affection and trust readily to others who reach out to support oneself—literally, through carrying.

The middle-class Euro-American pattern promoting independent spaces for infant sleep fits in with quite different ideological assumptions. Encouraging an infant to sleep in a separate space is consistent with the common middle-class Euro-American presumption (based nowadays on scientific models learned in school) that the newborn arrives in this world as a new genetic creation that had no previous existence prior to the uniting of an egg and a sperm inside the mother's body. At the symbolic level, it makes cognitive sense that a newly created biological entity deserves its own newly created sleeping space. Likewise, at the sociological level, the lesson conveyed by a bassinet, cradle, or crib that is placed in its own room at some point in the infant's first year is in keeping with the American-capitalist morality lesson that individuals ought to make their own way in the world on the basis of their own courage and efforts. In short, both Beng and middle-class Euro-American sleep decisions for infants make cultural sense in the cultural environments in which they are re-created daily.

In the next chapter, we will continue our investigation of the cultural construction of babies' bodily habits, moving on to a discussion of food.

CHAPTER EIGHT

Hungry Beng Babies

Breast Water/Ordinary Water/Sacred Water
and the Desire to Breast-Feed

Is there anything more natural than an infant breast-feeding while nestled against the warm body of a nourishing mother? Depending on one's museum-going and reading habits, the thought might evoke visions of a thirteenth-century Madonna and Child painting, a canvas in warm tones by Mary Cassatt, a Yoruba sculpture from Nigeria, or perhaps a pamphlet from La Leche League.[1] Disparate though their iconographic genealogies may be, these varied images all seem to say to the viewer: *With the intrinsic tie uniting them, this mother and child are perhaps the closest of any people. Before culture takes over to claim and reshape this baby in another form, its natural mother will feed her baby in the way that she believes comes naturally to them both.* The notion of the naturalness of mothering, as epitomized by breast-feeding, is especially strikingly envisioned in the Western art tradition in the central panel of a five-paneled painting by Belgian artist Léon Frédéric, *La Nature* (1897), in which the idea of "mother nature" is anthropomorphically portrayed as an actual human mother "who is feeding, or has already fed to stupefied reple-tion, all the little child-Seasons" (Nochlin 1980:143), which are depicted as a hungry and lush anthropomorphized cornucopia of flowers, grasses, fruits, and birds.

Seductive and even commonsensical though the image of nursing mother and baby as a natural pair may be, I want to propose in this chapter another conception of the breast-feeding duo. For some time anthropologists and other scholars have been suggesting that the empirical substances that any person or group terms "food" are as much culturally as biologically defined, and that eating is as much a socially constructed activity as it is a biologically necessary function (Mintz and DuBois 2002). Much of this literature has documented the richly developed systems of thought that lie beneath seem-ingly irrational food-related conventions such as food taboos and food prefer-ences.[2] The literature also includes explorations of the micropolitics of food practices in local social contexts[3] and political economic analyses emphasizing international trade systems that shape the production and consumption of foods.[4] Provocative as they are, for our purposes an obvious shortcoming of these otherwise intellectually rich works is that most focus on adults' eating habits while ignoring those of children.

At the same time, another group of scholars, among them anthropologists, historians, and demographers, have been exploring the ways in which infant feeding—including not only bottle-feeding and supplementation with solid foods, but also breast-feeding—is constructed by deeply social factors.[5] Some authors focus on nutrition, malnutrition, and other health issues;[6] others on demographic implications of infant feeding practices;[7] others on broad historical, political, and cultural factors;[8] still others on the politics of the specific controversy surrounding breast-feeding versus bottle-feeding in the "Third World."[9] The shared argument of these otherwise disparate works is that the feeding experiences of even the youngest infants are as much mediated by a variety of social, economic, political, historical, and cultural structures as they are dictated by biological urges.

In this chapter I aim to deploy the insights of these two bodies of literature in analyzing infant feeding practices in Beng villages. The anthropology of food has an especially strong contribution to make in giving us intellectual tools with which we can interrogate the overdetermined range of meanings that people bring to food as a cultural product. The gamut of social scientific approaches to breast-feeding and other feeding of infants offers a set of productive tools for looking at babies' eating practices as routinized by a broad array of social factors. Combining the strengths and insights of these two groups of writing should allow us to approach the meals of Beng babies as multiply determined events that say much both about Beng adults' views of infants and about Beng culture and society in general—and perhaps, to some extent, about Beng infants' own experiences.

Breast Water, Ordinary Water, Sacred Water

Water, Work, and Motherhood

When a young baby is obviously hungry, one might imagine that the first thing a nursing mother does is to position the baby comfortably to allow for breast-feeding. In Bengland, this is the second thing that a traditionally oriented breast-feeding mother does. Her first action is quite different. The mother scoops up a bowlful of cool water from her water pot, cups a small palmful, and, with her baby lying or sitting in her lap, offers some water to her child. If she is faithfully following tradition—which some but not all Beng mothers still do nowadays—the mother offers two more small handfuls.

A cooperative baby laps up these mouthfuls of water willingly from the mother's cupped hand—well and good. But an uncooperative baby balks. Then the mother of such a baby does what Beng women call *kami:* she forces her baby to drink at least a small amount of water. Depending on the baby's temperament or personality *(sie)* the mother may be somewhat violent in forcing water down the tiny throat. A baby with a *sie grégré,* or "difficult temperament," might start choking and gasping, trying desperately to spit out the liquid-that-is-not-breast-milk that is being sloshed into her mouth; perhaps such a child adds for good measure some dramatic thrashing about with tiny arms and legs, insisting, *"Listen to me! I don't want this water, I want that stuff from the breast!"* But the traditional Beng mother is trained not to take pity on such a rebellious infant before she makes sure that at least a few drops of water go down her baby's throat. Then and only then does she guide her child toward her nipple.

What accounts for this regular regime—marked as it sometimes is by a measure of maternal violence—that defines the nursing episodes of many young Beng babies? One mother proposed a medical explanation: If water is not drunk first, she suggested, a baby will develop heartburn. However, when I asked about *kami,* most men and women mentioned another factor: It is, they explained, a question of labor. As I probed for further explanation of this surprising claim, the systematic pattern of women's work habits as implicated cybernetically in children's breast-feeding needs began to make itself clear.

As we have seen, soon after giving birth—at least by the time the baby is three months old, and sometimes when the child is as young as one month—a new mother returns to farming, collecting water, and chopping down trees for firewood. Sometimes she brings along her baby for these tasks, but not always. Especially if she has other young children demanding her attention; or the baby is sick; or she is tired; or the weather is bad; or she knows she will return carrying a heavy load of wood or crops on her head and it would be too strenuous to carry a baby, especially an older, heavy baby, at the same time—in short, in any number of circumstances—a mother may not be able to bring her infant to work. During those times, as we have seen, a mother needs to find a *leŋ kūli*. Although on some days the *leŋ kūli* and baby may accompany the mother to work, on other days they remain in the village while the mother goes off without them. Thus at times an infant, even one who is not yet eating any solid food, may be separated from her mother. Such a child is ipso facto separated from her only source of nourishment.

Of course in such circumstances, the baby may become hungry. This is especially likely if a baby is accustomed to drinking small amounts of breast milk quite frequently—which, as we shall soon see, is the pattern for Beng infants. Baby bottles and commercially prepared infant formula are not sold in Beng village stores,[10] so what does a Beng caretaker do with a hungry baby whose nursing mother is not available and who is not considered old enough to eat solid food? Beng women and men alike told me that to prepare for such times, the child should learn to be satisfied with a drink of water. One male elder was careful to point out that ordinary water is just a temporary breast milk substitute: "He keeps on crying if we only give him water to drink. You must nurse him." A young grandmother added that three small handfuls of water is the most that a mother should force down her baby's throat: "Five handfuls of water would kill him." While acknowledging the risks of engaging in *kami* excessively, both these informants were nevertheless firm in underscoring the importance of the practice as a means to tide a hungry baby over until the time when the mother returns. Thus it is that from the start—ideally, the very day of birth—a mother tries to accustom her newborn to the taste of water.

This strategy frees a mother somewhat from her baby. It allows a village mother who is also a full-time farmer—which, as we have seen, is the case for virtually every Beng mother—to resume working, if only gradually, within a relatively short while after each delivery. From the baby's perspective, the practice of *kami* affords even a newborn a certain modest level of independence from the mother. If her hunger and thirst can be satisfied by someone other than her mother at least for a short time, the newborn has begun the move toward an active engagement with—and trust of—a wider coterie of persons. Although this is a move that all developmentally normal babies everywhere eventually make, Beng mothers are eager for their babies to make it as early as possible.[11]

The Sacred Nature of Water

If the practice of *kami* serves a critical role in enabling women to meet enormous labor demands, it also has cultural foundations beyond these instrumental considerations. For one thing, linguistic usage implies a culturally significant tie between water and breast milk. The Beng term for what is called "breast milk" in English is *nyo yi;* at a literal level, this translates as "breast water" (*nyo* = "breast" and *yi* = "water").[12] Thus *nyo yi* is not fully equivalent in semantic field to the English term *breast milk*. Moreover, the Beng term for cow's milk (whether fresh, powdered, or canned)—*nono* (a word borrowed directly from Jula)—has no etymological relation to the Beng term for breast water. Given that *water* and *breast water* are linguistically related in Beng usage, I suggest that the tie between the two liquids constitutes a culturally meaningful statement to the nursing mother that giving water to her infant, even by force, is something that makes cultural sense insofar as water inhabits the same conceptual universe as breast milk.

The local conception of water itself lends further cultural force to this association. Beng people, especially those who are not devoutly Christian or Muslim, consider water a ritually powerful substance. This general principle emerges in many arenas. For example, a Master of the Earth may sometimes present water as an offering to Earth spirits, especially in emergencies when a sacrifice is necessary to deal with a dangerous situation but no eggs or animals (the more common offerings to Earth spirits) are available.[13] Consider this case:

> Afwe was having a very difficult time in childbirth. A diviner pronounced that one of Afwe's female relatives was bewitching her, out of jealousy from an old resentment. In great alarm, Afwe's relatives immediately summoned a Master of the Earth.
>
> Ordinarily, the Master of the Earth would have offered an egg or a chicken to the Earth. But the Master of the Earth didn't have time to locate an egg or a chicken suitable for slaughter. In haste, he obtained a bowl of water and prayed over it, begging the Earth to strike down whoever was bewitching Afwe. He judged that this would allow Afwe's delivery to proceed without further delay.
>
> A few minutes after the Master of the Earth completed his prayer, a tree in the forest became uprooted for no apparent reason (it wasn't a windy or stormy day), knocking down a woman walking in front of it. The woman was an aunt of Afwe, and she died almost immediately. A few minutes later, Afwe gave birth to her baby. Villagers took this as a sign that Afwe's aunt had been killed by the Earth, which had caused the tree to fall on her after hearing the Master of the Earth praying over the bowl of water.

Here we see water as an effective medium of communication between human and spirit. Indeed, in this case water conveyed a curse that proved fatal to the aunt-witch, while it saved the lives of the laboring woman and her baby-trying-to-be-born. As this narrative reveals, water is clearly considered a locus of spiritual power in Beng ritual practice.

Some naturally occurring bodies of water (including small pools found next to a hill, as well as some rivers and streams) are seen by the Beng as the dwelling places of Earth spirits, which are named and classified as either malevolent or benevolent. Women who are experiencing fertility problems— having trouble becoming pregnant; remaining pregnant; delivering a live, healthy baby; or keeping a baby alive once born—may pray to the spirits residing in these waters, requesting that the spirits grant them a child. If a woman's prayers are successful, she incurs a permanent debt to the spirits of those waters. Every so often, at intervals specified by a diviner—perhaps once a week or once a month, but at least once a year—such a woman should come with an offering to the spirits of the pool or river, as thanks for their having granted her a healthy child. The offering itself is usually a gourd filled with water. Once again, the spiritual potency of water is affirmed.

Many Beng diviners use water in a spiritual connection. One of their divination techniques is to swirl milky water in a bowl.[14] This milky water is meant to attract spirits that are then said to speak to the diviners and allow them to understand the hidden causes of unfortunate occurrences such as illnesses, accidents, and so on. Other diviners use cowry shells for the same purpose. In this case, before a session the diviner drips water over the shells. The water is said to attract the spirits to the cowries, and the spirits then speak to the diviner.[15] With both divination techniques, water is a critical ingredient for attracting a spiritual presence to the human scene.

Another sign of the spiritually potent nature of water in Beng thought appears in common attitudes toward water and daily health. During our stays in Beng villages, Philip and I have always either boiled or filtered our own drinking water. To our dismay, our neighbors often derided our laborious efforts. One day we thought to explain our mysterious actions. The village had been experiencing an especially crippling outbreak of Guinea worm.[16] After reading about the disease, Philip and I were convinced that polluted drinking water was the cause of our neighbors' misery. We urged our friends to boil their water as protection against future infestation. But even our closest and most open-minded friends dismissed our suggestion with casual laughter.

"Can you see the worms in our water?" our friend Yacouba challenged us. We admitted we couldn't.

"There's nothing wrong with the water," he insisted. "Anyway, even if the Guinea worms come to us through the water, they're put there by witches." Yacouba added emphatically, "Boiling the water wouldn't stop the witches."

In this conversation, alternative systems of knowledge had confronted each other. Each of us remained convinced that our system of knowledge was correct, authoritative, incontrovertible. The entangled epistemological aspects of this point-counterpoint conversation are notable, but my aim in reporting it here is simply to illustrate the common Beng conviction that water is essentially health-giving. If and when it conveys disease, it is believed that the disease vector must have been introduced into the water by a human or extrahuman force that might just as easily have chosen another means to cause illness in a victim. The water itself is clean and cannot by itself be the source of illness.

I suggest that this view that water is inherently pure and is a frequent site of spiritual activity or a means of spiritual communication informs the Beng infant-care practice of *kami*. At one level, force-feeding water to a young infant enables women who are both full-time mothers and full-time farmers to do both the work of the farm and the work of child care. At another level, *kami* may be seen by women—perhaps in a less-than-conscious mode of perception—as a regular means to impart to their babies a substance that is closely related to breast water and that is considered intrinsically clean, health-giving, and spiritually valuable.

Furthermore, because infants are presumed to come from the land of the ancestors, where they were in close touch with spirits, and because the youngest of children are believed to still be spending considerable time in that other land, it may be appropriate that infants regularly drink water, with its ties to the spirit world. Although no Beng person offered this connection to me, I suggest that it exists as background knowledge informing the comfort level that women feel in forcing their babies—sometimes clearly against the babies' desires—to drink water before offering them breast milk. In short, *kami* is overdetermined, showing us how far we are from a naturalistic model of babies being subject to simple biological urges easily satisfied with a casually offered breast.

~

Once a baby drinks some water, whether or not willingly, the little one is finally offered the breast. If plain water is seen as clean, health-giving, and a potential site of spiritual communication and potency, how is breast water seen by the Beng?

The Nature of Breast Water

On the one hand, nursing Beng mothers say that the taste of whatever food they eat on a given day is not transmitted to their breast water. In fact, my women friends thought it a great joke when I asked about the possibility that after a mother had eaten especially spicy food the baby would be able to detect this when drinking from the mother's breasts. Here is one conversation I had with Amenan as we talked about her grandson, Sassandra, then six months old:

Amenan: Sassandra ate some sauce with chili pepper this afternoon.
Alma: Perhaps the chili pepper was mixed in with the breast water.
Amenan: Yih! I don't think so! [Turning to Sassandra] Sassandra, do you think it was mixed in? [Amenan laughs with abandon.]

So much for my trust in the breast-feeding advocacy literature that claims that the taste of breast milk changes according to what the nursing mother has recently eaten.[17] Beng women also assert that the constitution of their *nyo yi* does not alter as the baby grows older. These assertions suggest a fairly unremarkable view of breast milk.

However, other comments and practices reveal a far different sense of breast water as a bodily substance with meanings that are precisely and richly outlined in cultural ideology. These concern both risk and its obverse—vulnerability. Let us explore these in turn.

First, I frequently heard it said that when a woman is nursing a boy who happens to be naked (at least on the bottom), she must take care that her *nyo yi* does not drip onto the baby's penis. If the liquid does contact her son's genitals, the result is said to be catastrophic: once the boy comes of age, he will be impotent.

This is clearly a culturally constituted threat that must make sense in an intellectually coherent universe (Douglas 1985, 1992; Douglas and Wildavsky 1982). What puts it in meaningful perspective is that there is no corresponding risk said to threaten a baby girl if breast water drips on her vulva. Accordingly, I suggest that the threat posed by breast milk dripping on the genitals of boys (but not girls) signals a notion of inherent opposition between breast water, a symbol of female sexuality, and the ability to sustain an erection, a symbol of male sexuality. The knowledge of this culturally defined threat is common among Beng women. The mothers I have observed breast-feeding do indeed take care that their leaking breasts do not drip onto their baby boys' genitals. Daily practice thus replicates ideology in observable ways.

But what does the ideology mean? My interpretation follows the clues provided by related practices concerning sexuality. Although breast milk is clearly nourishing, in the case of baby boys it is a potential source of peril as well. In adults, when men's and women's bodily fluids are combined during sex, the result is also considered dangerous. As we saw in chapter 5, the contagious condition of *gbre,* or dirt—which is reportedly fatal to infants—is said to result when an adult fails to bathe in the morning after having had sex the previous night. Training infant boys to fear breast water when it may contact their own site of future sexuality may be seen as a way to prepare them for the notion that will be so important later—that sex itself, which likewise combines female and male bodily fluids, is potentially a source of danger. The lesson will stand them in good stead as adults, when they must discipline themselves to wash after each act of sex or risk symbolically polluting—and endangering the life of—a nearby infant.

Another breast milk–related practice pertains only to boys. So long as they are breast-feeding, baby and toddler boys may not eat what the Beng call "Earth meat" *(ba sòŋ)*—cooked meat prepared from domestic animals that were slaughtered for sacrifice by a Master of the Earth. Here the gender opposition has an asymmetrical impact: after weaning, boys will join men in eating "Earth meat," while girls and women will be forbidden to savor the dish.

Breast water may threaten infants of both genders in another way. There is one food that is taboo for a nursing mother to eat; if she violates the taboo—even unknowingly—she endangers the health of her baby, who may catch the disease the Beng call *gbre*. Once again, I suggest that the action of the disease operates on a symbolic level. The taboo food is a type of yam called *kpese ti*. Farmers grow this yam next to other yam types in order to "take the dirt out from sex." If an adult has sex one night and goes to the fields the next day before having bathed, people say that the "dirt" from sex that has not been washed off will ruin the yams that are growing in the fields.[18] In this case, it is said, some of the yams will rot *(ó sáŋ)*. If someone eats such a rotted yam, it could cause a skin rash *(wekewekeweke)*. To protect against this risk, farmers plant the *kpese ti* yam because, it is said, it will remove any dirt infecting other yams, ensuring that they remain edible and do not cause skin eruptions.

But because it removes this sexual dirt, the *kpese ti* is said to accumulate the dirt. This is why it is taboo for nursing women to eat *kpese ti,* for it is said that the dirt in these yams will enter the breast milk and afflict the nursing infant. As we have seen in chapter 5, the serious disease called dirt greatly concerns mothers of infants. Once again, the insistence that a breast-feeding child be kept at a distance from all sexual activity—including even indirect hints of such activity—is operating here.

Thus, although breast milk nourishes an infant, it can be a source of symbolically constituted danger as well. *Nyo yi* is also seen in the obverse way—as itself vulnerable. During the last stages of pregnancy, a Beng woman living in a village takes care to keep her breasts covered as long as she is out-doors, whereas before her pregnancy, she may have walked around the village or at least her own courtyard bare-breasted on occasion. The reason, I was told, is that during the last months of pregnancy the breast water that is start-ing to form inside a pregnant woman's breasts is vulnerable, as witchcraft may be directed against it. If another woman sees a pregnant woman walking around bare-breasted, the fullness of her breasts may arouse jealousy—espe-cially if the other woman has had trouble becoming pregnant, staying preg-nant, or keeping her babies alive. Such a woman may bewitch the breasts of a pregnant woman so that when the latter delivers her baby, her breast water will be spoiled. Thus we see that breast milk itself is considered susceptible to the depredations of witches.

Although the taste of breast milk is considered to be unchanged by diet, such is not the case for its nutritional content, which is seen as vulnerable to historically influenced social change. A conversation I had on this subject with Master of the Earth Kouassi Kokora made this clear:

> *Kouassi Kokora:* Some healthy mothers have good [breast]water. That helps the baby's skin stay healthier and [helps the baby] grow well. Some women's breast water is better [than others'].

Alma: In the old days, did mothers have good water in their breasts?

Kouassi Kokora: Yes, there were some medicines for that.

Alma: How do you explain the richness of breast water in the old days?

Kouassi Kokora: People of the old generation were totally different from those of today. In the old days, children were bathed with true medicines, real medicines *(la ti pɔ)*. People ate a lot of meals; that provided a lot of strength.

In this comment, we see yet another view of breast milk emerging. The richness of breast milk, the degree of nourishment it provides to babies, is considered subject to both cultural manipulation and historical change. Indigenous medicines used to be provided to nursing mothers to strengthen their breast milk and produce healthy children, but they no longer are. Here, my elderly informant was evincing a stereotypical historical nostalgia for the "old days" *(gbɔ gbɔ na)* that may have grounding in empirical fact (see chapter 11 for general discussion of historical change). In any case, once again, Beng women inscribe their bodies with historically and culturally inscribed knowledge. The substance that flows from their breasts is as much a cultural conception as an empirical liquid.

The Nursing Experience

The decision of when to breast-feed is likewise more determined by cultural factors than may be immediately apparent. In this section, I explore the perspectives of Beng women who must decide when to nurse their babies and how to judge their children's hunger.

Teaching First-Time Mothers How to Nurse

Before living in West Africa, I had unreflectively perceived breast-feeding as an intensely personal experience uniting just two people—mother and baby. In the United States, the few breast-feeding women I knew took great pains to find a quiet and private space to nurse their babies. Such spaces are frequently unavailable in the public world of restaurants, stores, malls, office buildings, post offices, and so forth.[19] After sizing up this situation, many new mothers living in the United States decide not to breast-feed, concerned that it will be too challenging to find private spaces when they are out and about with their babies.[20]

My own mother recounted just such a story. While pregnant with me in 1954, my mother told her obstetrician that she was inclined to breast-feed me. Her doctor talked her out of the plan by pointing out that it would be too difficult to find modest places to breast-feed when she took me on outings, and he didn't want to encourage her to stay home with me all the time. Although few biomedical doctors would likely counsel their patients in this way now, the basic warning offered by my mother's doctor long ago remains, unfortunately, all too relevant. In the United States today, breast-feeding mothers still lament their difficulty in finding suitable places to nurse their babies or pump breast milk, whether out and about with their children or at work. A small number of malls, stores, and offices are beginning to provide discreet breast-feeding or pumping stations, but the change is frustratingly slow and spotty for women who choose to breast-feed.[21] Moreover, the move to install discreet spaces for breast-feeding in public is itself an eminently cultural campaign founded in values that classify the breast as a fundamentally sexual rather than nutritional body part, and breast-feeding as a fundamentally solitary and private, not social and public activity (Dettwyler 1995a:188–89, 193–95).

In Beng villages (as throughout much of West Africa), things are quite different. Consider the following scene.

Amenan and I are visiting with her "granddaughter" M'ama Afwe, a young woman of sixteen or seventeen who gave birth to her first child two days ago.[22] Both mother and baby are indoors, recovering from the delivery and waiting for the newborn's umbilical cord to fall off before the baby can be taken outside. Stretched out on her bed with the baby asleep next to her, M'ama Afwe seems comfortable and content. But five minutes after I arrive, her new daughter starts to fuss, then defecates, then cries. After her own mother cleans up the mess, Afwe leans over her tiny child and tries to breast-feed. Afwe's breasts are huge, clearly ready for the baby. But in this leaning-over position, her nipples do not reach the tiny mouth, and there's nothing for the baby to latch onto. The infant becomes frustrated.[23]

Amenan observes the scene and immediately offers Afwe some advice: Why not try lying down next to the baby? Perhaps Afwe's nipple will fit into the little mouth that way, Amenan points out. Afwe immediately tries out the new position. It works: the baby nurses eagerly for ten minutes. Afwe appears grateful for her grandmother's advice.

However, immediately after nursing and being put down, the baby cries. Amenan instructs Afwe to pick up the girl and hold her. But Afwe is still tired from the delivery and the last two sleepless nights. Sensing her granddaughter's fatigue, Amenan takes the baby herself and holds her in her lap. The little one nods off to sleep this way while her mother lies resting.

Twenty-five minutes later, the baby awakes crying. By now, Afwe's mother has re-entered the room, and she instructs her daughter to nurse the baby. Afwe picks the little one up to do so, but then the baby stops crying, and Afwe starts to put her down on the floor again. Her mother disapproves. "Try nursing again," she instructs her daughter, "the baby isn't full yet." Afwe tries, and the baby sucks halfheartedly for a few minutes but then turns away. Afwe's mother is satisfied that the baby is content for now.

Every step of the way, Afwe was directed by someone. In this particular scene, it was her own mother and a grandmother who served as teachers. At any given point in the day, many others might play this role.

Indeed, during the first few weeks, a newly delivered woman—especially a first-time mother such as Afwe—has a constant stream of visitors, particularly women. Most have breast-fed many babies themselves, and they spontaneously share their nursing wisdom. Through them, a new mother is quickly socialized into accepting an almost continual round of breast-feeding suggestions dispensed by more experienced women. The need for a professional lactation consultant or a doula, as some middle-class mothers in the United States now seek, is obviated.

I was drawn into this ethos as I found myself one day offering nursing advice about repositioning her nipple to our neighbor Moya, who had delivered two days previously and whose newborn had not yet latched on to her breast to nurse. Accustomed as she was to receiving unsolicited advice from any number of people, Moya tried out my suggestion as trustingly as she did anyone else's. It was far more of a novelty to me to offer the advice than it was to Moya to accept it.

When to Nurse

Deciding when to breast-feed a baby may seem like an easy decision, but it is strongly determined by an array of cultural values and assumptions. Even within a single society, the question may provoke controversy. Over the course of the past century, there has been an ongoing debate within the United States on this question. Essentially two models are available to nursing mothers in the United States: "feeding on a schedule" and "feeding on demand." Although "feeding on a schedule" is, at least discursively, far more dominant, the alternate model of "feeding on demand" exists as a countermodel that is frequently both submerged and somewhat subversive.[24] In hospitals, maternity ward nurses and pediatricians routinely instruct new mothers to maintain the feeding schedules that the hospital has introduced once the mother and baby return home. Typically, that follows the official advice dispensed by the American Academy of Pediatrics, which is to breast-feed newborns every two to three hours (e.g., American Academy of Pediatrics 1997). Given that 98 percent of babies born in the United States are delivered in hospitals (Davis-Floyd and Sargent 1997:11), the vast majority of new mothers are likely to be instructed in the widely promoted ideal of "nursing (or bottle-feeding) on a schedule."

As a first-time mother I received more than my share of such advice myself. When our new son showed distressing signs of colic, the first—and often only—suggestion that pediatric nurses could offer me was to "put him on a schedule": the interval between "feedings" should be at least two hours, they specified, and preferably three. When I protested that my child sometimes seemed hungry after only an hour, they countered that "a regular feeding schedule is best for the baby." Not wishing to be cruel, the nurses sometimes suggested a pacifier, his own thumb or even water to mollify my son "between feedings." Through such advice, which pediatric nurses around the country offer regularly, sometimes because it is solicited and sometimes even though it is not, mothers in the United States and other Western nations learn to shape their infants' variable desires to the regular march of the clock.[25]

Those mothers who seek further advice from parenting books generally find the model of scheduled feeding reinforced. The latest edition of Dr. Spock's popular guide, widely regarded (perhaps inaccurately) as advocating "permissive" child-rearing, still urges parents to establish some sort of feeding schedule after the first few weeks, even if it is not as strict as the schedule that an earlier generation of Americans would have instituted (Spock and Parker 1998:158–65, 200–202). Establishing a predictable schedule should be the ultimate goal of all mothers, this discourse suggests, even if it takes a few weeks or months to reach. The rhetorical force of this discursive strategy is potent.

~

In Beng villages, a very different discursive strategy prevails. Here, nursing mothers are urged to breast-feed their babies frequently, and the younger the baby, the oftener the feeding. As soon as a newborn cries, any woman who happens to be visiting urges the new mother, especially a first-time mother, to breast-feed. The breast is nearly always the first resource for a crying baby as well as for a concerned mother. This is so much the case that many first-time mothers are baffled about what to do if a crying baby does not want to breast-feed. On one occasion I asked Afwe Akwe, a young mother of a two-week-old, what she liked and disliked so far about being a mother. Afwe answered without hesitating, "If she cries but she's not hungry, that makes me mad!" In those early days, all that Afwe had learned by way of comforting her new daughter was to breast-feed her.

If the baby nursed only a few minutes ago but is now crying, that is not considered a deterrent to nursing again. Once I asked Afwe Komenan, who had just given birth two days previously, how she knew her baby wasn't full after she breast-fed him. She answered unequivocally, "He cries when you take the breast out of his mouth." To a nursing Beng mother, crying after breast-feeding is almost always interpreted as an invitation by the baby to try more breast-feeding.

During one hour-long observation period with Afwe Akwe and her two-week-old, I counted that the newborn breast-fed ten times—an average of once every six minutes. So long as a given baby was awake, this nursing frequency was typical of other periods I spent with newborns. After their first month, most healthy infants tended to cry less frequently, and consequently their mothers tended to breast-feed them less frequently. Nevertheless, the "nurse on demand" principle remained relevant to older babies as well. In my sample of ninety-three nursing sessions observed for twenty-four babies aged between three and twenty-four months old, the average frequency of nursing was once every thirty-five minutes, with no significant differences between younger and older babies in this group.[26]

A corollary of this flexibility in breast-feeding times is a similar flexibility in breast-feeding spaces. So long as they are with their mothers, babies and toddlers breast-feed wherever they happen to be. For example, they may nurse while their mothers work either in the fields or in the village (figure 51), or while their mothers relax during a hairdressing session on a rest day (figure 52).

All of this contrasts significantly with the common pattern for middle-class Euro-American babies. In my own experience, pediatric nurses and pediatricians in the United States rarely interpret post-feeding crying as a statement of continuing hunger. Instead of more breast-feeding, biomedical personnel typically suggest burping, walking, or a nap in the crib. Dr. Spock validates this view by including a subheading for "crying doesn't always mean hunger" under the main heading of "Breast-Feeding" in his latest parenting guide (Spock and Parker 1998:889). Although a countercultural movement of "nursing on demand" is currently on the increase—partly associated with the "attachment parenting" trend now in vogue in certain social circles in the United States—the adherents of this breast-feeding style still constitute a very small and discursively almost invisible minority.

In Bengland, the principle that babies should nurse on demand extends to nighttime feeding. Unlike the many middle-class Euro-American women who hope that their children will sleep through the night as soon as possible after birth, Beng women neither expect this nor are they typically upset by nocturnal interruptions for nursing. Aya Kro described her nights with her newborn, then a little under a month old, in a matter-of-fact way:

Alma: Does she wake up at night?

Aya Kro: Yes.

Alma: Does she nurse?

Aya Kro: Yes, she does.

Alma: How often does she wake up during the night?

Aya Kro: Sometimes twice at night.

Alma: Does she go back to sleep after nursing?

Aya Kro: She sleeps again.

Alma: When the baby wakes up to nurse, does she wake you up also?

Aya Kro: I wake up too, then I go back to sleep.

Not only did she not complain, but Aya Kro was amused by my questions, which she seemed to find silly the way I might find silly a question such as "What should drivers do when they see a red light?" To Aya Kro, the answers to my queries were perfectly obvious, predictable, and unremarkable.

Experienced Beng mothers of older babies may remain half asleep as their babies quietly breast-feed while lying next to them without interrupting their own sleep in a serious way.[27] The subject came up in a conversation my friend Nakoyan and I had about her nine-month-old son:

Alma: Does he nurse at night?

51. *(below)* This toddler girl is old enough to breastfeed standing up while her mother works at crushing tobacco leaves into powder that she will sell in the market as snuff.

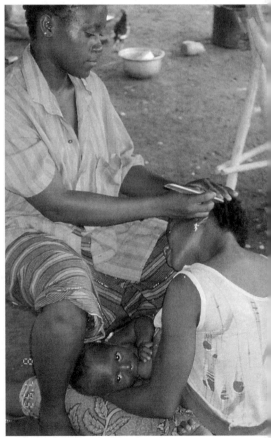

52. *(right)* Sassandra breastfeeds while his mother relaxes during a group hairdressing session on a rest day when everyone stays in the village.

Nakoyan: Yes, he nurses a lot at night.

Alma: How many times?

Nakoyan: I don't know the number. Sometimes, when I wake up, I see him nursing.

Alma: Because he can hold the breast now?

Nakoyan: Yes, while I sleep, he nurses.

Presumably Nakoyan knew at a subconscious level that her infant was nursing even as she more or less continued to sleep. Her vague knowledge of this nocturnal nourishment went hand in hand with a matter-of-fact attitude toward the topic.

However, as Beng babies grow into toddlers, their mothers may come to be mildly annoyed if their children continue to breast-feed actively through the night. One day Ajua Ba complained to me a bit laughingly about her fourteen-month-old daughter: "Amwe still doesn't sleep much at night—she does nurse all night, though! She sleeps a little, then nurses, then sleeps a little, then nurses—and it's like this all night long! [During the day], she doesn't eat much food, just rice. Mostly, she just nurses. She'll be very happy if she doesn't get a baby sister or brother any time soon, so she won't have to be weaned any time soon!" In some families, such a pattern of nighttime nursing can even last into middle childhood. My friend Amenan pointed out to me on several occasions—with, I thought, a changing mixture of amusement and disapproval—that her daughter Marie had loved breast-feeding so much that she'd had a hard time giving it up. During the day, Marie was ashamed to be seen nursing, but at night in bed next to her mother, she had breast-fed until she was six years old.

~

Although the model of breast-feeding a baby with every cry or whimper during the day or at night guides most Beng mothers' actions, there is one period when the model does not operate. In the early morning, as we saw in chapter 5, Beng babies may be awake for some time—even as long as two hours—before they breast-feed for the first time. Given how frequently babies otherwise nurse in Beng villages, what accounts for this delay?

Sometimes it is a question of women's labor. Between one and two months after the birth, most mothers begin to fetch water for their family's use. A mother may leave early in the morning when the baby is still asleep—in some cases I documented, before the first cock's crow, as early as 4:30 or 5:00 A.M.—but the baby may awaken soon after the mother is gone. When she returns, she does not breast-feed but rather embarks on the long bathing routine. Only when these procedures are over is the baby permitted to nurse.

A hungry baby may become quite impatient with the delay—a fact the mother certainly understands. When I asked Tahan one day why six-month-old Sassandra was whimpering through this long routine, she acknowledged, "He's looking for a breast to drink"—yet Tahan didn't speed up her routine to accommodate her young son's obvious hunger. Just as significantly, when Tahan did finally offer Sassandra her breast, the bath routine was not quite over. Medicinal eyeliner remained to be applied, to prevent Sassandra from developing any eye diseases. As he finally nursed eagerly, ravenous from the long morning of bath activities, Sassandra's eyes were propped open wide by Tahan, who carefully applied the paint around his eyelids. This ocular manipulation did not distract Sassandra from his own commitment to nursing.

What are the lessons of such an activity for Sassandra? At the most obvious level, he learns that having lines painted around his eyes is important. Perhaps he also learns that although breast-feeding is desperately important to him, it is not quite so critically important to his mother. And although he enjoys breast-feeding, it is not crucial that he do nothing else while he nurses. He can breast-feed while his mother is doing other things to his body—painting lines on his eyelids, repositioning him just right for the eyeliner—and he can shift his body accordingly to make sure that he still drinks breast water. Doing two things at once—or more precisely, doing one thing to his mother's body while his mother does something else to his body—is an acceptable compromise.

This morning routine with its breast-feeding delay that so frustrates many babies is an exception to an important rule. At virtually all other times, it is the baby who decides when to nurse, both in Beng ideology and, by and large, in daily practice as well. This strategy has medical advantages, but it also makes cultural sense. The practice echoes at a quotidian level the more general Beng conception that a baby is a complete person who has recently emerged from a previous life in *wrugbe*. At an ideological level, the practice is based on the local imperative to listen to and validate a baby's own desires.

When Babies Refuse to Breast-Feed
Just as it is the baby who largely decides when to nurse, the baby may also on occasion decide *not* to nurse. In Bengland, such a child is understood to be making a statement of volition. The worried mother of such an infant generally visits a diviner to discover what her young son or daughter is trying to communicate. This religious specialist informs the mother of the baby's intentions after listening to the *wrugbe* spirits that are said to remain in touch with the baby. The diviner then gives the mother instructions on how best to accommodate the baby's desires. Here is one example I recorded:

As a newborn, Baa's daughter went a few days without nursing. The family consulted a diviner, who pronounced that the baby was failing to nurse because no one was addressing her by her rightful name. She had been sent to this world by a particular spirit named Busu and thus wished to be called by that name herself. The family began calling her Busu, and she started nursing immediately.

That the notion of a baby deciding of her own volition not to breast-feed is an eminently cultural interpretation is made clear when we compare this with local interpretations elsewhere of babies who do not nurse. In the mountains of Tunisia, Khmir people say that breast milk conveys not only nutritional benefits to the baby, but spiritual blessings to the entire household. If a Khmir baby shows no interest in breast-feeding, women interpret this as a sign that the mother's milk has curdled and transmitted sickness to the baby (Creyghton 1992:45). Here, an infant is envisaged as a passive recipient of either beneficial or dangerous milk; either way, we are far from the Beng model with its insistence that it is the baby who decides whether or not to breast-feed, depending on desires he or she has retained from *wrugbe*.

Having explored the timing of breast-feeding, let us now explore the personnel. Once again the seemingly natural pair of nursing-mother-and-child is belied, for in the Beng case, the participants are not as predictable as one might assume.

Wet Nursing

In Europe, the history of wet nursing is associated with class difference replicating itself through gendered practices. Until early in the twentieth century, mothers of some means in many European countries employed poor women to breast-feed their infants. Wealthy families imported wet nurses from the countryside to the city, and lower-middle-class and working-class families sent their babies to live with wet nurses in the countryside.[28] In turn, the wet nurses sought other poor women from their villages to breast-feed their own infants. Ironically, this circulation of milk from rural peasant to urban elite allowed the privileges of class to continue even as the flow of body fluid across class lines contained the potential to symbolically challenge that hierarchy.[29]

In Beng villages, wet nursing tells a dramatically different story. Far from reproducing class difference, wet nursing creates a sense of shared identity among Beng women from different groups. It even erases age and status difference, as old women also comfort babies by offering their now empty breasts. The practice also inscribes, via the body, an important lesson in Beng infants: that any woman is potentially a source of breast water. For unlike the

European case, in which a single wet nurse was assigned to a single infant, sometimes via an employment bureau (Sussman 1982), in Beng villages the practice of wet nursing is largely a casual one, with spontaneous substitution of one woman's breast for another's, as the occasion arises.[30] For the baby, a commensurate lesson in sociability and its value to the developing person must be implanted. Let us explore several circumstances that might encourage someone other than a baby's biological mother to breast-feed a child.

First Days

During the first few days after birth, the new mother's breasts are usually filled with colostrum, not breast milk. As is the case in other parts of the world, Beng women do not consider this substance nourishing.[31] During this period, some Beng mothers give their newborns only water to drink; others seek another nursing mother who will breast-feed the new child until their own breast milk comes in. The wet nurse may well be the new mother's own mother, if she herself has a nursing baby at home.[32] If her own mother is unable to serve as a wet nurse, a woman may find another nursing mother— probably a close relative—to breast-feed her newborn during the first day or two after birth.

Breast-feeding a newborn around the clock once her milk comes in can leave a mother exhausted. A nursing mother who lives nearby or is visiting may feel sympathy for the new mother and her child if the newborn cries and the mother is sleeping or worn out, and she may casually nurse the newborn herself. Let us observe this scene with M'ama Afwe, the first-time mother of a two-day-old girl whom we encountered earlier:

> M'ama Afwe's tiny daughter has been sleeping, nursing, and fussing, generally at five-minute intervals, for the past hour and a half. At the moment, the baby is sleeping in her paternal grandmother's arms. A woman I don't recognize comes into the room and, after greeting and congratulating Afwe, takes the baby out of the grandmother's arms and looks at her. Satisfied at what she has seen, she hands the infant back to her grandmother.
>
> But the baby is unhappy at having been awakened and soon starts to cry bitterly. Her grandmother speaks softly to her, asking *"Je a dĩɛ—e loa?"*—Sorry, what's the matter? The newborn has no reply beyond further crying, and the grandmother offers her a breast. As a nursing mother of a toddler herself, this young grandmother still has milk in her breasts, and the little one nurses happily for five minutes before settling back into a comfortable sleep in her grandmother's arms.

Such scenes are common in the first days, and sometimes weeks, of a baby's life in this world.

Baby-Sitting

Baby-sitters may resort to wet nursing as a temporary measure when they are caring for a baby whose mother is not around. In this case, the momentary wet nurse is another nursing mother who may or may not be related to the baby's own mother.

A variation on this theme might be called "dry nursing."[33] Suppose a mother drops her baby off with a friend, neighbor, or relative and leaves for some time (perhaps to fetch water or chop wood). In a little while, the baby cries. Perhaps the baby is hungry, or perhaps he is missing his mother or the previous life in *wrugbe*—no one really knows. The baby-sitter offers water, but the infant refuses to drink it or fails to be satisfied by it. Any adult woman can offer to "breast-feed" the infant—even if she has no breast milk (figure 53). In effect, such a woman serves as a human pacifier.

Consider this scene:

53. Kouadio "dry nurses" for comfort from the empty breasts of his Aunt Amenan (his father's father's sister's daughter), who is baby-sitting for a short while.

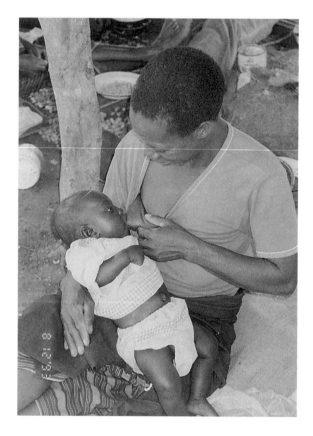

2:30 P.M.—Tahan decides to fetch water from the pump. On her return, she will be carrying water on her head, and it would be hard to carry six-month-old Sassandra without spilling the water; plus, the two loads together would be quite heavy. She decides to leave Sassandra with her mother, Amenan (who bore her last child eight years ago).

As soon as Tahan leaves the compound, Amenan pretends to breast-feed Sassandra. He is happy to suck but does not appear ravenous. Thinking Sassandra is in a mood to play, Amenan asks him, "*ŋo mí sí pɔ?*"—What's your name? Sassandra doesn't seem terribly stimulated by the question, and Amenan thinks he might be tired. He's only slept for a few minutes so far today, and he might be ready for a nap. Amenan says gently to her grandson, "*yilɛ mi delo, nyo mi nyɛ bedà*"—You're sleepy. Nurse, and then go to sleep.

3:05 P.M.—Still sucking on his grandmother's empty breast, Sassandra falls asleep.

3:25 P.M.—Sassandra awakes, and Amenan sits him up in her lap. She calls over to her ten-year-old daughter, Ajua, and playfully urges her to squeeze her mother's nipple—maybe some milk will come out for the baby. Ajua giggles with excitement at the idea of this game. She comes over and naughtily instructs her young nephew to bite his grandmother's nipple. Smiling, Amenan counters by cautioning Sassandra *not* to bite her, but Ajua mischievously stuffs her mother's nipple into the baby's mouth and teasingly encourages him to bite it. Afraid the little one—who is obviously pleased to be the center of so much attention—may oblige, Amenan removes her breast and instructs her daughter to carry Sassandra off to his mother at the water pump so that he can truly breast-feed.

But Ajua has caught sight of a picture book I have left lying around. She spots a photo of a baby bottle and shows it to Sassandra, telling him, "*a mí!*"—Drink it!

I find this very funny, but Sassandra doesn't laugh. Never having seen a baby bottle, he clearly doesn't understand the joke.[34] Besides, he's still sleepy. He's managing to keep himself awake, but not to be very lively.

4:25 P.M.—Sassandra falls asleep in his grandmother's arms. After a few false starts he nods off again, and even when another of his aunts transfers him to a mat on the ground, he stays asleep for some time.

In this situation, a grandmother's breasts have been used both as a serious pacifier and as a playful joke. Sassandra is a baby who does not nod off easily, and his grandmother has judged that the only way he will fall asleep—which, she thinks, he wants to do—is while breast-feeding. Since his mother is not around, his grandmother's own breast should do. Still, Amenan herself realizes the silliness of the gesture, and she is not offended when her own daughter turns the quasi-charade into a full-fledged prank.

In a communal baby-sitting setting, even a child may urge a nonnursing woman to pretend-breast-feed an unhappy young charge. Let us consider another episode, once again involving Amenan and two of her daughters:

> One afternoon a neighbor drops off her baby Eric to be cared for by the compound at large, and the baby gets passed around casually from person to person. For a few minutes Philip plays with Eric under the coffee trees, then Amenan's eight-year-year old daughter Lucy comes and carries Eric over to her older sister, thirteen-year-old Esi, who is sitting under the compound's granary. Five minutes later, Eric starts to fuss a bit. Esi brings Eric over to her own mother, Amenan, and Esi, now a bossy teenager, firmly instructs her mother, *"kà gba nyó!"*—Give him your breast! Amenan indulgently follows her daughter's advice and offers Eric a dry breast. Eric sucks contentedly, seemingly unaware of, or at least unperturbed by, the lack of milk.

These examples all speak to a rather casual attitude toward both wet-nursing and what I have termed dry nursing. This casualness is reflected in linguistic usage. It is significant that there are no words in Beng for either wet nursing or dry nursing. Both are simply called by the same word for breast-feeding: *nyo mialɛ* (lit., "to drink the breast"). I suggest that this linguistic inattention signals a broader-based inattention: the difference between the breast-feeding biological mother and another woman who might offer a breast—with or without milk—is not culturally valorized as significant.

Beng breast-feeding practices—like breast-feeding practices elsewhere—produce a particular lactational signature. In the Beng case, this signature is a markedly social one (see Kitzinger 1995:390). That is, although there is no doubt that most Beng newborns, like nursing newborns elsewhere, have an especially close relationship with their mothers, the intensity of that relationship—its monogamous nature, as it were—may be significantly mitigated beyond what it might be in other circumstances, in part due to the common practice of spontaneous wet and dry nursing. In the experience of many Beng infants, any woman's breast, even one that has no milk in it, is potentially a site for pleasurable sucking (if not nourishment). This must lead many babies to understand that a relatively large pool of people is available to satisfy two of life's earliest and strongest desires—the desire to satisfy hunger (by ingesting breast milk) and the desire to relieve stress and be comforted (by sucking).[35] Ironically, for some Beng babies, learning the value of sociability begins, literally, at the breast.

Introducing Solid Foods

When to Introduce Solid Foods

Biomedical researchers and pediatricians now assert that most breast-feeding babies—at least those whose mothers are not seriously malnourished—do not need any solid foods for adequate growth and development for the first six months of their lives.[36] In Beng villages mothers do take some note of their babies' ages before introducing solid foods, but this is not the most important factor in deciding when to offer new forms of nourishment. As Beng women explained it to me, the most important factor that helps a mother decide when to introduce solid foods into a baby's diet has nothing to do with nutritional or medical considerations. Instead, a sociolinguistic factor rules this important decision: a mother should only introduce solid foods to her baby "when the baby knows its name" *(o a tɔ dò)*. Why is this relevant to a decision that would appear to be more reasonably made by reference to biological or health-related considerations?

Once again, I suggest that the explanation lies in the afterlife. With an ideology that the child emerges only gradually from that place to inhabit living human space with clear awareness, eating solid foods that approximate what is eaten by adults and older children who are considered fully human constitutes a sign that the baby has reached another stage in leaving *wrugbe* behind and is becoming more human. Beng mothers judge that a baby is ready to take this step only when the little one demonstrates in another arena that she or he has taken another step in entering the human world by responding to other people's ideas of her or his humanity.

In the Beng world, a name not only is a marker of individual identity, it also tethers a child to a social universe. For example, if the child is given a "day name" associated with the name of the day on which the child was born, the little one is moored to a culturally constructed calendar that provides meaning to the movement of time. More traditional names can anchor a child to a human ancestor or to a particular spirit (see chapter 4). Either way, the connection to a world that is inherently social is made clear. When a baby recognizes that he or she is linked to such a name, this is taken as a clear sign t the child has begun to enter a meaningful space of human communica-ᴜn. That move then authorizes a parallel move in another arena: the world of food, which is also fully shaped by Beng canons of sociability.[37]

In Beng practice it is babies who, by clearly responding to the calling of their names, announce to their mothers that they are ready to eat solid food. By waiting for babies to communicate this readiness, Beng mothers attribute agency to their young children in the quotidian feeding practices that they jointly construct. In effect, they grant their infants the ability to negotiate their own subjectivity. Once again, the Beng conception of the afterlife, which creates a model of babies who are defined by intelligence and desire, asserts itself in daily praxis.

Which Foods to Introduce

Infant subjectivity and desire are equally validated in which foods are introduced and how. The commonest attitude is quite different from what we saw in *kami*. Although a mother may go so far as to force water down her very young infant's throat, I have never seen this done with solid foods. Instead, babies are allowed free range to encounter foods and manipulate them actively. Let us consider this scene:

> Six-month-old Sassandra is sitting up nicely on a mat. His eight-year-old brother, Meda, comes over and gives him a tiny piece of overripe pineapple. Sassandra is very curious about this new object. He inspects it, squeezes it, drops it on the mat, then picks it up. Again he inspects it, drops it on the ground, picks it up. Finally, he decides to taste it. It doesn't taste very good! He spits it out. But it is still interesting. Why not pick it up again? There comes another cycle of inspecting, dropping, picking up. . . . Fifteen minutes later, an aunt comes by and offers Sassandra a section of an orange. And so begins a new round of inspecting, dropping, picking up.

Absent in this scene is the common belief of many middle-class Euro-American parents (no doubt inherited, whether or not the parents are aware of it, from the Puritans) that "food should not be played with." Instead, the possibility of alternately eating and playing with food, or of alternately classifying something as food and as a plaything, is tolerated quite easily by Beng adults. Nor do Beng adults insist that food must be kept clean or that dirty food must be either washed off before being eaten or thrown away. Instead, babies are allowed to sit on the ground with food, and when they inevitably drop it in the dirt, no one comes to snatch it away from them in alarm. Medically, this practice is risky—parasites and bacteria may live in the dirt and can attack the baby's gastrointestinal system, with potentially damaging, even life-threatening consequences.

At the same time, the psychological attitude toward food that this practice fosters may be more beneficial than is the attitude conveyed by common Euro-American food practices. Fear of food, neurosis over food, obsession with food—the array of food disorders associated with so many middle-class Euro-American teenagers and adults, from unnecessary dieting to anorexia to overeating—are all conspicuously absent among the Beng. Although these Western food-related syndromes are certainly overdetermined—shaped by a complex mix of gender ideologies, class structures and other factors[38]—perhaps Beng adults' casual attitude toward food from babyhood on is one reason for the absence of such neurotic food-related syndromes among the Beng.

The nonchalant approach to food that Beng adults teach babies carries over into another arena. Let us return to the narrative of Sassandra encountering new treats. Notice who gave the two bits of food to him: in one case it was his older brother, in the second case it was a distantly related aunt. Both happened to be in the courtyard at the time, along with Sassandra's mother and several other people. This was a typical scene. On an ordinary day or evening at any given time, when there is no special ritual or festivity going on, a courtyard may have up to ten or fifteen people in it who come and go as they wish. Especially in the morning and late afternoon or evening, before and after a day in the fields, there is much traffic between compounds, much back-and-forth. Some visitors arrive with food. If children are around— and when aren't there children around in a Beng compound?—they may be offered a sample of whatever the visitor has in hand.

In my observations, the mother is never asked for permission to offer such food to her child. In this way, from a very young age a baby learns not only that she can be flexible about moving items in and out of the food category, but also that foods themselves pass hands easily from one person to another, and that in most circumstances she should accept food from anyone who offers it to her. A little later, when she is beginning to walk, a toddler learns to offer any food she has to others around her. Food is for eating, yes, but it is also for sharing. When any nearby adult or older child reaches out to request a bite of whatever a little one is eating, the child is expected to hand over a portion. If the toddler doesn't agree to share a tidbit, the child is immediately criticized—only half-teasingly—as "selfish" *(cēli)*.

This attitude continues into adulthood and extends beyond the sharing of food to the sharing of germs. Once I tried to politely decline when my friend Yacouba offered me some food from his hand—he had a cough that I was concerned not to catch. Yacouba was insulted at my refusal of his offering. I tried to explain as delicately as I could without hurting his feelings that I was worried about contagion. Yacouba laughed off my worry: "We're not concerned about that, Amwe. Don't you know that sickness belongs to everyone? It doesn't just belong to one person." It was a lesson that startled me because it made me realize that the notion that sickness is best suffered by the individual and that anyone who attempts to spread it to another is selfish at best, malicious at worst, is a value into which I'd been socialized. By contrast, in Bengland sickness is seen as existing on the same conceptual plane as food—both are meant to be shared. Food, then, is not only something to satisfy one's appetite and palette, it is also something to be regularly given to and given by others. Babies are taught this lesson early.

Weaning from the Breast

In the contemporary United States, women who breast-feed tend to switch to bottles quite early compared with many breast-feeding women elsewhere. There are many reasons for North American mothers' decision to wean their babies from the breast relatively early. Urging from interested relatives or friends; the notion that the only advantage of breast-feeding is nutritional and that this advantage dissolves by twelve months at the latest; a husband's jealousy over his wife's involvement in their new baby's nurture (Dettwyler 1995:189–91); the necessity of returning to work without easy access to the baby every few hours, coupled with lack of knowledge about pumping or access to an effective and affordable breast pump for expressing milk; the baby's development of teeth, with the troubling prospect of the baby biting the mother's nipples; the growing baby's own developing restlessness during breast-feeding; and the anticipated shame of an older nursing child who is sitting or even standing to breast-feed rather than stereotypically lying in the arms—any and all of these may deepen the conviction in the middle-class Euro-American mother that after a few short months it is no longer a good idea to nurse.

In Beng villages, none of these considerations is relevant to a mother deciding when to wean her child from the breast. Here, an entirely different set of factors comes into play.

Walking

Only after a baby starts to walk should a Beng mother think about weaning. Of course babies are quite variable in when they begin to walk. In the tropics, where infants and young children are vulnerable to a host of pathogens of both medical and political-economic origin, recurrent diseases, when they do not prove fatal, can cause developmental delays. As a result, many children wean later than they might in a more benign environment. Let us consider the story of one boy, told to me by his mother, Ndri:

> Kouakou was able to sit up on his own at slightly over five months. He crawled at a little over eight months. But he was a late walker. He wasn't even walking at two years. He started speaking well before he could walk. During his second year, he was sick a lot. He would develop a high fever that would last half a day, disappear, and return the next day for another half-day. This would last for five days, and on the sixth day he'd be fine. This pattern happened many times during his second year.
>
> Kouakou finally started walking at about twenty-seven months, and the fevers disappeared. That's when I weaned him.

As Ndri's story implies, a mother may decide to wean a baby simply by waiting until the child is a competent walker, whenever that occurs. Generally that is somewhere in the second year—usually several months earlier than with Kouakou. But this is not the sole consideration. Another factor concerns the social constitution of the family.

Pregnancy

When a mother discovers that she is pregnant with another baby, if she has a toddler who is still nursing, she often tries to wean the child quickly. Some women observed to me that once a nursing mother becomes pregnant, her breast milk changes in both color and taste. My friend Amenan claimed that the breast milk turns red and the breast becomes hot—both signs of infection.[39] Amenan further asserted that a nursing toddler can detect these changes and may opt to wean herself. Amenan recalled the experience of her own daughter Ajua, who was two years old when Amenan became pregnant again.

> *Amenan:* When I was pregnant with Lucy, when it [the pregnancy] started, Ajua decided to leave the breast. One day I gave it to her, and she said it didn't taste good. Since that day she refused to take the breast.
>
> *Alma:* When a pregnant woman doesn't wean her child, do people criticize the child or the mother?
>
> *Amenan:* The mother.
>
> *Alma:* What do they say?
>
> *Amenan:* To stop breast-feeding him, that the milk isn't good any more. It can give diarrhea.[40]

At the very least, if a toddler insists on nursing through the mother's new pregnancy, a Beng mother must ensure that the older child is weaned when the new baby is born. Except in the case of twins, it is considered unacceptable for a mother to nurse two of her own children simultaneously. I asked Amenan about this:

> *Alma:* Is it possible to breast-feed both children after the mother gives birth?
>
> *Amenan:* Never!
>
> *Alma:* Why not?
>
> *Amenan:* I haven't heard of it, they never do it.
>
> *Alma:* Is it taboo?
>
> *Amenan:* It's not taboo, but it's not good.
>
> *Alma:* It's not good for whom?
>
> *Amenan:* For the children. . . . I've never seen this before.
>
> *Alma:* Ah-heh. Do people say there's not enough milk for both children, or that it [the breast milk] is not good?
>
> *Amenan:* It's not that—it's shameful.
>
> *Alma:* Shameful to whom?
>
> *Amenan:* The mother.

Here, culturally mediated notions of shame and propriety vis-à-vis the mother herself prove paramount.

The mention of shame alerts us to another relevant factor: the act of sex that produces children.

Parents' Sexuality

If a woman begins to wean a child before the little one is walking and then resumes her sex life with her husband and becomes pregnant, Beng women say that the result could be catastrophic. Unless she obtains proper medicines, it is thought, the older child will never learn to walk and will eventually die.

In other words, Beng couples should not resume their sex life for a relatively long time after the birth of each baby. Parents explained this postpartum taboo in two different ways. Some said that couples may not resume having sex until their baby starts to walk; others said that they must wait until the baby is weaned from the breast. At first I was confused by this dual set of explanations, until I realized that the two events—the baby's development as a competent walker and the decision to wean a baby from the breast—are intimately interrelated. In effect, a woman should never wean her baby until the child can walk well; and, at least in theory, she does not resume having sex with her husband until then as well. Because weaning and walking should ideally coincide, both are invoked to explain the duration of the postpartum taboo on sex.

However, I believe it is breast-feeding rather than walking that is the determinative factor. My clue came when I posed a hypothetical question about bottle-feeding. If a rather modern Beng woman of my imagining decided to bottle-feed her baby, I was told, she could resume having sex with her husband whenever she wanted to, without harmful consequences to the baby. In other words, there is something in the fact that a woman breast-feeds her not-yet-walking baby that makes sex dangerous to the child. What could that be? I suggest that the reason has to do with Beng conceptions of sexuality and of infants' vulnerability. We have already seen that sex is believed to produce a symbolically potent form of "dirt" *(gbre),* which is perceived as dangerous to babies (chapter 5). Now we can specify that this vulnerability lasts as long as a baby is breast-feeding. Although no Beng person ever put it quite this way to me, semen and breast milk are apparently considered mutually incompatible.[41] This model echoes the danger vaginal fluids pose to infants, as evidenced by the requirement that the mother of a nursing baby wash the underwear *(cache-sexe)* that she wears twice a day; otherwise her breast-feeding child will catch the disease dirt *(gbre).*

Does this ideology concerning the incompatibility of sex and breast-feeding shape daily praxis in an observable way? Of course, definitive confirmation that particular couples are or are not observing the postpartum sex taboo would be hard to come by. But to the extent that indirect evidence is relevant, most Beng couples do appear to take the postpartum sex taboo quite seriously. From the male perspective, the taboo against sex with a breast-feeding wife is one frequently cited reason for the existence of polygyny. As long as both wives do not become pregnant simultaneously, the polygynous husband is guaranteed a legitimate way to remain sexually active during the years that one wife is breast-feeding. By contrast, a man whose two wives end up on a parallel fertility schedule—so that both are breast-feeding babies for a year or more—is the object of much sympathy from other men.

Monogamously married men may look for eligible women—young un-married women, divorcées, or widows—with whom to have sexual affairs dur-ing the long period ruled by the postpartum sex taboo. In the absence of such sex partners, the monogamous husband of a breast-feeding woman may even take up with a prostitute if the opportunity arises.[42] Villagers—both men and women—consider that a man has the right to visit a prostitute in this circumstance, although they acknowledge that he ought to be discreet about it and not flaunt the encounter in his wife's face. One bitter conjugal dispute I witnessed resulted from just such a situation:

> As the father of a nursing son of about nine months, Zi was feeling desperate for sex. When a visiting prostitute arrived in his village, he made his interest known to her. They negotiated a price and went off for their assignation. But once they had arrived at the agreed-on site, the prostitute recanted the agreement and demanded a higher payment. Zi had no more cash to offer, and a rowdy dispute ensued.
>
> The next morning, a neighbor in this small village leaked news of the night's events to Zi's wife, M'Afwe. A self-assured woman with impressive speaking skills, M'Afwe proceeded to chastise her husband in public. To my surprise, most onlookers sided with Zi, informing M'Afwe that her husband had the right to visit the prostitute since M'Afwe was nursing a baby and couldn't have sex with him. At the same time, neighbors faulted Zi for having made a spectacle of himself with the prostitute over the terms of the arrangement; for this reason, most agreed, "his name had been ruined."
>
> Following the incident, although nearly everyone had thought that M'Afwe had been in the wrong, Zi followed Beng protocol, which dictates that a husband always apologize to his wife after a marital dispute, and dispatched a mediator (in this case, a female cross-cousin of M'Afwe's) to apologize ritually to M'Afwe for him. On behalf of Zi, she declared: *mɔɛ à nínιɛ, ka je a dīɛ* (Mine was not sweet; please forgive me). The incident was considered closed.

If, unlike Zi, a man lacks either the opportunity or the desire to have a semi-licit affair while his wife breast-feeds their baby, he may grow impatient.

As the English saying might be amended to read, taboos are made to be violated. Although all Beng adults are well aware that it is taboo *(sō pɔ)* for a woman to engage in sex while she is breast-feeding, not all couples are equally vigilant in respecting the taboo. Here is a conversation I had with Asue about her adult daughter, N'Au, a woman in her twenties with a young son and daughter, Albert and Renée:

> *Asue:* It hasn't been too long since Albert has stopped nursing. Renée
>   weaned very early, [at] barely a year.
> *Alma:* What did the old women say when Renée stopped nursing early?
> *Asue:* They said she stopped nursing her early. They also thought she
>   did that because of sex.

Villagers assumed that N'Au was eager to resume her sex life with her husband and that she had weaned her daughter early to do so.

Neighbors and relatives may blame such early weaning on the mother's own desire for sex even if they recognize that her husband seduced or pressured her. Let us consider this story, recounted to me by a village gossip:

> Mo'kissi was always in a hurry to wean her babies. She always stopped nursing her babies just as soon as they started walking. Once she was nursing two babies at once—her own son and her [newly orphaned] nephew, Paul, who was six months younger. As soon as her own son started walking, she weaned him. Just as soon as Paul started walking, she weaned him too. She became pregnant right away. She was beaten a lot by male relatives for this. She refused to continue nursing Paul because she wanted to sleep with her husband, and she knew she couldn't if she was still nursing Paul! Maybe her husband always pestered her?

Here, my female informant acknowledged the responsibility of the husband in the violation of the taboo, but she downplayed it in recounting the situation. Ultimately, most women place the wife in the decision-making position concerning a couple's postpartum sex life.[43]

Late Weaning

Although a cultural script dictates when women should wean their children from the breast, it is far from slavishly followed. As Mo'kissi's story shows, some mothers wean their children earlier than they should according to local expectations. Others wean their infants much later than is common. Attitudes toward late weaning vary, but unless the child is chronically ill, most women nowadays disapprove of weaning a child later than two or two and a half years. Sometimes adults and older children will gently tease a three- or four-year-old who is still nursing—or they will mildly chastise the child's mother. Mélanie had a three-year-old son who was still nursing. I asked

Amenan about the boy. "He obviously likes to nurse!" she said, laughing—with a bit of disapproval hiding in her laugh, I thought. I began noticing other women poking fun of Mélanie for still nursing her son. But in each case, Mélanie seemed indifferent to their teasing. Beyond such gentle teasing, no more forceful effort is made to convince an older child to stop nursing or to persuade a mother to wean her nursing child. As we saw, Amenan nursed her last child at night as they slept side by side until the girl was six years old. Recounting the story to me, Amenan had laughed about it.

Determined by Gender

Once I asked a male elder if people treat baby boys and baby girls differently. To my surprise, the only thing that came to his mind concerned weaning. "Boys nurse more than girls do," Aba Kouassi stated. I asked him why that would be. He explained readily, "It's because a girl *knows* that if she nurses a lot, *her* children will nurse a lot too—to pay her back! Boys don't know this . . . so they just keep on nursing!" Interestingly, I never heard a woman offer this explanation. Ironically, the perception that breast-feeding is difficult work that demands much effort on the part of a woman may be a male viewpoint not shared by most Beng women. Although I did not observe that little boys generally breast-feed for a longer period than do little girls, Aba Kouassi's statement is intriguing insofar as it offers his understanding that there is solidarity among women and girls based on their shared knowledge of their difficult work burden.

However, Aba Kouassi immediately modified his statement. Gender is actually less definitive than birth order in determining the age of weaning, he explained.

Determined by Birth Order

Birth order may decisively affect when a given child is weaned. As we have seen, when a breast-feeding mother of a toddler knows she is pregnant, to avert disaster she endeavors to wean her child quickly. However, at a certain point in her life, a woman will be sure that the baby she bore most recently is her last, probably because she never resumed her menstrual cycle after the delivery. In this case, she is likely to allow the child to continue nursing long beyond the period she nursed her earlier children.[44] Of course, the most obvious reason has to do with the factor discussed earlier—if a toddler is not weaned while the mother is pregnant with her next child, once the new baby is born, the older child must immediately cease breast-feeding. By contrast, if there is no new baby to displace the nursing toddler, the child may continue to breast-feed—in theory, indefinitely. Recall the case of Marie, whose mother, Amenan, continued to nurse her at night for six years. The only way this could happen was that Marie was a last child—and the little girl knew it.

Although cultural ideologies sometimes have great staying power, they do not always persist against all odds. In Bengland, nursing patterns have purportedly changed dramatically in a relatively short time, at least in cultural memory. Master of the Earth Kouassi Kokora asserted to me, "Children of long ago used to breast-feed longer than today's children. Nowadays, young mothers have less time for their kids." He added, "That's why children [of long ago] had more energy and were blessed more than today's children are."

Amenan soon joined in this provocative conversation with her uncle. According to her, in earlier times a child used to be old enough to "grab a chair for her mother" before being weaned—that is, six or even seven years old.[45] Because the postpartum sex taboo requires that women remain celibate while breast-feeding, women's pregnancies would have been spaced apart far more than they are now. Ironically, the revolution in reliable birth control that has produced far greater intervals between children elsewhere has had no such effect in Bengland. Instead, there are now apparently shorter intervals between siblings due to earlier weaning and a correspondingly shorter period for the postpartum sex taboo.[46] Amenan added that the more widely spaced births were advantageous because young children have difficulty walking to the fields and often need to be carried, and it's difficult or impossible for a mother to carry two young children to the fields. Nevertheless, Amenan qualified her concern by noting that nowadays the shorter birth interval isn't so much of a problem because most men own bicycles and can take a young child, especially a son, to the fields on the handlebars, leaving the mother to carry the baby. Thus the apparently shorter birth interval has been accommodated to some extent by new technology.

Nevertheless, Amenan's uncle waxed nostalgic for the good old days when, he claimed, children nursed for many years. Recall that in his view, the breast milk of earlier times was richer and more nutritious. In this discourse, women's bodies become the focus of an idealized memory of a past era. Ironically, this elder described that time as "before independence" from France, rather than before colonial conquest. Constructed nostalgia may be at work in Kouassi Kokora's remembrance of earlier times, with women's bodies standing for tradition, purity, health, and notions of the ethnic group or the nation, as they often do elsewhere.[47]

Nutritional and Medical Benefits and Risks

If a child is sick and refuses to eat solid food, breast-feeding might be a significant factor in recovery. At least the child will not become dehydrated—

a risk that is far more serious in the tropics than it is in temperate zones. In addition, the nursing patient will continue to ingest some calories and nutrition. Beng mothers recognize this benefit. One day I asked Nesā why her eighteen-month-old son, who was quite an accomplished walker, was still nursing. She answered, "Because he's sick a lot. When he doesn't feel well, he doesn't eat." Indeed, when Nesā once brought over her son who had been sick for a few days, she explained, "He hasn't wanted to eat, but at least he can still nurse. Today, all he wants to do is nurse."

Allowing a child to continue breast-feeding into the second and even third year may thus be extremely beneficial in the short term.[48] Given that young children from impoverished families frequently fall ill with a variety of diseases, including intestinal sicknesses that leave them with no will to eat solid food, in some cases breast-feeding means the difference between surviving and succumbing.

Late weaning may not be beneficial for a child's health in the long term, however, as it may be associated with undernutrition or malnutrition (Maher 1992a). Nowadays at least, one reason for late weaning is that the mother is too poor to afford an adequate diet for her child. Lacking sufficient solid foods, she continues to breast-feed her growing child. Such a woman may herself be undernourished or malnourished because of her poverty. Breast-feeding weakens an undernourished mother's own nutritional status, in turn diminishing her milk supply (Popkin, Lasky, Spicer, and Yamamota 1986: 304). Moreover, the growing child needs increasing amounts of calories to sustain himself; the more he breast-feeds to satisfy his increasing hunger, the more he may compromise his mother's health. Such was the case with Mélanie, who suffered from pellagra—a disease caused by a serious deficiency of niacin, with symptoms including general weakness, mouth pain, amenorrhea, and skin disorders. Village women criticized Mélanie for continuing to breast-feed her three-year-old, but she confided to me that she had no money to buy her son food, nor much energy for farming to produce sufficient food herself. Mélanie was stuck in a rut and could see no way out.

Another risk to the health and nutritional status of an infant or young child comes when the mother or father dies. In particular, if a baby's mother dies and the father remarries or already has a second wife, the stepmother may neglect her stepchild, and the baby's health will be at risk. Amenan recalled one such case: "A woman died, leaving behind an infant of only two or three months. Her husband had another wife, but the stepmother refused to feed her stepson. [When he was a bit older] she didn't even let him roast yams on her hearth fire! Her husband was afraid of her and didn't criticize her for this." By contrast, Amenan claimed that this sort of neglect does not occur when grandparents raise a grandchild whose mother or father has died.

She also generalized that most foster parents do a good job of feeding and caring for their foster children. She cited a case I knew quite well: that of our neighbor, Amenan's own cross-cousin Aya, who has raised nine foster children who were born to her three sisters, one of whom had died in childbirth. Sometimes, Amenan maintained, Aya goes hungry all day herself in order to have enough food to feed her foster children. Kinship arrangements, then, provide a variety of options for an orphaned child, and some options are more congenial, nutritious, and safe than others.

Although women and men labor collectively to produce the varied foodstuffs that make up the Beng villager's diet, it is women who mainly control the day-to-day decisions about who eats what. Most mothers are benevolent and have their children's best interests at heart, my friends all claimed. Nevertheless, abuse and neglect do occur. In one case I heard of, a woman was so neglectful in feeding her own children that one day her oldest child, a boy of about eight or nine years old, fainted from hunger. Neighbors implied that some of this woman's children who had died had perished from similar neglect. And what of the children's father? In such cases, I am told, husbands often sit idly by without intervening. They either turn a blind eye to the neglect or are genuinely oblivious to it, at least for a time. In the case just mentioned, the husband was often away in the forest, farming in his distant fields, where he slept for days or even weeks at a time in a constructed shelter. For some time, my interlocutor claimed, it was possible that he truly had no idea of how his wife was neglecting their children.

Another situation that puts a baby at risk is the parents' economic situation. By world standards, all Beng villagers are poor, and those who are the poorest are undoubtedly the most at risk. The lesson seems simple enough in the abstract. We will follow the human dimensions of this bitter lesson in chapter 11.

Conclusion

In this chapter, we have considered breast-feeding and the introduction of solid foods as practices whose foundations are as much cultural as they are biological, medical, and environmental. In particular, the Beng ideology of the afterlife constructs an image of the infant as a being who has both desire and memory, and this image shapes the daily decisions that Beng mothers make concerning how, what, and when they will feed their babies. Classifying breast milk as a type of water associates the substance with the sacred liquid that is actual water, which in the Beng view resonates with articulated ties to the spirit world. This conceptual connection serves to legitimize the value of breast milk for the baby and the practice of nursing babies very frequently and for relatively long periods of time. It serves, as well, to pave the conceptual way for the common practice of force-feeding young infants ordinary water.

The ideology that the infant is a full person with independent conscious-ness also serves to socialize nursing mothers to look to the baby for cues about when to breast-feed and to seek the counsel of a diviner when a baby decides to boycott the breast. The various risks that Beng women associate with breast-feeding and solid food have eminently cultural foundations as well. Breast milk filling a pregnant woman's breast, leaking onto a nursing boy's penis, sucked by a child whose mother has given birth to another baby—all these evoke Beng ideas about the power and danger of the substance. The experience of breast-feeding takes its meanings from such ideas, as it takes its meanings from notions of the autonomous desires of the hungry baby.

~

In the next chapter, we consider another set of factors relating to the develop-ment of Beng babies' bodies: their linguistic, dental, and motor development.

CHAPTER NINE

Developing Beng Babies

Speaking, Teething, Crawling, and

Walking on (a Beng) Schedule

Nearly every Western-educated parent knows the important milestones to watch for in a young child's development. Smiling, rolling over, cutting the first tooth, crawling, sitting independently, uttering the first word, walking—these exciting firsts are regularly memorialized in the typical middle-class Western parent's baby diary. Such a parent may regularly compare her own baby's development with the charts featured in any number of parenting or pediatric guides to assess whether her child is on target for normal development or is exhibiting worrisome delays that call for an appointment with a medical specialist. The charts displaying these developmental averages are based on extensive research, so they must refer to universally valid norms and timetables . . . or do they?

The anthropological study of childhood teaches us differently. For one thing, as David Lancy has pointed out (1996:24–25), the milestones that Westerners look for as significant in their children's development are as much cultural as biological markers. What parents in one society deem important to observe as critical signposts of pediatric development may be considered far less relevant elsewhere. For example, in many West African societies, a major benchmark is "weaning from the back," when a mother no longer carries her child on her back routinely (Lancy 1996:25, citing Whiting and Edwards 1988:88). For Dani children in Irian Jaya (Indonesian New Guinea), the most important milestone in a young child's life occurs when the infant is brought out of the net bag in which virtually all waking and sleeping hours are spent for the first three to four months of life (Butt 1998:126). In Malawi, the major developmental events that are ritually celebrated for a Ngoni boy include his first nocturnal emission and the eruption of his second set of molars (Lancy 1996:24–25, citing Read 1960).[1] By contrast, none of these is especially significant for most Euro-American parents in the contemporary United States, where these developmental events typically remain ritually unmarked. The point is simple but powerful: what we take for granted as a naturally grounded developmental milestone is significantly shaped by cultural emphasis.

Moreover, behind the notion of norms is a generally unexamined assumption that typical development proceeds according to a biological timetable that is relatively fixed, thanks to a combination of evolutionary exigencies and genetic codes. In other words, the biological development of all healthy, well-nourished children is thought to progress at a relatively predictable pace no matter what the cultural environment. In this biologistic model of bodily development, infants' development in particular is seen as more or less automatic. Given that these assumptions are at once premised on a scientific model developed by scholars and a folk model accepted by many Euro-Americans, alternative cultural factors are not given much consideration by Euro-American parents.[2]

In this chapter, I follow some recent work that is starting to explore the ways in which culture joins biology in shaping motor development (e.g., Bril and Sabatier 1986) and offer a model of human development that emphasizes local meaning more than a universal standard so as to explore infant development from the Beng perspective. In so doing, I provide one ethnographic example of how the very events that we—whoever "we" might be—consider to be appropriate benchmarks of children's development are not universally considered as such. The Beng data demonstrate a related point that is equally significant at the theoretical level: even when the same milestones are celebrated as critical in a variety of societies, the reasons for highlighting those particular milestones and not others are sometimes surprisingly dissimilar. Bearing this in mind, then, let us inquire: What are the important milestones that Beng parents watch for in their infants and, more important, why are these particular milestones selected as the critical ones? What cultural sense does their selection make?

In the ensuing discussion I focus on four such markers: speaking the first words, sprouting the first tooth, crawling, and walking. I highlight these four because they are events on which Beng parents place great emphasis. Each of these achievements bears notable cultural significance, speaking actively and in multiple ways to key Beng values and systems of thought.

In Beng families, these milestones are noticed not only to observe that a child is developmentally normal. They are noticed for this reason, but they are also followed in order to ensure that the wrong developments do not occur at the wrong time. Additionally, they carry broader cultural significance beyond their obvious status as somatic achievements. In particular, three of the events I analyze—the utterance of the first word, the eruption of the first tooth, and the taking of the first steps—signal important spiritual connections relating to the well-developed ideology of reincarnation. The fourth benchmark that I will discuss, crawling, marks a crucial species distinction that speaks to broader conceptions of the cosmos. Taken together, these four mile-stones are highlighted by Beng parents in their daily interactions with their babies precisely because they carry a heavy burden of meaning that form part of a broader system of cultural significance. If they appear to coincide with popular Western benchmarks for infant development, the rationales for their importance in Beng practice—the indigenous meanings they bear at the local level—are, I suggest, more interesting for the analyst than is the mere fact of their co-occurrence with four commonly noted Western milestones.

Developmental Milestones in the Beng Cultural Universe

So far in this work I have emphasized the high level of volition, auton-omy, and personhood that Beng adults ascribe to infants. We have also seen that because of their spiritual connection to *wrugbe,* infants are deemed highly vulnerable to a host of dangerous diseases and conditions. In this chapter, we will follow up on this perceived vulnerability at the same time that we explore its closely linked obverse: the danger that infants can pose to adults because of this strong spiritual connection.

Their intimate ties to *wrugbe* afford babies a spiritual power that is more than an object of frustration, curiosity, and awe to their parents; sometimes this spiritual power proves dangerous, even lethal, to others in this life—espe-cially elderly people. Beng adults say that infants ought to develop certain behaviors and bodily habits according to a strict schedule. If an infant unwit-tingly diverges from these culturally prescribed timetables, the occurrence is said to constitute what the Beng term *tete,* which I translate as "a bad omen." In the following four sections we explore the implications that the notion of *tete* holds for the Beng theory of infant development as well as for the day-to-day decisions that adults—especially, but not exclusively, parents—make concerning that development.

I first discovered the importance of such omens when my friend Yacouba and I were looking through a popular parenting book. I had brought along *The First Twelve Months of Life* (Caplan 1984), which is amply illustrated with photographs of infants in various positions and situations, for the purpose of eliciting local interpretations of young childhood. Yacouba and I were en-joying looking through the volume when my companion became visibly upset by two photos. In one picture (p. 70), an infant of unidentified age was shown creeping or slithering, belly to the floor; in another illustration (p. 215), a different infant, again of unidentified age, was shown with a full set of teeth before the age that Yacouba judged to be appropriate for walking. My friend judged both situations to be bad omens *(tete),* and he was shaken at the images of infants who appeared to be contravening these Beng expectations.

Indeed, Yacouba speculated that the inappropriate developments shown in the photographs had resulted in the death of relatives of the two babies shown in the photos, most probably a grandparent of each of them.

How can we interpret Yacouba's reaction? To understand the source— and force—of his anxiety, we must examine a range of developmental norms on which Beng adults focus when looking to verify that their babies' physical development is progressing appropriately. Yacouba's concerns make sense as part of a system of thought concerning a group of bad omens that may be presented by infants. Let us explore the four most significant of these, as I have come to understand them.

Speech

If a newborn or a young infant should happen to utter one or more real words in a known language, this extraordinary event would be taken as a bad omen *(tɛtɛ)*. This interpretation by Beng adults may come as a surprise when we recall that the Beng believe infants understand all languages, and that adults therefore speak frequently to and for babies and encourage babies themselves to engage in babble.

While they encourage baby babble, Beng adults recognize that young infants are not capable of articulately speaking actual languages. At the same time that they are said to understand all languages, infants speak only the language of *wrugbe,* which is said to be incomprehensible to all other living humans other than diviners. If an infant were to speak real words in a language of this world, this would indicate that the young child had completely left *wrugbe* behind and had fully entered this world. As we have seen, this is a process that normally ought to take several years. For this reason, the premature uttering of articulate speech is interpreted as a sign that a close relative, often a parent or, more usually, a grandparent, will soon die.

In other words, the development of comprehensible speech is subject to a culturally prescribed timetable that itself articulates with broader conceptions of the afterlife. Here we are far from a Chomskian notion of biologically mandated language development regardless of local context.

Teething

Beng parents and their relatives are extremely anxious about the appearance of their babies' teeth.[3] They pay careful attention to when and where their infants' teeth erupt through the gums. A mother may string a special teething necklace on her infant to ensure proper dental development (figure 54). Beng adults assert that there is a normal time and place for the various teeth to appear. If any of four variations on the norm occurs in the teething

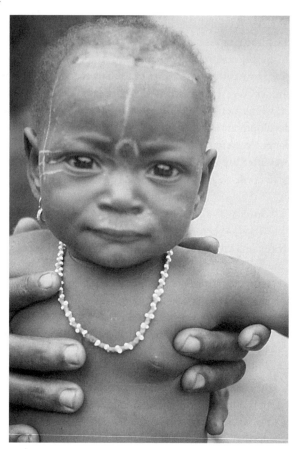

54. This baby wears a "teething necklace" to ensure proper dental development. The baby died a few days after the photo was taken, probably from malnutrition.

history of a particular infant, it is considered a disaster for the baby or the family.

First, as far as the Beng are concerned, all babies should be born toothless *(trobi trobi),* and the first tooth should appear several months after a baby's birth. This is, of course, exactly what happens in the vast majority of children. But on rare occasions a baby is born with a tooth, or even two or more teeth, already visible in the mouth.[4] In Beng villages, the presence of a natal tooth is classified as *tetɛ* and is considered a harbinger of tragedy. In precolonial days, a baby who was born with a tooth already erupted was killed immediately—drowned in a bucket of soapy water by a female elder of the baby's matriclan—and the corpse buried hastily in the bush, with no ritual attention.

In the local view, the reason for this drastic treatment of newborns with teeth had to do with the anticipated consequences of allowing the baby to live. If the baby's life were spared, adults were certain that someone else, generally an elderly relative in either the baby's own matriclan or that of the baby's father—probably one of the infant's grandparents—would soon die. I received contradictory interpretations of the baby's role in such a tragedy. Most people maintained that it was not the baby who would kill the elderly relative, but rather that the little one's tooth was a premonition of such a death. A few others, however, implied that the baby would be responsible for killing the elder, although perhaps unintentionally. In either case, removing the baby with the offending tooth from this world was considered the only sure means to avert the tragedy.

The second problematic teething scenario in Beng thought concerns the tooth that first erupts after birth (*sɔ gɔlɛ:* to grow a tooth). In the vast majority of cases, the first tooth to erupt is one of the two lower central incisors. However, the Beng have observed, in rare cases the first tooth to erupt is one of the upper central incisors. This anomalous teething schedule is also considered a disaster and is classified by the Beng as a bad omen—*tɛtɛ*.[5] Again, in earlier times such a baby was killed immediately by a female elder in the baby's matriclan and buried hastily in the bush. And again, the reason cited was that it was necessary in order to spare the life of an elder in the baby's family, who, it was supposed, would otherwise die prematurely.

Naturally, parents want to avoid such a tragedy. To do so, the concerned mother of an infant whose first tooth has not yet come in takes ritual precautions. After washing the bark-cloth mats *(zɔ)*, or nowadays, cotton cloths, or *pagnes,* on which her infant normally lies, she takes care to dry the mats or *pagnes* by spreading them on the ground rather than by elevating them either on a rooftop or on a modern clothesline. This action bears metonymic power: just as the mat remains low, it is supposed, the first tooth that comes into the infant's mouth will cut through the lower, not upper, gum. By contrast, if a mother of a young infant were to dry her child's mats or *pagnes* up high, villagers assert, the infant's first tooth would erupt through the upper gums, and in earlier times the unfortunate child would have been killed.

The third teething disaster, teething too late, is considered equally catastrophic. Beng parents maintain that it is normal for babies to learn to speak only after their teeth have begun to come in.[6] If a baby learns to say a proper word in the Beng language before the first tooth has erupted, this is classified as *tɛtɛ,* and once again it is expected that someone in the baby's family, usually an elder, will soon die. For this reason, in the early months after the birth, mothers and other relatives eagerly look for the appearance of a baby's first tooth—not only to ensure that it erupts on the lower jaw, but also that it erupts before the infant has begun to speak a recognizable word. When the first tooth does erupt, as long as it does so on the lower jaw and before the baby has spoken a first word, its appearance is often cause for spontaneous celebration by any in the courtyard who observe the event. Catching the general sense of relief, an older sibling may break out into song: *"sɔ kaeèèènà!"* ("There's a tooth!").

A child should also cut the first tooth before learning to walk. Of course, this happens in the vast majority of cases.[7] But in the rare instance of an infant learning to walk before having cut the first tooth, *tete* is invoked. It is thought that if the child survives, a relative, probably an elder in the child's matriclan or the father's matriclan, will soon die. Once again, to avert this situation such a child might have been killed in earlier days.

And what about contemporary times: Are babies whose teeth come in too early, in the wrong place, or too late still killed? I received contradictory answers to this question from a variety of people. Most adults asserted that such babies would not be killed nowadays for a pragmatic reason: the act would be illegal according to national law, and a person who killed such a baby could be sent to jail if the act were reported to the police.[8] In one case that Master of the Earth Kouassi Kokora recounted to me, a Beng baby was born with two natal teeth in the medical dispensary in the nearby town of M'Bahiakro. The attending medical personnel judged that the optimal solution was for a dentist to extract the teeth, and the baby was taken to the nearest large city, Bouaké, for this purpose, since there was no dentist in M'Bahiakro. The Bouaké dentist was unable to extract the teeth. Indeed, Kouassi asserted that such teeth can never be removed and that if the dentist had somehow been able to extract them, the baby would have died right away. The Master of the Earth added ominously that if the baby survived infancy without having had the teeth extracted, the little one would surely grow up to be a witch.

In contrast to the above case, a few people whispered to me that even today it is possible that a baby born with a natal tooth will be killed clandestinely. The decision would be made by the family, depending on their own sense of the perceived risks and consequences of killing versus not killing the child. Of course the great sensitivity of this issue made it difficult to discuss particular instances.

Regardless of the current negotiation of individual cases, what do we make of these general practices regarding teething? Most Beng are certainly not cruel in general, nor are most Beng parents homicidal toward their young children. I suggest that a full understanding of these lethal practices must take us back to Beng religious ideology—to the afterlife. Given that every baby is seen as a reincarnation of someone who was recently living in *wrugbe*, a baby who cuts his first tooth in the womb has demonstrated that he is in a rush to trade places with an elder who is still living in this life. Teeth, we might say, are taken as the somatic locus of a mystical relationship between babies and elders. This somatically articulated tie makes cultural sense when considered in relation to the local ideology of reincarnation.

Babies normally move from having no teeth *(trobi trobi)*, to having only a few teeth, to having a full set of teeth. Elders are in a structurally similar but temporally reversed position: they move from having a full set of teeth, to having a partial set of teeth, to (potentially) having no teeth *(trobi trobi).*[9] The dental histories of babies and elders are thus likely to be parallel—but in a temporally inverted order. Given this pair of inverse transitions through time, I suggest that teeth constitute an appropriate symbol of the complex tie uniting infants and elders. At a general level, these two groups appear, paradoxically, quite similar—even though they occupy opposite ends of the life cycle. Beng adults would surely find wisdom in Shakespeare's comments on the affinities between infancy and old age:

> Last Scene of all,
> That ends this strange eventful history,
> Is second childishness, and mere oblivion,
> Sans teeth, sans eyes, sans taste, sans everything.
> *(As You Like It,* II.7, 164–67)

Indeed, with an ideology of reincarnation such as that developed in Beng thought, the connection between elder and infant is even closer than the general connection posited by Shakespeare. Through passage in a culturally constituted afterlife, the one (the elder) is said to become, not just to approximate, the other (the baby). In the Beng model of reincarnation, the dental cycle of gaining and losing teeth becomes an appropriate metaphor for the cycle of life itself.

In addition to observing teething patterns, Beng families are also vigilant about the motor development of their babies. Crawling and walking represent culturally significant milestones that relatives observe very carefully to ensure that both skills develop in locally appropriate ways and at locally appropriate times.

Crawling

There are two potential problems with inappropriate crawling that Beng relatives watch for with anxiety. First, they hope that the baby is not delayed in learning to crawl. Beng parents observe that as long as a baby is healthy, the little one should be crawling by the age of six months; they further point out that some healthy babies crawl as early as four months old.[10] But in some cases, an otherwise healthy baby does not crawl by six months. This situation is described by the phrase, *a wɔ diŋ a sɛ̃,* meaning "his/her wrists hurt him/ her." The anxiety exhibited by parents and other relatives about this delay refers to a cultural agenda quite different from that provoking Western parents' concern about a biomechanical deficit.

It is true that Beng ideology shares a general concern of the scientific model, that motor development ought to progress normally according to a predictable timetable. But the Beng model allows for the possibility that certain cultural conditions may disrupt this normal progression. That is, unlike the scientific model, which emphasizes biomechanical development exclusively, the Beng model accepts the chance for significant delay in biomechanical development due to the violation of cultural norms in the form of behavior that is locally classified as forbidden. In this model, human moral systems, as much as bioevolutionary systems, can influence the development of biomechanical skills.

Given this cultural foundation of knowledge concerning motor development, villagers blame the parents if an infant's crawling is delayed significantly beyond about six months. Neighbors and relatives may start to gossip that the parents resumed their sex life prematurely, in violation of the postpartum sex taboo. This lack of restraint on the parents' part is considered a grave danger to their baby. The child is inevitably said to have come down with the sexually transmitted disease dirt, and unless the proper medicines are obtained quickly, it is widely presumed that the child will never learn to crawl and will soon die.

The appropriate medicine *(la)* for this condition is constituted of symbolically significant components. It works on the homeopathic principle we have seen elsewhere in Beng medical practice, that "like cures like." In this case, symbolically resonant sexual dirt is used to cure the sexual dirt that is said to be afflicting the unfortunate baby. Early in the morning, the baby's mother removes the underwear that she wore the previous night, and she holds it over an illumined kerosene lamp to warm the fabric.[11] Then she puts the heated cloth around the baby's wrists, and she pulls the tiny wrists with the cloth.

Sexual dirt is relied on to address the condition called dirt not only curatively but also preventively. In this case, the mother of a not-yet-crawling baby administers an enema whose ingredients are gathered in a symbolically significant manner. She identifies a left-handed person, who locates any shrub that happens to be growing on a mound and digs up the plant to give to the baby's mother. The mother then crushes the leaves well with some chili peppers (which are an ingredient in most enema recipes) and uses the mixture as an enema for the baby for several consecutive days (three days for a girl, four for a boy).

The culturally important aspect of this treatment is the left-handedness of the person gathering the herb. Left-handedness is culturally disapproved of in Beng villages, as it is in many societies, both Western and non-Western (Needham 1973). Normally one should use the left hand only for wiping after defecation, and, as we have seen, feces themselves are classified as bad *(à gɛŋɛ)*. Someone who is left-handed and is collecting herbal remedies with the left hand is thus going against the grain of normally approved human activities and, in a sense, polluting the medicinal herbs. But let us recall that a baby who is slow in learning to crawl is considered to be polluted by the dirt of his parents' premature sex; the homeopathic principle of like curing like is therefore operative here.

In addition, as we have seen with Yacouba's comment, creeping or slithering with belly on the ground, rather than crawling with stomach raised, is considered unacceptable by Beng parents, who do all they can to reorient a baby who seems inclined to slither rather than crawl. One is reminded here of Mary Douglas's (1966) analysis of the dietary laws laid out in the Old Testament. Other than the famous pork, the long list of foods considered unacceptable to ancient (and, to varying extents, contemporary) Jews includes meat from animals that creep or slither rather than walk. According to Douglas's symbolic analysis, this mode of locomotion is classified as falling between clearly constituted categories and hence unacceptable. The Beng appear to be following a similar logic.

Significant deviance from what adults recognize as the norm for the appropriate motor development of infants is thus interpreted according to principles that make sense in a culturally constituted universe. In the following section, we will see how this is applied with equal insistence to the development of the next stage of motor skills.

Walking

In the mainstream medical model, the biological mandate for walking is overwhelming. As one textbook sums it up unambiguously, walking is a "natural activity" whose "limits are set largely by the rate of physical maturation" (Bornstein and Lamb 1992:138–39).[12] The Beng model of motor development contrasts significantly with this one. Unlike the scientific perspective, the Beng knowledge system posits limits set largely by culture rather than nature. That is, in the view of most Beng parents, there is an optimal time for a baby to begin walking, and adults should regulate this milestone actively by deliberately delaying its occurrence during the first year and deliberately encouraging its occurrence during the second year.

As is common with culturally proscribed behavior, the indigenous rationale for maintaining the taboo is that this is necessary to avoid the consequences of violating it. If a baby begins to walk too early according to the cultural script, this is considered a disaster for one reason. On the other hand, if the baby is delayed in learning the skill, this is interpreted as a disaster for another reason. Both situations are interpreted according to a system of cultural logic whose roots lie in broader conceptions of the life cycle and its spiritual basis.

As soon as a baby starts to crawl, as we have seen, Beng parents are excited and proud, for they recognize this achievement as a prelude to their child learning how to walk. However, parents learn from elders that they must discourage their baby from progressing from crawling to walking until the baby is a year old. To keep track of their infants' ages so as to avoid inadvertently violating this taboo, parents might consult a male elder who specializes in the calendar. In the village of Asagbe, for example, an elder named Kouakou Latɛ and his son were widely considered "human calendars": they kept track of time according to seasonal agricultural labor, and they could reliably give any infant's age.[13] Other adults, including mothers, may also keep track of the passage of time informally.

Parents should take care in calculating an infant's age because early walking is not considered inevitable for a given child; instead, early walking is to be actively prevented. Thus Beng parents might take any or all of three direct measures to ensure that their children refrain from walking before a year of age. First, if a younger-than-one-year-old baby shows signs of precocious motor development, the baby's father is urged to spank his child whenever he sees the little one trying to take independent steps. Of course, spanking does not always have the desired effect—as Western-trained psychologists observe.[14] Beng parents recognize this awkward truth as well. Amenan mentioned to me that her own daughter Amwe was able to walk at nine months. Amwe's father kept spanking her to discourage her, but baby Amwe's youthful urge toward locomotion proved stronger than her father's efforts.

Perhaps because they recognize that spanking is not always effective, Beng parents have two additional options at their disposal. If a mother observes that her infant seems determined to walk before the first birthday, she is urged by her elders to keep the young child strapped to her (or someone else's) back as much as possible. Such physical restraint is complemented by yet another means: a mother may also buy a *lagba* bead from itinerant Hausa traders from Nigeria and string it onto a cord that she ties around the baby's waist. This belt is said to exert a magical influence over the baby: as soon as the bead is put on the baby's waist, the baby reportedly will just sit still and no longer feel the urge to walk. In this way, cultural practice is said to actively inhibit any natural inclination to take those first steps.

The impetus to slow down motor development also has the effect of slowing down the culturally significant movement away from *wrugbe*—a movement that is otherwise encouraged. This makes the practice we are exploring seem contradictory (Nancy Abelmann, personal communication). Although no Beng adult ever mentioned it in this context, one pragmatic factor may be relevant: in an outdoor setting with ground-level cooking fires, snakes, goat droppings, and so on, early walking can be especially dangerous. The older the child is when she begins to walk, the more physically coordinated she is, and also the more cognitively ready to assess dangers realistically. Here, then, the cultural script may be tempered by pragmatic exigency. The cultural ideology specifies that although movement away from *wrugbe* is desirable in the first years of life, it should nevertheless be relatively slow and prolonged over the course of those years. Overly hasty extraction from *wrugbe* is considered as dangerous as prolonged habitation of that cultural space.

Nevertheless, early walking is not always considered a spiritual threat any more. Times have changed, and some young parents have begun to reject the ritual injunctions of their elders and are allowing their babies to walk before a year. These parents consider early development as a hallmark of modernity. Accordingly, they look for ritual herbal or magical medicines to encourage their babies to walk early. Village elders are appalled by this recent development, which they view as a threat to the integrity of the indigenous religion.

Once the baby reaches a year of age, parents must make sure that their child does not start to walk too late, for delayed walking is another cause for anxiety. As with delayed crawling, if an infant does not take those first steps soon after a year of age, people say *ŋo wɔ diŋ ŋo sɛ̃*—"his/her wrists hurt him/her." Villagers may start accusing the parents of having resumed their sex life without waiting for the child to begin walking so the child could be weaned. Forbidden sex can cause a very serious condition that the Beng call "split leg" *(gã wilɛ)*, which can prevent a child from ever learning to walk. If relatives suspect that this could be the cause of a child's delay in learning to walk, the parents are urged to consult a diviner, who will prescribe certain remedies. Without ritual treatments, it is thought, the child will soon depart this world.[15]

There is a pragmatic personal reason impelling parents to encourage those first steps as well. As we have seen, until their baby is weaned and can walk properly, a couple is forbidden to resume their sexual relationship. Maintaining this postpartum sex taboo is considered critical to protecting a child. If a nursing mother of a nonwalking baby resumes her sex life and becomes pregnant before her baby learns to walk and is weaned, it is said that the developing fetus will steal breast milk from the nursing child. The older sibling will never learn to walk properly, and eventually the poor child will die.

Once a child has passed the first birthday, therefore, the baby's mother has a strong incentive to encourage her child to learn to walk, for this will permit her to legitimately resume her conjugal sex life. This may especially be a concern to her if she is married monogamously, for if her child does not start walking soon, her husband may be tempted to have an affair, visit a prostitute, or take an additional wife. If he does none of these, he might pressure her to resume their sex life prematurely, which could lead to both gossip and tragedy.

Thus some women avail themselves of local magical techniques to hasten their children's motor development. My friend Amla was eager for her thirteen-month-old baby, Sunu, to begin walking, so she put a silver anklet around each of her daughter's ankles, which is said to speed up the process. However, soon after doing so, Amla lost one of the silver anklets. She temporarily replaced it with a copper anklet until she was able to buy a new silver one. Other mothers administer an enema concocted with particular ingredients (such as the crushed small fruit of the *telu* vine) that are said to influence the baby to walk soon. Recipes for herbal bath washes are also available to anxious mothers.

Yet not all mothers are concerned for their babies to begin walking soon after they turn a year old. One mother told me that she was not at all worried that her sixteen-month-old son, Anie, had not yet begun to walk. She claimed, "We don't teach children to walk at all." She did say that if her son was not walking at two years, she would search for medicines for him, but that he was still too young for this.

In short, the development of the ability to walk is influenced by the individual inclinations and circumstances of both the child and the parents. It is also deeply enmeshed in a matrix of beliefs and practices concerning the life cycle, reincarnation, and human sexuality.

Bad Omens

The Beng judge each of the situations we have examined as a form of liminality that is symbolically dangerous. Creeping is an inappropriate form of human locomotion: mammals with legs ought to use them to walk with, while slithering or creeping is best left to other species, notably snakes and other reptiles. The cases of speaking, walking, and teething at inappropriate times or in inappropriate sequence are related, although here the form of liminality is temporal rather than spatial: there is an absolute time that is considered to be appropriate for the onset of speaking and walking. Regarding the latter, there is a relative time as well, after the first tooth has been cut but before the full first set has appeared.

Why should violation of these culturally dictated schedules be seen as producing such a drastic result as the premature death of another person, especially an elder? Amenan explained that in the "old days" it was said that if a baby walked before turning a year old, the infant "walked on a grandparent's spirit." This comment returns us to the demographics of *wrugbe* as Beng adults conceive of them. Let us recall how Kouakou Bah explained Beng population dynamics (chapter 4): births and deaths in this life have their counterparts in *wrugbe*, making the two sites interconnected, with souls crossing back and forth between the spaces.

Bearing this in mind, it makes sense that infants can be seen as responsible for the deaths of old people, for the babies themselves have emerged only recently from the land of the dead, bringing with them the identity—sometimes known to others in this life, sometimes not—of a deceased ancestor, and they sometimes opt to return to the other life. For their part, very old adults have an equally fragile hold on this life as they approach their journey back to *wrugbe*. If a baby exhibits a kind of liminal behavior or trait judged unacceptable to the Beng, this can result in the infant taking the place of an old person. The connection between infant and elder is made all too explicit, and the passage from one stage to the other is believed to be hastened prematurely. The symbolic logic operates in such a way as to make clear, even literal, the diffuse ties that normally exist between the youngest and the oldest people, who are at the two extreme ends of the human life cycle—the two points closest to *wrugbe*.

Old people who are close to death nevertheless occupy a space in this life, and the action of *tete* hastens a death that, while it was close at hand, had not yet occurred. An inappropriately timed activity on the part of an infant is thus capable of upsetting the balance of lives in this world vis-à-vis those in *wrugbe*, and therefore of precipitating the untimely death of a relative, especially an old relative. The Beng themselves do not elaborate on the mechanisms at work. Certainly, most do not allege that the infant in such a scenario is the advance reincarnation of the elder who is dying from *tete*, nor do most adults commenting on a case of *tete* accuse the infant of taking an active hand in killing the unfortunate relative. Rather, they simply point to the convergence between the recent birth of the infant and the hastened death of the elder, and because of a tragic transgression of culturally prescribed development norms, they claim a vague causal relationship. In the minds of most people who explained *tete* to me, it seemed a relation of logic more than one of intentionality: there is a terrible symmetry at work such that one ill-timed or ill-spaced event precipitates, in an unspecified way, another. The spiritual nature of infants thus asserts itself with a malevolence that Beng adults themselves find disturbing.

Conclusion

In this chapter, I have investigated several domains of physical development, presenting an indigenous model that is quite different from the accepted scientific model. Within the literature on infant development in both psychology and anthropology, the surprisingly meager literature on non-Western infants' development has focused overwhelmingly on the issue of precocity. This issue has especially pervaded a body of articles that have addressed the continent of Africa, and the weight of professional opinion suggests that on the whole, African infants are precocious when it comes to motor, social, and cognitive development especially for the first six months of life, and decreasingly so up to the age of approximately two years.[16]

What, exactly, is meant by such assertions of precocity? Implicit in the very term is the assumption that there is a single set of norms for the development of motor, social, and cognitive skills that is relevant for all human populations. In the literature, deviants from these norms are labeled either precocious or delayed. As it happens, the set of norms against which all infants' development is measured in these studies has been formulated on the basis of research conducted overwhelmingly with middle-class Euro-American and, to a lesser extent, European infants. This research has set an excellent standard for researchers to follow up in other parts of the world while allowing for the possibility of shifts in content. Such shifts, however, have hardly happened. Instead, textbook after textbook offers norms for infant development on the basis of research with Euro-American and European children while claiming universality for those norms. The sole important exception has been this literature on African precocity.

Why is it that Euro-American and European infants have been considered the "norm" against which African infants have been measured? For argument's sake, let us imagine that the power relations of the world run in the opposite direction from that in which they currently run. In this scenario, African researchers, on the basis of extensive research on their continent, would consider African infants' development as the norm, and when they finally decided to turn a curious eye on a few token Euro-American and European infants—who are, after all, a small minority in the world's youth population—they would find these infants to be lagging woefully behind their African counterparts. Such children would be classified as developmentally delayed.

We know, of course, that this has not happened. If we tried to make the development of non-Western infants the norm, psychologists might counter that the scenario would not make for good science insofar as we would be constructing a norm with supposedly universal relevance on the basis of a culturally restricted subject pool. By the same token, I suggest, the current norms, based overwhelmingly as they are on Euro-American and European populations, do not make good science. As Irene Rizzini and Andrew Dawes have recently written: "The standards employed in modern psychological discourse about child development are in fact minority (first world) standards" (2001:316).[17]

Keeping this in mind, I propose that it would be intellectually prudent to temporarily suspend the notion of norms in the universal sense altogether until we have a much larger and more diverse base on which to posit a set of them. The new norms might be expressed in terms of ranges—far broader than those currently imagined in the infant development literature—rather than in terms of discrete target dates. At the same time, we ought to consider the theoretical possibility that such norms may prove meaningless at the local level and that local models of appropriate development need to be privileged as much as "objective" standards that are based on a single set of cultural values.

In the next chapter, we move to a consideration of another set of local models, these focusing on Beng ideas about the causes of and cures for young children's illnesses.

CHAPTER TEN

Sick Beng Babies

Spirits, Witches, and Poverty

Alma: When children die, is it related to malnutrition?
Amenan: Maybe.
Alma: Is it related to their parents' poverty?
Amenan: No, it's often a problem of witchcraft.

It is a paradox of Beng conceptions of infancy that adults view babies as at once extremely hardy and extremely vulnerable. Both perceptions are shaped by a cultural imaginary. Although the outsider might predict otherwise, infants' purported hardiness emphasizes the spiritual side of their existence, whereas their conceived vulnerability emphasizes their somatic life—but both are, I suggest, as much culturally as biologically constructed. In this chapter, we explore the ways in which caretakers, especially mothers, conceive of the day-to-day interventions necessary to ensure their young children's health as they negotiate the symbolic contours of illnesses as they are imagined.

We start with a simple fact. In Beng villages, babies fall sick often. Many recover, but some die. Most mothers keep track of the proportion of their living children compared to the total number of children they have borne, though some have lost so many children that they have lost count. Ama Au was able to recall easily that of the fifteen children she had borne, eight remained. Kolia had to count up her twelve pregnancies in order to subtract the five children still alive and arrive at the number of seven representing those she had lost. M'Akwe presented a happier story; she had lost only one child. Other women are even luckier: they have never suffered the death of a child. But these women are rare. In most villages, everyone knows who those fortunate women are—the short list is part of common knowledge.

The first time a Beng couple experiences the death of a child, people expect that the parents will be traumatized. Parents living in poverty who are likely to experience the deaths of many children are no less emotionally affected by such events than are parents in privileged circumstances.[1] However, the two sets of parents may mark their reactions quite differently. In Beng villages, a special funeral for the first-time loss of a child requires a range of stringent ritual activities for and around the mourning parents. Only other parents who have experienced such a funeral for one of their own children may attend most components of the ritual. In this way, the village at large is made aware of which parents have and which have not had tragedy strike their growing family.

In Beng villages, so many babies and young children die that there is a special name for a baby born following the consecutive deaths of two older siblings. If such a baby is a boy, he is inevitably named Wamyā; if the baby is a girl, she is named Sunu. The special status of these children is not only reflected in their names, it is etched on their bodies. All Wamyās and Sunus boast three cicatrices carved into each cheek, permanently radiating out from their mouths like cats' whiskers. Through such surgical alterations, Africa's tragic infant and child mortality statistics are inscribed.

~

As I mentioned earlier, in 1993, much of my fieldwork on infancy was conducted around the amateur nursing station that my husband, Philip, and I set up every morning in Amenan's compound. As with families elsewhere in the "developing" world, Beng mothers and other caretakers are constantly on the lookout both for new ways to protect their children from sickness and new cures to administer when their children do become ill. Given a bricolage approach to healing that characterizes most villagers' medical strategies (Lévi-Strauss 1966), the bandages, pills, and book knowledge that Philip and I offered easily found a place in the heterogeneous pharmacopoeia most every Beng mother manages in her mind.

As the epigraph to this chapter implies, while living in Beng villages my inclination has been to seek the prime cause of children's illnesses and deaths in the domain of political economy. However, most of my respondents have usually looked elsewhere for explanations of their children's health problems. Spirits of the bush, spirits of the Earth, spirits of the ancestors, and the evil intentions of witches all seemed more probable causes of illness to most of the Beng women and men with whom I spoke than did the ravages of poverty—ravages that, I hasten to add, they know far better than I. To ensure that we listen to these voices, throughout this chapter I constantly try to keep in mind the ways, both great and small, in which culture constructs the contours of the perception of medical risk. I begin by focusing on the indigenous emphasis on the spiritual connection. Later I add my outsider's analytical perspective, while endeavoring to allow these two types of explanation to remain in conversation with one another. In the next chapter, I continue by focusing on political economy as another way to explain the toll that living in a postcolonial village of the West African rain forest takes on young children's bodies.

The Spiritual Connection

Many dangers threaten Beng infants. Although Beng adults perceive babies as harboring a great deal of spiritual resilience, they also acknowledge that babies' bodies are remarkably vulnerable. The contrast between presumed spiritual energy and evident somatic weakness is striking to an outside observer. Yet Beng parents do not necessarily perceive contrast in this dual state of affairs. Indeed, in the Beng view, the two factors are often linked causally rather than contradictorily. That is, precisely because they are said to have a strong spiritual profile—to be leading, in effect, a double life—Beng infants are often perceived as making the decision to fall sick and die so as to return to the halcyon space of *wrugbe*. In this model, their spiritual strength is considered responsible for their bodily weakness.

Although Beng infants are understood by adults to innately wield spiritual power, they are nonetheless considered far from omnipotent. Their spiritual connection also produces a certain vulnerability against which their mothers in particular should be constantly vigilant. Adults believe that babies are imperiled by a variety of diseases and conditions whose nature and origins the Beng judge to be spiritual, though their effects are decidedly physical.

Their recent exit from *wrugbe* gives Beng infants an insufficient hold on life in this world and makes of them an easy target for witches and other spiritual forces that may readily overpower the fragile beings. Living, as Victor Turner might have put it, "betwixt and between" two worlds, babies are seen as only weakly attached to each world while they slowly make the transition from one to the other. Beng women warn that indifference to a baby's medical vulnerability can easily result in the infant's death—an all-too-common occurrence in Beng villages. In this way, indigenous religious beliefs intersect with poverty, providing an explanation for the appallingly high infant mortality rate that looms large in the consciousness of every Beng mother with whom I have spoken.[2]

Yet Beng women see themselves and their infants not only as victims but also as agents. Infants—and, by extension, their mothers—are victims of the spiritual dangers whose manifestations take the shape of diseases caused by poverty. At the same time, mothers are agents insofar as they believe they have a culturally meaningful tool kit at their disposal with which to protect their babies against these dangers and their manifestations especially if they work in tandem with diviners. Beng women are, of course, realistic about the limits of their methods; they recognize that these tool kits are all too far from perfect. They are also convinced that as conscious subjects themselves, babies may not always cooperate with their mothers' efforts to keep them in good health.

The Baby as Agent: The Will to Die

The Willful Fetus

In the view of Beng adults, a baby may decide to die even before being born. A woman who experiences difficulty delivering her baby may first try herbal treatments. If these have no effect, a relative will consult a diviner to discover whether there are deeper reasons for the complications. The diviner may identify any of several causes. The diviner may have heard from the spirits that the baby-still-in-the-womb is not joining this world because no one is calling the infant correctly—by the name that the baby prefers. We have already considered the case of one woman who was having a very difficult delivery (chapter 4). Only after a diviner pronounced that spirits had named the baby "Mo Jaa" and the attendant women called the baby-in-the-birth-canal by this name did the baby emerge. Claiming that a baby requires a particular name as a prerequisite for descending down the birth canal is a way of imputing to the newborn a wish to be welcomed into her new incarnation with the identity she brings from her past life.

After the birth, as long as life in this world seems hospitable to a Beng infant—if relatives are warm and loving; if they offer the baby plenty of breast milk and, later, good food; if they entertain the little one, find effective medicines when the child is sick, wash the baby twice a day, and adorn the baby's body with the jewelry the little one craves from a remembered life back in *wrugbe*—if all these conditions are met, an infant should be content and should opt to stay in this life, or at least will try to do so. Nevertheless, long after birth, young children continue to reside mentally and emotionally in the invisible realm of *wrugbe*. A child who is neglected or abused in this existence may decide to fall sick and return to the more purportedly idyllic other world, hoping to be reborn next time into a more congenial family.

The baby may also recall gifts that the ancestral parents presented the little one back in *wrugbe*. If the parents of this world neglect to consult a diviner who will interpret those longings to them, the little one will have no way to communicate those desires. Recalling the treasures of *wrugbe*, the infant may decide to return to the ancestral parents who, it is said, were kinder.

Beauty and the Lure of *Wrugbe*

A baby or toddler can decide to become ill and die for another reason. A very young child who looks into a mirror and is not pleased with the reflection may become unhappy. The little one may say, "I'll die and come back with a beautiful face." Alternatively, the reflected image may startle the child simply because it is so unexpected, and the little one may die of fright or shock. When my friend Yacouba and I were looking at a book about infants that is filled with photos (Caplan 1984), he grew disturbed when he spotted a toddler of uncertain gender gazing in a mirror (p. 208): "This is a black child. S/he isn't walking well yet. S/he's looking at her/himself—this isn't good! If s/he doesn't like her/his face, s/he'll return to *wrugbe!*" To prevent such a calamity, a vigilant mother never allows her infant or toddler to play with a mirror. Other adults and children in the village know never to show a baby his or her reflection. In Beng villages, a gift of an unbreakable mirror— so popular in certain baby-shower circuits in the United States—would be a horrible present for a newborn. Indeed, the presentation of such a gift might be seen as a death sentence, or even an act of attempted murder.[3] One wonders how Lacan might have revised the imputed universality of his theory of the "mirror stage" if he had encountered this aspect of the Beng theory of human development.

Adults say that twins are especially sensitive regarding their appearance, and like people elsewhere, Beng adults see infant twins as having a special vulnerability. If a visitor happens to remark that one baby twin looks healthier, has grown more, or is more beautiful than the other twin, the sibling who has been slighted will be gravely insulted. In a fit of anger, the resentful baby may decide to fall ill and return to the afterlife. Likewise, when presenting a gift to a Beng twin, one must always offer an identical gift to the other twin; otherwise the neglected one may be offended enough to return to *wrugbe.* When infants thus assert their intimate ties to *wrugbe,* they are ironically exhibiting both agency, by making a decision to return to the afterlife, and— from the perspective of their human parents—weakness, by leaving this life.

All of this implies an extraordinary level of self-determination on the part of infants. Beng adults assert, in so many words, that their babies have consciousness and volition. In conversations about babies, one often hears the phrase, "*o vī . . . ni*"—"S/he wants . . ." These reported desires are not only biological, as is the emphasis in most middle-class Euro-American discourses about infant appetite; they are also sociological and emotional. Beng mothers take great pains to interpret the longings of their babies, especially for jewelry and clothes that infants reportedly miss from the other life, because a disappointed baby who is denied a desired item may decide to exit this life. In this model, adults hold babies themselves accountable for their survival or early demise.

Baby as Victim: Spirits and Witches

Infant agency is far from the whole story, however. Given the large number of infants and children who die in Beng villages, parents and other relatives may actively seek alternative explanations. Beng adults perceive babies as highly vulnerable to the nefarious machinations of evil others. Whereas some infants reputedly make the choice to die, others are classified as victims—of bush, Earth, and ancestor spirits, or of witchcraft. This model also refers back to the connection that infants are believed to retain to their previous existence. Because part of their consciousness is still back in *wrugbe*, in the Beng cultural imaginary babies do not have a complete hold on, or commitment to, life in this world, and this makes them especially vulnerable to an array of malevolent forces that threaten their health. Barren spirits eager for a human child to raise; a watchful Earth wreaking revenge on a sinner in the clan; malevolent spirits ruled by their own evil; human witches consumed by jealousy—all of these forces pose culturally constituted dangers that demand vigilance on the part of the baby's relatives, or tragedy may occur.

Spirits of the Bush

The Beng world is populated not only by beings that are visible to the human eye—people, animals, plants—but also by forces that are equally present and potent even though they are invisible to humans. It is true that a gulf separates humans from spirits, but paradoxically, the lives of spirits parallel the lives of people in uncanny ways. For example, Beng adults envisage bush spirits *(bɔŋzɔ)* as living in the same sorts of family arrangements that characterize human lives. They are believed to be governed by the same desires and to suffer from the same lacks. As with the ancient Greek pantheon, the Beng spirits are ruled by passion and caprice as much as by logic.

One implication of this can prove devastating for Beng children. Adults perceive young children to be open to the vengeance of beleaguered spirits. Because most spirits are not associated with particular human families or clans, infants are considered vulnerable generically to any *bɔŋzɔ*. If a bush spirit is barren or sterile, the spirit may covet a human child. If it sees a young child wandering alone in the forest, it may take advantage of the situation and snatch the child, then take the little one off to the spirit world. If a child becomes lost in the forest, a diviner should be enlisted right away to speak to the spirits and discover what they would accept in exchange for the child; otherwise the little one will be lost to his or her parents forever. Here is a narrative I recorded of one such near disaster:

> A woman took her grandson to the fields with her and lost him there: she couldn't locate him anywhere. When news reached the village, the male chief sent around a young messenger to ask everyone in the village to look for the little boy, but no one could find him. The child remained all night in the forest.
>
> After consulting a diviner, the family offered up many white chickens as sacrifices to the forest spirits, to ask that they release the child. The next day the family discovered the little boy in the same spot where they had last seen him the previous day. Most villagers agreed that spirits had abducted the young child, then returned him after receiving the family's offerings.

To prevent such a tragedy, some mothers pin their hopes on the ritualized protection afforded by a local system of color symbolism. The spirits of the forest are said to be especially partial to red and white—in fact, spirits themselves reportedly wear *pagnes* of these two colors. Accordingly, some Beng mothers take care never to dress their toddlers in red or white when they will be going into the forest, so as to minimize the chance that bush spirits will be drawn to their children and attempt to kidnap them.

Other spirits may have a different motive for stealing a human child: revenge against a person who offended the spirit in some way. Let us consider this narrative:

> A young boy named Janvier went to the fields with his mother, Amlan. She was holding his hand, but he started saying, "Let me go, let me go," and pulled away from her. Instantly he vanished! Amlan tried to find her son, but she couldn't.
>
> It happened that many other women were farming in nearby fields that day, and they all started yelling for the little boy. Finally they found him. When he returned, they asked him where he had been. Janvier replied that an old man had come to take him away, but the old man became annoyed when he heard the women yelling, and he allowed Janvier to return to his mother.

Popular interpretation of this ordeal quickly embraced the theory that the old man was really a spirit who lived in a water hole that adjoined the fields where the boy had disappeared. Women from this region know the water hole well, and they say it houses spirits that impose a demanding set of taboos that women must obey if they want to draw water. Villagers reasoned that the water-hole spirits must have been angry with the village. Probably a woman who had come to draw water had violated one of the taboos demanded by the resident spirits. In their anger, the spirits had abducted the young child.

Perhaps Janvier's own mother had violated a taboo, but perhaps not. In the social universe of the Beng, the community is considered responsible for any resident's misdeeds. Accordingly, villagers think it reasonable that spirits may abduct any child from the village as a way to punish whoever the sinner might be. The notion of a moral community operates very actively in such a model. This narrative also speaks to the Beng conviction that because children have recently come from the spirit world, they may be easily seduced by the *bɔŋzɔ* spirits of the bush, who may remind them of the ancestors' spirits they knew back in *wrugbe*.

Spirits of the Earth

Infants are also subject to the wrath of the Earth itself (*ba*), whose spirit messengers *(bɔŋzɔ)* may convey punishment to infants when adults have violated the Earth's taboos or when the Earth has been invoked as a curse *(ba tō)*. A baby is believed to be vulnerable to spirits of the Earth while still in the mother's womb. Some time before the seventh month of his wife's pregnancy, a husband should sacrifice an egg to the named Earth that is associated with their village. Those who adhere to the local religion are confident that after receiving the sacrifice, the Earth will protect the woman and her fetus through the rest of the pregnancy and the delivery. By contrast, if the husband should neglect to sacrifice an egg, the lives of both mother and baby will be in jeopardy. The only men who are considered exempt from this religious obligation are those who have become devout Christians or Muslims and reject the Beng pantheon for a single god. Yet, to be on the safe side, even some Muslim and Christian husbands continue to offer such sacrifices, in case the Earth spirits are more real than the Muslim holy men and Christian preachers claim (see Gottlieb n.d.a).

Animists maintain that the fetus remains vulnerable to vengeful Earth spirits later, when it is time for the pregnant woman to deliver. As we have seen, if a woman is having trouble delivering her baby even after receiving the usual herbal treatments, a relative may consult a diviner. One diagnosis may be that either the woman herself or a member of her matriclan has committed a sin against the Earth. She may have violated one of the Earth's taboos without acknowledging the lapse and may therefore have neglected to sacrifice something by way of apology. Even if the violation was unintentional, the woman remains responsible for rectifying the wrong. In this case, a relative must immediately offer a sacrifice, usually a chicken, to the Earth to apologize. Then the birth should proceed without problem. Scenarios that explain various forms of fetal distress during labor by reference to spiritual dissatisfactions are common.

~

After a successful delivery, the baby remains susceptible to diseases brought by Earth spirits. The egg the father offers to the Earth during his wife's pregnancy is conceived as a type of spiritual debt incurred by the father toward the Earth *(pɔ gba a pɛŋ wo mi mã*—lit., "the Earth sacrifice has a debt on you"). Soon after the baby is born, the child's mother or father should offer a chicken as sacrifice to the Earth *(tõ bolɛ)* as thanks to the Earth for having protected the baby inside the womb and as repayment of the spiritual debt. People maintain that if this second sacrifice is offered, the Earth will continue to watch over the baby. If the parents neglect the follow-up sacrifice, others worry that the baby is at risk. The Earth will be angry that its debt remains unpaid and may punish the parents for their neglect by making their baby fall ill. If a diviner is not dispatched quickly to diagnose the root of the problem, the infant will soon succumb.

Another common risk to an infant concerns the past behavior of the mother. When a young woman marries for the first time, she must ritually confess the names of any lovers she had before the marriage. If she conceals any names, the Earth may later make her first baby sick. If she consults a diviner soon enough after the baby falls ill, the diviner may discover the cause of the illness and recommend that the proper sacrifice be made immediately— usually an egg, a chicken, or some palm wine. Failure to offer the sacrifice soon after the child's illness begins is said to result in the child's death.

I was once chatting with an aging friend about her life as she lamented the seven children she had lost. Later, a mutual friend explained that at least some of the children had most likely died as punishment of the mother by the Earth. Apparently, as a young woman my companion had neglected to confess the identity of the lover(s) she had had before her marriage. The Earth was displeased and later killed many of her children—or so the village gossips had it. Once again infants had proved vulnerable to the avenging Earth and its spirits. Returning to the *wrugbe* from which they had departed only recently, they had left their mother to grieve.

The Earth may remind a sinner of a spiritual debt by making a baby sick if someone in the extended family of either the baby's mother or father has violated any of the Earth's many taboos and has not yet offered a sacrifice as apology. Because of their continuing ties to *wrugbe,* babies are defined by a high level of vulnerability to the spirits of the Earth that the Beng say normally protect their lives. They are vulnerable to the influence of their ancestors' spirits as well.

Spirits of the Ancestors

Spirits of the bush and of the Earth are joined by a third set of spirits that pose a threat to infants' health. Although a baby leaving *wrugbe* gains a new set of parents in this life, the previous, invisible set of parents from the other world are said to retain their interest in their child. In certain circumstances, these spirit-parents may decide to lure their infant back to *wrugbe*, especially if the *wrugbe* parents are discontent with the parenting behavior of the couple who has inherited their child in this life. For example, if a new mother does not nurse her baby enough or if she neglects to seek adequate medicines when her baby falls sick, the child's *wrugbe* parents may call back their suffering child. The souls of ancestors may also curse infants or young children to avenge their personal disappointments, as in the case of the poorly attended chief recounted in chapter 4.

And then there are witches.

Witches

Witches occupy a vexed space in the Beng cultural imaginary. Most Beng people believe that the workings of witchcraft exist at the same level of "really real"(Geertz 1973a) as the workings of a machete. That does not mean, however, that the work of witches is welcome. On the contrary, many Beng people, whether they live in the village or in the city, make frequent efforts to rid their lives of the threat of witchcraft and fervently wish for a witchcraft-free world. Yet given that witchcraft is said to stem from envy and greed, and that envy and greed seem intrinsic components of the human psyche, all Beng people with whom I have spoken about the subject are resigned both to living in a world that contains witches, and to having to combat witchcraft in their own lives (cf. Geschiere 1997). For their part, despite Western involvement in witchcraft in many eras and places, from colonial Salem, Massachusetts (Demos 1982), to early modern Italy (Ginzburg 1983) to the contemporary United Kingdom (e.g., Luhrmann 1989), many Western observers have long relied on African witchcraft practices as a rationale for racist condemnation of what is dismissively classified as superstition—as if any assertion of access to mystical power, or, for that matter, to any invisible spiritual entity, whether monotheistic or polytheistic, Judeo-Christian or local, male or female, benevolent or malevolent, had any greater claim to incontrovertible reality than any other.

In the Beng world, the level of people's vulnerability to witchcraft is said to form a continuum. Those who are least vulnerable have made efforts to gain spiritual protection and have thereby become the most powerful. But ironically, the powerful include both those who use power licitly to protect the innocent—kings, queens, village chiefs, and matriclan chiefs (Gottlieb 1989b)—and those who use it illicitly to harm others: witches. At the other end of the spectrum, those who are the most vulnerable include infants as a class—tiny creatures who have barely made the transition from their previous life to this one.

To begin our discussion of witches, let us consider this life history:

One day back in 1985, an elderly woman named Afwe Zi came to Philip and me to ask if we could treat a persistent cut on her leg. We tried every curative cream we could find in the pharmacy, but the cut stubbornly refused to heal. We fretted aloud about the mysterious wound, and we began hearing that Afwe had suffered with this cut for many years. It never got worse, never got better—it just stayed there. Later, back in the United States, I had occasion to ask a biomedical doctor about the puzzle, and he suggested that perhaps the wound was ulcerated, which would explain why it had not responded to antibiotic treatment. But the Beng explanation was quite different. In the eyes of the people I spoke to, this persistent wound must be the result of witchcraft.

Afwe Zi had always seemed to possess tremendous poise and calm, an almost uncanny ability to endure the hardship of her wound without complaint. Back in the village in 1993, I started hearing more of Afwe Zi's troubles, and in the process, I discovered the source of her ability to withstand her suffering so patiently. One day, she sat down to tell me her tragic story.

Afwe Zi had given birth to fifteen children. All but one had died as babies or toddlers. Indeed, she had only had more than two children living at the same time on one occasion. For the rest, each of her children had died while she was pregnant with the next one *(dó à do dá lòɛ)*. Eleven had departed this life before learning to walk, although some had been crawling. The remaining three had already begun walking when they died. Each time Afwe told me of another child dying, she clapped her hands and then opened them with an empty gesture—a conventionalized hand sign to denote the concept of zero, nothing (figure 55).

Afwe explained to me that the same disease had killed all fourteen children. As she described it, their heart beat very fast, and they became "as white as paper." On both sides of their rib cage, there was a depression like two holes right under the breastbone. This was where the disease was lodged. Sometimes at night when her babies slept, Afwe saw these depressions move up and down under the *pagne* covering them.

Afwe went on to say that the disease is not all that rare. In Beng, it is called "cut the sides" *(blɛ cīlɛ)*. It seems to come in clumps—many children come down with it at the same time, usually during the dry season when it is very dusty. The illness can attack children from the newborn stage through the time that they can walk and beyond, up to when they are five or six years old; on occasion, even ten year olds can become afflicted with this disease.

Only one of Afwe's fifteen children escaped the terrible illness: her second child, the one who managed to survive childhood. He grew to adulthood, married, and became a father. But a few months before Afwe and I spoke, during the season for clearing the yam fields (which is usually January through March), her adult son's health had started to decline, and he was diagnosed with yellow fever. He recovered somewhat and returned to working on his farm. He cleared new fields and started to make yam

55. After telling her tragic story of having lost fourteen children to the same unknown disease, Afwe Zi makes a hand gesture to indicate, "nothing left."

mounds. But then he fell sick again. One of his sons took him to a hospital in the closest large city, Bouaké, where he was treated and appeared to have been cured. The doctors told him he could return to the village. However, on the evening he was supposed to leave the city, he developed a fever, and he died that very night. His corpse was brought back to the village for burial. It was yellow fever that killed him. He had not been vaccinated against it.

As Afwe Zi told me her life story, she dabbed her eyes with a small square of bark cloth, meant to be carried as a handkerchief of sorts by anyone in mourning to absorb the inevitable waters of grief. Afwe's small bark-cloth fragment, once rough as sand paper, had become as soft as cotton from a lifetime of tears. Clutching the small square of comfort, Afwe told me that on the day before, she had cried all day after hearing the chief announce the funeral of a woman in the village who had just died. Mention of the woman's name reminded Afwe of her son who had recently died, as both he and the woman had initially fallen sick at the same time. Straining to imagine the depths of Afwe's heartache, I could not imagine what to say.

To fill in the silence of suffering, my friend Amenan added her commentary to the melancholy chronicle of Afwe's lost children:

> Children who are afflicted with this disease can only be cured if the disease hasn't been caused by witchcraft. If there's no witchcraft involved, it isn't hard to cure. You get *wrú taà* leaves ("spirits' tobacco") and crush them with the juice of some white kola nuts. You do this behind an old mortar that's no longer used by anyone. You use this to massage the baby with, on the shoulders, back and sides: three times for a boy, four times for a girl.

Amenan also noted that the disease brings a cough with it and added that there is a separate herbal cure for the cough.

Finally, Afwe rejoined the conversation, insisting, "There was witchcraft involved: *jáni*"—there's the reason! I asked Afwe who was responsible for the witchcraft. She replied:

> My mother tried to find out by doing sacrifices. They sacrificed sheep, they sacrificed sheep, they begged them. . . . Me, I've been called a witch, but never, never!! My mother offered palm wine. . . . She gave *sráká* sacrifices to children. It was a diviner who told my mother to offer these sacrifices. She did a lot of them! She asked the witches to release my children.

I asked Afwe if she had ever discovered the identity of any of the witches who had killed her children. She replied, "I know who killed my [adult] son. This is the only witch we were ever able to identify." She explained that the witch was a member of her matriclan (as is usual in most cases of Beng witchcraft) (Gottlieb 1996b:60–62), a female relative I will call Jataa. Afwe added that Jataa was a young woman in her mid-thirties and commented that it is difficult for a witch this young to kill a mature adult of her son's age. But, Afwe claimed, her relative confessed to the deed after the young woman herself fell ill. I must have betrayed a skeptical look, for Afwe quickly insisted that Jataa was such a notorious and active witch that if children spent time with her in the fields, after returning to the village they all came down with a fever. Amenan, who was following the conversation, corroborated Afwe's claim. She added that Jataa was responsible for the current serious illness of a male matriclan elder as well. Amenan also mentioned sotto voce that during the funeral for Afwe's son, Afwe had hurled a number of strong insults at the mother of the young witch.

Another day, I asked Amenan if she had any theories about who had killed Afwe's other fourteen children. Amenan answered, "Some said it was

Afwe's own witchcraft. Last year a boy died. People accused Afwe of killing him. She came here to cry that they had blamed her wrongly. Aba Kouassi and I spent all day consoling her." Through this statement, Amenan implied that she rejected the rumor that Afwe was to blame for her own children's deaths. As her comment reveals, although the identity of witches is often widely agreed on, there is sometimes controversy surrounding a given accusation (see Douglas 1970).

~

I was haunted by Afwe's story, and on our return to the United States, I felt driven to discover the likely biomedical cause of the fourteen infants' deaths. I asked my son's pediatrician if he had any theories and expected to hear of a congenital heart condition or some rare incurable disease. He surprised me by replying that it would be statistically almost unthinkable that such a congenital condition would occur in so many children of the same family. Rather, it sounded to him as if all fourteen babies had died of asthma. Although it would be unusual for asthma to occur in so many children of a single family, this was far more likely than any other scenario he might imagine. When I asked about the "holes" in the chest that Afwe had reported for all her infants, my doctor-consultant explained that if a very observant mother were paying close attention to the breathing pattern of her asthmatic infant who was gasping for breath, this might indeed be how she would describe what she saw (Daniel Picchietti, personal communication, 1993).

Could it really be something so simple? Of course, asthma is a potentially fatal disease, but it can usually be brought under control with Western medicines. If Afwe's fourteen babies had had access to biomedical treatments, conceivably they could all be alive today. Why were these medicines unavailable?

The simplest answer is that no biomedical drugs against asthma were sold in the villages, and a trip to the nearest pharmacy in M'Bahiakro would have been prohibitively expensive. Besides, at thirty miles down the dirt road, the town was a world away. Another narrative illustrates the vast geocultural distance that a villager must travel in search of biomedicine even when the drugs are brought right into the village. As a means of investigating how local belief, cultural practice, and poverty can intersect in the health of Beng infants, let us consider the short biography of a child who lived for a brief time in the same village as Afwe Zi.

The Ways of Witches versus the Wages of Poverty:
A Case Study of Tetanus

One morning, I was about to get my day's work organized when a young woman I didn't recognize entered our compound holding a newborn who was screaming hysterically. Like others in the compound, I was startled by this unusual sound: living most of their lives attached to someone's back, Beng babies are rarely so miserable. I asked what the problem was. The mother said she didn't know but she was searching for medicines, and she wanted to know if I had any.

I looked questioningly across the courtyard at Amenan, who walked over to examine the baby. As she did so, the infant screamed again, and his arms and legs stiffened up noticeably, his back arching in a posture reminiscent of the startle pose. Alarmingly, the miserable infant repeated this disturbing routine every few minutes.

"I'm sure it's tetanus," Amenan whispered to me.

"How do you know?" I asked skeptically.

"I saw lots of cases in the villages when I did that rural health program with the nuns," she answered matter-of-factly. "Once you've seen a case, you can never make a mistake about it. Look at how stiff his arms and legs are."

Amenan scolded the young mother, whose name, I discovered, was Au: "Why didn't you bring the baby over sooner?" News of the free daily health clinic that Philip and I offered was quite public in the region.

"He wasn't that sick until today," Au answered, "and besides, I've been looking for *sɔŋ ti la*"—"African"(herbal) medicines—"the past few days."

I reached deep into my memory to recall what little I knew about tetanus: I recalled my mother always warning me about playing with rusty nails. What would a newborn be doing touching old hardware? Remaining doubtful of Amenan's diagnosis despite her remarkably accurate diagnostic record, Philip and I flipped through our medical text until we reached the page about tetanus. Slowly, sadly, we read the description. On each point it matched the infant we saw before us. The final sentence was the most alarming. In the best of circumstances, with prompt injections of penicillin, we read, a case of tetanus has only a 50 percent chance of being cured.[4] We knew quite well that there was no injectable penicillin in the village.

Sighing as the weight of this terrible prediction began to sink in, Philip and I offered to drive Au and her baby to wherever we could find the nearest penicillin. Amenan mentioned, "A van of nurses came to Totogbe yesterday to give people shots. Maybe they have the medicine the baby needs." This was welcome news, as the Beng village of Totogbe was less than five miles away. Even on the dusty, bumpy dirt road, we thought we could drive there in under half an hour. Philip and I informed Nathaniel of the new plan for the day. Playing with some children at the edge of the compound, he did not protest at this interruption. By then, several weeks into our stay in a Beng village, Nathaniel was used to the unexpected.

Meanwhile, I informed Au that we lacked the proper medicines for the baby, but that we were willing to drive her and her son to Totogbe.

"Isn't there anything you can do here?" Au asked, looking worried.

We repeated that we did not have the proper medicine. She hesitated and, frowning, mumbled that she had to return to her house to get ready. Half an hour later she returned, baby in arms and accompanied by her mother.

When we arrived in Totogbe, we rushed out of the car to find the nurses and blurted out the problem. They shook their heads in regret, explaining that they did not have the right form of penicillin—the form they had was too strong for a newborn. They advised us to drive to the closest dispensary, in M'Bahiakro. We were dismayed by this advice because it was a Sunday, and we worried that we might not find the doctor in. Moreover, because the nearest phone was in M'Bahiakro itself, we had no means to call ahead to inquire. Thirty more bumpy, dirt-road miles separated us from this knowledge. Nevertheless, we knew they represented the baby's only hope for recovery.

We explained the situation to Au and her mother. The two women exchanged unhappy glances. Au confided that she and her mother were concerned about how much money would be necessary for the trip: they knew they would have to buy both food and medicines while in M'Bahiakro, and they didn't have any cash at all.

Philip and I offered to support the medical and food expenses. Au and her mother discussed our offer at some length. Finally, they accepted it—though not, it seemed to us, without some reluctance. This unexpected reaction did not escape Philip, who commented to me, "They don't seem to want to go to M'Bahiakro even if we pay for everything. What's the story?"

"I don't know, it's strange," I replied, frustrated that I had no anthropological expertise to offer. At a loss for an explanation, we both suspected witchcraft.

～

Arrived in M'Bahiakro, we were relieved to find that the overworked doctor was in his office, seeing patients on Sunday. He examined the baby perfunctorily and confirmed the diagnosis of tetanus. He informed us glumly that the baby had at best a 50 percent chance of surviving, and he did not seem to believe the hopeful half of his statistics. Without the air of urgency that we anticipated would signal some cause for optimism, he instructed us quietly, "Go see the nurse in the next building. He'll give the baby a shot."

Quickly we crossed the courtyard to the hospital building and found the nurse on duty busy on his rounds. We explained the situation and he told us casually that we would need to buy the necessary medicines and supplies in the pharmacy in town. We were appalled to learn that the hospital did not have penicillin, syringes, needles, IV drips, Valium, or bandages. The medical system was supposedly subsidized by the state. At the time of our last visit eight years before, all these supplies would have been routinely stocked; this unwelcome news was a disturbing sign of how the economy and basic infrastructure of Côte d'Ivoire were in shocking decline.

We soon returned to the hospital with the various medicines and supplies on our list. I expected the nurse to start the IV drip right away. However, he hesitated when he noticed several homemade bracelets wrapped around the baby's wrists. Dismissively, he asked the mother in French, *"Tout ça, c'est quoi?"*—What's all this stuff?

Au did not understand a word of French, but clearly she understood the patronizing sense of superiority underlying the remark. I responded for her: "They can't harm the baby, just leave them there and let's start the IV, okay?"

Every Beng mother lovingly crafts these bracelets, often from recipes handed down by her mother, her grandmother, her aunts. As an Ivoirian himself, surely the nurse was aware of the local cultural value of the jewelry. His question was merely meant to provoke and to show disapproval, to exhibit his superiority, his cultural distance from the village, his immersion in modernity.

Finally he started the IV drip and the Valium began to take effect, calming the screaming newborn. At least for the moment, the baby seemed to have stabilized. We left several days worth of food money with Au and her mother, and we returned to the village, at once exhausted, depressed, and outraged.

Two days later, up in the village, we heard bad news. Au had returned but the penicillin had not worked: the baby was declining rapidly, and he might not last another day. A hospital nurse had told Au that she had better take the baby back up to the village to die, for if he died in M'Bahiakro it would be very costly. There would be fees for the cemetery, fees for the casket, fees for the death certificate to be issued at the mayor's office, and fees paid to the gravediggers. It was much cheaper to die in the village.

That evening, Amenan and I forced ourselves to visit Au's compound and offer our condolences about the now officially dying baby. I was shocked to see that the newborn, who was not yet dead, lay on his back covered head to toe in cloths, as for a corpse. Amenan whispered to me grimly, "It's as if he's already dead. One could say he is dead." I had brought along a camera to record this tragedy for a scholarly presentation some day, but faced with the unutterably sad scene, I could not even bring myself to remove the lens cap. I tried to plan how I would break the awful news to Nathaniel. A middle-class boy raised in America, he had never considered the idea of a baby dying.

~

We started with a single, simple fact. A newborn was struggling for his life, his tiny body thrashing and convulsing in his mother's arms, his grand-mother's arms, my arms. Two days later, he was dead of tetanus. How do we comprehend this tragedy? There are many layers of explanation. Let us start with the local.

The Beng would ask a version of the same famous question that the Azande of the Sudan have posed for several generations of anthropologists (Evans-Pritchard 1937): Why did *this* baby come down at *this* time with *this* sickness? We were dealing with a newborn who, at only about ten days old, had barely entered this life; in Beng eyes, he was still mostly living in the afterlife. Did he miss his former home too much and had he decided to return? That was one plausible local explanation, considering, as we have seen, that Beng infants are accorded as much volition as are adults.

However, in Beng villages, as in much of Africa, social ties also rule bio-logical processes in tangible ways. It was possible that the baby's life in this world was cut short by problems festering in his social universe. Suspecting such processes at work, I queried Amenan to see if she had any theories. She proceeded to tell me that there were many social ruptures in the biography of the baby's mother, Au, that might indeed be relevant. Thus, expanding the Azande question outward sociologically, we might ask: Why should *this mother* suffer at this time with this baby's sickness?

When Au came of age some years ago, her parents told her that they wanted her to marry someone "in the family," in conformity with the complex set of arranged marriage rules that still determine many Beng young women's first marriages (Gottlieb 1996b:72–96). Au had a lover—we'll call him Yao—so she tried to refuse this arranged marriage. But she was forced to marry her arranged-marriage partner. Yao was so jealous that he consulted a distant Muslim magician (*clameau*) who works with charms. The *clameau* bewitched a *pagne* cloth that Yao then presented to Au's new husband as a present, aiming to make the husband impotent and ruin the marriage. Soon after re-ceiving the cloth, the husband fell sick, and he consulted a diviner to discover the cause of his mysterious illness. The diviner revealed the story of the *pagne*. Because the husband had discovered the magic soon after the *pagne* had been bewitched, its magic had not entirely taken effect—which is to say that he had not yet become impotent. However, he was so distressed by the story the diviner told him that he soon divorced Au and fled the village for a job in the city.

Au took a new lover, with whom she became pregnant. But while she was pregnant, this man left her. She took another lover, her current partner, who agreed to serve as the father of the baby still in her womb once she went through childbirth—with the afflicted infant whose life we had tried in vain to save. For his part, Au's father, Jean-Paul, remained adamantly opposed to this latest union, as it perpetuated the rupture of the legitimate marriage he had arranged for his wayward daughter. Thus, when Au gave birth to her son, Jean-Paul rejected his daughter's current lover as the legitimate father of his new grandson. To signal his rejection of this union, Jean-Paul bestowed his own family name on his new grandson, refusing to allow his daughter's current lover to name the boy. He did this in full knowledge that this naming decision violated the current laws of his country. The Ivoirian government had recently issued a proclamation that a child could only be given the family name of his father, not that of his grandfather, unless the grandfather or another relative petitioned the local justice office, and Jean-Paul was aware of the law.

Clearly such an act of legal defiance could only be motivated by a deep commitment to traditional marriage practices and an insistence on the legitimacy of arranged marriage—even one that had ended in de facto divorce. For her part, Au was well aware of her father's act of subversive naming, as her divorce from her arranged-marriage husband had long been a source of family dispute.

What role did this family drama have in the infant's birth and death? Sociologically, it must have had much to do with his fate. In American terms, this baby was far from a "wanted child"—the deathly ill newborn was literally conceived in trouble. Both reflecting and further contributing to this social drama, as Victor Turner would have termed it (1957), was gossip about the possible involvement of witchcraft. Those familiar with the drama expressed to me their hunch that the baby was being bewitched by members of his would-be father's family, who were angry that the infant's maternal grandfather had, in their view, illegitimately claimed him. Let us recall that once the infant fell sick, his mother hesitated for two days before bringing him to see Philip and me to request medicines. And once she did, Au hesitated further before agreeing to go first to Totogbe, then to M'Bahiakro in search of the necessary injections for her infant. Could it be that Au was not fully motivated to save her son's life?

Such an interpretation sounds harsh, defying as it does the common Western belief in every mother's dedication to her children's survival due to the widely posited biological urge toward maternal nurture. But this assumption of a maternal instinct may be an ethnocentric one, and in any case, it does not appear warranted in the case at hand. Perhaps a more reasonable interpretation would be the following: Au felt wildly ambivalent—though perhaps, like many people who might find themselves ensnared in such a situa-

tion, inarticulate about that ambivalence—as she was caught between circumstances that both echoed and perpetuated her structural misery. On the one
hand, she had the usual mother's love for her infant. This surely motivated
her to seek indigenous herbal medicines—*sɔŋ ti la*—for her sick child in the
first instance. When it became undeniably clear that these medicines were
having no effect, her mother's love must have motivated her to follow the next
available route, that of requesting medicines from visiting "white people." On
the other hand, her ambivalence may have led her to hesitate in seeking such
medicines actively and in accepting them once the economic cost became
apparent. If witchcraft was involved, she may have wondered, would any
Western medicine be effective?

The complex social entanglements of this ten-day-old child further exacerbated the witchcraft now threatening him. The baby was the product of a
voluntary union, but one that had ended before Au had given birth. Au was
currently involved with another man who was devoted enough to accept social
paternity for the child still in her womb. Yet Au's own father continued to
reject this man as the social father of her child. The rejection signaled that
the family remained deeply divided over Au's reproductive life. Perhaps an
unconscious understanding of all this is what prevented Au from coming to
Philip's and my informal health clinic before it was too late.

Once she consulted us and we told her the bad news—that we would
have to take extraordinary measures if we were to have hope of saving her
child—perhaps it became clearer than ever to Au what the costs would be of
maintaining this infant born amidst a complex set of entanglements. To put
it crudely, it may have been the disastrously high economic price of saving
the baby that told Au just how much at risk this infant was in the broader
sense—a sense encompassed by the sociology of the newborn's young but
fraught life. As others have argued in investigating the agonizing decisions
mothers living in poverty have to make when faced with their children's illnesses (e.g., Einarsdóttir forthcoming), the failure to take every possible measure to acquire costly health care is far too complex a decision to be judged
easily by an observer.

~

So we have answered the sociological part of the famous Azande question:
We know why it was *this baby*, and even more broadly, why it was *this mother*
of this baby, who suffered. But what about the medical aspect of the Azande
question—why was the newborn afflicted with *this* particular sickness and not
another?

Although the tragedy may have resulted from the simple failure to seek
an effective remedy in time, charting the contours of this failure takes us to

a wider circle of investigation. Do the Beng have indigenous methods of preventing tetanus? I learned that there was an indigenous preventive medicine, but that it was no longer considered effective. Amenan commented: "A lot of Beng people ruined the medicine with witchcraft. In fact, the old women say that almost *all* indigenous medicines have been ruined by witchcraft nowadays [since independence]. One reason is that witches' medicines are shown on television and thus have become more widespread!" This attitude betrays a certain hopelessness: a rise in tetanus and other diseases is inevitable if the local preventive methods no longer work. Witchcraft serves here as a convenient explanation, perhaps taking on the metaphorical burden of the evil rampant in modernity.

I learned that there was also an indigenous cure for tetanus but that this was no longer effective either: "People say that in order to treat tetanus once someone has contracted it, the healer would need to kill another child [by witchcraft] in place of the one that would be saved, and nowadays few people want to go to this drastic length to treat someone." In the previous comment, the rise in witchcraft was imputed as the reason for the failure of traditional medicine; here the increasing *fear* of witchcraft is operative. Although seemingly opposed, the two comments are linked in a chain whose effect is increasing inaction in the face of increasing scourge.

Beyond such local techniques, surely the infant should have received protection against tetanus through the umbilical cord. Scientists have gathered ample evidence that the vast majority of newborns are well protected against tetanus if their mothers have been inoculated with at least two doses of tetanus toxoid prior to becoming, or while, pregnant (Dietz, Galazka, van Loon, and Cochi 1997). Indeed, medical researchers know that protecting newborns from tetanus "depends exclusively on maternal antibody transfer." Given this, the World Health Organization (WHO) now recommends that all women be vaccinated every ten years (the estimated duration of the vaccine's effectiveness) to protect both themselves and their current and future newborns from tetanus (Pasetti, Dokmetjian, Brero, Eriksson, Ferrero, and Manghi 1997: 255).[5] If Au had been up-to-date on her tetanus vaccinations, her infant probably would not have contracted tetanus at all.

In fact, Au had never been vaccinated against tetanus. In the late twentieth century, some sixty years after dissemination of the tetanus vaccine became widespread (McGrew 1985:335), how is such a lapse possible? A tetanus vaccination program had been in place in rural Côte d'Ivoire for several years, with medically equipped vans sent to even the remotest Beng villages at regular intervals. Ironically, I had witnessed the arrival of one such van just two days before Au presented her newborn to our compound.

So why had Au not availed herself of the opportunity to be vaccinated? "Because it was too expensive," a friend explained on Au's behalf. My recollection of the medical van scene of two days earlier gained new poignancy. The nurses had told me that the shots are free, but villagers had filled in the missing footnotes. One friend explained:

> You have to pay for the needle. That costs 25 CFA.[6] And then they have to record it in your little medical record notebook *(cahier)*. If you don't have one already, you have to buy one. That's really expensive. If you buy it from the nurses, they charge 100 CFA. So you see, the shot's not free at all. That's why a lot of villagers don't get one.

Au had apparently belonged to this category.

My ethnographic observations of the encounters between Beng villagers and the non-Beng nurses uncovered further possible factors that discouraged people from receiving shots. The nurses had acted arrogantly. Although none of them spoke the Beng language, many of them could speak either Baule or Jula, both widely spoken languages in Côte d'Ivoire in which most Beng are quite competent. But the nurses chose to parade their modernity by speaking—or rather, barking—their orders exclusively in French.[7] Since very few village women speak any French at all, the nurses' instructions mostly fell on deaf ears. Those women who did stand in line for shots for themselves or their children simply did so on faith. When I asked them from which illnesses the shots would be protecting them or their children, the women I questioned simply shrugged and replied that whatever illnesses the shots prevented, the shots were good.

With such facts we can begin to understand why Au and her newborn were unprotected against tetanus. But what happened with the infant himself? In his short time in this life, how did he manage to contract the fatal disease?

The available biomedical literature explains that neonatal tetanus is "usually due to infection through the open end of the severed umbilical cord" (*Stedman's Illustrated Medical Dictionary* 1982).[8] Prime among the suspects for the agent of such an infection is whatever device was used to sever the umbilical cord. I asked what had been used during Au's childbirth.

"An old razor blade," Amenan told me.

"Why not a new one?" I asked, dreading to hear the answer I could now anticipate.

"I'm sure it was because she couldn't afford to buy a new one," Amenan answered plainly. In the villages, the price of a package of new razor blades at a boutique is roughly the equivalent of twenty-five cents in the United States. Given that this seemingly modest but locally prohibitive price makes the use of unsterile objects inevitable, the very first act of bringing an infant into this life thus becomes the potential agent of its death.[9]

This leads us to the next in the ring of questions we must force ourselves to ask. How common are such deaths in villages such as the one I have described—was this death an isolated one, or was it part of a broader pattern? If the specific concatenation of social circumstances leading to neglect of this particular sick baby is now accounted for, his contraction of the disease remains to be contextualized. Here is where numbers accrue a horrifying force. Some researchers estimate that as many as "400,000 deaths occur annually from neonatal tetanus" (Dietz, Galazka, van Loon, and Cochi 1997); others offer estimates of up to 500,000 (Stanfield and Galazka 1984, cited in Koenig 1992:18). The death we witnessed is therefore an infinitesimally tiny part of an enormous medical trend. How do we begin to make sense of mind-numbing statistics such as these? One way is to tell stories such as Au's. Behind each one of those 400,000 or 500,000 deaths there is a family who mourns—and perhaps a mother who is wildly ambivalent, trying to find ways to cure her sick child even as she weakly hesitates because some problematic aspect of her biography discourages curing this particular baby.

Another way to understand these overwhelming figures is to locate them at a broader level yet. These roughly half a million deaths are far from evenly distributed worldwide. In 1998, only forty-five deaths from neonatal tetanus occurred in the United States (Centers for Disease Control and Prevention n.d.), and a country such as "Sweden records less than 10 tetanus deaths annually" (McGrew 1985:335). Each one of the deaths behind such impressively low figures must be attributable to an odd concatenation of peculiar circumstances converging in an unlikely scenario. By contrast, 80 percent of the more than 400,000 deaths from neonatal tetanus each year now occur in merely twelve of the world's countries. Six of the twelve countries are located in West, Central, and Northeast Africa; the other six are in East, South, and Southeast Asia (World Health Organization 1996). India and China alone account for about 100,000 each of those deaths. With such a skewed distribution, omitting the entire continents of Europe, the Americas, and Australia from statistically high rates of occurrence, clearly the worldwide pattern of neonatal tetanus incidence is anything but haphazard.

And so what seems incomprehensible suddenly becomes obscenely predictable, part of a broader trend of almost unthinkable disparity between the health and disease patterns of the so-called First and Third World (Muller 1982). Yet when the grotesque becomes understandable, that is no place to stop, which leads us to yet another, more globalized version of the famous Azande question: Why should *any* babies *anywhere* contract tetanus? My answer must be a heterodoxically un-Azande one: They should not.

～

What about the ethics of conducting fieldwork in such circumstances? When indigenous beliefs about tetanus challenge those of Western biomedicine, how should the visiting anthropologist mediate that conceptual canyon? In the case I have reported, Philip's and my chain of decision making was overdetermined; the reasons behind it require the proverbial more hands than two to elucidate. In the worldview to which we subscribe, not only is each human life sacred, but each person—male or female, infant or adult, rich or poor—is worth as much as every other. When we were faced with a dying person, my husband's and my commitment was almost unthinkingly to do what we could to reverse the seemingly doomed biomedical direction in which the unfortunate baby appeared headed, even if his mother and grandmother seemed less than fully committed to such an effort. Our worried young son's urgings only echoed our own inclination to intervene.

And yet in retrospect, it was clear that the sick baby was doomed. Shouldn't I have seen this? Shouldn't paying careful attention to the social circumstances of the baby's life—my stock in trade, after all—have alerted me to his fate? Moreover, had Philip and I performed a quick, insurance company–style cost/benefit analysis and come up with the negative scenario as the likeliest one, should we not have made the rational choice to forego treatment? While this might have appeared cold-hearted, perhaps in the end it would have been the opposite. On the financial side, we would have conserved scarce resources—my grant funds—for patients who had a far better chance of survival according to sociological as well as medical indications. On the social and psychological side, we could also have considered the quality of life. If the miraculous had come about and the afflicted baby survived his early medical ordeal, would the life facing him as an illegitimate child who was subject to an early custody battle have proved a long and fulfilling one? Or would his mother have hesitated at the time of the next inevitable illness due to the same uncertainty about her maternity and its responsibilities, pulled in two directions as she was by father and lover? Did this newborn have much chance of surviving past childhood in any case? If not, did it make sense—to put it in the crudest terms—to invest in him?

These questions unsettle, but anthropological fieldwork challenges us to jump outside our skins and reimagine reality from another perspective. Thus the best question under these circumstances may not be whether it made sense generically to put forth every effort to save this dying baby. Rather, perhaps we might more productively ask whether it made *Beng* sense to put forth such effort. Here, the answer appears to be no. Will this answer change my behavior if I am confronted by a similar scenario the next time around in Bengland? That I cannot yet predict. Understanding the contours of social life and living by that understanding are two somewhat distinct intellectual and emotional universes. At least the anthropological project can offer us the possibility of both their imaginings.

~

The local and the global, we now know, are inextricably intertwined. One can hardly comprehend one segment of social life without exploring the other, even if the local is, like the Beng village I have discussed here, seemingly quite removed from global concerns. Fair enough. But what do we do when the two systems of knowledge embodied in these cultural zones collide?

On the one hand, we have a local system of knowledge that, like local systems of knowledge everywhere, concentrates on the local. In the case I have detailed here, reputed witchcraft activity and social disruption surely played a determining role in the medical decisions that Au made for her child each step of the way. On the other end of the spectrum, the global factors I have hauled out for our depressing perusal focus on big numbers, big programs . . . big failures. As scholars have charted for some years now, African poverty is overdetermined. Several centuries of European extraction of scarce natural and human resources have combined to make a mockery of the Western model of development (see chapter 11).

In the intersection between these two sets of factors, a baby lives a brief ten days, then dies a violent, convulsive death. Throughout the world, 400,000 or 500,000 more stories each year offer their own tragic contours. In one small corner of the West African rain forest, where is the best space for a Beng parent to mourn?

Fewa Funerals: A First Time to Mourn

As I mentioned earlier, the funeral for the first child to die in a family has a special name: *fewa*.[10] For Beng speakers, the very name *fewa* conjures up an especially painful dose of grief. Upon hearing the news that parents have experienced the death of a child for the first time, relatives and neighbors immediately describe the death by saying in hushed tones that convey an extra measure of sadness, "It will be a *fewa* funeral." So long as one or both of the parents are still alive, the ceremony is conducted for the first child in a family to die no matter what the age of the one who died—even if the deceased is an adult.[11]

As a parent who has never lost a living child, I find it impossible to deploy my anthropological imagination to its full extent in envisioning this scenario. The act of empathy is often premised on a Stanislavskian leap: in the early twentieth century, when student actors had difficulty finding their way into the consciousness and, especially, the feelings of a character they were to play, the great Russian theatre director Constantin Stanislavski advised his pupils to try imagining an analogous event that had occurred in their own lives and then to transfer the emotion the memory engendered toward the character they were trying to inhabit (Stanislavski 1948, 1977). Many cultural anthropologists are, if unknowingly, Stanislavskian in their approach to ethnography. Both in the field and in the classroom, we often seek parallels from our own experiences to help us envision the emotional burdens, frustrations, and pleasures of the lives of anthropological Others. Some of the most evocative writing in anthropology is premised on this approach.

A reader can also find a cognitive pathway into an alien practice if some analogy, even a distant one, can be identified from his or her biography. Suddenly the alien, the exotic, the Other appears far less so, and the possibility of empathy is created; simultaneously, any latent impulse toward ethnocentrism or racism is diminished.

When it comes to the issue of dying babies, however, it is too painful for me to take the Stanislavskian challenge. Unlike many parents in the developing world, most parents in the urban West have the luxury of never having to experience—or even to imagine—the deaths of our children, and we gladly exercise this option. I believe that most Beng parents would approve of this emotional and cognitive timidity. As we have seen, local etiquette forbids villagers who have never lost a child to attend a *fewa* funeral, and especially to enter the room in which the cadaver is laid out (which is invariably the kitchen or salon of the house in which the child lived). In earlier times, when villagers lived in round houses with crown roofs, no woman who had never lost a child was even permitted to enter the courtyard of the mourning household, even if the mother of the deceased was as closely related as her own full sister. Beng children are even more strictly barred from *fewa* funerals than they are from attending other funerals.

Should anyone violate this rule and witness a *fewa* funeral without having lost a child, they would put at risk the lives of all of their offspring, including those who are not yet even conceived. To avoid such a tragedy, the cadaver should always be buried very soon after the death, in order to minimize the time during which mourners might have exposure to the corpse. Although such haste is generally practiced for all deaths occurring in the village, it is especially imperative in the case of a *fewa* funeral.

The rituals surrounding a *fewa* burial are considered difficult (*grégré*).

They include the obligation both to wash frequently with certain herbal con-coctions that are considered to be very powerful ritual medicines *(la)* and to engage in what are considered embarrassing sexual practices. To some con-temporary parents, these ritual requirements seem such a traumatic ordeal that if they claim adherence to Christianity or Islam, they may opt not to undergo the demanding rituals when they lose their first child, invoking their religious affiliation as their reason. Nevertheless, other mourning parents con-tinue to endure the ritual. Two consultants outlined for me what happens to the mourning parents, and their descriptions closely matched what I saw when I discreetly observed one *fewa* ritual that occurred near our compound.

The Fewa Ritual: A Case Study of Mourning

For some time, our neighbor Akissi and her husband KofiKro had been endeavoring to help their young son, Pierre, to walk. He was over two years old but still had not mastered this critical skill. His parents tried all manner of indigenous treatments to no avail. They even asked Philip and me for pills. We were pained to acknowledge that we knew of no medicine to facilitate success in the challenging task of learning to walk.

I knew Akissi and KofiKro were eager to help Pierre for two reasons. First, of course, was the obvious worry about their young child's development. But they also had a more personal concern: so long as Pierre was not yet walking, his parents were forbidden to resume their sex life. As theirs was a monoga-mous marriage, this was a more onerous burden for KofiKro than it would be for a polygynously married man. According to village gossip networks, the couple was desperate.

Meanwhile, Pierre was looking more and more frail. Every day seemed to bring less hope that he would ever learn to walk. Finally, one day, the drums pounded out the sad but not unexpected news: Pierre had died.

I soon made my way over to the courtyard and found Akissi and KofiKro sitting, solemn and obviously grieving, in the salon of their house with two other women. In the kitchen, following *fewa* custom, their son's body was already lain out on top of a white bark cloth and white sheet and covered with another white sheet; a small cotton ball was located near his head. Five female elders who had themselves been through *fewa* sat nearby, one of them fanning the cadaver with leaves to chase away the flies. Soon, a few men came to carry away the small body for burial. The mourning parents remained in the room—it would be too painful for them to watch the burial—but all the other women left for the gravesite. The cadaver was interred quickly at the edge of the forest. As is customary for a *fewa* funeral, from the moment fol-lowing the burial it was henceforth taboo to cry any more about the death.[12]

After the burial, the *fewa* rituals began in earnest. Philip and I watched from a distance, reluctant to intrude. Pierre's mother untressed her long, thick hair, achieving the intended effect of looking a bit wild, and she removed her clothes, which would be replaced by a white bark cloth wrapped around her body. Pierre's father put on a similar bark cloth from the waist down. A woman from the village who had herself undergone *fewa* brought in a large calabash filled with ritual medicine with which she would wash the parents. Soon she accompanied KofiKro and Akissi to their baby son's new grave, where they stooped in front of a nearby rotted tree trunk and stripped so the ritual specialist could wash them.

Following this, the mourning parents entered a new house constructed for the purpose of the ritual. There they sat . . . and sat. They stayed there for three days, with two or three female ritual specialists remaining with them to oversee their activities. It was said that the behavior of the mourning parents during the ritually charged period of *fewa* would determine their future behavior, so it must be especially meritorious. For example, during the daytime, Akissi and KofiKro were not permitted to nap. If they were to doze off, people believe, after the period of mourning the couple would sleep excessively for the rest of their lives. Of course, lazy parents would never produce enough food to feed their children, so this would be a disaster.

Right after dawn on the morning of the third day, another attendant came to lead Akissi and her husband off to the edge of the forest. There the attendant shaved all the couple's body hair and, for KofiKro, all the hair on his head. On Akissi, just a small, round tuft of hair was left in the front of her head, in a style that is also worn by new widows and widowers. During the day, Akissi and KofiKro's ritual attendants made beadless string necklaces to put on them.

Early on the morning of the fourth day, an elaborate and especially "difficult" (*grégré*) portion of the ritual occurred. Women who have never lost a child may not even look over in the direction of the ceremony. I learned this as I was heading over to observe the activities and was chased away quite brusquely. Taking it as a personal rebuff, I returned, dejected, to my home, where some neighbors came to console me. They assured me that they were not permitted to witness the ritual either, as they had not lost any children themselves. Later I heard a description of the activities I had been forbidden to witness.

Akissi and her husband were ritually washed, and a set of elaborate medicinal paints and jewelry were applied to their bodies by two elderly female specialists, who painted some of the green herbal medicine on their own faces as well. Water was poured into the gourd containing the herbal medicine, chalky white clay *(sɛpɛ)* was crumbled into it, and to this *nonú* leaves were added. The couple took this mixture with them as they walked around the village to greet everyone and thank them for having helped them through the *fewa* ritual. As they approached each compound, they dipped some *nonú* leaves in the herbal mixture and sprinkled the mixture around, and Akissi ritually stamped her foot on the doorway. After they reached the last compound, they passed by the old women sitting near their son's grave to report that they had finished their circuit. Then they returned home.

At their house, the women in charge of the ritual directed Akissi and KofiKro to sit down on chairs and then rise four times before allowing them to sit on their own. Finally the couple was allowed to sit quietly and wait for everyone from the village to come to their compound and greet them in turn. As the villagers reached Akissi and KofiKro's house, they ritually welcomed the couple back to the village, then washed their own hands, heads, shoulders, and chests in special medicinal water. All the women of the village brought their young children to wash their hands in this purifying water.

Later, Akissi and KofiKro went to the grave site. Akissi carried a hoe and KofiKro carried a machete—the prime agricultural tools for women and men, respectively—and they also each held a piece of a gourd. When they arrived at the tomb, they put the gourd fragments on the ground. With their backs to each other, they each put their right foot on their gourd piece and, on instructions from the ritual specialist, they pressed down on the pieces at the same time to crack them. Were they symbolically smashing the life of their child who was still alive only four days ago—and undoubtedly was still alive in their hearts?

Following a full month of these and other *fewa* funerary ritual practices, the mourning couple offered their clothes as payment to one of the attending ritual specialists. This marked the close of the *fewa* season. Akissi and KofiKro might someday suffer the misfortune of losing another child, but they would never again have to undergo the rigors and humiliations of *fewa*.

Conclusion

As we have seen, a view held commonly by rural Beng adults is that babies usually decide to remain in this world as long as life seems hospitable—if the mother and others in the family are warm and loving, offer the baby plenty of good food, entertain the little one, find effective medicines when the child is sick, and wash the baby twice a day and decorate the baby with jewelry that the infant craves from *wrugbe*. If all these conditions are met, an infant will normally be content and will opt to stay in this life, or at least the baby will try to do so. Still, the depredations or temptations of spirits or witches may ultimately prove overwhelming.

With such a model accounting for infant survival and infant mortality, it is clear that most Beng adults privilege the role of the spiritual in seeking an explanation for the medical suffering that so many of their infants endure. At the same time, Beng villagers, youths and adults alike, are, of course, acutely aware of their poverty. Some see the two phenomena as interlinked, but others see them as independent of each other. Before moving on in the final chapter to a more theoretically engaged discussion of the relations between these two explanations, let me end this chapter with a narrative.

One morning, an acquaintance—I'll call her Ajua—came over to tell me about two maladies that were afflicting her. First, she had a skin eruption that was bothering her, and she asked me for medication to clear it up. I asked her to tell me more about the symptoms, and Ajua told me that she had already been to the medical clinic in town, where she had been diagnosed with pellagra. The clinic staff had given her medications, which had been effective, but she had no money to renew the prescription once her first supply was gone, and the symptoms were starting up again. Secondly, Ajua confided that she had not gotten her period since her last child was born about three years before.

After consulting a medical text, I glanced up and noticed Ajua's three-year-old son's severely distended stomach. From my reading, I was fairly sure that this was produced by the same cause as was his mother's condition: malnutrition. I shared the diagnosis with Ajua. She seemed quite discouraged by the news, but she did not dispute its accuracy. She agreed to accept the vitamins and cans of sardines I offered her. To complement them, I offered an explanation of basic nutrition Western-style, complete with recommendations I knew she could not possibly afford to enact. As she nodded, agreeing to search for eggs, vegetables and meats to cook more regularly, we both knew her search would prove in vain, hampered by her lack of funds.

A little later, her cousin, who had been listening to the conversation, confided that Ajua was not only suffering from pellagra, she was also being bewitched. Indeed, it was witchcraft that had brought on the disease in the first place, her cousin alleged, and witchcraft that accounted for the return of the symptoms as soon as Ajua finished the various medicines people gave her.

After I have lived for so long in Beng villages, both explanations—witchcraft and poverty—have come to seem to me equally plausible, equally real. Overdetermination, I was convinced, was surely the most realistic way to account for the complexities of Beng realities.

CHAPTER ELEVEN

From Wrugbe to Poverty

Situating Beng Babies in the World at Large

> Understanding a form of life, or anyway some aspects of it to
> some degree, and convincing others that you have indeed done
> so, involves more than the assembly of telling particulars or the
> imposition of general narratives. It involves bringing figure and
> ground, the passing occasion and the long story, into coincident
> view.
>
> CLIFFORD GEERTZ, *After the Fact: Two Countries,*
> *Four Decades, One Anthropologist*

> In the world of supermodernity people are always, and never, at
> home.
>
> MARC AUGÉ, *Non-Places: Introduction to an Anthropology*
> *of Supermodernity*

When I first came to Bengland, I often observed young babies grinning and
even giggling as only babies can while someone—a parent, an aunt or uncle,
a cousin or older sibling, a neighbor—propped them up into a semisitting
or semistanding position on their lap and sang rhythmically: *ceŋ káká, ceŋ
káká, ceŋ káká,* over and over. The older person would gaily chant these ono-
matopoetic words—meant to imitate the surprisingly delicate ringing of iron
bells—while holding the tiny child under the armpits and merrily raising and
lowering the baby in rhythm to the lilting melody. From this routine, infants
learned to associate the crooning and bouncing of *ceŋ káká* with joy.

Given this pleasurable association, if a baby cried for no apparent reason,
one method to cheer up the unhappy child was to sing *ceŋ káká* and dance
the baby gently up and down. Moreover, the song's rhythmic tune was intended to echo the sound of the drums that are played during the Crui dance
that tradition-minded Beng girls and young women put on yearly to honor
their Muslim neighbors celebrating the end of Ramadan (figure 56). Thus
the singing of *ceŋ káká* to infants was additionally meant as a precursor for
teaching them to perform the associated Crui dance, which made the *ceŋ káká*
routine as much a dance lesson—and a lesson in religious tolerance—as a

56. "Animist" girls and women dance "Crui" to honor their Muslim neighbors who are celebrating the end of Ramadan. Photograph by Philip Graham.

singing session. Indeed, as babies grew into toddlers, older people began to teach the little ones the steps to the Crui dance, providing a small gourd or other object as a rattle for the young child to shake gleefully while dancing.

But in the summer of 1993, I never saw adults or older children bouncing babies while singing *cɛŋ káká* to them—neither to entertain them, nor to comfort them, nor to teach them to dance. Amenan corroborated my impression that people were no longer training their babies in the rhythms of Crui drumming. This, she explained, was because the Crui dance itself was not being staged very much any more, and for one simple reason: few teenage girls and young women remained in the village to perform it. Fed up with their poverty, Amenan estimated that many, perhaps even most, teenage girls had left the village, seeking work on plantations or in towns, especially in the southwest portion of the country. And since babies were not being taught to associate *cɛŋ káká* with pleasure in anticipation of someday dancing Crui, there was no use in singing them the song to comfort them when they were distressed.

Amenan added that if people nowadays were crooning any tunes to their infants, it was usually Protestant hymns that they learned from those who attended church. However, the meaning of this significant shift in infant music strategies was not as transparent as it might seem. For, interestingly enough, the singers were not primarily Protestants who were singing to their babies to train them in their new faith. Rather, they were largely those who remained faithful to the Beng religion and were singing the new songs with an ironic air, as a way to gently poke fun at their Protestant neighbors.[1]

For example, in the village in which I lived in 1993, people sang these Christian tunes to baby Hallelujah as a way to tease her father, Dieudonné. The young father had abruptly left the Catholic church to become a Protestant a scant week after he had finished the prescribed mourning period for his wife, who had died tragically young. Dieudonné explained his abrupt conversion by pointing out that the Protestants of the village had taken good care of him while he was in mourning. However, his non-Christian neighbors had little sympathy for the sudden conversion, and they indicated their disapproval by intoning Protestant hymns in an ironic voice to his infant daughter. From this story, we see that the practice of singing to infants has diverged drastically from its earlier goal. Previously it constituted a means of socializing children into the rhythms of traditional, albeit interfaith, dances. More recently, it has become a means to take note of—and to mock—religious change as introduced by foreign Christian missionaries.

~

In this chapter I articulate issues that emerged intermittently in previous pages and now come to the fore. I refer to the engagement between the local and the global as this engagement shapes the nurturing of infants in Beng villages that seem at once remote from and deeply tied to global structures.[2] In the previous chapters I emphasized the cultural logic that underpins daily childcare practices; in some places, I also explored how these intersect with economic realities. In this chapter I privilege these economic realities, which in turn circumscribe cultural practices.

Marc Augé has recently observed of the contemporary world: "Thought based on place haunts us still" (Augé 1995:114). As members of that unspecified "us," the Beng remain very much attached to their sense of place. However, the geocultural foundations of the space that the Beng inhabit, like those of all cultural spaces of the postmodern era, are rapidly shifting. As the site of active reproduction and negotiation of central cultural values and beliefs, infants represent an especially rich lens through which to observe the tectonic shifts that are taking place as Beng families endeavor to retain their moorings in a slipping terrain. As I try to chart the contested arenas and sometimes dizzying transformations, overdetermination will be the perplexing theme of this chapter, as it is of the lives of Beng villagers striving both to preserve and to reforge their commitment to a cultural space that is constantly altering.

We begin with some critical economic realities.

Poverty

In Côte d'Ivoire overall, the annual per capita income as of 1996 was officially $600. In Beng villages, this figure is certainly far lower. My village data contain only a small range of annual incomes: the highest annual man's income I have recorded, in the flush year of 1980, was approximately $500; the lowest was under $15. Most Beng adult men's incomes probably fall in the bottom half or below of the space spanned by those two figures; adult women's incomes are typically far lower. By this conventional standard for measuring economic status, then, the Beng are among the world's poorest people. If, as scholars such as Paul Farmer (1999) and others argue, poverty constitutes a form of structural violence, then the Beng are indeed victims of violence.

The historical and political causes of Beng poverty are multiple and over-determined.[3] Here I want to focus on the contemporary ramifications of those causative factors.

Is there no way for the Beng to extricate themselves from their poverty? In a capitalist economy such as that adopted by the Côte d'Ivoire, one source of improvement to people's lifestyle is traditionally offered by loans. Most economists and economic historians see access to credit as critical to development in economically underdeveloped regions. Even microloans can enable those living in poverty to make investments in profit-generating activities that can make a difference in lifestyle. Independent nonprofit agencies (such as Finca International, Lift above Poverty Organisation, and others) that now offer such loans often produce modest yet significant economic improvements in the local communities in which they operate.

In Côte d'Ivoire, the major source of loans until recently has been the Banque Nationale pour le Développement Agricole (BNDA), an economic agency of the Ivoirian government that was founded to provide credit to farmers. But the agency no longer exists, and to my knowledge the gap has not been filled by another.[4] As a result, small-scale farmers such as the Beng no longer have consequential amounts of credit available to them.[5] This presents new impediments to rural Ivoirians who aspire to improve their material standard of living.

As an example of the impact this change has had on people's lives, let us consider the case of André Kouassi M'Be, one of our village hosts. In 1994 a motorized, multipurpose mill that hulls rice and performs other labor-saving functions was donated to his village (Gottlieb and Graham 1999). Eager to take advantage of the possibilities for economic expansion offered by the machine, André hoped for extra cash that would enable him to buy additional seeds to plant a much larger rice field than usual. But with no access to a low-interest loan, André was able to expand neither his rice field nor his profits. He lost the chance for economic improvement that the newly introduced technology offered.

Sadly, in such circumstances, training children to accept the pains and challenges of poverty becomes one of a parent's goals. Lest this claim appear hyperbolic or implausible, let us consider a conversation I had with Amenan:

Alma: Do [Beng] people love their children?

Amenan: Yes, but they don't say it or show it directly. Maybe by buying good food for them.

I asked Amenan to elaborate. To my surprise, she continued by recounting the following story, which seemed to undercut her first response:

> One father in the village bought cooked rice and meat for his children every day in the market, as long as it was available. He spent 200 CFA a day![6] But people criticized him because he'd stolen the money from a collective fund [that was established] to buy a camera for the village. In fact, even if he'd used his own money, they would have criticized him (though not as much) because it's not good to spoil children. If you do, and then the parent dies, the children will be used to getting a lot of food and other goods, and they'll turn into thieves to get their own food and whatnot!

Amenan's statement attests that families are realistic about the likely limits of their children's economic future. Bearing this bitter knowledge in mind, Beng parents endeavor to implant what they consider a sober sense of economic goals in their children's consciousness. Indeed, as Amenan implied, they may even train their children for the possibility of being orphaned and suffering the plunge into even greater poverty that such an event might produce. Parents hope this training will ensure that their children will not be disappointed or frustrated later, nor act out of unfulfillable hopes and expectations.

Let us consider another incident:

> Amenan's young daughter, Lucy, awoke in the middle of the night. She was hungry and asked her mother to cook her a yam. Amenan refused, explaining that the middle of the night was not an appropriate time for cooking. But Lucy continued to complain, plead, and cry off and on for the remainder of the night. In the morning, Lucy begged her mother to buy her a particular bread roll sold in the marketplace

for her to eat for breakfast. Amenan refused this request as well, even though she happened to have the necessary cash (25 CFA, about $.05 U.S.). Amenan explained to me that she didn't want to spoil her daughter, who would then come to expect such treats regularly, and what would Amenan do on the days that she didn't have extra pocket money? Better for Lucy not to count on special market tidbits even if Amenan could afford them on a particular day.

In ways such as these, Beng parents implant in their young children the cognitive underpinnings of poverty. But what is the source of this scarcity, and how is it perpetuated? Given that the Beng are primarily farmers, let us explore the nature of their agricultural system to discover how it continues to produce not only crops but also poverty.

Farming

Like other farmers in tropical Africa, precolonial Beng farmers relied on shifting cultivation and mixed planting of crops, or intercropping, accompanied by an extended fallow period for their fields. Describing the advantages of this system for subsistence agriculture, Paul Harrison recently wrote:

> The conventional wisdom used to be that intercropping was primitive and untidy. Most development projects aimed at replacing the practice with neat monocropping, which made it easier to apply fertilizers and pesticides, and easier to mechanize the harvest. But research over the past decade has confirmed that the peasants had it right all along. Intercropping is superior to monocropping in the African environment. Like mulching, intercropping provides a better protective cover of vegetation, and so lowers soil temperature, and saves labour on weeding. It reduces the incidence of pests and diseases, which cannot spread so easily when their host plants are separated by other species (1996:109).[7]

As it did elsewhere in Africa, the French colonial occupation in Côte d'Ivoire transformed Beng agricultural techniques.[8] Encouraged by agricultural extension officers, smallholder farmers such as the Beng changed much of their planting regime from intercropping to monocropping. After continuous years of this significant change, as documented by soil specialists working in a variety of "Third World" regions, crops' resistance to insects and other pests significantly decreased. At the same time, when coupled with population growth and restrictions on land, the new agricultural practices shortened the available fallow period, which further depleted the nutrients in the soil (cf. ter Kuile 1987:103–4).

All this and more have occurred in the Beng region. Beng farmers told me that their precolonial ancestors typically maintained a fallow period of fifteen to twenty years before replanting. According to contemporary Beng farmers, this is the optimal duration of a fallow period in this ecosystem, affording enough time for the fragile tropical soils of the region to replenish their fertility and allowing a maximum crop yield once fields are replanted. Western researchers confirm this assertion (e.g., Hart 1982:36, 55). In the current era, the typical Beng farmer has reduced the fallow period to between five and seven years—or even shorter. Consequently, the soils have become unable to replenish their organic matter at the level that the longer fallow periods allowed, and an increase in erosion has resulted (Harrison 1996:195). "Third World" poverty furthermore means that the use of chemical fertilizers to compensate for depletion of soil nutrients does not accompany this change. A decline in soil fertility is inevitable—as is a decline in crop yields.[9] In turn, lower crop yields lead both to smaller amounts of food grown for household consumption and to decreased access to cash from food grown for sale. In this way, the cycle of poverty is doomed not only to perpetuate itself but—for ecological reasons—to worsen.

Beyond such ecological risks, a heightened dependence on a smaller number of crops for access to cash also carries with it a high level of risk related to the vagaries of the global economy. Smallholder farmers rely increasingly on market forces well beyond their control that can significantly affect their ability to sell their crops. The Beng have been caught by this net of enmeshing factors.

In the mid-twentieth century Beng farmers, encouraged by the state, began to specialize in coffee as their main cash crop.[10] In the years following World War II, this was part of a national strategy of such importance that "coffee was a substantial part of the Ivory Coast's post–World War II export boom" (Hart 1982:63; also see Amin 1967). The strategic concentration on coffee left Beng farmers extremely vulnerable to the fall in world coffee prices in the 1980s and 1990s that followed a rise in the 1970s. Both the rise in prices and the subsequent fall were partly due to significant fluctuations in weather patterns and the coffee harvest in Brazil—the world's leading coffee producer. However, the price changes were also influenced by the international agency headquartered in London that set world coffee prices and export quotas from 1963 to 1989 and by this agency's local Ivoirian counterpart, which set (or, in later years, recommended) all purchase prices for Ivoirian coffee growers until 1998–1999.[11]

In 1993, Ivoirian traders who came to Beng villages to buy coffee offered only 25 CFA/kilogram—compared to the local buying price of 300 CFA/kilogram that I had recorded in 1980. Recounting the precipitous rate drop to me, one farmer lamented, "It was insulting!" Discouraged by the low payment offered by the buyers in the 1990s, many Beng farmers judged that the labor required to harvest and sell their coffee beans was not worth the effort. Leaving their coffee trees to flower, farmers stared bitterly at the coffee berries that fell of their own accord onto the forest floor.[12]

In short, because of intertwined factors relating to colonial and postcolonial economic history and the increasing insertion of Beng farmers into the world capitalist economy, the availability of cash to Beng families has diminished significantly in recent decades. How does this poverty resonate with the Beng conception of babies' existence that we have traced throughout the preceding chapters? To answer this question, let us begin once again with the Beng cosmos.

Wrugbe as Political Allegory

I have already discussed the childrearing implications of the Beng ideology that infants retain an active memory of their previous lives, which adults envision as situated in a space of both pleasure and plenty. Here I focus on the envisioned nature of *wrugbe*, and specifically on the Beng idea that in the afterlife there is no material want. In *wrugbe*, currency in two ancient forms is said to be abundant: precolonial cowry shells and early French colonial silver coins. Those living in this world claim that unlimited access to both these currencies allows the residents of *wrugbe* to buy whatever goods they need.

Why is *wrugbe* envisaged as a place of plenitude, and why is it located in a historically identified past? I suggest that a critical clue to the broader meanings embedded in these twin cultural imaginings is found in the nature of the currencies said to be used in the afterlife. At one level, the historical past of earlier monetary systems seems to echo the past of the human life cycle. This interpretation is premised on the fact that in the Beng cultural imaginary, *wrugbe* serves as a springboard for reincarnation—which itself represents a collapsing of time in which past and future exchange places. If, as Elizabeth Tonkin has written, "'the present' is a perpetually disappearing moment" (1992:2), it disappears with especially significant and culturally resonant force in a cognitive system such as the Beng model of reincarnation. In such a system, the present folds not only into the future but also into a past defined by particular cultural contours. Which leads me to my next point.

At another level, I suggest, we can read the cultural construction of *wrugbe* as a political allegory. Infants' reputed memories of halcyon days lived at another point in the life cycle can be coded as a metaphorical model of cultural nostalgia for an imagined precolonial past.[13] In other words, the collective envisioning of the past as a safer time and as a place where all was right with the world constitutes a discourse through which contemporary adults express their own current sense of loss. That loss revolves around a widespread conviction that, in general, life is far worse today than it was long ago.

In Beng villages, old people regularly claim that nowadays more children and adults fall sick than did previously, and they especially note an increase in tetanus, malaria, eye diseases, and yellow fever. They also allege that more women die in childbirth than before. They explain that all these changes for the worse are due to an increase in witchcraft activity and that indigenous medicines, both preventive and curative, are no longer as effective against these and other conditions as they once were. I have not tried to substantiate or quantify these claims about declining health through the scanty historical record, but for the present purposes what is significant is the perception that is broadly held by older Beng adults—and that may be counterintuitive to many Western readers—that Westernization and modernization have produced deterioration rather than improvement in the quality of daily life.

By contrast, *wrugbe* takes on an image of economic plenitude as well as spiritual and emotional fulfillment. The model of ancestors living in *wrugbe* provides, as Andrew Orta says of certain Aymara rituals in Ecuador, "a local framework of copresence with the ancestors, a footing for lived history, a legitimating memory center" (2002:490). In effect, *wrugbe* might be translated not only as the afterlife but also as the imagined precolonial life. The infinite supply of cowry shells—seen by the Beng as the major precolonial currency[14]—suggests that the envisioning of *wrugbe* as a space of economic plenty serves as a means of reimagining the precolonial past. We might call this a cultural variation of the evolutionary principle that ontogeny recapitulates phylogeny. That is, through the "ontogeny" of infant-based *wrugbe*, Beng adults read onto infants' attributed other-world experiences their reflections on what has been lost with, and since, the "phylogeny" of colonialism.

I suggest that the attribution of heightened infant memory of an idyllic *wrugbe* serves as an indirect critique of French colonialism and its aftermath, the period of independence to which older Beng refer with some irony—for poverty has worsened, health has deteriorated, witchcraft incidents have increased, and interpersonal strife has intensified. Thus, what appears to be the most traditional of Beng beliefs about the cosmos and the place of people in it may be a relatively recent reinterpretation of colonial history.

Currently we cannot know what the precolonial vision of *wrugbe* looked like. It may have approximated most components of the contemporary ideology that I have summarized here. But even if this were so, I contend that its meanings would have been significantly different. Surely, envisioning the past as an idyllic space of harmony and affluence must have different connotations in precolonial, colonial, and postcolonial epochs. In the contemporary era, reclaiming the past as a time of harmony and affluence must serve at one level as a critique of the effects of the French colonial and neocolonial presence, which has brought layers of misery to West African peasants such as the Beng for over a century.

But let us recall that *wrugbe* is imagined as the site not only of precolonial wealth—in the form of the cowry shell—but also of colonial wealth—in the form of early French coins (figure 57). French currency in the form of silver franc coinage was "used extensively in the groundnut trade [in West Africa] as early as the 1850s," and a French bank was established in Senegal in 1854 (Hopkins 1973:49n50, 206). During the colonial era, the five-franc piece was in widespread use in francophone West Africa (Austen 1987:134). In 1945, "the franc zone was created and a separate currency issued for the colonies," to be regulated by a currency board (Hopkins 1973:207–8; see also Bourdin 1980; Hopkins 1970). The introduction of the new coins seems to have transformed the earlier coins into items of local prestige value, imbuing them with the sort of mystical power I discuss here.

The addition of colonial French coins necessarily adds complexity to our discussion. When the French invaded West Africa, they brought many goods

57. A baby wearing colonial-era French coins on his necklace

with them, but more than any other material reality, their silver coins symbolized the capitalist system that would transform African life in short order. By 1900, the French had imposed a head tax on each household (construed as male-headed) that was required to be paid in cash. In order to gain access to the necessary cash, African farmers were obliged to convert a good portion of their labor from farming subsistence crops to farming cash crops that the colonial rulers introduced. In the Beng region, these cash crops were especially coffee and, to a lesser extent, cocoa and rice.[15] The transformation to a tax-oriented cash economy proved so grueling that in order to discuss anything having to do with "taxes," rather than adopting (or adapting) the French word *impôt,* the Beng instead coined the Beng phrase, *"nen zra,"* which means, literally, to "throw away [one's] soul." Clearly early colonial-era Beng farmers recognized with searing clarity the upheaval in their lives that was already being produced by the forced introduction of a capitalist economy.

Given this critical perspective, how did the early colonial French coins take on a positively coded semantic field in the culturally imagined space of other-worldly pleasure and plenty that is *wrugbe?* A particular type of revisionist fantasy may be at work here: the Beng may be creating what some social scientists would term a counterfactual.[16] They appear to be speculating, What if the French introduction of a capitalist economy, as symbolized aptly by their silver coins, had produced wealth for us rather than poverty? It provides a bittersweet fantasy.

The bitterness proves an especially difficult pill to swallow when it comes to infants. After exiting both the mythical, precolonial realm of *wrugbe* and the historical realm of colonialism, infants are said to endeavor all too often to return to the plenitude of that other life. If they return definitively, they add to the appalling infant mortality statistics that plague West Africa. Ironically, the envisaged return of babies to an imagined paradisiacal precolonial/ prehuman life presupposes their death. Through this ideology, colonialism and its aftermath continue to violate villagers' family lives.

Medical Issues

As we have seen, in the 1990s many Beng families had little or no access to cash during much of the year. How do poverty and the associated imperative that parents rear children for a life marked by material deprivation affect young children? The most obvious and most dangerous effect is on their bodies. In many ways the reduction in household income has taken its greatest toll on children's health. Babies and toddlers now fall sick in increasing numbers due to the confounding effects of poverty.

In the "Third World" at large, one of the most widely reported forms of infant illness are gastrointestinal infections from polluted water and lack of access to basic modern sanitation. This is certainly the case among Beng farming families. Although they pump water from government-dug wells, the water from the wells is not treated chemically and may contain harmful microbes. Moreover, at the height of the dry season, the water in these wells often dries up and women draw water from forest pools that contain harmful parasites and bacteria. Due to the traditional practice of *kami*, or force-feeding infants water (chapter 8), Beng infants are susceptible to water-borne diseases from a very young age.

Moreover, as is true in many parts of Africa, older Beng children now consume a less nutritious diet than their counterparts did in the past, due to a variety of factors. Both colonial and "post-"colonial regimes have encouraged farmers to plant new food varieties; sadly, many of these have lower nutritional content than their earlier counterparts.[17] For example, Beng farmers used to grow an indigenous strain of red rice that had higher nutritional value than the new forms of imported white rice they now plant. In addition, to the extent that farmers now spend more time cultivating cash crops such as coffee, cocoa, and rice, time is taken away from both growing and gathering other nutritious vegetable crops that provide vitamin and mineral variety to their diet (see Hart 1982:127).

Because of the additional labor requirements demanded by growing and processing cash crops, people also have less time now to hunt, so there is less animal protein in the diet. For women of reproductive age, this can create anemia, which tends to reduce its victims' energy and make women susceptible to a host of infections and other illnesses, including chronic gastritis, peptic ulcers (Konno et al. 2000), and even cardiac problems (Bard et al. 1998). Anemic children may also suffer these symptoms. In breastfeeding women, anemia can result in an insufficient milk supply, perhaps because of the mother's fatigue, which is exacerbated by the anemia, and can shorten the period of breastfeeding and lead to early weaning (Henly et al. 1995).

In a pregnant woman, severe anemia can cause low birth weight in her newborn (Dettwyler and Fishman 1992:182). In infants born prematurely, anemia is associated with cardiac stress (Bard et al. 1998). In all infants and young children, "iron deficiency anemia . . . is associated with diminished cognitive function, changes in behavior, delayed infant growth and development, decreased exercise tolerance, and impaired immune function" (Bogen et al. 2000:1254; also see Lozoff, Jimenez, and Wolf 1991; Pollitt 1997; Ryan 1997a; and Walter et al. 1989). For this reason, pediatricians in the United States are seeking more effective screening methods to identify children at risk for anemia so they can intervene early (Bogen et al. 2000).[18] Protein deficiency brings with it additional risks, including impediments to full cognitive development in growing children (e.g., Klein, Irwin, Engle, and Yarbrough 1976).

In the 1990s, Beng infants and young children fell sick with much greater frequency than they had in the previous decade. Mothers reported this change to me regularly, and my observations bore out their reports. In 1979–1980 and again in 1985, Philip and I had typically devoted one to two hours daily to providing basic medical treatment for sick people—both children and adults—who requested health care. In 1993, lodged in the same village in which we had resided in 1985, we typically devoted about three to four hours daily to such nursing care, and the vast majority of our cases involved infants and young children. Two factors accounted for the large increase in cases brought to us. First, more children were falling sick. Secondly, fewer families of sick children were able to scrape together the funds to pay for an expensive bus ride to take a sick child to the government-funded dispensary in the nearest town—where they expected to be issued a prescription to buy prohibitively expensive drugs at the local pharmacy. In 1993 some mothers could not even afford to take their babies to village-based diviners or healers, who charged fees for their services and remedies that were extremely modest even by local standards.[19]

One day in 1993 the elders of one Beng village met to discuss why so many people, especially children, had fallen sick recently. They decided to travel in their dreams to *wrugbe,* where they would ask the ancestors to reveal the cause of their collective misery. When the elders arrived in *wrugbe,* the ancestors informed them that many people were falling sick in the village because a European trader had recently stolen the savanna king's regal treasure. The ancestors added that the trader himself had died immediately after the sale. In other words, the illicit alienation of a culturally valued item meant to exist entirely outside the sphere of monetary circulation, in a parallel plane of a nonalienable economy, was seen to occasion a rupture in the somatic lives of all involved, even those who were involved only peripherally—the village's children. In this way, the notion of a moral economy asserted itself as still relevant in a world otherwise driven by amoral capital.[20] But the Beng recognize that their morality-driven model of economy is under siege. As that model is violated by those who reject its relevance, the bodies of even the youngest members of the Beng community, may—and do—suffer.

Such is the Beng explanation of their children's increasing medical vulnerability. What of a Western explanation?

Vaccinations

In many, perhaps most, medical regimes, it is a truism that preventive medicine is the most effective form of health care. This is no less the case in

Bengland than it is in the West. In the world of biomedical treatments, a prime focus of preventive medicine is the administration of a series of vaccinations in early childhood that prompts the body to manufacture its own immunity to a variety of dangerous diseases that would otherwise imperil children's lives. Over the past century, scientists have made extraordinary breakthroughs in creating vaccines with remarkable effectiveness. In the economically developed nations of the world, the diseases that are almost universally prevented by these vaccines—measles, mumps, rubella, diphtheria, whooping cough, tetanus, and polio—are barely a bad memory.[21] But the situation is drastically different in the rest of the world. Especially in Africa, but also in parts of Asia and Latin America, these diseases, which have no technical or moral reason to exist, continue to claim millions of lives annually. Let us explore briefly the day-to-day realities of vaccination culture in one small corner of the economically developing world: the world of Beng villages, where many residents never receive any vaccines, and where those who do often receive only incomplete doses.[22]

In Beng villages, vaccines are sometimes available, but the nominally free administration of the serums by government nurses imposes hidden costs that, while seemingly modest, often prove prohibitive. In the larger villages, another option exists: some villagers buy syringes and medications that they use to inject fellow villagers with various medicines for a modest fee. The major advantage of receiving shots from these untrained healers is that the healers do not require patients to maintain a medical record, thus villagers do not have to spend 350 CFA to buy the required notebook. In light of this, many villagers, including those who are literate or have experienced biomedical treatments in towns and cities, opt to receive shots from village injectors rather than from biomedically trained nurses. But they pay a different sort of price. As the village injectors are not formally trained in biomedical techniques, including sterilization procedures, people who subject themselves to their needles incur many health risks. Villagers themselves claim that people who receive many shots from these injection assistants often develop boils on their skin. To date, I have not heard of hepatitis, HIV, or other serious bloodborne diseases being spread through these needles, but the possibility surely looms large.

Moreover, as far as I was able to ascertain, the medicines that the village healers offer their patients are not preventive—they include no immunization serums. Rather, they usually consist of antibiotics and are meant as one-time cures of specific symptoms, although some villagers assume they are protecting themselves against the same illnesses for which the visiting biomedically trained nurses offer protection. The children who receive these shots remain unprotected against the classic killer diseases of childhood.

These diseases continue to claim many lives. Tetanus in particular is so common that some families expect to encounter it. Once, when I was video-taping a one-month-old baby girl being bathed by her mother, I chatted with both parents about their daughter. The young father, Bande, told me that he was working outside of the village when his daughter was born. He explained that he had not made an effort to return to the village for the delivery because he and his wife had lost their two previous children prior to this baby's birth. The first child had died of a mysterious skin disease, and the second had died of tetanus about a week after being born. When he heard that his wife had delivered their third child, he did not hasten to return to the village, as he was not optimistic that this baby would live either. By the time he spoke to me, he had begun to allow himself to be happy about the baby's birth, but he told me that he was still not entirely confident that she would survive. The devastating loss of his first two children had made Bande emotionally wary and had caused him to anticipate an early death for his new child as a real likelihood.

Other diseases that ought to be prevented by vaccines continue to claim lives as well. In 1985 my friend Amenan told me that in early 1982 "all" the children then living in the village died of whooping cough (pertussis)—a disease that is prevented by the DPT vaccination series (diphtheria-pertussis-tetanus) that is administered routinely to babies in postindustrialized nations. Amenan said she had counted over a hundred Beng children who died that year. She added, "Every day, two or three children died. Even children up to eight to ten years old died." The fact that every one of these children's deaths was most likely preventable renders their early demise absurd.

Childbirth

Calculating the percentage of women who die in childbirth is another conventional, if gruesome, scholarly means for measuring poverty. In Côte d'Ivoire overall, maternal mortality is currently listed at 0.6 percent (that is, 600 laboring women die per 100,000 live births) (UNICEF 2000). Wall estimates that "in remote rural areas, the rate is an order of magnitude higher" than the WHO rate of 0.64 percent for Africa overall (1996:115). What are Beng perspectives on this figure? In the villages, elders told me that they observe far more cases of women dying in childbirth nowadays than they used to observe. While I have not tried to quantify this claim using oral or written records, I witnessed and heard about enough such tragedies to confirm the fact that childbirth still represents a very serious risk to women's lives.

As of now, there are still no trained midwives, obstetric nurses, or doctors in any but one Beng village, and the dispensary in that village often has no nurse available. This means that, as elsewhere in the "Third World" (see Allen 2002), in the case of a difficult childbirth with serious medical complications, a Beng woman may have few options.

Let us consider the case of Aya, who was having a very difficult delivery. Her husband wanted to transport her to the dispensary in M'Bahiakro, where there is usually a midwife on duty. However, taking advantage of the situation, the bus driver (who was not Beng) raised the transportation fee over fortyfold, from the usual 700 CFA to an exorbitant 30,000 CFA. Not surprisingly, Aya's husband lacked the necessary funds. Aya remained in the village and suffered through what turned out to be an exhausting breech delivery that killed the baby and produced a torn placenta, nearly killing her as well.

Elsewhere I have recorded stories of other Beng women who were not so lucky (Gottlieb and Graham 1994). Although I have critiqued hospital maternity wards in the United States for promoting excessively technologized births for routine pregnancies (Gottlieb 1995a), my observations in rural West Africa testify that appropriately used technological intervention can certainly save lives in some contexts.

Major Health Problems

In Beng villages, surviving birth often means entering a life of further serious medical risk. For one thing, in the tropics, where infants and young children are vulnerable to a host of pathogens, if recurrent diseases do not prove fatal, they can cause developmental delays. I have also mentioned that the diet of many Beng villagers has changed significantly over the past century. Echoing disturbing trends throughout the continent, lower levels of protein, iron, and a variety of vitamins and minerals put Beng children at risk for all manner of illnesses. As Harrison recently wrote with bitter irony, "Poverty and malnutrition are the main growth sectors in Africa" (1996:21).

In 1993 I observed two severe cases of malnutrition for the first time (figure 58). Let us explore one of these:

> One day a young but haggard-looking woman came to me with a child folded into her arms. The child appeared curled into a snail shell, retreating into a womb, but too old to retain active womb memories. I asked the woman what the problem was. She said simply, quietly, "*à kenè*"—he's not well. My friend Amenan cast me a knowing glance that I couldn't interpret. I looked at the child, so docile yet clearly unhappy, staring vacantly into space. Suddenly I understood: he was far older than his size suggested. Suspecting malnutrition, I took out the malnutrition measuring tape I had brought along with me and had hoped—foolishly, as it turned out—never to use.
>
> Shrunken into his mother's arms, the boy's sad, wise face suggested he must have

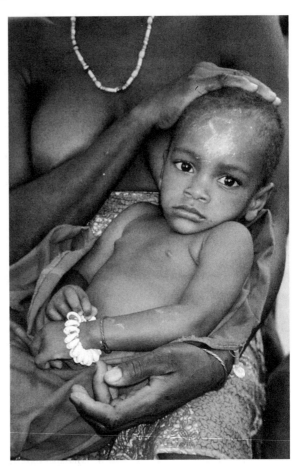

58. This sad,
malnourished child is
wearing a full cowry
bracelet. He died a few
days after the photo
was taken.

been at least three, maybe even four years old. However, his tiny bones told another
story. The boy's skinny wrist occupied enough of the measuring band to reach only
the "severely malnourished" line. My mind flashed back to television images of severely
malnourished children from the political crises of the last cruel century: Auschwitz,
Biafra, Somalia, Bosnia. . . . But the Beng were not at war. How could this level of
malnutrition occur in the very village of farmers in which I was living?

I couldn't help feeling anger at the boy's mother for not having managed to feed
her child. Yet my anthropological training reminded me not to blame the victim. This
impoverished woman was suffering from structural inequities that allocate so many resources to a small part of the world but so few to the rest, wealth to the few elites of
her country and suffering to the many peasants such as herself. Still, that classic Azande
question plagued me: Why *this* woman? There was plenty of poverty to go around, but

other mothers of the village managed at least to get a bare minimum of calories into their children to stave off the hungry god of malnutrition. Why couldn't this mother do the same?

Amenan interrupted my gloomy thoughts. "Why didn't you come to see Amwe sooner?" she snapped disapprovingly at the unhappy mother.

"No reason," the woman mumbled.

Amenan turned to me in disgust and switched to French. "This woman could have saved her child if she'd come earlier. Now, look. It's too late." With that final pronouncement, Amenan returned to her breakfast dishes.

"But wait," I said, pursuing her across the courtyard. "Maybe it's not too late. I can try and build up the boy's strength. Let's get him some nourishing food. I have a can of sardines in the house, let's start with that. Let's tell the mother to bring him by every morning and I'll give him breakfast."

"If you like," Amenan muttered, unconvinced.

I went into the house to find a can. Returning outside with it, I opened it and told the unhappy mother of my plan.

"No, that's not the problem," she said. "He doesn't want to eat. I offer him food and he refuses. He's sick, can't you see? He needs medicine. Can't you give him any medicine?"

"This food will be his medicine," I countered with as much confidence as I could muster. With that, I removed a sardine from the can and held it out to the boy. He cast a sidelong glance at it, then looked away, disinterested. His mother gave me an I-told-you-so look. Undaunted, I pinched off the tip of the sardine and tried gently to insert it into the boy's small mouth. But rather than gobbling it up with relish, he let it sit on his tongue a few seconds, then tried weakly to spit it out.

Young as he was, he had apparently decided it was time to die.

Imbued with my culture's can-do Yankee spirit, I found this capitulation to defeat impossible to accept. Amenan mocked me; Philip gently rebuked me; even the boy's mother discouraged me. Did it make sense to confer precious resources on an obviously dying child when there were so many others who were at risk for the same fate but not yet so enfeebled, who might still be nourished back to health? Yet who was I to play God and decide to give up on one life, however fragile it was, in favor of another? It was a decision I was wholly unprepared to make.

In the end, unable to abandon the dying boy, I asked the mother to bring him by twice a day, and she halfheartedly agreed. Morning and evening I embarked on the same doomed routine: I tried to tempt him back to life with a new tasty morsel—a tiny piece of bread with peanut butter, a thimble-size piece of scrambled egg, a section of an orange to suck on. Twice a day he reaffirmed his refusal. After two days of this grim game, he made his final assertion. The death was announced quietly to me by a distant relative who mechanically thanked me for my efforts.

The second case of malnutrition I observed had the same outcome:

> One day a mother of a young child came to me with a sad-looking boy. Because of his
> size, I first judged that he must be a baby, but when I looked more closely, I saw that
> he had the uncanny look of an older child about him. The malnutrition ribbon con-
> firmed the sorrowful hunch. Two days later, the funeral drums beat in the village: the
> boy had died.

Ironically one Beng interpretation of these deaths seems to endorse the
common Western belief in free will more than my own analysis does. In spite
of several centuries of post-"Enlightenment" thought leading me to see the
individual as paramount, my discipline has trained me to seek the structural
causes that sentenced these small persons to death. But many of my village
neighbors did not see it this way. The boys had made their own decisions,
some Beng people asserted. Alternatively, others maintained that the first
boy's mother was responsible because she was probably a witch, hungry for
her own son's meat. With regard to neither case did anyone mention the

59. Akissi holding her
adopted son, who has
been sick for several
days with an
unidentified illness

International Monetary Fund, with its bitter pill of structural adjustment and that policy's devastating effects on the country's economy. Nor was the impersonal notion of fate evoked. Ultimately, in most Beng people's view, it is *individuals* who are responsible for lives and deaths—their own or others'. Impersonal forces, including structural agencies, do not enter the local equation.

Yet health problems in babies and young children are not only troubling or tragic for the individual child; their effects can ricochet sociologically. When a young child falls sick, someone must take care of the little one. That someone is usually the mother. During this time, the mother cannot work in the fields; perhaps she cannot even chop firewood or collect water (figure 59). If this occurs for a day or two, the implications are not serious. For a longer illness, the consequences can be devastating. Let us consider another case (figure 60).

60. Baby Kouadio was born with a herniated testicle. Because it hurt him to be held on someone's back, he spent most of his days seated in the lap of his mother or various relatives, such as this girl, his second cousin Tupé (the maternal granddaughter of his paternal grandfather's sister).

Shortly before I arrived in the village in 1993, a young mother named Amwe had given birth to a boy, Kouadio, who was afflicted with a herniated scrotum.[23] With this condition, the baby suffered great pain when anyone tried to carry him in the usual piggyback position. His mother explained to me: "If I try to carry him on my back, he cries because his testicle hurts." This was presumably because his enlarged scrotum was pinched against his mother's back. Amwe added that she could hold her son on her back if she tied the *pagne* very loosely, but, she said, "I can't carry him tightly" *(mà zi a dodo grégre)*. What she did not say—presumably because it was so obvious to her— was that the *pagne* needs to be wrapped tightly if the child is to remain securely attached without risk of falling, especially if the carrier is to walk any appreciable distance. As luck would have it, Amwe's fields happened to be located quite far from the village, in an area known as a camp (*namwe*, or *campement* in French). In such distant fields, Beng farmers construct crude houses in which they sleep for several nights rather than walking the long distance back and forth to the village every day.

With her infant son's medical problem, Amwe could not work in her faraway fields. Baby Kouadio would not tolerate being carried on her back such a long distance—his crying would communicate his outrage and pain quite effectively. Nor could the nursing baby remain in the village the whole day for another to care for him. The village boutique sold neither baby bottles nor infant formula, and without having any milk to drink all day, young Kouadio would surely be ravenous and miserable. Leaving him with a baby-sitter in the village in such circumstances was out of the question. Given this predicament, Amwe's fields went untended that summer. Fortunately for her household, the extended family had enough other working members to feed her and her husband.[24]

Had Kouadio's condition gone uncorrected, Amwe would have remained unable to work in her fields for an indefinite period, presumably until Kouadio's hernia became strangulated and he died. Had the baby survived into a second planting cycle, the family's food supply would almost certainly have become imperiled. As it happened, the intervention of a visiting anthropologist's family to provide funds for surgery changed the course of a medical crisis that would have otherwise had a very different outcome.

Although Kouadio's medical condition is relatively rare, many other medical situations in infants and young children produce parallel socioeconomic effects. Not only are sick children miserable; their illness has the potential to disrupt the household in ways that can be catastrophic for a family that is already living on the edge (Popkin, Lasky, Spicer, and Yamamota 1986).

Invisible Deaths

Another fact renders the deaths of infants and young children troubling at a different level. The passing of many babies goes unnoted in official records. Residing in each region of rural Côte d'Ivoire is a government bureaucrat whose job is to keep written records of all births and deaths in a group of villages. The bureaucrat's recording notebook has neatly spaced lines and columns that produce the convincing appearance of a rationalized system of clear accountability. However, the system is far from flawless and far from impervious to a cultural calculus.

For one thing, not all Beng parents go to the trouble of recording their children's births. The Beng civil servant based in one village lamented to me that people from one of the smaller neighboring villages rarely made the trip to his village to report births and deaths. Therefore, the residents of that village were almost completely invisible in government records. Lack of transportation thus skews the records significantly, with the population of smaller or remoter villages substantially underrepresented.

This civil servant complained to me that even in his own village he was able to record births and deaths only when he was officially informed of them by a relative. In summer 1993, he told me that he knew of thirty-one babies born in his own village so far that year, but he had only recorded five births because those were all he had been officially told about by the infants' parents. If any of the twenty-six unrecorded babies were to die, their deaths would ipso facto have to go unrecorded as well. Parents might neglect to register their children's births and deaths for any number of reasons beyond transportation. If a marriage is unhappy, for example, if the baby is unwanted, or if some other social drama entangles a family, the chances are greater that a baby will remain officially unaccounted for.

Another, more systematic gap concerns a particular group of newborns. This same civil servant told me that during his training a higher government official had instructed him to record births only after newborns had reached the age of two weeks. Consequently, if a baby should die within the first two weeks, the death would never be registered. The record keeper's own newborn grandson had recently perished. However, neither the infant's birth nor his death appeared in his grandfather's notebook because the baby had died within his first two weeks of life, so his brief existence was unrecorded.

The relationship between the invisibility of these very early deaths and their cause is often not coincidental. Significantly, the vast majority of neonatal tetanus cases occur within the first two weeks of life. Reciprocally, it is likely that a significant proportion of infants' deaths that occur within the first two weeks are due to tetanus. Hence the government record-keeping policy of noting births only two weeks after the delivery has the effect—whether or not intended—of concealing most deaths from neonatal tetanus. It is as if babies killed by tetanus had never existed.

Aside from the troubling ethical implications of this record-keeping practice, serious pragmatic issues also arise. As the passionate wrangling over the U.S. census has demonstrated over the past decade (e.g., Scott 2001),[25] both governmental and nongovernmental agencies make major decisions about asset allocation on the basis of such official statistics. In the case at hand, significant undercounting of Beng infants' medical problems might result in fewer funds for health care. If the number of deaths from neonatal tetanus were widely reported in Côte d'Ivoire, would there be more local political will—or more international political pressure—to make the tetanus vaccine universally available?

Birth Control

For the first time in 1993, I began hearing some women of childbearing age assert—sometimes sotto voce, sometimes in surprisingly open fashion—that they had had enough children. They told me that if they had the resources, by which they meant the money, the knowledge, and the access, they would seek reliable birth control methods to prevent further pregnancies. When I inquired further, I often received answers that directly invoked poverty.

For example, one young woman, Boussou, explained to me that she had not been able to interest a baby-sitter in helping her with child care because, as she put it, "I won't be able to offer her anything." Boussou had in mind the cash necessary to buy gifts for a *leŋ kũli*. As a result, she had not even tried to find a caretaker. Boussou added that because of her inability to solicit child-care help, raising children "tires you out." She medicalized the sense of exhaustion that she said she frequently felt by saying, "We don't have medicines to take." Boussou was recalling a time when diviners offered effective energy-giving preparations to postpartum women.

Another mother, Ajua, lamented the effects of poverty on her youngest child's diet. For the first few months of her five-month-old son's life, all Ajua had to eat was manioc (or cassava)—a notoriously nonnutritious food that is "a relatively poor source of minerals and vitamins" (Balagopalan et al. 1988: 13).[26] Let us listen to Ajua's own perception of her situation:

> My son was born five months ago. For a while, I had nothing to eat but manioc. My breastwater dried up completely! Now I'm starting to eat some corn, and I expect that some breastwater will come back in.
>
> I have four children living in the village now. Four more are living elsewhere in the country . . . somewhere.
>
> I would stop having children if I could.

On another occasion, Ama, a mother of two, voiced similar sentiments. As her year-old daughter crawled around us, I asked Ama what she thought was the hardest part of raising children. She immediately replied that the greatest challenge was simply getting enough money to buy the bare necessities of household maintenance: soap for laundry, kerosene for lamps, and similar products. She added: "It's very hard to be a mother without enough money. This is especially so if you don't have enough money to have a babysitter for the baby—if you don't have money to buy *pagnes* for her as a present." Lamenting these challenges of motherhood reminded Ama of her older sister, who had tragically died in her seventh month of pregnancy while working in the fields. Ama's point seemed to be that even before women begin raising children, one of the most difficult aspects of motherhood was simply surviving pregnancy and childbirth. To conclude our discussion, Ama sighed that she would like to leave her husband so as not to have any more children at all—that children are too hard. For her, sexual abstinence represented the only reliable and realistic route to birth control, and divorce was the only imaginable route to abstinence.

Yet, for all her frustration with motherhood and poverty, Ama seemed a perfectly competent mother. At one point during our discussion, her year-old daughter Aya fussed, and Ama immediately picked her up. Facing her daughter, Ama asked tenderly, *"o leà? mo!"*—What's wrong, sweet girl? She gave her a little hug, which seemed all Aya wanted, for Aya then detached from her mother to play contentedly with some copper anklets. Overall, I did not see signs that Ama was so overly stressed by poverty and motherhood that she was either abusing or neglecting her infant daughter. Her loving attitude proved extraordinarily resilient in the face of the challenges confronting her.

Ama's situation may seem familiar to Western readers who likewise privilege finances in their decision making about regulating their fertility. Other Beng women seek birth control methods for completely different reasons that have cultural foundations.[27] Let us consider the case of a young woman, Joelle, as recounted to me by one of her distant relatives, a middle-aged woman with several children of her own:

> When Joelle was giving birth to her last baby, the umbilical cord emerged at the same time that the baby's body was coming out [prolapse of the umbilical cord through the cervix]. Miraculously, both Joelle and the baby survived the ordeal. An old woman in the village said that Joelle's maternal aunt, Aukro, had bewitched her niece during her labor. Aukro had been working in the fields that day—which is why she had bungled the job. If the aunt had been in the village, she surely would have killed Joelle!
>
> Aukro is being initiated into a Beng women's ritual cult that teaches adepts how to administer ritual medicines to new widows and widowers. Any time a mar-

ried woman or man dies, unless the widow or widower is a Muslim or a Christian, the bereaved spouse must take a ritualized medicinal bath. The ritual occurs the very evening on which the dead spouse is buried. [The medicine used to be administered continuously for three months; now the period has been shortened to one or two weeks.]

About eight years ago, Aukro decided to join the group of older women in her village who administer this medicine. The women are called *sua laboli*—widow/er medicine gatherers. Everyone knows that there are always four women who do this in Asagbe, and the four women are always members of the same matriclan *(wla)*. Aukro is the youngest of the four women elders in Asagbe, and she's still being initiated into the cult. She is replacing another woman who died recently. The price of initiation into the cult is extreme *(grégré)*. The initiate must provide the soul of a woman who died in childbirth. That is, she must kill someone during childbirth. Aukro had tried to kill her niece Joelle in childbirth for this reason. Once she succeeds in fulfilling her obligation, she may administer the ritual medicine to widowers and widows innumerable times without having to kill another relative in childbirth ever again.

Because Joelle's aunt hasn't yet killed anyone in labor, people in her family are very worried about childbirth. Joelle's younger sister is pregnant now. She's young, only about fifteen years old. The whole family is very nervous for her, frightened that the aunt will try to kill her during her delivery. Once any woman in the matriclan dies in childbirth, then all the other women of the clan will no longer be nervous, as Aukro must kill just one person, and everyone will say that Aukro was responsible for the death. Once this happens, as long as Joelle isn't the victim, she won't be nervous about childbirth any more. If she's managed to get birth control, she'll stop using it then.

In Joelle's story, we see culture and the technology of modernity intersecting in surprising ways. Women seek reliable means to regulate fertility for a wide range of reasons. They expectedly invoke the problem of limited resources, both financial and physical, but they also refer to situations shaped by culture-specific contexts and meanings that would be unlikely elsewhere. Joelle's case reveals a motive for seeking birth control that is quite different from that of Ama and Boussou. In contrast to the other two women, Joelle invokes not poverty, but ritual as her motive for seeking to regulate her fertility.

In any case, dependable means of birth control are currently unavailable in the villages, in both the technological and the sociological sense. Regarding the technology of fertility regulation, most Beng have access only to local herbal methods whose reliability I have no way to judge because knowledge of these methods is classified as top secret. Female elders have a monopoly on knowledge about the relevant plants, and they only share their knowledge with younger women on an individual basis, depending on the circumstances. Having been judged too young myself to merit access to the occult knowledge, all I have been able to ascertain is that the women of reproductive age who succeed in gaining access to this information are few in number. Most women who inquire about the methods are informed firmly that they are too young and have not yet had enough children to merit the right to cease bearing children. Only one woman told me that she had successfully campaigned for access to the local methods. A mother who had borne ten children and lost only one, she had sought and received infertility medicines because one of her last labors had been quite difficult.

Given the quasi-taboo nature of traditional birth control methods, where do factory-produced methods fit in? Interestingly, despite their very different origins, these latter methods are grouped conceptually with the local techniques. That is, as with the herbal technologies, only women who have already borne and reared a large number of children and are approaching the biological end of their childbearing years are normatively accorded the right to modern contraceptives. In 1993, I made it clear through village gossip networks that I had brought along a large number of condoms that I would give out at no charge to anyone who wanted them.[28] Only one man asked for them. As for the women I spoke with or whose views I heard about, all said that their husbands would never agree to use the condoms. Not one woman asked for so much as a single free sample—including those who expressed the desire to cut short their reproductive years. However, one young woman who had recently had a dangerous delivery did ask me to explain the rhythm method, since she thought she might be able to accomplish this without her husband's knowledge. Intervention at a less-than-obvious level might be worth trying as it posed a relatively low level of cultural risk.

Baby-Sitting

The challenges of poverty and the gendered structures of labor are closely interlinked. In much of the "Third World," and especially in rural Africa, the combination of the work of mothering with the work of farming produce very long, often exhausting days for women.[29] This is certainly the case for Beng women of reproductive age, who find it essential to regard child care as a potentially collective enterprise to which a large pool of colleagues might contribute at any given time. Thus an important strategy soon after each childbirth is the identification of one or more baby-sitters *(leŋ kūli)*. The ability to find a baby carrier is especially critical to successful farming for those mothers who also have a toddler and another young child under their care, as is often the case. If the pool of potential baby-sitters were to become significantly constricted, this could have dangerous effects on the labor capacity of Beng women. In recent years, this is exactly what has happened, for two interrelated reasons. The first concerns the age of available baby-sitters; the second concerns changes in agricultural practices.

In earlier times, Beng mothers typically sought baby carriers among the group of unmarried village girls who were aged between about seven and seventeen years old. This cohort regularly helped their mothers in both domestic and field work, but their mothers might liberate them to help with baby-sitting (either for their younger sibling or for someone else's baby) when the need arose. These girls were not allotted their own fields to farm until after they married, which was typically around seventeen years of age. Hence as long as they remained unmarried, their agricultural work, while important to their families, was sometimes considered expendable for restricted periods of time, especially if there were other siblings to fill in for their lost labor.

However, in the current era, youths are being allotted their own fields to work well before they marry—usually by the time they are twelve or thirteen years old. During my last stay in Bengland, Amenan's fifteen-year-old daughter Esi had her own rice field. She did the bulk of adult-level work in her field and was thus no longer available as a reliable baby-sitter. Even some children as young as ten or eleven are now acquiring their own fields to farm. As a result, most teenage girls are no longer available to serve reliably as *lɛŋ kūlí* because they are often too busy working in their own plots to care for babies—even their own siblings. Thus the group of available baby-sitters has diminished.

This significant shift in field ownership began in the late 1960s following independence from France, when Beng farmers began extensively planting rice and corn, as well as coffee and cocoa, as cash crops. Youth became interested in the income possibilities of such cash crops, and over the course of the next few decades have convinced their elders to allot them fields of their own.

The shortage of baby-sitters occasioned by the change in land ownership has recently been exacerbated for two additional reasons relating to poverty. First, some women must now find a baby-sitter earlier than they would like to following childbirth. For example, let us consider a conversation I had with "Afwe," a mother of three whose youngest child was currently a two-month-old girl. At the time that we spoke, Afwe told me that she had already returned to work in the fields a month previously, when her baby daughter was only one month old. Afwe acknowledged that her aunt had discouraged her from going back to work so early—older Beng women generally urge new mothers to wait at least two and preferably three months after delivery before returning to work in the fields full-time.

Afwe lamented that she had to resume her farm labor early because there happened to be a famine in the village that year. (The famine's natural causes would have been exacerbated by the change from intercropping to mono-cropping, and from subsistence farming to the cultivation of cash crops.) If Afwe didn't return to her agricultural work soon after childbirth, she feared, her two older children would have nothing to eat. To take care of her young infant while she was working in the fields, Afwe was lucky enough to be able to engage the services of her oldest child, Aya, as a *leŋ kũli*. However, Aya was still quite young—only seven years old. Every day, the little girl carried her baby sister on her back to and from the fields as best she could while her mother toted farm tools and crops on her head.

Teenage girls are less frequently available as baby-sitters nowadays for a second reason. Although the villages are not entirely depleted of teenage girls when adolescents leave the villages to work as laborers on commercial planta-tions—they usually leave only for a contractual period of a year and then return—so many girls are leaving that the overall pool of potential teenage baby-sitters is significantly diminished.

In short, in the postcolonial era, labor changes have produced new hard-ships for women even as the government has undertaken development efforts such as the installation of water pumps to improve women's lives.

~

Baby-sitting is but one arena in which the effects of poverty shape Beng wom-en's lives. As we have seen, Beng poverty is produced by a complex array of factors that includes such global forces as the recent decline in local coffee prices, which are dictated by the world market. For those who survive infancy and toddlerhood, the local and the global announce their interconnections in children's lives in another direct way: through their engagement—or non-engagement—with formal education.

Education

Access to formal education presents a challenge to Beng families that may be hard to imagine for those who live in industrialized nations that have had universal publicly funded education for the better part of a century. Nation-ally, Côte d'Ivoire is ranked 118th in the world (out of 198 countries) for adult male literacy. According to government figures, adult male literacy is 50 percent and adult female literacy is 30 percent. Among the younger gener-ation, the figures are higher, though still distressingly gender-skewed: according to one set of figures, 80 percent of boys and 58 percent of girls attend primary school (Population Concern 1998). Another source claims that only half of primary school–age children are actually attending school (World Bank 1997: section 28).

The situation at the village level, as usual, is worse. Although Western-style schools have been a part of the Beng landscape for many decades, the villages are far from having available the universal education for all primary school–age children that exists on the books.[30] The first school in the region was built in the nearby town of M'Bahiakro in 1921. Yet today, only five of twenty Beng villages have an elementary school, and none has a junior high school *(collège)*, let alone a high school *(lycée)*. For the majority of villages that lack even a primary school, a family wishing to educate one or more of their children must send them to another village. Given that most villages are separated from one another by several kilometers and that there is no reliable mode of transportation between Beng villages other than walking and biking, most schoolchildren lodge with a relative living in the village that houses the school and return home on weekends and holidays. As most children start school at age six or seven, this living situation presents a dramatic rupture in daily life that not all young children easily tolerate.

The emotional risk is complemented by economic risks. From the perspective of the family, the more years a child stays in school, the less the child will be adequately trained in farming techniques. This would not pose a major labor loss to a large family with many children if only one is sent to school and the others remain to learn and perform farm work, but in families with many children it is rare for all or even most of them to be sent because parents must ensure that there is an adequate labor supply on the farms. For a family with only a small number of children, the labor lost in sending even one child to school is often judged untenable. Likewise, a family with several sons but only one daughter would be unlikely to send the daughter to school, as they would have no female labor supply among their children; the obverse would be true of a family with several daughters but only one son.

For those children who are allowed to begin school, passing from one grade to the next is far from automatic. A recent World Bank report on Côte d'Ivoire acknowledges this problem at the national level: "The internal efficiency of the system has suffered from high repeating and dropout rates; 20 student years of primary school are required to produce a primary school graduate, rather than the 6 years required in an ideal world" (World Bank 1997: section 29). In Beng villages, this shocking statistic is rehearsed annually in a ritualized performance. At the end of the academic year, the local school director holds a public meeting at which he ceremoniously announces the results of the year's tests, indicating which students have passed into the next grade and which have not. The proportion is quite different from what is typical in schools in the United States. In 1993, I recorded these figures from one village school:

CP1 (equivalent to first grade in the United States): only 28 of 39 students passed; 28 percent failure rate

CP 2 (second grade): 21 out of 26 students passed; 19 percent failure rate

CE 1 (third grade): 9 students failed, 1 stopped coming[31]

CE 2 (fourth grade): 9 out of 16 students passed; 44 percent failure rate

CM 1 (fifth grade): 16 out of 23 students passed and 1 was expelled; 30 percent failure rate

CM 2 (sixth grade): 26 out of 36 passed and received their elementary school degree (C.E.P.); 28 percent failure rate. Of the 26 who passed, 23 were candidates for the C.E.P.E. test that would allow them to attend junior high school *(sixième/collège)*. Of the 23 eligible candidates, 13 students passed the exam and were eligible to continue on to junior high school. Considering this, that year there was an overall failure rate of 64 percent for eligibility of sixth grade students for junior high school.

Villagers are acutely aware of these distressingly high failure rates. Many parents calculate quite explicitly that the odds of their child succeeding at school are so low that it is not worth pulling them from work in the fields to enroll them. To their minds, the economic risk is unacceptable.

A consideration of the economics of formal education must also take into account the question of feeding the students during the school day. The Ivoirian government sends village schools free staple foods for the students' lunches: generally rice, canned sardines, oil, and tomatoes. The state also pays the salary of a chef—a local woman who cooks these ingredients into a hot lunch for the children every day. As in the United States, the price that families pay for their children's hot lunch in rural Ivoirian schools is quite modest by local standards. In 1993, a child's hot lunch cost 25 CFA (currently between about 4 and 12 cents U.S.) in the villages—a price that Beng farmer-parents should be able to afford at least once or twice a week, if not daily, for a child in school. But one consultant noted bitterly that in her village the teachers skimmed a good portion of the supplies for their own needs. She complained that if the government sent thirty bags of rice, the teachers often took twenty bags for themselves.[32]

The government sent food every three months, but since the teachers were in the habit of appropriating much of the food for themselves, the bags did not last anywhere near the intended amount of time. The results of skimming became apparent in the students' lunches. When the new food sacks had just arrived, my consultant observed, the children's lunch plates were full. But soon the portions became smaller and smaller as the cook realized that the ingredients would not last to the end of the three-month period. My informant claimed that sometimes the sacks of food lasted only two days. After they ran out, the schoolchildren had to either return home for lunch—if there was someone there to cook for them—or go hungry. Given that most able-bodied adults work in their fields all day, the second scenario was not uncommon.

Cooked lunches—when they are available—are not the only expense incurred by Beng parents of schoolchildren. Far more significant is the outlay of cash required at the beginning of the school year for two categories of purchases: school uniforms, and supplies such as notebooks, pencils, and books. African authors who have grown up in poverty have noted with poignant detail the hardship school expenses created in their own families and the barrier they constituted to attending school (e.g., Laye 1955; Mathabane 1986). When I asked Beng parents whether they would be sending their children to school, many said that they would send either none or one. Most cited economic reasons for not being able to send more.

The education level of the Beng as a group reflects this very low level of school attendance in the villages. As of this writing, fewer than a dozen Beng students have ever lived abroad to pursue higher education (including only two in the United States). To my knowledge, although quite a few Beng girls have attended high school, only a handful have yet begun studies at the university level. Nationally, there are fewer than two dozen Beng high school teachers. No Beng student has yet trained at the Ecole Normale Supérieure in Abidjan to qualify to serve as a *sous-préfet* in the government administrative structure (a position roughly equivalent to a county supervisor in the United States). In short, in striking contrast to so many other ethnic groups in Côte d'Ivoire and elsewhere, among the Beng there are only the bare beginnings of an educated middle-class. As long as the majority of rural families judge the costs of sending their children to school as too high—or, put differently, as long as school remains so inaccessible in all senses (economically, politically, pragmatically, sociologically, and symbolically)—this underrepresentation of Beng in the urban middle class will persist. However, among the small but growing group of urban Beng, a larger proportion of both boys and girls are now attending schools; it is this group that will probably be responsible for significantly expanding the still miniscule educated middle class in the near future.

Migration

Because there is too much poverty, too much sickness, and too little reason for hope to transcend these ills within the villages, many Beng villagers are now joining the long-standing colonial and postcolonial African march out of the village with the expectation of finding more lucrative work situations elsewhere. Yet this does not always amount to participation in the infamous rural-urban exodus that has marked—and often plagued—so much of Africa over the past century.[33] Until recently more Beng villagers have probably left for paid farm work elsewhere than have left for the cities.

Plantation managers in other parts of the country are aware of the grinding poverty of Beng villages and for many years sent representatives regularly to recruit laborers in the Beng area. In 1985, one consultant, Pierre, noted, "Many people are leaving the villages now. They realize they can make more money elsewhere—if not in a city, then in another forest area, such as near San Pedro, to work as laborers or farm hands." That same year, another consultant estimated that perhaps half of all those who had been born in her village were currently living elsewhere in the country, either temporarily or permanently. "When all the young people in the cities are called back to the villages for meetings," she noted, "there are many, many people here!" Since the death in 1993 of long-time president Félix Houphouët-Boigny, the economic downturn and political upheaval in Côte d'Ivoire have contributed to the common conviction among rural residents that opportunities in cities and on plantations may ameliorate the increased harshness of conditions in the villages.

Yet the promise of an improved life elsewhere does not always bear fruit. The expectations of greater life chances either in a town or on a commercial plantation are often unmet. One consultant commented on the economic seduction that lures Beng youth out of the village:

> A Baule woman came to the village recruiting teenagers to work on a plantation. She promised a salary—but often the young workers were sent back to the villages after a year [of hard field work] with no money at all. If they did make any money, they had to hand over their entire salary to their parents. It was as if they were sold as slaves for the entire period. One girl had claimed 15 CFA [equivalent to between about 3 and 8 cents U.S.] of her salary to spend on something for herself, and she was put in prison [by the plantation manager] for her troubles.

The exploitation endemic to such plantation work is troubling.[34] Yet until recently, increasing numbers of Beng youth were so dissatisfied with the hardships of life in their villages that they were willing to take their chances elsewhere—even if their predecessors continually return to the villages empty-

61. A meeting of the Beng "youth" in Abidjan; meetings such as this are held every two weeks in Abidjan.

handed and disillusioned. The optimism of youth evidently enabled them to believe that perhaps their situation would be different.[35]

In the past decade more Beng youth have left for the cities than for the plantations. In Abidjan, a regional association of Beng youth (called *Ye Do*— "One Mouth") now meets every other Sunday (figure 61). Whereas the first generation of Beng migrants to Abidjan tended to live in isolation, now ten or twelve Beng residents occupy some urban courtyards. One Abidjan resident estimates the Beng population of that city at between one thousand and fifteen hundred people (Boussou Koffi, July 2001). Some of the larger cities outside Abidjan likewise have notable Beng populations, and there is now a national association of Beng youth that coordinates activities among Beng people scattered throughout the country.

What is the effect on village life of what is amounting to a systematic exodus of young people in search of more lucrative work? For a farming community whose lifestyle is dependent on a reliable and abundant labor supply, the impact is punishing. In 1993, two women friends complained to one another that "all" the young people had left the village to go work elsewhere in the country. Members of this age group were normally responsible for chasing birds away from the young rice plants growing in the fields. With young people left to chase the predators, the two friends lamented, the birds were eating more rice than usual. Even though their claim was exaggerated, they had legitimate worries that there would be little if any rice to sell for cash, and that perhaps there would not even be enough for household consumption.

Beyond such economic ruptures, the increasing out-migration also affects the quality of culture more broadly speaking. Consider these comments one consultant made in 1985:

> A young man invented the Beng dance, "Jeunesse" ["Youth"] in Asagbe. He has recently left Asagbe to go to Agboville, where he's tapping palm wine [as a paid laborer]. Since he left the village, no one can dance "Jeunesse" any more, since he was chief of the dance. As a result, the Beng are back to where they started: they're not singing in Beng any more; it is just as it was before.[36]

Despite the upheavals that the new economy is producing, the effects of modernity are neither easily predicted nor entirely one-way. In recent years, scholars working in a variety of sites throughout Africa have charted the multiply surprising ways in which modernity is now being experienced, interpreted, and revalued (see note 2, above). Here I highlight the confounding nature of the migration and, as elsewhere, the reverse migration of Beng people.[37]

Over the past two decades, I have consistently observed that those who leave Beng villages do not necessarily sever all ties to home. In fact, the opposite is more usually the case: many emigrants endeavor to maintain an active relationship with their relatives and friends still living in the villages. Several categories of Beng people leave the Beng rural area. They include young children who are sent to live with relatives in a town or city for various reasons, teenagers or young adults who go to find work in the cities or are recruited as laborers to work on commercial plantations, and adults who flee the village after an unhappy engagement with particular village practices or expectations. Let us explore each of these groups briefly.

Young children are often sent to live with others, usually relatives, in a town or city. Sometimes this is meant to benefit the child, at other times to benefit the relative. In either case, although this system has certain similarities to the Western system of foster care, there are critical differences. Whereas in the West it is generally a specific crisis in the family—the child is orphaned or there is extreme neglect or abuse—that occasions a child being fostered out, in the Beng situation this is not the commonest reason for foster care.

Rather, devoted parents may decide to send their child far away to be raised by a relative or friend for the sake of convenience, training, or improvement in life situation.

When the decision is made for the child's sake, it is generally so the child can go to school. Either the child's natal village does not have a primary school, or the child has graduated from elementary school and has passed the eligibility test for middle school or high school. As we have seen, this necessarily requires moving to a town or city, as there are no middle or high schools in any Beng villages.

On other occasions, a child, especially a boy, is sent as an apprentice to live with an urban-based relative or friend who is pursuing a relatively lucrative trade. One Beng man I will call Marc works as a tailor in a nearby town. He generally has several young village boys, mostly Beng, living with him as apprentices. No money passes hands between Marc and the boys' families. The boys live with Marc and his family, who provide them with food and shelter. In return, the boys serve as Marc's assistants—taking customers' measurements, cutting fabrics to his specifications, handing him the proper threads as he sews, and so on. The boys' parents expect that over the course of a few years as apprentices, their sons will learn enough of the trade to work successfully as tailors once they come of age.

Other children are sent to live with family members in towns or cities as a favor to the relatives. Girls, especially, occupy this position, although occasionally boys do as well. Generally the children learn useful domestic skills such as cooking, cleaning, and taking care of even younger children. In some cases the situation becomes disturbingly exploitative, with a young child doing a large amount of work day in and day out with little time left for the pleasures of childhood.

The variety of fostering practices clearly constitute a modern response to the options and constraints that urban life presents in Africa, but they have a traditional analogue in local practices. Within the villages, as we have seen, Beng children move about frequently: both literally, from one back to another, as infants; and sociologically, from one household to another, as older children. From the first days, babies are raised to appreciate multiple attachments and to feel comfortable with strangers. This child-rearing strategy has proved adaptive in the contemporary context, when multiple and regular migrations out of the village are a necessary strategy for an increasing number of families. Thus I suggest that this deeply ingrained sense of comfort with movement and multiple caretaking contexts from the earliest ages serves as a template for what appears to be a far different situation under conditions of modernity, with children moving, sometimes quite frequently, from village to city and back again.

Depending on how often they go back and forth and how much time they spend in the village between city visits, many children who leave the village regularly or for long stretches of time nevertheless continue to see their natal village as home or as a second home. This remains the case even when interethnic marriages create their own strains. Consider this narrative:

> Nguessan has three children, but at varying points, she has left them all with her older sister Aya, who is barren, to raise in the village while she has gone elsewhere. The children's father is a member of an unrelated ethnic group who is working as a teacher in a distant town. Their oldest child, a boy named Clovisse, lived in his mother's village until he was about eight years old. Then his father returned to the village to fetch Clovisse and take him to town, where he would begin first grade (CP1 in the French system). At that point, Nguessan herself left the village to go work in the southwest of the country for a year. She took her youngest child with her—a baby named Gbagbo— but she left her six-year-old daughter, Joselle, in the village in the care of her sister Aya. While she was gone, the children's father returned to the village to take Joselle to Abidjan, where she would live with his adult sister, whom the girl had never met, while attending first grade. Apparently his sister had requested Joselle to keep her company, claiming that her brother didn't need any more children because he already had a lot of them from his three wives.
>
> Soon, Nguessan again left the village in search of work in town, again taking her youngest son Gbagbo with her. This time her destination was Yamoussoukro, where she found a job working as a live-in housemaid. But her boss did not appreciate having her worker's child underfoot, so Nguessan felt obliged to send Gbagbo, by then about two years old, back to the village to be raised by his Aunt Aya. All the while, many of Nguessan's husband's relatives continued to visit her village often, and her husband himself continued to send money regularly to his aging and blind father-in-law even though Nguessan was not living in the village.

In this case, as in so many others I have observed and recorded, one sees a steady traffic in children between village and town and between the mother's and father's families. A systematic demographic study of migration patterns would present methodological challenges insofar as the composition of most households is so fluid, with so much coming and going into and out of the villages.

Beyond childhood, this regular traffic between town and country produces its own quotidian system of cultural expectations for adults. Because few Beng people own cars, when they must travel long distances they rely on the country's public transportation system. Beng passengers who ride the buses carry news of their own and their Beng neighbors' lives back and forth from village to city. But the transmission of such news of major life events— births, weddings, illnesses, deaths—does not depend only on Beng passengers riding the buses. The non-Beng drivers of those buses who regularly travel the route between Bengland and various towns and cities near and far often become integrated into Beng social networks and serve to convey not only bodies but also information from one place to another. Through these non-technological yet efficient means of communication, news travels with surprising rapidity—not quite as quickly as e-mail, to be sure, but nevertheless quickly enough. The demise of a Beng person living in a distant city is generally announced on the drums of whatever villages are affected—often hundreds of miles away—on the day that the death occurs.

Even those Beng who leave their villages in bitterness as adults because of what Victor Turner might have called social dramas enveloping their lives often return, sometimes many years or even decades later, to reconcile with their families. One young woman left the Beng region to marry a man from a neighboring ethnic group. Years later, in 1980, her grown daughter Mo'kissi left the village in disgust after her extended family tried to force her to accept an arranged-marriage husband whom she found odious (see Gottlieb and Graham 1994). I was amazed one day in 1993 to see my old friend Mo'kissi show up unexpectedly in the Asagbe *marché*. Here is what I wrote in my field notes for the day:

> Mo'kissi looks as young and beautiful as I remember her from 1980. Nevertheless, she tells me, to my astonishment, that she's had six children since then. At some point, Mo'kissi came back to Ndogbe and lived with her first husband. She had two children with him, then left him and returned to Manigbe. There she found a Mossi husband with whom she had a child. But she didn't want to stay with him, so she returned to Kosangbe to live with her mother, who had returned to the village after all those years. Even more astonishing, three of the children have died, and three are left: a boy, a girl, and the baby on her back.

I later asked a neighbor of Mo'kissi what explained the decision that both she and her mother had made to return to their village, a decision that was, to me, so unexpected. His response was simple: "You can't stay away for too long if your relatives are still in the village—eventually you must come back."

This imperative to come back now has a systematic structure organizing many urban Beng people's lives. For some years the national association of Beng youth living throughout the country has arranged an annual meeting for all members. Significantly, although the meeting is scheduled according to the Christian calendar—during the Easter weekend—it is held, in rotation, not in any of the cities but in one of the Beng villages. And the agenda often consists of discussion of future rural development plans that the youth who are now living in towns and cities would like to see implemented in their home villages. In this way, the road from village to city and back again is traveled regularly, metaphorically as well as literally.

An Endangered Religion?

Throughout both my earlier writings about the Beng and this book, I have sought to document a vibrant local religious tradition built around complex cosmological precepts and associated moral and ritual obligations. But the indigenous religious tradition of the Beng is now under siege on multiple fronts. Most obviously, Islam and Christianity tempt young people with their various promises of salvation, sobriety, and marriages based on love rather than family preference. At the same time, the rigors of maintaining faith in indigenous, Earth-based religion seem increasingly demanding to people for whom the terms of poverty are already strict. To some young skeptics, sacrificing chickens is simply a waste of good resources.

More importantly, a potential succession crisis is brewing. The Beng religion is dependent on a small group of specialists, often (though not always) elderly, who serve the spirits of the bush and the Earth and the ancestors in the afterlife. Without their dedicated religious practice week in and week out, the religion would wither. Currently there is reason to envisage just such a scenario. Some devout villagers worry that there will be no eligible replacements for the current group of Masters of the Earth when they eventually die. This is because the position requires that the occupant fill several requirements that are increasingly difficult to meet:

he may not have joined another religion;

he may not have been circumcised (this would be taboo to the Earth *(ã ba sõ pɔ)*;

he must have been born to parents who were wed in an arranged marriage;

he must belong to the proper matriclan (specified for each village);

he must be male; and

he may not be left-handed.

In some villages, it is not clear whether any young men fulfill all these requirements. For one thing, a great many young men are converting to either Islam or Christianity, thus violating the first requirement. Three Christian Internet sites now list the Beng as ripe for missionary activity, with chilling implications for the future of the indigenous Beng religion.[38]

Moreover, even many young men who have not converted to Islam, which requires male circumcision, are deciding to be circumcised; it has become the fashion because they fear that no young women will consent to sleep with them if they remain uncircumcised.[39] Therefore, the second requirement is proving increasingly problematic when it comes to finding eligible candidates for Master of the Earth. The requirement concerning arranged marriage is likewise proving an obstacle, as couples increasingly contract marriages that are based on love rather than family preference. As youth contest the arranged-marriage system, this prerequisite will become more and more difficult to fill, but there are some indications that it may be waived if the other criteria are filled and the candidate is generally a respected person of the correct lineage. This combination of six criteria is proving increasingly rare in some villages.

Will there be heirs to replace the current group of Masters of the Earth when they die? This question is for the moment unanswerable. Nevertheless, not all elders perceive the future as a gloomy time of loss. Some maintain a realistic engagement with modernity in what they foresee for the future. The late Kouassi Kokora, who served for many years as a Master of the Earth, once shared with me his reasons for guarded optimism about the changes of the future. He explained that in the days when people slept in the traditional large, round houses, the frightening *alufyɛ* bush spirits that can be seen with human eyes were unable to enter the courtyard because around the time of night when they normally came into the village (at about 10 P.M.), the doors to the houses were already closed. But now that the enclosed round houses are gone, having been replaced with small rectangular huts, the *alufyɛ* can enter the courtyards late at night. Because of the presence of the *alufyɛ* in the courtyard, people are often afraid if they awaken at night.

On the other hand, because the courtyards are no longer enclosed and because they lack doors to be locked, the *wru*, or souls, of the ancestors can also enter the courtyards any time they wish in the evening. As a result, people sleeping in the courtyards feel protected: the intermittent presence of the *wru* partly nullifies the otherwise threatening presence of the *alufyɛ*. Kouassi Kokora explained further: "The *wru* of your family will always follow you, no matter where you are: even if you move to a big city, your parents' souls will accompany you. This is true even if your family splits up: the *wru* of your parents and other close relatives will still accompany you in all your scattered locations." Here, the elder displayed a confidence that the visible changes brought by the technology of modernity will remain subordinate to the less visible structures of cultural tradition, which will continue to serve as a moral and affective anchor. To conclude, Kouassi Kokora asserted that he and other elders are not angry that their traditional house style has been forcibly changed. As he put it wisely: "Every epoch has its own style."

~

In this book I have explored how a cultural model of life and death, and of their interrelation via reincarnation, shapes in often unexpected and profound ways how infants are viewed and raised in Beng villages. The conception of a dual economy locates a contemporary postcolonial economy in one space (this life) and a precolonial/colonial economy in another space *(wrugbe)*, with the two maintaining an active interrelationship via the ideology of reincarnation. In the preceding chapters I have sought to chart how this cultural ideology makes itself felt in a child-rearing agenda that dictates a range of quotidian practices from bathing to adornment, from sleeping to eating. At the same time, poverty dramatically structures the bounds of cultural experience.

I conclude this work with a brief story. On the bodies of Beng infants a perverse new relationship between life and death, and between the present on the one hand and the past and future on the other, is now asserting itself. I have heard it reported that thieves have stolen some ancient colonial coins off of the necklaces that Beng babies still wear. Apparently the antique jewelry now fetches a good price in the cities. According to what I have been told, a coin bearing the colonial imprint of 25 CFA may now be sold for as much as 1,000–1,500 CFA each in the cities. The economic inflation signaled by these sales serves to remind us that as the moral and economic compasses of village and city collide on the bodies of Beng babies, there is much to be gained—and lost—on each side.

NOTES

Chapter One

1. Recent examples, including some experimental pieces, include Behar 1993; Cesara 1982; Gottlieb and Graham 1994; Stoller and Olkes 1987; Williams 1994; and Wolf 1992. For an engaging collection of essays chronicling relations between personal and scholarly interests in anthropologists' field research projects, see Okely and Callaway 1992. For a few rare personal accounts of female anthropologists' lives as mother-scholars both in the field and out, see Schrijvers 1993; Shostak 2000; and Sutton 1998. Other intriguing autobiographical chronicles of the person behind the scholar include Behar 1996; Geertz 1995; Grimes 1995; Myerhoff 1980; Myerhoff and Littman 1976; and Schneider 1995. A related group of provocative writings exploring the sometimes subtle, sometimes not-so-subtle dynamic of power relations and gender bias in ethnographic fieldwork includes Abu-Lughod 1990; Bell, Caplan, and Karim 1993; Callaway 1992; Caplan 1988; Golde 1986; Gregory 1984; Lewin and Leap 1996; Rosaldo 1989; Smith 1999; Warren 1988; Whitehead and Conaway 1986; D. Wolf 1996; and Yanagisako and Collier 1987; among others.

2. For descriptions of some Beng childbirths, see Gottlieb and Graham 1994.

3. For a penetrating recent discussion on the risks and complications of transporting women in labor to hospitals, see Davis-Floyd 2003.

4. For a playful critique of this genre, see DeLoache and Gottlieb 2000.

5. For a key article on this phenomenon by psychologists, see Hunziker and Barr 1986.

6. For further discussion of Nathaniel's experiences that summer, see Gottlieb, Graham, and Gottlieb-Graham 1998. For other accounts of children's effects on their ethnographer-parents in the field and vice versa, see Butler and Turner 1987; Cassell 1987; Fernandez and Sutton 1998; and Flinn, Marshall, and Armstrong 1998.

7. For more on this spatialized cosmology, see chapter 3 below and Gottlieb 1996b.

8. Bertin Kouadio and Augustin Yao were among the handful of young Beng men who had studied at the national university of Côte d'Ivoire. (No Beng women had yet studied there.) They had been living in Abidjan for some time and returned to the village to work for me full-time while I conducted my research that summer. A few months after completing the project, Bertin came to the United States to complete his B.A. in political science and M.A. in African studies at the University of Illinois; he is currently working on a doctorate in international relations at Florida International University.

9. A standardized block of 2¼ hours proved convenient for two reasons. That seemed about the natural limit for an observer to keep focused, continuous attention on a baby, and rows and columns for recording that amount of time fit legibly on a single sheet of paper, making it convenient for the recorder to work with the forms.

10. In common English, a first cousin once removed.

11. For an account of our efforts to engage in longer-term assistance, see Gottlieb and Graham 1999.

12. For an excellent overview of recent research on infant cognition, see Gopnik, Meltzoff, and Kuhl 1999.

13. Medical research has demonstrated that especially in the perinatal period, but also to some extent beyond, twins have notable medical vulnerability; see, for example, Baldwin 1994 (87–167); Buekens and Wilcox 1993; Little and Bryan 1986; and Powers and Kiely 1994.

Chapter Two

1. One internationally oriented journal, *Childhood,* begun in 1994, includes some anthropological discussion of children, but most of the articles treat contemporary social problems in urban, industrialized nations largely from a socioeconomic, rather than cultural, perspective and rarely address the lives of infants as opposed to older children and youth.

2. One brief methodological manual by a sociologist on working with older children as research subjects is also helpful to anthropologists (Fine 1988), as is a recent article on using various writing- and drawing-based methods with older children (Punch 2002).

3. Notable studies include Goodwin 1990; Heath 1983; Ochs 1988; Ochs and Schieffelin 1984; Schieffelin 1990; and Schieffelin and Ochs, eds. 1986. For overviews, see Bavin 1995; de Boysson-Bardies 1999; and Schieffelin and Ochs 1986.

4. The two journals devoted to infancy are *Infancy* (published by the International Society on Infant Studies, which hosts a biannual international conference) and *Infant Behavior and Development.* These are augmented by an annual series, *Advances in Infancy Research.* Additionally, the following journals specializing in child development frequently include articles on infancy: the *British Journal of Developmental Psychology* (published for the British Psychological Society), *Child Development* (the journal of the Society for Research in Child Development), *Developmental Psychology* (a journal of the American Psychological Association), *Developmental Review, Developmental Science* (published by the European Society for Developmental Psychology), *Early Childhood Research Quarterly* (the journal of the National Association for the Education of Young Children), the *Journal of Experimental Child Psychology,* and the *Merrill-Palmer Quarterly.*

Despite the plethora of research, developmental psychology is hampered by significant limitations. For one thing, psychologists specializing in infants have tended to concentrate their research on a very narrow spectrum of the world's babies—those belonging to Euro-American middle-class families (DeLoache 1992). Moreover, the overwhelming majority of psychological studies are based on observations of infants in laboratories, far from babies' daily lives (see Goldberg 1977). For a recent article exploring current alternatives for developmental psychology that are more informed by the anthropological emphasis on the cultural construction of experience, see Cole 1999; for a historical review of relations between anthropological and psychological work on children, see LeVine 1998.

5. Other partial reviews, annotated bibliographies, and discussions include Hardman 2001; Harris 2000; Lallemand 2002; Morton 1996; Toren 1999, n.d.a.

6. For example, see Whiting 1963; Whiting and Edwards 1988; Whiting and Whiting 1975; and Whiting 1977.

7. For example, Kakar 1981; Parin, Morgenthaler, and Parin-Matthèy 1980.

8. For example, several late essays by Meyer Fortes (1987) contain scattered but rich material on children and religion.

9. Important recent works include Fajans 1997 (83–112); Friedl 1997 (59–117); Hollos and Leis 1989 (68); Lancy 1996; and Morton 1996 (60–66).

10. For examples, see Aijmer 1992; Davis-Floyd 1992; Geurts 2002; Héritier 1994, 1996; Jordan 1993; Jorgensen 1983; Morgan 1997, 1999; Nourse 1999; Sargent 1989; and Weiner 1978.

11. For an early review, see Ginsburg and Rapp 1991. More recent works include Bledsoe 2002; Davis-Floyd and Dumit 1997; Davis-Floyd and Sargent 1997; Delaney 1991; Feldman-Savelsberg 1999; Franklin and Ragoné 1998; Ginsburg and Rapp 1995; Inhorn 1994, 1995; Jordan 1993; Rapp 1999; Roth 2002; Strathern 1992; and Tremayne 2001.

12. For example, see Allen 2002; Davis-Floyd, Cosminsky, and Pigg 2002; Geurts 2001; and Maust, Piñeda, and Davis-Floyd forthcoming.

13. For example, see Anagnost 1997; Rajani, Mann, and Ledward 2000; Richards 1984; Rwomire 2001; Scheper-Hughes 1992; Scheper-Hughes and Sargent 1998; and Stephens 1995.

14. Recent works focused on children's labor include Schlemmer 2000 and Woodhead 1998; for a review of earlier literature, see Nieuwenhuys 1996. On homeless children, see Filho and Neder 2001; Mickelson 2000; Kilbride, Suda, and Njeru 2000; and a review by Panter-Brick (2002). Writings on youth popular culture include Amit-Talai and Wulff 1995.

15. Foundational writings by anthropologists privileging a global perspective include Abu-Lughod 1998, 1999; Appadurai 1996; Comaroff and Comaroff 1991, 1997; Dirks, Eley, and Ortner 1993; Gupta and Ferguson 1997a, 1997b; Hannerz 1996; Marcus 1999; and Piot 1999.

16. Key works include Butt 1998; Harkness and Super 1983, 1996; Kilbride and Kilbride 1990; LeVine et al. 1994; Munroe and Munroe 1980; Riesman 1992; and Super and Harkness 1980, 1986.

17. For example, see Bonnet 1988; Erny 1988; Harris et al. 2000; *Journal des Africanistes* 2002; Koubi and Massard-Vincent 1994; Lallemand 1991, 1993; Lallemand and LeMoal, eds. 1981; Toren 1993; and UNESCO 1988.

18. For example, see Alanen 2000; Bose 1995; Hunt 1999; Kinney 1995; Michel 1999; Viazzi and Corsini 1997; and West and Petrik 1992.

19. For an overview of much of the key recent interdisciplinary literature on children (again, with little discussion of infants), see James 1998.

20. For example, *Asian Journal of Social Psychology* 2000; Cole 1996; Shweder 1990; and Small 1998. For a biography of Lev Vygotsky, whose work is an early precursor of many of these studies, see Kozulin 1990.

21. For other ethnographic examples of this common tendency found among peoples as diverse as the Ijo of Nigeria and the Lurs of Iran, see, respectively, Hollos and Leis 1989 (66–67) and Friedl 1997 (xiv–xv).

22. For a somewhat different but complementary set of reasons for the anthropological neglect of children as suggested by a psychologist, see Hirschfeld 2002.

23. I am indebted to Simon Ottenberg for this insight (personal communication, 15 January 1999).

24. For notable exceptions, see two excellent scholarly studies of children by nonparent anthropologists: Briggs 1998 and Ottenberg 1989.

25. For a piece that advocates a subject/agency-centered approach to children (albeit beginning at the age of four years), see Hardman 2001 (504).

26. For an unusual case of fathers routinely carrying their babies, see Hewlett 1991; for other considerations of fathers, see Hewlett 1992.

27. Critical discussions of the notion of maternal instinct include Badinter 1982; Dettwyler 1994; Einarsdóttir forthcoming; Gottlieb 1996a; Pollitt 1993; and Scheper-Hughes 1992. Theoretical and critical discussions of the notion of instinct in general include Bateson 1972; Senchuk 1991; and Varela 2003. Related thoughtful discussions on the nature/nurture debate and works that problematize the notion of human nature include Bock 1980 and Paul 1998.

28. For works on women who choose not to have children, see, for example, Campbell 1999; Ireland 1993; Lewis 1986; Morell 1994; and Veevers 1980.

29. For incisive analyses of particular instances of such behavior, see, for example, Korbin 1989, 1991; Scheper-Hughes 1987.

30. Some important works include Boone 1992; Davin 1997; Dyhouse 1978; Koven and Michel 1993; Marsh and Ronner 1996; Michel 1999; Perry 1992; and Swerdlow 1993.

31. For a variety of other perspectives on the social construction of motherhood, also see Blum 1999; Bornstein et al. 1992; Chodorow 1978; Frydman 1987; Glenn, Chang, and Forcey 1994; Hansson 1996; Harkness and Super 1996; Harwood 1992; Holloway and Minami 1996; Leiderman 1974; Lewis 1980; Crouch and Manderson 1993; Pateman 1992; Ransel 2001; Rich 1976; Roiphe 1996; Rothman 1989; and Tulkin 1977.

32. Ahead-of-their-time approaches include Minturn and Lambert 1964 and Etienne 1979. More recent works include Bianco 1991; Hyatt 1997; LeVine 1987; Lewin 1993; Ragoné 1994; Ram and Jolly 1998; and Schrijvers 1985, 1993.

33. For classic examples, see Barthes 1972, 1982, 1983; for a theoretically oriented review of the issues involved, see Hanks 1989.

34. For one direction pursued by the new "critical medical anthropology," see, for example, Scheper-Hughes and Lock 1987.

35. Some key texts include Farnell 1994, 1995; Farnell, ed. 1995; Howes 1991; Stoller 1989b, 1997; and Strathern 1997. For a helpful early review, see Lock 1993. Other examples are Ask 1994; Rasmussen 1999; and Roberts and Roberts 1996.

36. For a prescient early study, see Caudill and Plath 1966; for a recent assessment of that study, see Shweder, Jensen, and Goldstein 1995.

37. See especially the provocative work by James McKenna on the protection that co-sleeping may offer against SIDS (e.g., McKenna 2001; McKenna and Bernshaw 1995; McKenna, Mosko, and Richard 1999). For an appreciative review of this literature, see Small 1998 (109–37).

38. On sexuality, see Bunzl forthcoming; Caplan 1987; Lancaster and di Leonardo 1997; and Manalansan 2003. On breast-feeding, see Maher, ed. 1992. On menstruation, see Buckley and Gottlieb 1988; Hoskins 2002; and Van de Walle and Renne 2001. On eating, see Counihan and Van Esterik 1997.

39. I am grateful to Philip Graham for bringing this passage to my attention.

40. For example, see Briggs 1998; Crapanzano 1980; 'Elota 1983; Ongka 1979; Ottenberg 1996; Shostak 1981; and Werbner 1991.

41. For example, Fischer and Abedi 1990; Gudeman and Rivera 1990; Whitten, Whitten, and Chango 1997.

42. For example, Bertaux 1981; Buckley 1987; Crapanzano 1984; Dwyer 1982; Okely and Callaway 1992.

43. For important early examplars, see Mintz 1985; Roseberry 1989; and Wolf 1982.

44. For a few recent stimulating discussions of this long-vexing issue, see Bock 1980; Carruthers 1992; Lewontin 2000; Paul 1998; Sahlins 1976; and Senchuk 1991.

Chapter Three

1. For a similar perspective on a marginalized group in Indonesia, see Tsing 1993 (28 *et passim*).

2. For a general ethnography of Beng society, see Gottlieb 1996b; for a narrative of fieldwork among the Beng, see Gottlieb and Graham 1994.

3. In 2001, the first Beng person appointed to a national position was Koffi Boussou, named Directeur Général des Eaux et Forêts (Director of Waters and Forests).

4. The Beng religion does include the legitimate possibility of murder by mystical rather than empirical means. Although it is considered deplorable (*à geŋɛ*), witchcraft is not classified as taboo (*sō pɔ*). The distinction between the two means of killing is critical in the local system of significance.

5. For the definitive history of Samori, see Person 1968, 1975. Additional works include Azarya 1980, 1981; Dussart 1984; Georges 1991; *Mande Studies* 2001; Oloruntimehin 1971; Person 1979; and Tymowski 1988. For a short and somewhat hagiographic biography of Samori, see Fofana 1998. For brief discussion of an assertion that Samori's troops did succeed in extracting tribute from the Beng in the form of kola nuts, see Gottlieb 1996b (6, 143–5).

6. On military resistance against the French by the neighboring Baule, for example, see Weiskel 1980.

7. For a brief general overview of trade in this region of West Africa, see Kelly 1997. For discussion of kola nuts in particular in the history of the regional economy, see, for example, Austen 1987; Hopkins 1973; and Iliffe 1995 (82). Hopkins notes that kola remained an important export of Côte d'Ivoire throughout the colonial and early postcolonial periods (1973:246–48).

8. Beng men used to manufacture bark cloth in great quantity, both for their own and their wives' use as well as for trade with neighboring groups that did not have the technical skills, knowledge, appropriate trees, or inclination to manufacture it. Older villagers told me that in earlier times every Beng man knew how to make bark cloth. The bark cloths (*zɔ*) that the Beng manufacture come from a tree of the same name (*zɔ yírí*). The manufacture of bark cloth involves an ingenious and arduous process. Men fell a tree, strip off the bark, and wash the bark with a mixture of water and lemon or lime juice to soften it. After squeezing the bark to dry it, they stretch it, then finally sew it into various items. Nowadays, Beng men still fashion bark cloth into washcloths for herbal baths, hunting bags, napping mats, and men's traditional style underwear (used for certain ritual occasions). Occasionally, police officers come to the weekly village market from the nearby town of M'Bahiakro and confiscate any bark cloths they see being sold, claiming that Beng men are depleting the forest of *zɔ* trees. Villagers vigorously dispute this assertion, maintaining that the trees grow abundantly and quickly.

9. For a brief but cogent overview of the place of the Mande family in the broader schema of West African languages, see Williamson 1997; for an overview of Mande languages as part of the Niger-Congo family, see Williamson and Blench 2000 (18–21); for a dictionary of the Beng language, see Gottlieb and Murphy 1996.

10. For more on Beng religion, see Gottlieb 1996b (19–45) and Gottlieb and Graham 1994.

11. To specify this localized spiritual understanding, I capitalize *Earth* in my discussions of Beng religious practice.

12. To honor this strong preference, I do not divulge their names in any of my writings.

13. For some comparative discussion of this trend in Africa, see Gottlieb n.d.a and Ray 1999.

14. On Beng diviners as intermediaries, see Gottlieb 1996b (chap. 2) and Gottlieb and Graham 1994.

15. For line drawings of the round houses and round fields, see Gottlieb 1996b (42, 65). One round field that I measured had a diameter of about 868 feet and was said to be somewhat typical of such fields (or perhaps slightly smaller). This particular field had twenty-two pie-slice-shaped fields within it. Each man was allocated one or more slices of the pie, and those with multiple slices allocated some of their holdings to their wives and sisters. Slash-and-burn techniques necessitate the annual establishment of a new round field for each group of male farmers.

16. For further discussion of the relation between witchcraft and kingship/queenship, see Gottlieb 1989b.

17. The vagueness of this number is due to the fact that some villages are, it is said, "going Baule": their residents have begun to speak the Baule language rather than the Beng language. This is a complex process of cultural-linguistic transformation that has yet to be studied systematically.

18. For comparative data on this increasingly common situation, see Stephens 1995.

19. The CFA is used in fifteen largely Francophone nations of West and Central Africa. Since 1994, the exchange rate has floated, generally ranging from 200 to 600 CFA = $1 U.S.

20. For example, D'Alisera 1998, 2001, forthcoming; Hutchinson 2001; Johnson 2001; Stoller 1996, 2002.

Chapter Four

1. Of course Westerners with active religious affiliations may involve their infants to some extent (and their older children far more so) in religious activities geared to the life cycle, including baptisms, circumcision rituals, and adolescent initiations (see Kirshenblatt-Gimblett 1982). Members of certain contemporary Western religious communities, including the Amish, some Mennonites, and Chasidic Jews, also promote systematic child-rearing agendas based explicitly on religious doctrines.

2. In Africa, the notion that babies are reincarnated ancestors is fairly common—e.g., among the Ijaw of Nigeria (Leis 1982), the Mossi (Bonnet 1981) and Bobo (LeMoal 1981) of Burkina Faso, the Akan peoples of Ghana and Côte d'Ivoire (Ephirim-Donkor 1997), the Yoruba (Okri 1991; Oluwole 1992) and Igbo (Bastian 2002, Uchendu 1965) of Nigeria, and many others (e.g., Creider 1986; MacGaffey 1986; Orubu 2001). Even when infants are not seen as full reincarnations of ancestors, they are frequently said to harbor special ties to the world of spirits, animals, and witches (e.g., Fermé 2001:196–218). For reincarnation beliefs among Native Americans, see Mills 2001 and Mills and Slobodin 1994; for these beliefs in Tibet, see Gupta 2002.

3. As with so many other semantically rich words, the term *afterlife* is not a perfect translation. *Afterlife* implies that the ordinary or unmarked place and time of orientation are this human existence and that once one dies one goes "afterward" to a space where one stays, presumably for eternity. In contrast, Beng souls go to *wrugbe* as a way station of sorts; after

a period of time, the duration of which varies, they are reborn as infant humans. In some ways, "this life" is seen by at least some Beng—certainly by religious specialists (diviners and Masters of the Earth) and others who think deeply about such eschatological matters—as the ephemeral site of transit whose ultimate goal is to reach the land of the ancestors. For a similar case among the BaKongo, see MacGaffey 1986.

4. Compare Ardener 1989 (117, 123, and passim) on "demographic false consciousness" and "folk-demography."

5. John Peel has noted that a somewhat similar contradiction (by Western standards) exists in Yoruba thought: ancestors are said to exist at two levels simultaneously, both individual and collective, and no problem is perceived concerning what appears, in Western logic, to be internal inconsistency (personal communication).

6. I will discuss this ghostly commuting further in chapter 11.

7. In one study of infants born vaginally in Seattle, the mean number of days for umbilical cord separation was 12.9 (Novack, Mueller, and Ochs 1988:221), though the range was wide—from 3 to 45 days. The mean appears to be shorter in developing countries (for an explanatory hypothesis, see Novack, Mueller, and Ochs 1988:222). For example, in a study of infants born vaginally in India, the mean number of days was 5.2 (Bhalla et al. 1975). At the time of my fieldwork, there were not enough newborns for me to observe this phenomenon at a statistically significant level.

8. Extended symbolic elaboration or ritual treatment of the umbilical stump in one way or another is not uncommon in West Africa. For a notable example from the Igbo of Nigeria, see Uchendu 1965 (58–59).

9. The initial, ritual enema must be administered with a bulb-shaped gourd (*beŋlɛ*), which women grow in this shape for this purpose. Subsequent enemas may be administered using an industrial version of this object: a rubber clyster purchased in a local market.

10. In chapter 6, I discuss a more pragmatic rationale for this toileting practice from the perspective of the mother and her labor demands.

11. Since this jewelry ritual may take some time to organize and carry out, it occurs on the same day that the umbilical cord stump falls off only if the stump breaks off in the morning; if the stump drops off in the afternoon, the jewelry session will usually be delayed until the next day (which, as with the traditional Jewish calendar, begins at sundown for the Beng).

12. The gradualness of this process has been noted elsewhere in Africa (e.g., for the Ijaw of Nigeria, see Leis 1982 [154]; for the neighboring Akan of Côte d'Ivoire and Ghana, see Ephirim-Donkor 1997 [84]), as well as in other areas of the world, such as Indonesia (Edward Brunner, personal communication; Diener 2000). Edward Bruner has observed that in Indonesia a culturally defined gradual process of entry into "this world" often correlates with a gradual process of exiting from it, as evidenced by a long and drawn-out set of funeral rituals (personal communication; see also Peacock 1973).

13. Spirits are said to take food from people's crops for their own nourishment. For this reason, farmers often do not ask questions if there is some food missing from their fields; they assume that the spirits must have taken it to feed themselves.

14. Typically their services cost 50 CFA.

15. The ancient French coins are sometimes sold in local markets, although they are increasingly rare. The tie between infants and cowries is found elsewhere in West Africa. For example, the Mossi of Burkina Faso may, for a sum of cowry shells, mock-sell to someone else a new infant born to a woman who has lost many children to stillbirth or later death,

as a ritual means of protecting the newborn against tragedy (Skinner 1962:274). For further discussion of the meaning and place of cowries in Beng child care, see chapter 11.

16. In the case of "Ajua," the Beng are referring to the seven-day calendar and associated naming system, which they have borrowed from neighboring Akan peoples. In other contexts, they rely on their own six-day calendar. I lack space to elaborate here on the complexities of the interrelations between these two calendrical systems in Beng daily life.

17. When I presented an early version of this chapter at a conference in England during the height of the controversy over "mad cow disease" I became especially sensitive to what may be a panhuman tendency to read symbolic danger into sick and dead animals. For a recent anthropological analysis of foot-and-mouth disease as it is currently being culturally constructed in England, see Franklin 2001. On other uses of animals in Beng thought, see Gottlieb 1986b, 1989a.

18. For their part, adults can be "caught" by a human corpse only if they have direct contact with it—if they wash the cadaver itself, or if they washed the deceased's laundry right before the person died.

The general tendency to take notice of and to symbolically elaborate on the rotten smell of a human corpse is widespread (for an example from Amazonia, see Crocker 1985 [160]).

19. I had been enlisted by a distant relative to contribute to the cause of feeding the chief, as he was not being well attended by his immediate family. This woman criticized the family for having neglected the chief during his illness. She claimed that he had been a great chief, continually giving away large sums of money to help others in need until he was virtually destitute; thus his *wru* was justified in seeking vengeance for unfair treatment by his kin.

20. For the first month of her widowhood, a woman must wash daily with ritual "medicines" to chase away her husband's spirit. The medicines must be cooked in a pot over a fire separate from her normal cooking hearth, and the ashes from this fire, which are deemed polluting, must be disposed of in a discrete pile, not dispersed. Otherwise, women who are not yet widowed might touch the ashes inadvertently, killing their husbands.

21. For scientific discussion of the neurological foundations and processes of memory both in those afflicted with Alzheimer's and in others, see, for example, Kostovic et al. 1992; for a moving set of photo essays of individuals diagnosed with Alzheimer's with texts written by relatives, see Smoller 1997.

22. Although the literature in developmental psychology classifies this phenomenon under the rubric of the development of object permanence rather than under the rubric of memory, surely memory is central to the story.

23. For a review of the now abundant literature on infant memory, see Mandler 1998.

24. For discussion of the social and historical construction of memory in recent years, see Bloch 1998; Cole 2001; Connerton 1989; Foucault 1977; Halbwachs 1992; Küchler and Melion 1991; Litzinger 1995; Lowenthal 1985; Roberts and Roberts, eds. 1996; and Tonkin 1992.

25. Variations on this theme exist elsewhere in Africa. Among the Sukuma/Nyamwezi of Tanzania, people possessed by ancestral spirits often inexplicably speak in the languages of surrounding ethnic groups (especially the Maasai and Taturu peoples)—languages that neither they nor their Sukuma/Nyamwezi audiences understand (Allen 2002). A notion of a multilingual "afterlife" in which all languages are mutually comprehensible, not unlike that envisioned by the Beng, may be at work here.

26. For helpful summaries of the innatist and nativist theories of language development on the one hand versus the behaviorist and social interactionist theories on the other, see Cole 1999 (95–98) and Hulit and Howard 1997 (14–53). For some examples of cultural

perspectives on language development, see Bruner 1982 and 1983 and Elman, Bates, Johnson, Karmiloff-Smith, Parisi, and Plunkett 1996. For a recent enunciation of the Chomskyian (innatist) perspective, see Pinker 1995.

27. On the striking congruence of the Beng model with another widely accepted scholarly model of early language development, however, see Werker 1989.

28. In the short run, infants and toddlers who are addressed directly and regularly tend to begin speaking somewhat earlier and to acquire larger and more precise vocabularies than do their counterparts who are not (Judy De Loache, personal communication; Smiley and Huttenlocher 1995). In the long run, however, virtually all healthy humans learn to speak their native language with a high degree of fluency no matter how often adults or older children spoke to them directly when they were infants (e.g., Snow, de Blauw, and van Roosmalen 1979:287).

29. Some scholars have claimed that the special speech style used to address infants and to teach them language—sometimes called baby talk or motherese—has identifiable features that are universal (e.g., Ferguson 1977; Snow 1977). Critics, however, have pointed out that the scarce cross-cultural data on this speech style do not all support the theory (e.g., Ochs and Schieffelin 1984; Crago 1992:31). The term *motherese* is itself a Eurocentric one based on the Euro-American pattern that it is mothers who overwhelmingly talk to infants. Although the Beng pattern does appear to uphold the theory, I remain cautious about using these data to make more general claims until a far more comprehensive comparative database is assembled.

30. For example, see Bavin 1995 (379–81); Caudill 1972; Ochs and Schieffelin 1984; Snow, de Blauw, and van Roosmalen 1979.

31. The Beng pattern of mothers addressing their newborns and older infants face-to-face on a regular basis challenges a widely discussed hypothesis, suggested by Robert LeVine (1984, 1987), that rural, unschooled women living in the technologically underdeveloped world are too preoccupied with ensuring the physical survival of their infants to enjoy the luxury of speaking to them face-to-face and to enjoy a high level of emotional involvement with them (LeVine 1973, 1977; LeVine et al. 1994:196–223). Although LeVine's theory has found some ethnographic support (e.g., Goldschmidt 1975), it has also been criticized on the basis of other data from East Africa (e.g., Kilbride and Kilbride 1983; Super and Harkness 1974). The Beng practice further challenges the applicability of LeVine's hypothesis to all of sub-Saharan Africa, signaling that the model must be modified to accommodate local cultural variation. Moreover, LeVine's explanation, which is based on essentially economic and related ecological concerns, is monocausal. The Beng are at least as impoverished as are the rural populations with whom LeVine has worked in Kenya, yet cultural factors, especially religious ideology, inspire Beng mothers and other caretakers to speak directly to infants no matter what their economic constraints and anxieties.

Chapter Five

1. Usually it is the mother who bathes the young infant, but for the first two months an older woman who lives nearby, most likely the mother's own mother or mother-in-law, may take over this task.

2. In precolonial and early colonial days, Tahan would have used a handmade wooden basin, a *yiri gbɔ* (lit. "old wood/tree"), made by a Beng man with carving skills.

3. Kola nuts come in two varieties, white (*pu*) and "red" (*tɛ̂*) (a deep magenta). Sometimes one color is specified when the nut is used for ritual purposes.

4. For an ethnographic application of this approach to childbirth practices in rural Tanza-

nia, see Allen 2002. A cultural perspective on risk is equally illuminating when applied to Euro-American settings. For a psychocultural analysis of risk applied to American adolescents' behavior, see Lightfoot 1997.

5. Women who are especially sought after for making infant jewelry may also make the jewelry for their own babies. In this case, the woman might describe her role by saying, *n títí, ma wroná,* which means literally, "I alone, I took them [the beads] out [of a basket to string them]."

6. Other Beng mothers living in cities do know such procedures, however—the level of knowledge of such traditional techniques varies among urban Beng women.

7. White beads are *baŋlɛ pu,* tiny brown beads are *cecɛŋwlɛ,* large brown beads are *bomblo trí,* blue beads are *flɔwlɛ,* striped beads are *wlewlɛ,* green beads are *baŋlɛ gbégbé,* and red beads are *gbɔ tɛ́.* A necklace is *wɔze baŋ,* a bracelet is *wɔ diŋ baŋ,* and an anklet is a *gã diŋ baŋ.*

8. Women make use of the lemon's pungent smell in other contexts: they sometimes wash themselves with lemons to hide the smell of breastmilk or menstrual blood.

9. According to one Beng mother, another reason to apply the oral lemon treatment is to promote good speech development in the child later on.

10. Lemons are also used as a component of medicinal concoctions that a woman in labor may drink to promote an easy delivery, and they can be added to an herbal preparation bought from Jula healers to treat stomachache.

11. From a woman's perspective, the disease *gbre* may be described as *gɔŋ klɛ yilɛ gbre*— "dirt from sleeping with a man."

12. In addition to posing a danger to infants, such dirty adults are also at risk themselves: it is said that they will soon be bitten by a snake.

13. This belief is only held in the Forest region, not the Savanna region of Bengland.

14. Normally, a young woman's first marriage is arranged by her family, traditionally while she is a teenager, according to specific principles of alliance (Gottlieb 1996b: chapter 4).

15. Violation of the rule confining young female sexuality to a prearranged alliance, rather than any intrinsic notion of female sexual pollution per se, accounts for the ideology of dirt. For an elaboration of this interpretation, see Gottlieb 1990.

16. Another is a belt made from pineapple bark onto which is strung a small brown bead, a large black bead, and two red, black, and white striped beads (*gbongbo trí*), with a conspicuous knot dangling down from the beads.

17. This linguistically constituted disease has been noted elsewhere in West Africa, as linguistically far afield as among the Fulani of Niger (Johnson 2000b; Riesman 1992:174–75), as well as among the linguistically closer Mandinga of Guinea-Bissau (Michelle Johnson, personal communication, 29 August 2001). Some Muslim groups elsewhere endorse related beliefs (for example, for Iran see Friedl 1997:87–89).

18. These bracelets may take quite different forms. One *ye baŋ* had four white beads and a brown bead hanging down from the wrist cord; another bracelet had a blue bead and a brown bead dangling from the cord; and a third had four black beads and a brown bead hanging down. Another baby wore a bracelet consisting of four green beads dangling down from the wrist strap, and a yellow and red striped bead at the bottom of that row. Still another newborn—this one ten days old when I observed his jewelry—wore four mouth cords with variations on the above bead themes and the addition of a tree root, a shell, and a lock of his mother's hair strung into some of the bracelets.

19. In fact, contact with a corpse is considered dangerous for all people, with the youngest people being the most susceptible. Although most cases of *gale* are said to result from contact with a human corpse, rare cases are said to be caused by exposure to the cadaver of an animal, especially a dog, which has special ties to humans (Gottlieb 1996b: chapter 5). Given the continuity between the human and animal world that marks Beng ecothought, this makes local sense.

20. Since one of the symptoms of *gale* is a fever, another popular remedy is to wash the afflicted baby with plants used to cure babies' fevers.

21. See figure 28 below.

22. The other two are palm trees (which produce the multiply useful palm nuts as well as palm wine), and kapok trees (which are ritually planted in every village for symbolically critical reasons) (Gottlieb 1996b).

23. By contrast, urine is not considered mystically powerful. As a result, mothers do not spend much time or energy training their infants to urinate at a specific time or in a specific place. If babies happen to urinate on someone while being held, the event is not considered problematic or offensive. Accordingly, the bathing routine does not include practices related to regulating urination.

24. According to pediatrician Melvin Tyrone, a warm, pulsing, or bulging fontanel spot may indicate a serious illness in an infant—perhaps roseola, encephalitis, or meningitis (personal communication, April 1996).

25. The fontanel is the subject of ritual attention in many societies; for a strikingly similar rationale in Tonga, see Morton 1996 (62); on related haircutting rituals in Thailand, see Rajadhon 1965 (188–89).

26. During my own children's pediatric visits, male biomedical doctors tended to discount the possibility that teething can bring on fevers, whereas female pediatric nurses (perhaps on the basis of their own mothering experiences) tended to accept the possibility of a causal association. If there is indeed a biochemical connection between teething and fevers, it remains to be documented and explained by Western science.

27. Remedies for infant fevers not caused by teething involve a variety of other herbal products, such as leaves from the tomato plant (*tomati*), bitter berry plant, *nonú pléplé* plant, or *boŋ ti kondro* plant.

28. As Michelle Johnson has pointed out (personal communication, 29 August 2001), kaolin has widespread currency in ritual contexts throughout sub-Saharan Africa. In particular, it is used in girls' (and sometimes boys') initiation rituals among several groups on the continent (e.g., Bledsoe 1984; Boone 1986; Leopold 1983; MacCormack 1979; Philips 1995; and Turner 1967).

29. I take this description from field notes written in 1980; MoKla died in 2003.

30. T. Berry Brazelton, "Dr. T. Berry Brazelton on Toilet Training: Online Chat, Pampers Parenting Institute," available online at <www.babycenter.com/general/4526.html>.

Chapter Six

1. For an early statement on how interactions between infants and their major caretakers shape the lifelong structure of cognition as children mature into adults, see Isbell and McKee 1980.

2. Two notable exceptions documented in the ethnographic literature are the cases of the rural Maya in Mexico and the Dani of Irian Jaya. In both groups, young infants are cared for mostly or exclusively by their mothers and are kept in very quiet, dark places for several

months (Brazelton 1977; Butt 1998). These examples remind us not to generalize about "the non-Western world," which itself contains a diverse collection of practices overdetermined by historical layers of culture and political economy.

Some scholars have recently begun to document contemporary challenges to the traditional non-Western model of collective child care involving a variety of local and, increasingly, global factors (e.g., Swadener, Kabiru, and Njenga 2000). Such sweeping changes have not yet affected Beng village-based child-rearing structures to the extent that they have elsewhere; in chapter 11, I discuss other changes that are more pertinent to the Beng context.

3. Dieudonné Kwame Kouassi carried out most of the observations in this quantitative portion of the research. In total, we observed 25 babies in 43 observational sessions over a total of 5,745 minutes, or 95.75 hours. Of the 43 sessions, 41 were 135 minutes in duration; one was 120 minutes in duration; and one was 90 minutes in duration. The babies ranged in age from three months to 24 months, with the average age being 11.4 months.

4. On the problematic nature of the popular nostalgia for an imagined utopic community of an earlier America, see, for example, Coontz 1992 and May 1988.

5. As elsewhere throughout this work, my generalizations in this chapter concerning middle-class, Euro-American families are founded on a combination of published research and my own positioning as a "native anthropologist." The applicability of my observations concerning strangers may vary when it comes to American families with other ethnic and class backgrounds, as well as to Europeans and citizens of other postindustrialized nations.

6. The acronym stands for Drug Abuse Resistance Education. According to its website, as of 2002 the program was active in nearly 80 percent of school districts in the United States and was present in over fifty-four countries internationally (<www.dare-america.com>).

7. A rich literature is now accumulating on this topic. For especially stimulating reflections, see Bauman 1995, 1997, and 1998. For two earlier essays reflecting a less stark portrait in which the stranger is far less demonized than in the more contemporary portrait I am drawing here, see Schütz 1944 and Simmel 1950.

8. In his later work, Bowlby himself—the father of attachment theory—acknowledged the historical and cultural influences that shape contemporary attachment patterns (e.g., 1988), but he continued to maintain that women are more naturally suited than men to child care (Karen 1998:314 and 463n3). For helpful summaries of recent attachment research that emphasizes cultural influences, see Harwood, Miller, and Irizarry 1995; Karen 1998 (411–25). For a balanced summary of the strengths and weaknesses of the attachment literature, see Cole 1999 (91–95).

9. For research on relations with fathers, largely focusing on European and other postindustrialized nations, see especially the work of Lamb and his colleagues (e.g., Lamb, ed. 1987, 1997, 1999; Lamb, Hwang, Ketterlinus, and Fracasso 1999). On meaningful emotional attachments between young children and their caretakers, including day care teachers in postindustrialized settings, see, for example, Cummings 1980; Kearsley, Zelazo, Kagan, and Hartmann 1975; Lamb 1999; Lamb, Sternberg, Hwang, and Broberg 1992; and Sroufe, Fox, and Pancake 1983. For helpful overviews of this controversial literature, see Karen 1998 (313–44) and Sroufe 1996. For parallel work looking at the lives and experiences of fathers cross-culturally (mostly conducted by anthropologists), see Hewlett 1992.

10. I will deploy the term attachment, but in a somewhat looser way than that in which my developmental psychology colleagues usually deploy it. I do so deliberately, in order to expand the parameters of discussion to encompass indigenous models of attachment whose content may look somewhat different from that of the models that have been identified by Western-trained researchers for Western and Westernized populations. Researchers steeped

in Western contexts may be surprised to learn of the relatively large number of meaningful emotional attachments that infants among the Beng, and among many other groups in West Africa, have with a large array of adults and older children.

In this chapter, I also link two bodies of work: research by historians, sociologists, and other scholars on strangers, and work by developmental psychologists on emotional and social attachments as well as on relations of infants to strangers. Concerning the latter, I further combine discussion of two technical bodies of literature in developmental psychology: writings on attachment and writings on fear of and wariness toward strangers. In some works by developmental psychologists, these two topics of inquiry have been inextricably linked; in other works they have been considered independent; and in still others they are seen as related, but in complex and not easily predicted ways. I lack space here to expound on the implications inherent in this issue (for one thoughtful early discussion, see Clarke-Stewart 1978). Briefly, my perspective is that the two parameters, attachment on the one hand and young children's attitude toward strangers on the other hand, are indeed linked, in compound and subtle ways. In referencing these discrete bodies of literature by developmental psychologists, I will explore how the issues implicated in their otherwise distinct writings speak to each other in striking ways in Beng villages.

11. One might imagine a direct relationship between anxiety toward strangers and strangers' relative rarity. Thus one might predict that the more rare strangers are, the more anxiety they might produce, and vice versa. This commonsensical prediction is problematic, however, because cities have both high numbers of strangers and high levels of anxiety concerning them. The inverse is untrue as well. Contrary to the prediction, Beng villages have moderate numbers of strangers but low levels of anxiety about them. Clearly, other factors are at work.

12. This echoes an observation Jan Jansen makes regarding the linguistically related northern Mande groups: "A stranger in Mande is, in fact, not 'strange' at all; the term 'stranger' is as neutral as, for instance, the term 'hunter' or 'brother'" (1996:26).

13. For example, in French, the semantic scope of *étranger(e)* is similar to that of the English *stranger*, while *invité(e)* (derived from Latin, *invitare*) corresponds to the English *guest* (derived from German, *gest*). According to the 1993 *New Shorter Oxford English Dictionary*, the English term *guest* also denoted what we now term "stranger" for a period from the mid-twelfth through the late sixteenth centuries, but this meaning is now obsolete. It is tempting to speculate that the relatively brief period during which the English term *guest* also meant "stranger" is precisely the late medieval/early modern period leading to the rise of European urbanism—a psychologically threatening time when guests might have been increasingly likely to be encountered, and perceived, as strangers. However, I leave it to linguists and historians to pursue this line of inquiry. My point refers to the modern period following the late sixteenth century, when the two meanings of the English words *guest* and *stranger* have been, and continue to be, quite disjunct in daily parlance.

14. For a related argument concerning the situation among Fulani people of West Africa, see Riesman 1977. For a contrasting description of the length of time and high degree of cultural effort typically required for a stranger to become incorporated into contemporary urban, industrialized societies, see Schütz 1944.

15. The pattern I have described may be common in other villages throughout West Africa; for a Ugandan case with certain similarities to what I have described, see Obbo 1979.

16. In Beng, the greeting for a female host welcoming a male visitor, which incorporates words from the Baule language, is as follows (there are minor variations for different gender combinations):

Female host: aba ka kweŋ. (Father, welcome.)

Male guest: maa, nye wiau. ([Male response.])

Female host: aúŋ. blíni ka. we nã ŋo grè? ([Female response.] Have a seat. How are the people over there [where you are coming from]?)

Male guest: we nã ŋo myankalo. (The people over there are fine.)

Female host: aúŋ. mú wiyau. ([Female response.])

Male visitor: màà. ([Male response.])

17. Amy Gajda, "Legal Issues in the News" (commentary on "duty to rescue"), WILL-AM Radio, Urbana, Ill., 22 March 1999. The New Hampshire legal case cited is *Buch v. Amory Mfg Co.*, 44 A. 809 (N.H. 1898).

18. In the case of a very difficult childbirth in the village, a male healer may be called in to administer herbal remedies, or a male Master of the Earth may enter to offer prayers and sacrifices.

19. Infants vary in their level of alertness during their first few hours, and even days, postpartum. However, some Western researchers are now suggesting that the increasing number of "floppy," nonalert babies in hospital newborn wards may be in part explained by the pain medication that is administered routinely to laboring women. This occurs even more in the case of caesarean-section deliveries (e.g., Rook 1997:471–74). In the United States, "in many hospitals, 80 percent [of laboring women] receive epidural anesthesia" (Davis-Floyd and Sargent 1997:11). In rural West African villages such as those I am describing, such drugs are unavailable. It may be that Beng newborns on the whole are more alert than most newborns born in Western hospitals at least in part because of this difference. My informal observations in both contexts would support this hypothesis.

20. Beng terms for relatives group together individuals of different genealogical categories to place them in the same conceptual universe according to a combination of complex principles. For instance, one's "little mother" might be the younger sister, first- or second-degree matrilateral or patrilateral parallel cousin, or even a more distantly related clanmate of one's parent. The details of this system are not relevant to this discussion. Suffice it to say that on learning that, for instance, a boy is called an elder brother, a young girl does not confuse this boy with her own genealogical brother, but comes to understand that the two boys are of the same generation and gender and may also belong to the same matriclan or patriclan as herself. In Beng villages, only children younger than one are addressed by name; all others are accorded kinship terms as a sign of respect, whether or not the two people are actually related. This means that virtually everyone an infant meets—including strangers—will be introduced by a kin term and not a name.

21. The practice of waking a sleeping baby for introductions to visitors has been documented elsewhere in West Africa (e.g., among the Fulani—see Riesman 1992:113 and Johnson 2000b:185) and may be fairly common on the continent. We will see in chapter 7 how this practice forms part of a broader structure of Beng infant sleep practices.

22. On the common practice of children circulating among households in a variety of "traditional" societies, see Lallemand 1993.

23. "Baby Health and Safety: Limit Visitors to Keep Baby Healthy," *Parents*, November 1996, 47.

24. The tendency to restrict social engagements during an infant's first few months of life is not monopolized by Western societies—some non-Western societies have their own reasons for restricting social contacts to an even greater extent than is common among the contemporary Euro-American middle-class. Writing of the Dani of Irian Jaya (Indonesia),

Leslie Butt explains that during the first three to four months of life the young infant is never exposed to the sun (1998:119). Instead, the child is almost constantly wrapped up in several layers of net bags and stays in virtual darkness: "The point is not to stimulate the child, but to sedate through darkness, quiet, routine breastfeeding on demand, and through providing stimulation only when the child comes to demand it" (15). During these early months, when a mother takes her infant to the gardens, she encloses her child in ten or twelve bags to protect her against the sun, and there it is so cool and dark that the baby can often sleep for hours. The rationale for this set of practices is well thought out: young babies are said to be frightened easily and are also considered vulnerable to spirits' or ancestors' attacks that can sicken the child (121–22); in the face of these culturally constituted risks, Dani parents maintain that babies grow best without too much talking or stimulation (119). It is only by the fourth or fifth month that Dani mothers allow their babies to play with other adults (122).

25. William Sears, "Answers from Dr. Sears: Soothing Stranger Anxiety," *Parenting,* May 1999, 37–38.

26. For an incisive comparative analysis of the cybernetic relations among mothers, infants, and others in the family as they concern the household food supply, see Popkin, Lasky, Spicer, and Yamamota 1986. For further discussion of food and Beng infants, see chapter 8.

27. The likelihood that a particular Beng baby who exhibits stranger anxiety would be classified by a developmental psychologist as emotionally healthy and properly "attached" (to the mother) depends on several factors about which the relevant psychology literature has much to say. A discussion of the nuances and technical details underlying the classificatory schema is beyond the scope of this chapter. For one clear summary of the relevant issues, see Sroufe 1996 (112–13).

28. For an example of a society in Micronesia where it is taboo to leave a baby alone, see Le 2000 and Lutz 1988.

29. These informal situations of separation and reunion that I observed in daily life loosely approximated the "Strange Situation" test that is administered by attachment researchers to determine the degree and kind of infants' attachments to their mothers or other primary caretakers. However, I did not administer the formal "Strange Situation" test during field-work for a variety of reasons, including the pragmatic consideration that it would not have been possible to replicate the carefully controlled laboratory conditions created for such studies by most developmental psychologists.

Chapter Seven

1. See the Sleepnet.com archived infant sleep forums at <www.sleepnet.com/infant/infantinf.html>.

2. For scholarly documentation of this broad trend, see, for example, New and Richman 1996; Super et al. 1996; and A. Wolf et al. 1996. For a small but perhaps representative sample of the abundant popular literature exhibiting the tendency to unquestioningly promote these goals, see, for example, Condor 1999; Salmon 1996; Symon 1999; and United States Consumer Product Safety Commission 1999.

Several recent studies have documented the fact that some U.S. populations other than middle-class Euro-Americans—including African-Americans and impoverished residents of Appalachia—regularly practice some variety of co-sleeping with their babies, and sometimes with their toddlers and young children (e.g., Abbott 1992; Litt 1981; Lozoff, Wolf, and Davis 1984). Even some middle-class Euro-American parents are beginning to consider the possible virtues of co-sleeping. A series of articles and letters to the editor in the mainstream magazine *Parents* hints at the diversity of opinions to be found among middle-class parents on this issue (July 1996 and November 1996). Contemporary countertrends toward co-sleeping and the "family bed," sometimes marketed as "attachment parenting" or "natural parenting," are increasingly evident (see, for example, Breazeale 2001; Granju and Kennedy 1999; Jackson 1999; *Mothering* 2000; Thevenin 1987; and co-sleeping advice at <www.babycenter.com>). It remains to be seen whether the practice will make sufficient inroads to modify the dominant pattern of middle-class Euro-American parents. At the same time, another countertrend is underway: some members of non-Euro-American subgroups who have access to the abundant popular literature and the broad cultural practices around them are now adopting mainstream parenting practices. Such mixing of cultural practices is a hall-mark of the dynamic geocultural space that is the United States.

3. For this set of observations, my research assistant was Dieudonné Kwame Kouassi.

4. The exact figures for this paragraph are: 72.2 percent (26 naps) were 30 minutes or less; 22.2 percent (eight naps) were between 35 and 60 minutes; and 5.6 percent (two naps) were between 65 and 90 minutes. The mean duration of the 36 naps was 20.4 minutes. I note that several of the naps included in this number either commenced an unknown number of minutes before or ended an unknown number of minutes after the observation period. I have included them in my figures, however, because excluding them would have resulted in excluding four of the six very long naps observed (50–90 minutes), thereby significantly skewing the statistical means. All factors considered, I estimate that the overall effect of in-cluding these naps in the figures reported here does not significantly distort the general statis-tical pattern observed.

5. Some middle-class Euro-American parents initially have their infant assume a different position, in a lap, stroller, baby carrier, or car, in order for the baby to fall asleep. But in most cases, once they feel confident that the baby is in a sound sleep, such parents transfer the baby elsewhere, usually to a crib. The goal is to encourage the baby to continue napping for as long as possible while lying down and stationery.

6. The exact figures are 59.4 percent for vertically positioned napping; 35.4 percent for horizontally positioned napping; and 5.1 percent for lap napping.

7. The exact figures are: 64.6 percent for sleeping attached to someone, and 35.4 percent for sleeping independently.

8. The figures are: 88.6 percent (775 minutes) of all observed nap time was outdoors, whereas 11.4 percent (100 minutes) of observed nap time was indoors.

9. During light, passing rains, napping babies may remain outdoors under a thatched open-air pavilion; during heavy rains and thunderstorms and in strong winds, most people congregate inside their houses until the bad weather passes.

10. My formal observations did not include any instances of this scenario, so I have no quantitative data on this point.

11. For a needlepoint design kit available online (for $39) that announces, "Sh-h-h Babies Sleeping," go to Elaine Magnin Needlepoint at <http://store.yahoo.com/elainemagninneedlepoint/babiessleeping.html>.

12. Bruce A. Epstein, "Sleep Disorders in Children," available at America on Health, <www.americaonhealth.com/aoh/child/child_sleep_disorders.html>. See also the Sleepnet.com archived infant sleep forums at <www.sleepnet.com/infant/infantinf.html>.

13. In precolonial times, Beng villagers used locally crafted lamps to achieve the same effect. They burned karity (or shea) butter, which they made themselves or bought in a village market, using a wick set in a rounded iron cup forged by local (non-Beng) blacksmiths. One

elderly informant recalled that with this technology a ball of karity butter as large as one's fist could burn for as long as five nights if the lamp was lit for a few hours each evening.

14. In monogamous Beng marriages, married couples usually share a bedroom. In polygynous marriages, each wife has her own bedroom, and the husband rotates among the bedrooms on a fixed schedule. In most cases husbands have no bedroom of their own. If a husband needs to sleep apart from his wife (or wives) for any reason, he typically retires for the night in the house's salon (*faà*). This latter practice usually applies as well to a monogamously married man whose wife is still breast-feeding their baby, whether she is sleeping in her own bedroom or that of her mother.

15. Somewhere between the ages of ten and thirteen, girls move out of their mother's room and find another space to sleep. Boys generally move out slightly earlier—somewhere between the ages of about nine and twelve. After these older children leave their mother's bedroom, they might sleep in the large salon of their own house or a friend's house, in their guest room, or in their mother's kitchen. Below these ages, children typically continue to sleep next to their mothers. On nights when their parents make love, older children—usually those above the age of four or four and a half—are moved out of the room temporarily into the room next door (which in some houses is separated only by a hanging cloth). Contra Freud, the thought that children may hear their parents' sexual activities is not upsetting to Beng parents, who do not judge this as traumatic.

16. According to the president of the company that manufactures the Bedside Co-Sleeper, sales of the product actually soared in the late 1990s (Douglas Tharalson, personal communication, 1999), though clearly not in my hometown. The president thinks it likely that most of his customers are parents who are consciously resisting the cultural norm I have described and are trying out various attachment parenting techniques (see note 2, above).

Chapter Eight

1. For reproductions of and a brief text about the Madonna and nursing baby Jesus, see Steinberg 1996 (131–33 and figures passim); for an assortment of reproductions of Madonna and Child paintings on the Internet, see the fine-art section of ProMoM's Breastfeeding Gallery at the Web site of Promotion of Mother's Milk, Inc.: <www.promom.org/gallery>. For reproductions of relevant Mary Cassatt paintings, see Barter 1998 (plate 85) and Breeskin 1970 (plates 186, 311, 314, 503, 504). For reproductions and brief discussions of a variety of European symbolist and impressionist paintings of breast-feeding infants (by Paula Modersohn-Becker, German artist Fritz Mackenson, Swiss painter Giovanni Segantini, Italian painter Teofini Patini, and especially Belgian painter Léon Frédéric), see Nochlin 1980.

2. For example, see Bulmer 1967; Douglas 1966, 1975a, 1975b, 1984; Douglas, ed. 1987; Khare 1979, 1992; Lévi-Strauss 1997; Meigs 1997; and Tambiah 1969.

3. For example, see Allison 1997; Scheper-Hughes 1992; Sobo 1997; Stoller 1989a; and Sutton 1997, 2001.

4. For example, see Counihan 1997; J. Goody 1982, 1998; Jing 2000; Mintz 1985, 1996; and Weismantel 1988.

5. For reviews of relatively recent literature in several fields relating to infant feeding patterns cross-culturally, see Dettwyler and Fishman 1992 and Van Esterik 2002.

6. For example, see Cassidy 1980, 1987; Chavez, Martinez, Muñoz, Arroyo, and Bourges 1972; Draper 1977; Engle et al. 1996; Falkner 1991; Guldan 2000; Klein, Irwin, Engle, and Yarbrough 1976; Klein, Lasky, Yarbrough, Habicht, and Sellers 1977; and Lepowsky 1985.

7. For example, see Ellison 1995, 2001; Harkness and Super 1987; Hull and Simpson 1985; Hunt 1997; and McLaren 1985.

8. For example, see Maher, ed. 1992; Marshall 1985; Popkin, Lasky, Spicer, and Yamamota 1986; Quandt 1995; Raphael and Davis 1985; Whitaker 2000; and Zeitlin 1996.

9. For example, see Baumslag, Michels, and Jolly 1995; Fernandez 1979; Gottschang 2000; Manderson 1982; and Van Esterik 1989, 1995.

10. Beng women living in villages are aware that some urban women use bottles and formula, but they do not consider these as available to them. From a medical as well as an economic perspective, this is undoubtedly just as well. The biomedical community worldwide is in virtually full agreement that breast-feeding is a far better choice for almost all babies because of the variety of epidemiological and other medical benefits it conveys both in the short and the long term (for overviews of the relevant literature, see Cunningham 1995 and Wray 1991). And even if baby formula were readily available, rural Beng families are too impoverished to buy enough of it to mix in the proper proportion for adequate nutrition for a young infant. The medical risks of diluting infant formula—and of mixing it with polluted water—are now notorious. For a tragic case study from northeast Brazil, see Scheper-Hughes 1992.

11. For a comparative analysis of breast-feeding as it relates to women's work demands in Nepal, see Panter-Brick 1992.

12. The Beng word for water, *yi,* is probably derived from the Jula/Bamana word for water, *ji.*

13. For more on the ritual potency of water in a variety of other sub-Saharan African cultural traditions, see Zahan 1979 (20–23).

14. The milkiness is caused by the addition of kaolin, a fine white clay (*sɛpɛ*) that is said to attract spirits and is used in a variety of ways—including, as we have seen, being patted on babies' skin.

15. The symbolically meaningful convergence of water and cowry shells occurs elsewhere in West African religious traditions; for the Yoruba, see Falola and Lawuyi 1990 (32–33).

16. For a description, see Gottlieb and Graham 1994 (259–61).

17. For example, the authors of a guide published by the breast-feeding advocacy group La Leche League write, "The taste of the milk changes with the diet of the mother. You could say that your milk is programing your baby's taste buds for the coming fare on the dinner table" (La Leche League International 1981:300). I am not aware of any scientific research supporting this assertion.

18. Although all adults know that they should bathe every morning, especially if they had sex the night before, not everyone follows the rule. Elders complain that teenagers are especially likely to be offenders—and oblivious offenders at that.

19. For critical discussions of breast-feeding in the contemporary United States, see Blum 1999 and Dettwyler 1995a.

20. In 1995, only 59.4 percent of new mothers in the United States who delivered in hospitals even tried breast-feeding. By the time their babies were 6 months old, the percent of mothers who were breast-feeding had declined to 21.6 percent (Ryan 1997b, cited in American Academy of Pediatrics 1997); according to 1990 figures, by twelve months only 6.2 percent of mothers were breast-feeding (Dettwyler 1995a:168).

21. For a recent popular article on both failed and successful attempts at placing lactation stations in corporate workplaces, see Laurie Saloman, "Formula for Success," *Working Mother,* June 2001, 11, 13–14, 16.

22. Afwe is the daughter of Amenan's cross-cousin. According to Beng kinship rules, this makes Afwe a classificatory granddaughter of Amenan.

23. Mothers do not offer newborns water until they have learned to latch on to the breast.

24. As Michael Woolridge has pointed out, the term *feeding on demand* itself connotes "negative implications—the baby is a demanding tyrant, and controls the mother and the household." Woolridge prefers more neutral terms: "baby-fed" or "baby-controlled" breast-feeding (1995:237n2). However, Sara Quandt cautions, even these terms speak to an easy contrast between two models that may each conceal significant complexities (1995:130). Other authors, including biological anthropologist Meredith Small (1998:183–84) and popular authors Katie Allison Granju and Betsy Kennedy (1999:161–66), prefer to speak of "cue" feeding.

25. For an Italian example, see Balsamo et al. 1992:73–75; for a discussion of "the place of the clock in pediatric advice" overall, see Millard 1990; for a much broader and historically situated discussion of the development of standardized time zones in Western nations, see Zerubavel 1982.

26. My assistant or I observed twenty-four babies on forty-two occasions for a standardized period of 2¼ hours each. During these times, the average baby breast-fed 3.875 times, which is equivalent to 1.72 times nursed during a one-hour period, or once every 34.88 minutes. The breakdown is as follows: during the forty-two observational periods, two babies did not breast-feed at all, thirteen babies breast-fed once, ten babies nursed twice, ten babies nursed three times, five babies nursed four times, and two babies nursed five times.

It is worth noting that the general pattern of "nursing on demand" has been noted for other non-Western populations—for example, for !Kung hunter-gatherers of southern Africa (Konner 1977a; Konner and Worthman 1980). Physician Michael Woolridge (1995) argues that frequent ("demand" or "baby-led") breast-feeding provides optimal nutrition more effectively to an infant than does feeding on a fixed schedule; on this point, also see works by biological anthropologists Katherine Dettwyler (1995a:192) and Meredith Small (1998: 189–90).

27. This pattern has been noted elsewhere; see, for example, Konner 1977b on the !Kung of southern Africa. In the United States breast-feeding enthusiasts (sometimes called "lactivists") often evoke this knowledge in their effort to increase breast-feeding rates by pointing out the nighttime sleep advantage for the mother of breast-feeding over bottle-feeding (e.g., Granju and Kennedy 1999:187–88).

28. For a range of perspectives on wet nursing, see Faÿ-Sallois 1980; Fildes 1995 (102–103, 109–110); Klapisch-Zuber 1985; McLaren 1985; Nochlin 1988; Sussman 1982; and Van Esterik 1995 (148).

29. For more on the subversive potential of "flow," see C. Taylor 1992 and Turner 1982, 1985.

30. A more permanent wet nurse, typically a close kinswoman, is sought in Beng villages when a nursing baby's mother tragically dies. In one case I heard of, a young woman died, leaving behind a baby of only three months. The baby's paternal aunt, who was living in the city of Bouaké at the time, happened to be nursing her own nine-month-old son, and she immediately came to the village to begin nursing her young nephew. After a week, she returned with both babies to Bouaké, where she continued to breast-feed them both until they were walking.

31. For brief discussions of this issue for several culture areas and historical eras, see Fildes 1995 (116–17) and Stuart-Macadam 1995 (85); for more extended discussion concerning

a nearby region of West Africa, see Gunnlaugsson and Einarsdóttir 1993, and concerning Malaysia, see Manderson 1982, 1984.

32. Keeping in mind women's fertility cycles, this is likely to happen with the first grown daughter or two. The vagaries of demography of course increase or decrease the likelihood that a given older woman and her grown daughter are both nursing mothers at the same time. For example, if a woman bears her first child at the age of eighteen and that child is a girl who likewise bears her first child at the age of eighteen, there may be five to ten years during which both mother and daughter are bearing—and breast-feeding—children. However, if a woman bears her first child when she is in her twenties and her first and second children are male, an overlap in fertility with a grown daughter is less likely.

33. My use of the term *dry nursing* differs from conventional usage, which generally refers to the practice of raising an infant on solid foods rather than any form of milk (whether human or animal) (e.g., Fildes 1995, Stuart-Macadam 1995). I find the latter usage misleading, however, and prefer the meaning I have indicated in the text as more appropriate.

34. Even if he recognized the function of the bottle, he would be too young to understand the joke, as babies of this age do not have a developed sense of the difference between two- and three-dimensional objects (see DeLoache, Pierroutsakos, Utall, Rosengren, and Gottlieb 1998).

35. The act of actually feeding the infant is probably not as significant for forming meaningful multiple emotional attachments as is the act of providing nurturance and comfort (Sarah Mangelsdorf, personal communication, 16 July 2001).

36. For example, see American Academy of Pediatrics 1997 and Popkin, Lasky, Spicer, and Yamamota 1986 (91). For an ethnographically based challenge to this increasingly common biomedical recommendation, however, cf. Maher 1992a, 1992b.

37. In other arenas people elsewhere likewise validate the crucial role that language development plays in allowing a baby to become human, as culturally understood. For example, the Laymis, an Aymara group of Bolivia, assert that a baby develops gender when the child can speak (Harris 1980:72). The role of speech in signifying the development of personhood or humanity seems a fertile topic for comparative investigation.

38. For two incisive discussions on anorexia nervosa in particular, see Bordo 1993 and Brumberg 1988.

39. For an American midwife's corroboration of Amenan's claim, see Gaskin 1987 (69, 116).

40. Many African women elsewhere share this belief. For the Luo of Kenya, for example, see Cosminsky 1985; the belief is also reported for Papua New Guinea (Jenkins and Heywood 1985), as well as for parts of early-modern Europe (Klapisch-Zuber 1985).

41. In many other places in Africa, as well as in the Pacific, parents must avoid sex until the baby is weaned (see Einarsdóttir forthcoming; Maher 1992b:13–17; Popkin, Lasky, Spicer, and Yamamota 1986:178). The underlying ideology connecting abstinence and breast-feeding to a perceived incompatibility between semen and breast milk has been reported elsewhere as well (Hull 1985; Hunt 1999:244).

42. A few Ghanaian prostitutes have resided in the Beng village of Asagbe for some years. Other traveling (non-Beng) sex workers arrive in the villages from time to time.

43. For a case from nearby Guinea-Bissau in which men may decide when their wives wean their children so as to enable the couple to resume their sexual relationship, see Einarsdóttir forthcoming.

44. This pattern may be common elsewhere in Africa. For a case from Guinea-Bissau, see Einarsdóttir forthcoming.

45. According to some biological anthropologists, there is a "hominid blueprint" for relatively late weaning in human evolution. Scholars estimate this from a low of two to three years (Stuart-Macadam 1995:94) to perhaps four to five years (Dettwyler 1995b; Konner 1977a) or even longer (Dettwyler, personal communication, 15 July 2001). In part they base their estimate on the fact that in "traditional" societies around the world today, "most children . . . [are] weaned between 2 and 4 years of age" (Dettwyler 1995b:39). If these scholars are right about the evolutionary tendency, the traditional Beng pattern, at least as it is reported by some elders, would have approximated or even surpassed this evolutionary norm. Other biological anthropologists, however, posit a somewhat earlier weaning age in the evolutionary record (e.g., Bogin 1999:173–78).

46. This unexpected pattern of shorter rather than longer birth intervals is documented elsewhere in Africa. For one example, see Harkness and Super 1987 on the Kipsigis of Kenya.

47. For a variety of cases that exhibit their own particularities but nevertheless speak in some way to this constellation of issues, see Bowlby 1990; Chatterjee 1993 (116–57), Delaney 1995; Enloe 2000; Friedlander 1995; Lakshmi 1999; Mani 1998; Moghadam 1994; Nefsky 1991; Ong 1995; Ortner 1996; Parker, Russo, Sommer, and Yaeger 1992; Saigol 1999; and Webster 1998.

48. For a similar case from Guinea-Bissau, see Einarsdóttir forthcoming.

Chapter Nine

1. According to medical research (presumably based largely on research with Western children), the second set of permanent molars erupts on average between the ages of twelve and thirteen years of age (Behrman, Kliegman, and Arvin 1996:42, table 11-6).

2. I make this claim on the basis of my own positioning as a "native anthropologist" to the culture about which I am writing. However, ethnographic fieldwork systematically investigating the issue in the Euro-American community remains to be done. It is possible that such fieldwork would uncover variations on the basic theme that I have posited.

3. I am not aware of many sustained anthropological treatments of children's teeth, although brief comments about teething in infants appear in some discussions of child care (e.g., for Tibet, see Maiden and Farwell 1997:17). For a rare analytic article on children's teeth—analyzing the extraction from young children of extra teeth that are classified as plastic by the Haya of Tanzania—see Weiss 1992.

4. For a timetable of the typical appearance of teeth after birth—presumably based largely on research with Western infants—see Behrman, Kliegman, and Arvin 1996 (42, table 11-6). According to medical research, one in two thousand newborns infants is born with natal teeth, as dentists call them (Johnsen 1996). In some cases, such teeth present medical risks: the teeth may make it difficult for the infant to breastfeed; "the infant may have injured the tongue, lips, or maxillary ridge" (Jedrychowski 1982:84); if the tooth is loose, the infant risks swallowing it (Fawcett and Varon 1999); or the teeth may be associated with any of several other medical conditions (Johnsen 1996). According to experts in pediatric dentistry, "Decisions regarding extraction of prematurely erupted primary teeth must be made on an individual basis" (Johnsen 1996); if the natal teeth are deciduous incisors and not "supernumerary" (extra) teeth, an alternative to extraction "should at least be attempted" (Jedrychowski 1982:85).

5. This ritual concern has been reported in several other places. In Kenya, the Giriama are concerned if the first two teeth to erupt appeared on the upper jaw; as with the Beng, such a child was formerly drowned (Parkin 1985). For a variety of related practices in Guinea-Bissau, see Einarsdóttir forthcoming. In Tibet, parents make offerings to a local deity to

ensure that the first tooth erupts on the lower, not the upper, jaw (Maiden and Farwell 1997:77). By contrast, modern dentists do not seem concerned when the first tooth erupts on the upper jaw. I could find no mention of this anomaly in the pediatric dentistry literature I consulted. My own dentist told me that the situation is so statistically rare that he had never seen or heard of a case in his own practice (Scott Anderson, personal communication, 2 January 1999).

6. Scientific research shows that most first mandibular central incisors erupt between five and seven months (Behrman, Kliegman, and Arvin 1996:42, table 11-6). According to this literature, significant delays in the eruption of all teeth "may indicate systemic or nutritional disturbances" (Johnsen 1996). Also, having teeth permits clear articulation. The vast majority of babies do develop teeth before beginning to speak; my own dentist speculated that it would be very difficult to make clearly understandable sounds in the absence of any teeth, and he had never heard of a baby doing so (Scott Anderson, personal communication, 2 January 1999). I am not aware of any scientific studies investigating the unusual case of infants who begin speaking before teeth erupt. By contrast to Beng thought, in which great attention is paid to the unlikely possibility, the situation seems to have no significance to Western medicine or science (Judy DeLoache, personal communication, 29 December 1999).

7. The age at which children learn to walk is quite variable. In the United States and Europe, most children begin to walk between 11.4 and 14.5 months (Malina 1980).

8. According to local gossip networks, at least one Beng village houses a Beng man who is widely suspected of being a paid informer (*yayereyáná*) to the (non-Beng) police officers stationed in the nearby town of M'Bahiakro. Given his presence, villagers are aware that any actions they take that contravene national law may bring about their imprisonment.

9. No modern dentistry services are available to Beng villagers. Thus it is not unlikely that as they age, village-dwelling adults may lose teeth due to decay. Although I have not conducted a systematic survey of this question, I have noticed quite a few Beng adults with less than a full set of teeth.

10. Elsewhere in Africa, crawling on all fours may, by contrast, be discouraged, as it is taken as a style of locomotion appropriate to animals but not humans (e.g., LeVine et al. 1994). Sometimes this is associated with encouraging infants to sit unassisted very early as a mark of social engagement with others (Kilbride and Kilbride 1975). By contrast, Beng parents do not disapprove of crawling.

11. Women's underwear takes the form of a piece of cloth, or *pagne,* that is worn in the *cache-sexe* style, attached to a string of waist beads.

12. Two recent developmental psychology textbooks acknowledge the role of cultural factors in regulating the timing of motor development: Bukatko and Daehler 1992 (217–22); and Siegler, DeLoache, and Eisenberg 2003 (184–86).

13. There may well be such elders in all Beng villages—I did not investigate this systematically.

14. For a review of relevant literature, see Miller 2000. The American Academy of Pediatrics (1996) discourages the practice of spanking children younger than two years old. For a popular child-care guide on the subject, see Hyman 1997.

15. For discussion of one ritual cure for late walking involving rich gender symbolism, see Gottlieb 1990 (121–22). If a baby is slow not just in walking but in other ways as well, such as not talking on time, this may be interpreted as a sign that the mother committed a serious violation while pregnant. For example, if she ate food while walking along a forest

path, the child may have been transformed into a snake in utero. In this case, there is no effective medical treatment: it is presumed that the child will never be human. If the parents can afford an expensive ritual treatment, they consult a specialist. In a secret ritual in the forest, the specialist will offer the child a substance that appears to be medicine but is really snake food. If the child ignores the food, it probably means that the little one is actually human and that there is some other reason accounting for the developmental delay. But if the medicine seems delicious, the baby will eat the food and immediately start turning back into a snake and slither off into the forest. If the parents are lucky, the creature will not return the next time the mother becomes pregnant, and she will give birth to a person. If parents suspect that their seeming infant may really be a snake, they are urged to have this ritual performed as soon as possible. The longer they wait, the more money the ritual specialist will charge for his services, and the harder it is for the medicine to take effect; in the end, the parents may be left with a snake-child. The creature will never have a family, it is thought, for who would marry a snake?

16. Studies finding motoric precocity among African infants include Geber and Dean 1967; Kilbride 1969; Kilbride and Kilbride 1975; Kilbride 1980; Konner 1977b; Leiderman, Babu, Kagia, Kraemer, and Leiderman 1973; Super 1976; and Werner 1972. One study that disputes the validity of the model for a sample of infants in Uganda, however, is Warren and Parkin 1974.

17. One developmental psychologist has mentioned that many of his colleagues specializing in motor development are keenly aware of this bias but that this awareness has not yet been actively discussed in print and has not yet shaped research agendas (Karl Rosengren, personal communication, 14 February 2003).

Chapter Ten

1. For an extended discussion of this claim for northeastern Brazil, see Scheper-Hughes 1992; for a critical discussion of that work, see Einarsdóttir forthcoming.

2. As elsewhere in Africa, the infant mortality rate in Côte d'Ivoire is disturbingly high: about 11 percent of infants die before the age of one year (United States Department of State 2001), and 17 percent die before the age of five years (UNICEF 2000). By contrast, in the United States the mortality rate for infants under one year is about 0.7 percent (Centers for Disease Control 2001).

3. See Fernandez 1986 on the symbolic importance that mirrors hold in some African and other religious traditions.

4. In one study in Java, the fatality rate for neonatal tetanus was as high as 90 percent (Over 1984:15).

5. The extent of protection against tetanus in individual newborns may vary. There is evidence that a case of malaria that is active at the time of the injection may decrease the body's immune response to the vaccine, as may a deficiency in vitamin A. In addition, when the vaccine is administered to a pregnant woman, its effectiveness for the fetus may be lessened if the doses are not spaced according to an optimal schedule vis-à-vis the woman's pregnancy (Dietz, Galazka, van Loon, and Cochi 1997), or if only one dose is administered, rather than two or three (Koenig 1992). Notwithstanding such factors, the likelihood of significant protection in newborns in general is high enough for the WHO to recommend vaccination for all women of reproductive age.

6. The exchange rate usually fluctuates between about 200 CFA = $1 U.S. and 500 CFA = $1 U.S.

7. For an analogous case of local nurses insensitively displaying their modernity in small-town clinics in Tanzania, see Allen 2002 (chapters 9 and 10).

8. "Tetanus is . . . caused by *tetanospasmin,* an element in the toxin secreted by the bacterium *Clostridium tetani.* The tetanus bacillus . . . toxin follows the nerve channels toward the spinal cord, where it becomes fixed in the anterior horn of the gray matter of the cord. Once it is established, the symptoms of tetanus begin" (McGrew 1985:335). For more on the biochemistry of the bacterium, see Rood et al. 1997.

9. There are several other possible opportunities for contact between the not-yet-healed umbilical stump and something infectious. McGrew notes that the bacterium causing tetanus is common "where there are numbers of domestic animals" (1985:335). In farming communities such as those of the Beng, it is conceivable, though not likely, that a newborn might have contact with the feces of a domestic animal kept nearby, perhaps a chicken, goat, sheep, or dog.

10. The term is Baule, and one consultant maintained that the entire funeral ritual is borrowed from the Baule, who reportedly require even harsher measures at some points. I have not seen any published descriptions of this funeral in the ethnographic literature on the Baule.

11. For a baby, *fewa* is performed only if the child's navel stump has fallen off. If a newborn dies before this occurs, it is considered that the child was not born at all; hence no funeral (*fewa* or otherwise) is celebrated.

12. The following description is partial. I have deliberately omitted quite a few details: some because they are considered highly sensitive or secret, others because they are less important than the actions I do report.

Chapter Eleven

1. Given the nation's French colonial heritage, Protestants came to Bengland later than did Catholics. The first generation of educated Beng students attended a Catholic mission school in the nearby town of M'Bahiakro and, if they were successful, continued on to a Catholic high school in Bouaké; the first Protestant missionaries came to reside in one of the villages, Asagbe, only in the early 1980s. As of 1993, there were still fewer Protestants than Catholics among those in Beng villages who counted themselves as Christians. In Côte d'Ivoire overall, statistics from the 1988 census claim that 22.7 percent of the nation's population is Catholic and 6.6 percent is Protestant (Europa Publications 2000:431). One Protestant missionary organization claims that 3 percent of the Beng are Christian (Bethany World Prayer Center, "Prayer Profile: The Ngan of Côte D'Ivoire," available online at <www.bethany.com>). All these figures must be regarded quite cautiously, however, because, as people elsewhere in West Africa, many Ivoirians feel comfortable embracing multiple, overlapping religious identities in a nonexclusive fashion (see Gottlieb n.d.a).

2. For a selection of the increasingly rich and voluminous literature on relations between local and global structures in and out of Africa, see, for example, Appadurai 1996; Ciekawy and Geschiere 1998; Comaroff and Comaroff 1993; D'Alisera 2004; Fermé 2001; Gable 1995, 2000; Geschiere 1997; Johnson n.d.; Masquelier 2001; Piot 1999; Shaw 2002; Weiss 1996; Werbner 1998; and Werbner and Ranger 1996.

3. For an early argument articulating what has come to be known as dependency theory, which holds European colonialism responsible for Africa's poverty, see Rodney 1982. For a brief discussion of several theoretical models assessing responsibility for Africa's poverty, see Austen 1987 (1–8). For some recent critiques of development theory and counterproposals

of various versions of the dependency model, see Amin 1992; Escobar 1995; Ferguson 1994; and Larrain 1989. For an attempt at a compromise position between development theory and dependency theory, see Toye 1993. For a recent sympathetic critique of dependency theory, see Leys 1996.

4. The BNDA, which succeeded two previous, colonial-era farm credit programs, was established in 1968 under the Ministry of Agriculture and the Ministry of Economy and Finance with the federal government holding two-thirds of the total stock. Some observers noted early on that the agency was "seriously threatened by low repayment rates" (Yabilé 1982:13); by the time it was liquidated in 1991, it "had a loan portfolio of 64 bn [billion] CFA francs, mostly unrecoverable" (*Africa Today* 1996:633). A significant amount of embezzlement of funds by regional loan officers—some of whom were imprisoned for their deeds—further accounts for its collapse.

5. Tiny loans are sometimes available from village-run credit societies (*tontines*) or from successful businessmen and traders who on occasion advance very small amounts of cash to reliable customers.

6. Most Beng farmers living in the village are more or less self-sufficient and typically spend very little cash to feed themselves on a regular basis, except for purchase of two staples—oil and salt. Occasional purchase of such items as bread (50 CFA), a can of sardines (200 CFA), or a plate of ready-made fish and *attieké* (a couscous-like dish prepared from manioc) in the weekly market are considered luxuries. Only wealthy merchants (and the odd visitor such as an American fieldworker) spend money daily to feed themselves in the villages.

7. For other discussions of the limits as well as merits of intercropping, shifting cultivation, and the bush fallow system, see Barrett, Barbier, and Reardon 2001; Ruthenberg 1980; and ter Kuile 1987.

8. For a general history of the French colonial conquest of West Africa, see Manning 1998. For overviews of the impact of European colonialism on agriculture in West Africa, see Hart 1982 and, more briefly, Lewis and Barry 1988 (79–82).

9. In any case, in Africa the use of commercial fertilizers does not always lead to higher crop productivity, as inappropriate fertilizers are often offered by poorly trained extension officers (Bates 1981:55–56n4).

10. For a discussion situating the colonial introduction of coffee to Côte d'Ivoire in the broader historical context of the late-nineteenth- and early-twentieth-century French political economy, see Nyong'o 1977.

11. For an account of Ivoirian coffee production and prices through the 1970s and early 1980s, see Ayemou 1983; for data through the mid-1980s, see Akiyama 1988; for data through the 1990s, see Food and Agricultural Organization n.d. For a summary of the International Coffee Agreement regulating world production and prices, see Europa Publications 1999 (36); for a discussion of Caistab (Caisse de stabilisation et de soutien des prix des production agricoles), the Ivoirian agency that sets coffee prices, see Hodgkinson 1999 (403). For an argument that the Ivoirian government's policy of setting prices inhibits technological innovation that would improve both crop productivity and farmers' standards of living, see Ridler 1990. Finally, for a discussion of climatic and other risks related to growing coffee in West Africa, see Ruf and Ruf 1989.

12. In 2000, the local buying price of coffee as well as cocoa was raised to 700 CFA/kilo (Bertin Kouadio, personal communication, 3 January 2001).

13. This is a rather different—though equally culturally shaped—form of nostalgia from

that which has been charted so perceptively by Renato Rosaldo (1989) in the context of the imperial project.

14. For brief discussions of cowries as currency in West Africa, see Hopkins 1973 (68–70); July 1975 (247–50); and Zeleza 1993 (282–84). Jan Hogendorn and Marion Johnson (1986) argue that the cowry-based economy in West Africa expanded significantly with the Atlantic slave trade, which would make the cowry a largely colonial rather than precolonial regional currency. Falling indirectly within the orbit of the slave trade, the Beng would have felt these economic repercussions even if (as they claim) they had no direct involvement in the trade. For a more cultural analysis of cowries as embedded in a rich symbolic and social matrix elsewhere in West Africa, see Falola and Lawuyi 1990, writing of the Yoruba. Charles Piot suggests that the Beng custom of adorning babies with cowry shells implies an emphasis on separation from the other world that echoes separations experienced elsewhere in the circulation of cowry shells—for example, in the market ("between persons and their products") and, in the Voltaic area of northern Togo and Ghana, between the living and the dead (personal communication).

15. Concerning coffee in particular, see Nyong'o 1977. For overviews of the European colonial tax structures and their sociopolitical effects in Africa, see, for example, Iliffe 1995 (196–98, 207), Lewis and Berry 1988 (81), and Manning 1998 (51–56, 70–71, 75–76, 123–26). For analysis of several cases of colonial taxation in West Africa, see Guyer 1995.

16. For a stimulating collection of essays using counterfactual models, see Tetlock and Belkin 1996; for a philosophically oriented discussion of the concept of counterfactuals, see Wilson 1986.

17. On a similar shift to a less nutritious food base in Central Africa, see Zeleza 1993 (102–103).

18. Iron-deficiency anemia is an enormous problem worldwide. According to one estimate, it affects about two billion people (Ryan 1997a), including about 51 percent of all children under five years old (Bogin 1999:21).

19. A recent article claims that the strong social ties of extended families in Côte d'Ivoire enable even impoverished rural patients to scrape together funds to pay the new "user fees" the government now imposes on health care. Sadly, this is rarely the case in Beng villages nowadays, where cash is in too short supply for most people to help even close relatives in dire medical need (Ayé, Champagne, and Contandriopoulos 2002).

20. For a stimulating collection of articles analyzing intersections between morality and capital, see Parry and Bloch 1989.

21. Successful and systematic vaccination against major diseases was introduced between 1798 and 1981 (Plotkin and Plotkin 1994); for a general account of the history of vaccines, see Chase 1982.

22. For comparable cases from Thailand and Uganda, see Cunningham 1970 and Whyte 1997 (26, 233), respectively; for an account of a vaccination culture of another sort, in Cameroon, see Feldman-Savelsberg, Ndonko, and Schmidt-Ehry 2000.

23. This rare condition, technically known as an indirect inguinal hernia, occurs in 1–2 percent of infant boys at birth (Yale University, "Pediatric Surgery for Parents: Inguinal Hernia," Yale University, Department of Surgery, Yale University, available online at <http://yalesurgery.med.yale.edu/surgery/sections/ped_surg/hernia.htm>. In industrialized nations, biomedical doctors nearly always perform surgery to avoid the risk of the hernia becoming strangulated, a situation that is life-threatening.

24. That summer, Philip and I also contributed food indirectly to this extended family's food supply as we were living in an adjacent, related household.

25. Stephanie Coontz, "Not Much Sense in Those Census Stories: The Way We Read the Numbers Doesn't Match the Way We Live," *The Washington Post,* 15 July 2001; Mark Levin, "First, Let's Get the Head Count Right on Redistricting," *The Houston Chronicle,* 5 June 2001; Robert Rosenblatt, "Census Bureau Is Losing Authority to Adjust the 2000 Count," *Los Angeles Times,* 17 February 2001.

26. Beng farmers recognize that manioc is deficient in nutritional value. Most say that they view manioc as a "starvation food." They grow it because it is easy to cultivate: even with droughts and floods, manioc still comes up, and farmers know they will have something to eat if all their other crops fail. But it is hardly a prestige food, and many Beng villagers disdain it. The leaves of the cassava plant have much higher nutritional value than do the tubers, but this Beng mother's diet was most heavily dependent on foutou made from the tubers. Another health risk posed by a diet high in manioc results from the fact that the plant has dangerous levels of the toxin cyanide, which has been shown to be associated with serious neurological and other disorders, possibly including mental retardation, in people whose diets contain manioc as a staple. Although some methods of processing manioc for cooking reduce the toxic levels of cyanide, the amount reduced is variable and the evidence to date is contradictory (Balagopalan, Padmaja, Nanda, and Moorthy 1988:15–16, 22–23, 25–29).

27. For a recent work exploring the cultural foundations of birth control elsewhere in West Africa, see Bledsoe 2002; for Indonesia, see Tsing 1993 (104–20).

28. My thanks to the Planned Parenthood chapter of Champaign, Illinois, for donating these supplies.

29. For the classic early statement on this issue, see Boserup 1970; for more recent discussions, see, for example, Bryceson 1995 and Coquery-Vidrovitch 1997 (9–20).

30. For a discussion of several factors, including child labor, that contribute to low school attendance rates in Côte d'Ivoire, as well as in Ghana and Zambia, see Canagarajah and Nielson 1999.

31. Regrettably, I did not record the total number of students in this class.

32. Recently, a strict accounting system for the school lunch program has been introduced throughout Côte d'Ivoire to eliminate such excesses; its results in Beng villages have yet to be studied.

33. See Ankerl 1986; Becker, Hamer, and Morrison 1994; Lewis and Berry 1988 (339–65); Touré and Fadayomi 1992; Farvacque-Vitkovic 1998; Todaro 1997.

34. For discussion of exploitative child labor on cocoa plantations in Côte d'Ivoire, see Child Labor Coalition n.d. and Greenhouse 2002.

35. For a tragic enactment of such misplaced optimism among airplane stowaways flying to Europe, see Lambert 1999.

36. Until recently, all songs were sung either in Jula or Baule. Only in the 1970s did Beng youth begin to compose lyrics in their native language.

37. On contemporary "reverse migration" of African-Americans from the North to the South, see Stack 1996.

38. The three are: Bethany World Prayer Center, "Joshua Project II. Original Joshua Project—Unreached People Profile. Ngan (Nguin, Gan, Beng)," available online at <www.joshuaproject.net>; the Wild West Africa Connection, "Beng of Côte d'Ivoire. The Wild West Africa Connection, available online at <www.wwac.org/beng/>; and 2001-Pray, "Africa. Beng of Côte d'Ivoire," available online at <www.2001pray.org/PeopleGroups/Beng.htm>.

39. This appears to be a trend in other places as well; for contemporary Japan, see Miller 2003.

REFERENCES

Abbott, Susan
  1992 "Holding On and Pushing Away: Comparative Perspectives on an Eastern Kentucky Child-Rearing Practice." *Ethos* 20 (1):33–65.
Abu-Lughod, Lila
  1990 "Can There Be a Feminist Ethnography?" *Women and Performance: A Journal of Feminist Theory* 5 (1):7–27.
  1999 "The Interpretation of Culture(s) after Television." Pp. 110–35 in *The Fate of "Culture": Geertz and Beyond*, ed. Sherry Ortner. Berkeley: University of California Press.
  ———, ed.
  1998 *Remaking Women: Feminism and Modernity in the Middle East*. Princeton, N.J.: Princeton University Press.
Africa Today
  1996 "Country Survey: Côte d'Ivoire." Pp. 617–41 in *Africa Today*, ed. Raph Uwechue. London: Africa Books.
Aijmer, Göran, ed.
  1992 *Coming into Existence: Birth and Metaphors of Birth*. Göteburg, Sweden: Institute for Advanced Studies in Social Anthropology, University of Gothenburg.
Ainsworth, Mary D., Salzer, M. C. Blehar, E. Waters, and S. Wall
  1978 *Patterns of Attachment: A Psychological Study of the Strange Situation*. Hillsdale, N.J.: Erlbaum.
 ̣yama, Takamasa
  1988 "Cocoa and Coffee Pricing Policies in Côte d'Ivoire." Working Papers, International Commodity Markets Division, International Economics Department Policy, Planning, and Research Complex. Washington, D.C.: International Bank for Reconstruction and Development/The World Bank.
Alanen, Leena
  2000 "Review Essay: Visions of a Social Theory of Childhood." *Childhood* 7 (4):493–506.
Allen, Denise Roth
  2002 *Managing Motherhood, Managing Risk: Fertility and Danger in West Central Tanzania*. Ann Arbor: University of Michigan Press.
Allison, Anne
  1997 [1991] "Japanese Mothers and *Obentos:* The Lunch Box as Ideological State Apparatus." Pp. 296–314 in *Food and Culture: A Reader*, ed. Carole Counihan and Penny Van Esterik. New York: Routledge.
American Academy of Pediatrics
  1996 "The Short- and Long-Term Consequences of Corporal Punishment [Consensus Statements]." *Pediatrics* 94 (4, part 2):853.

1997 "Breastfeeding and the Use of Human Milk." *Pediatrics* 100 (6):1035–1039. Available online at <www.aap.org>.

Amin, Samir
1967 *Le développement de capitalisme en Côte d'Ivoire*. Paris: Les Editions de Minuit.
1992 *Empire of Chaos*. Translated by W. H. Locke Anderson. New York: Monthly Review Press.

Amit-Talai, Vered, and Helene Wulff, eds.
1995 *Youth Cultures*. New York: Routledge.

Anagnost, Ann
1997 "The Child and National Transcendence in China." In *Constructing China: The Interaction of Culture and Economics*, ed. Kenneth G. Lieberthal, Shuen-fu Lin, and Ernest P. Young. Ann Arbor: University of Michigan Center for Chinese Studies.
2000 "Scenes of Misrecognition: Maternal Citizenship in the Age of International Adoption." *Positions: East Asia Cultures Critique* 8 (2):390–421.
n.d. *Maternal Perversities: Class, Race, and Gender in American Middle-Class Parenting*. Unpublished manuscript.

Ankerl, Guy
1986 *Urbanization Overspeed in Tropical Africa, 1970–2000: Facts, Social Problems, and Policy*. Geneva: Interuniversity Institute/INU Press.

Appadurai, Arjun
1996 *Modernity at Large: Cultural Dimensions of Globalization*. Minneapolis: University of Minnesota Press.

Arad, I., F. Eyal, and P. Fainmesser
1981 "Umbilical Care and Cord Separation." *Archives of Disease in Childhood* 56:887–88.

Ardener, Edwin
1989 [1974] "Social Anthropology and Population." Pp. 109–26 in *The Voice of Prophecy and Other Essays*. Edited by Malcolm Chapman. Oxford: Basil Blackwell.

Arens, William, and Ivan Karp, eds.
1989 *Creativity of Power: Cosmology and Action in African Societies*. Washington, D.C.: Smithsonian Institution Press.

Ariès, Philippe
1962 [1960] *Centuries of Childhood: A Social History of Family Life*. Translated by Robert Baldick. London: Jonathan Cape.

Asian Journal of Social Psychology
2000 *Special Issue: Indigenous, Cultural, and Cross-Cultural Psychologies. Asian Journal of Social Psychology* 3 (3).

Ask, Karin
1994 "Veiled Experiences: Exploring Female Practices of Seclusion." Pp. 64–100 in *Social Experience and Anthropological Knowledge*, ed. Kirsten Hastrup and Peter Hervik. London: Routledge.

Augé, Marc
1995 [1992] *Non-Places: Introduction to an Anthropology of Supermodernity*. Translated by John Howe. London: Verso.

Austen, Ralph A.
1987 *African Economic History: Internal Development and External Dependency*. London: James Currey.

Ayé, Marcellin, François Champagne, and André-Pierre Contandriopoulos
2002 "Economic Role of Solidarity and Social Capital in Accessing Modern Health Care Services in the Ivory Coast." *Social Science and Medicine* 55 (11):1929–46.

Ayemou, Afla Odile
1983 "An Analysis of the Supply of and Demand for the Ivory Coast's Export Coffee." M.A. thesis, Department of Agricultural Economics, University of Illinois at Urbana-Champaign.

Azarya, Victor
1980 "Traders and the Center in Massina, Kong, and Samori's State." *International Journal of African Historical Studies* 13 (3):420–56.

1981 "State Intervention in Economic Enterprise in Pre-Colonial Africa: Massina and Samori's State." University of California at Los Angeles, African Studies Center, Occasional Paper No. 22.

Badinter, E.
1982 *The Myth of Motherhood: An Historical View of the Maternal Instinct*. London: Souvenir Press.

Bakhtin, Mikhail
1968 [1965] *Rabelais and His World*. Translated by Hélène Ifwolsky. Cambridge: M.I.T. Press.

Balagopalan, C., G. Padmaja, S. K. Nanda, and S. N. Moorthy
1988 *Cassava in Food, Feed, and Industry*. Boca Raton, Fla.: CRS Press.

Baldwin, Virginia
1994 *Pathology of Multiple Pregnancy*. Heidelberg: Springer Verlag.

Balsamo, Franca et al.
1992 "Production and Pleasure: Research on Breast-Feeding in Turin." Pp. 59–90 in *The Anthropology of Breast-Feeding: Natural Law or Social Construct,* ed. Vanessa Maher. Oxford, U.K.: Berg.

Bard, Harry, et al.
1998 "Myocardial, Erythropoietic, and Metabolic Adaptations to Anemia of Prematurity in Infants with Bronchopulmonary Dysplasia." *The Journal of Pediatrics* 132 (4):630–34.

Barnett, Ola W., Cindy L. Miller-Perrin, and Robin D. Perrin
1997 *Family Violence across the Lifespan: An Introduction*. Thousand Oaks, Calif.: Sage.

Barrett, Christopher B., Edward B. Barbier, and Thomas Reardon
2001 "Introduction: Farming the Garden of Eden." *Special issue: Agroindustrialization, International Development, and the Environment. Environment and Development Economics* 6 (4):503–509.

Barter, Judith A., ed.
1998 *Mary Cassatt: Modern Woman*. New York: Abrams/Art Institute of Chicago.

Barthes, Roland
1972 [1957] *Mythologies*. Translated by Annette Lavers. New York: Noonday Press.

1982 [1970] *Empire of Signs*. Translated by Richard Howard. New York: Hill and Wang.

1983 [1967] *The Fashion System*. Translated by Matthew Ward and Richard Howard. New York: Hill and Wang.

Bastian, Misty
2002 "Irregular Visitors: Narratives about *Ogbaanje* (Spirit Children) in Southern Nigerian Popular Writing." Pp. 59–66 in *Readings in African Popular Fiction,* ed. Stephanie Newell. Bloomington: Indiana University Press.

Bates, Robert
    1981 *Markets and States in Tropical Africa: The Political Basis of Agricultural Policies.*
    Berkeley: University of California Press.
Bateson, Gregory
    1972 "Metalogue: What Is an Instinct?" Pp. 38–58 in *Steps to an Ecology of Mind.* New
    York: Ballantine.
Bauman, Zygmunt
    1995 *Life in Fragments: Essays in Postmodern Morality.* Oxford: Blackwell.
    1997 *Postmodernity and Its Discontents.* New York: New York University Press.
    1998 *Globalization: The Human Consequences.* London: Polity Press.
Baumslag, Naomi, Dia L. Michels, and Richard Jolly
    1995 *Milk, Money, and Madness: The Culture and Politics of Breastfeeding.* Westport,
    Conn.: Bergin & Garvey.
Bavin, E. L.
    1995 "Language Acquisition in Cross-Linguistic Perspective." *Annual Review of Anthro-
    pology* 24:373–96.
Becker, Charles M., Andrew M. Hamer, and Andrew R. Morrison
    1994 *Beyond Urban Bias in Africa: Urbanization in an Era of Structural Adjustment.*
    Portsmouth, N.H.: Heinemann.
Behar, Ruth
    1993 *Translated Woman: Crossing the Border with Esperanza's Story.* Boston: Beacon.
    1996 *The Vulnerable Observer: Anthropology that Breaks Your Heart.* Boston: Beacon.
Behrman, Richard E., Robert M. Kliegman, and Ann M. Arvin, eds.
    1996 *Nelson Textbook of Pediatrics*, 15th ed. Philadelphia: W. B. Saunders.
Bell, Diane, Pat Caplan, and Wazir Jahan Karim, eds.
    1993 *Gendered Fields: Women, Men, and Ethnography.* London: Routledge.
Ben-Amos, Paula Girshick
    1995 [1980] *The Art of Benin,* rev. ed. Washington, D.C.: Smithsonian Institution Press.
Bertaux, Daniel, ed.
    1981 *Biography and Society: The Life History Approach in the Social Sciences.* Beverly Hills,
    Calif.: Sage.
Bhalla, J. N., et al.
    1975 "Some Observations on Separation of the Umbilical Stump in the Newborn." *In-
    dian Journal of Pediatrics* 42:329–34.
Bianco, Barbara
    1991 "Women and Things: Pokot Motherhood as Political Destiny." *American Ethnolo-
    gist* 18 (4):770–85.
Bledsoe, Caroline
    1984 "The Political Use of Sande Ideology and Symbolism." *American Ethnologist* 11:
    455–72.
    1990 "The Politics of Children: Fosterage and the Social Management of Fertility among
    the Mende of Sierra Leone." Pp. 81–100 in *Births and Power: Social Change and the
    Politics of Reproduction,* ed. W. P. Handwerker. Boulder: Westview.
    1993 "The Politics of Polygyny in Male Education and Child Fosterage Transactions."
    Pp. 180–92 in *Sex and Gender Hierarchies,* ed. B. Miller. Cambridge: Cambridge
    University Press.
    1995 "Marginal Members: Children of Previous Unions in Mende Households in Sierra

Leone." Pp. 130–53 in *Situating Fertility*, ed. Susan Greenhalgh. Cambridge: Cambridge University Press.

2002 *The Contingent Life Course: Reproduction, Time, and Aging in West Africa.* Chicago: University of Chicago Press.

Bloch, Maurice

1998 [1996] "Autobiographical Memory and the Historical Memory of the More Distant Past." Pp. 114–27 in *How We Think They Think: Anthropological Approaches to Cognition, Memory, and Literacy.* Boulder, Colo.: Westview.

Blum, Linda

1999 *At the Breast: Ideologies of Breastfeeding and Motherhood in the Contemporary United States.* Boston: Beacon.

Bock, Kenneth

1980 *Human Nature and History: A Response to Sociobiology.* New York: Columbia University Press.

Bogen, Debra L., et al.

2000 "Screening for Iron Deficiency Anemia by Dietary History in a High-Risk Population." *Pediatrics* 105 (6):1254–59.

Bogin, Barry

1999 [1988] *Patterns of Human Growth*, 2nd ed. Cambridge: Cambridge University Press.

Bonnet, Doris

1981 "Le retour de l'ancêtre." *Journal des Africanistes* 51 (1–2):133–49.

1988 *Corps biologique, corps social: Procréation et maladies de l'enfant en pays Mossi, Burkina Faso.* Paris: ORSTOM.

Boone, Sarah S.

1992 "Slavery and Contract Motherhood: A 'Racialized' Objection to the Autonomy Arguments." Pp. 349–66 in *Issues in Reproductive Technology.* Vol. 1: *An Anthology*, ed. Helen B. Holmes. New York: Garland.

Boone, Sylvia Ardun

1986 *Radiance from the Waters: Ideals of Feminine Beauty in Mende Art.* New Haven: Yale University Press.

Bordo, Susan

1993 "Anorexia Nervosa: Psychopathology as the Crystallization of Culture." Pp. 139–164 in *Unbearable Weight: Feminism, Western Culture, and the Body.* Berkeley: University of California Press.

Bornstein, Marc H., et al.

1992 "Maternal Responsiveness to Infants in Three Societies: The United States, France, and Japan." *Child Development* 62:807–21.

Bornstein, Marc H., and Michael E. Lamb

1992 *Development in Infancy: An Introduction*, 3rd ed. New York: McGraw-Hill.

Bornstein, Marc H., S. Toda, H. Azuma, C. S. Tamis-LeMonda, and M. Ogino

1990 "Mother and Infant Activity and Interaction in Japan and in the United States, II. A Comparative Microanalysis of Naturalistic Exchanges Focused on the Organization of Infant Attention." *International Journal of Behavioral Development* 13:289–308.

Bose, Pradip Kumar

1995 "Sons of the Nation: Child Rearing in the New Family." Pp. 118–44 in *Texts of Power: Emerging Disciplines in Colonial Bengal*, ed. Partha Chatterjee. Minneapolis: University of Minnesota Press.

Boserup, Ester

1970 *Woman's Role in Economic Development.* New York: St. Martin's Press.

Bourdin, Joel

1980 *Monnaie et politique monétaire dans les pays africains de la zone franc.* Dakar: Nouvelles Editions Africaines.

Bowlby, John

1969 *Attachment and Loss.* Vol. 1: *Attachment.* New York: Basic Books.

1973 *Attachment and Loss.* Vol. 2: *Separation: Anxiety and Anger.* New York: Basic Books.

1980 *Attachment and Loss.* Vol. 3: *Loss: Sadness and Depression.* New York: Basic Books.

1988 *A Secure Base: Parent-Child Attachment and Healthy Human Development.* New York: Basic Books.

Bowlby, Rachel

1990 "Breakfast in America: *Uncle Tom's* Cultural Histories." Pp. 197–212 in *Nation and Narration,* ed. Homi K. Bhabha. London: Routledge.

Boyden, Jo, and Judith Ennew, eds.

1997 *Children in Focus: A Manual for Participatory Research with Children.* Stockholm: Rädda Barnen (Swedish Save the Children).

Brazelton, T. Berry

1977 "Implications of Infant Development among the Mayan Indians of Mexico." Pp. 151–187 in *Culture and Infancy: Variations in the Human Experience,* ed. P. Herbert Leiderman, Steven R. Tulkin, and Anne Rosenfeld. New York: Academic Press.

Breazeale, Tami E.

2001 "Attachment Parenting: A Practical Approach for the Reduction of Attachment Disorders and the Promotion of Emotionally Secure Children." M.A. thesis. Bethel College, School of Education.

Breeskin, Adelyn D.

1970 *Mary Cassatt, 1844–1926.* Washington, D.C.: National Gallery of Art.

Briggs, Jean L.

1998 *Inuit Morality Play: The Emotional Education of a Three-Year-Old.* New Haven: Yale University Press.

Bril, B., and C. Sabatier

1986 "The Cultural Context of Motor Development: Postural Manipulations in the Daily Life of Bambara Babies (Mali)." *International Journal of Behavioral Development* 9: 439–53.

Brumberg, Joan Jacobs

1988 *Fasting Girls: The Emergence of Anorexia Nervosa as a Modern Disease.* Cambridge: Harvard University Press.

Bruner, Edward, and Victor Turner, eds.

1986 *The Anthropology of Experience.* Urbana: University of Illinois Press.

Bruner, Jerome

1982 "Formats of Language Acquisition." *American Journal of Semiotics* 1:1–16.

1983 *Child's Talk.* New York: W. W. Norton.

1990 "Culture and Human Development: A New Look." *Human Development* 33:344–55.

Bryceson, Deborah Fahy, ed.

1995 *Women Wielding the Hoe: Lessons from Rural Africa for Feminist Theory and Development Practice.* Oxford, U.K.: Berg.

Buckley, Thomas
1987 "Dialogue and Shared Authority: Informants as Critics." *Central Issues in Anthropology* 7 (1):13–23.

Buckley, Thomas, and Alma Gottlieb, eds.
1988 *Blood Magic: The Anthropology of Menstruation.* Berkeley: University of California Press.

Buekens, P., and A. Wilcox
1993 "Why Do Small Twins Have a Lower Mortality Rate than Small Singletons?" *American Journal of Obstetrics and Gynecology* 168 (3, pt. 1):937–41.

Bukatko, Danuta, and Marvin W. Daehler
1992 *Child Development: A Topical Approach.* Boston: Houghton Mifflin.

Bulmer, Ralph
1967 "Why Is the Cassowary not a Bird? A Problem of Zoological Taxonomy among the Karam of the New Guinea Highlands." *Man* 2 (1):5–25.

Bunzl, Matti
Forthcoming *Symptoms of Modernity: Jews and Queers in Late-Twentieth-Century Vienna.* Berkeley: University of California Press.

Butler, Barbara, and Diane Michalski Turner, eds.
1987 *Children and Anthropological Research.* New York: Plenum Press.

Butt, Leslie
1998 "The Social and Political Life of Infants among the Baliem Valley Dani, Irian Jaya." Ph.D. diss., Department of Anthropology, McGill University.

Callaway, Helen
1992 "Ethnography and Experience: Gender Implications in Fieldwork and Texts." Pp. 29–49 in *Anthropology and Autobiography,* ed. Judith Okely and Helen Callaway. London: Routledge.

Campbell, Annily
1999 *Childfree and Sterilized: Women's Decisions and Medical Responses.* London: Cassell.

Camus, Albert
1946 [1942] *The Stranger.* Translated by Stuart Gilbert. New York: Alfred A. Knopf.

Canagarajah, Sudharshan, and Helena Skyt Nielson
1999 "Child Labor and Schooling in Africa: A Comparative Study." SP Discussion Paper #9916 20456. The World Bank. Available online at <www-wds.worldbank.org>.

Caplan, Frank, ed.
1984 *The First Twelve Months of Life.* New York: Bantam.

Caplan, Pat
1988 "Engendering Knowledge: The Politics of Ethnography." *Anthropology Today* 4 (5):8–12; 4 (6):14–17.

———, ed.
1987 *The Cultural Construction of Sexuality.* London: Tavistock.

Carruthers, Peter
1992 *Human Knowledge and Human Nature: A New Introduction to an Ancient Debate.* Oxford: Oxford University Press.

Cassell, Joan, ed.
1987 *Children in the Field: Anthropological Experiences.* Philadelphia: Temple University Press.

Cassidy, Claire
1980 "Benign Neglect and Toddler Malnutrition." Pp. 109–39 in *Social and Biological Predictors of Nutritional Status, Physical Growth, and Neurological Development*, ed. L. S. Greene and F. E. Johnston. New York: Academic Press.
1987 "Child Malnutrition and Worldview Conflict." Pp. 293–324 in *Child Survival: Anthropological Perspectives on the Treatment and Maltreatment of Children*, ed. Nancy Scheper-Hughes. Boston: D. Reidel.
Caudill, William
1972 "Tiny Dramas: Vocal Communication between Mother and Infant in Japanese and American Families." Pp. 25–48 in *Mental Health Research in Asia and the Pacific*. Vol. 2: *Transcultural Research in Mental Health*, ed. W. P. Labra. Honolulu: The University Press of Hawaii.
Caudill, William, and David W. Plath
1966 "Who Sleeps by Whom? Parent-Child Involvement in Urban Japanese Families." *Psychiatry* 29:344–66.
Centers for Disease Control and Prevention
2001 Deaths: Final Data for 1999. NVSR 49 (8) (PHS) 2001–1120. Available online at <www.cdc.gov/nchs/data/nvsr/nvsr49/nvsr49_08.pdf>.
n.d. "What Would Happen if We Stopped Vaccination?" Atlanta: Centers for Disease Control and Prevention. Available online at <www.cdc.gov/nip/publications/fs/gen/WhatIfStop/htm>.
Central Intelligence Agency
2001 "Côte d'Ivoire." *The World Factbook 2001*. Central Intelligence Agency. Available online at <www.cia.gov/cia/publications/factbook/geos/iv.html>.
Cesara, Manda
1982 *Reflections of a Woman Anthropologist: No Hiding Place*. New York: Academic Press.
Chase, Allan
1982 *Magic Shots: A Human and Scientific Account of the Long and Continuing Struggle to Eradicate Infectious Diseases by Vaccination*. New York: William Morrow.
Chatterjee, Partha
1993 *The Nation and Its Fragments: Colonial and Postcolonial Histories*. Princeton, N.J.: Princeton University Press.
Chavez, A., C. Martinez, M. Muñoz, P. Arroyo, and A. Bourges
1972 "Ecological Factors in the Nutrition and Development of Children from Poor Rural Areas." Pp. 265–69 in *Proceedings of the Western Hemisphere Nutrition Congress*. Vol. 3, ed. P. L. White and N. Selvey. Mt. Kisco, N.Y.: Futura.
Child Labor Coalition
n.d. "There's Nothing Sweet about Child Slave Labor in the Cocoa Fields." Available online at <www.stopchildlabor.org/internationalchildlabor/chocolate.htm>.
Chodorow, Nancy
1978 *The Reproduction of Mothering: Psychoanalysis and the Sociology of Gender*. Berkeley: University of California Press.
Ciekawy, Diane, and Peter Geschiere, eds.
1998 *Special issue: Containing Witchcraft. African Studies Review* 41 (3).
Clarke-Stewart, K. Alison
1978 "Recasting the Lone Stranger." Pp. 109–76 in *The Development of Social Understanding*, ed. Joseph Glick and K. Alison Clarke-Stewart. New York: Gardner.

Cole, Jennifer

2001 *Forget Colonialism? Sacrifice and the Art of Memory in Madagascar.* Berkeley: University of California Press.

Cole, Michael

1983 "Society, Mind, and Development." Pp. 89–114 in *The Child and Other Cultural Inventions,* ed. Frank Kessel and Alex Siegel. New York: Praeger.

1996 *Cultural Psychology: A Once and Future Discipline.* Cambridge: Harvard University Press.

1999 "Culture in Development." Pp. 73–123 in *Developmental Psychology: An Advanced Textbook,* 4th edition, ed. Marc H. Bornstein and Michael E. Lamb. Mahwah, N.J.: Lawrence Erlbaum.

Comaroff, Jean, and John Comaroff

1991 *Of Revelation and Revolution.* Vol. 1. *Christianity, Colonialism, and Consciousness in South Africa.* Chicago: University of Chicago Press.

1997 *Of Revelation and Revolution.* Vol. 2. *The Dialectics of Modernity on a South African Frontier.* Chicago: University of Chicago Press.

———, eds.

1993 *Modernity and Its Malcontents: Ritual and Power in Postcolonial Africa.* Chicago: University of Chicago Press.

Comaroff, John

1987 "Sui Genderis: Feminism, Kinship Theory, and Structural 'Domains.'" Pp. 53–85 in *Gender and Kinship: Toward a Unified Analysis,* ed. Jane Collier and Sylvia Yanagisako. Stanford, Calif.: Stanford University Press.

Condor, Bob

1999 "The Great Sleep Debate: The Experts Answer a Crying Need for Shut-Eye." *Chicago Tribune,* October 31.

Conklin, Beth A., and Lynn M. Morgan

1996 "Babies, Bodies, and the Production of Personhood in North America and a Native Amazonian Society." *Ethos* 24 (4):657–94.

Connerton, Paul

1989 *How Societies Remember.* Cambridge: Cambridge University Press.

Coontz, Stephanie

1992 *The Way We Never Were: American Families and the Nostalgia Trap.* New York: Basic Books.

Coquery-Vidrovitch, Catherine

1997 [1994] *African Women: A Modern History.* Translated by Beth Gillian Raps. Boulder, Colo.: Westview.

Cosminsky, Sheila

1985 "Infant Feeding Practices in Rural Kenya." Pp. 35–54 in *Breastfeeding, Child Health, and Child Spacing: Cross-Cultural Perspectives,* ed. Valerie Hull and Mayling Simpson. London: Croom Helm.

Counihan, Carole

1997 [1984] "Bread as World: Food Habits and Social Relations in Modernizing Sardinia." Pp. 283–95 in *Food and Culture: A Reader,* ed. Carole Counihan and Penny Van Esterik. New York: Routledge.

Counihan, Carole, and Penny Van Esterik, eds.

1997 *Food and Culture: A Reader.* New York: Routledge.

Crago, Martha

1992 "Ethnography and Language Acquisition: A Cross-Cultural Perspective." *Topics in Language Disorders* 12 (3):2–39.

Crapanzano, Vincent

1980 *Tuhami: Portrait of a Moroccan.* Berkeley: University of Chicago Press.

1984 "Life-Histories" [review article]. *American Anthropologist* 86:953–60.

Crawford, C. Joanne

1994 "Parenting Practices in the Basque Country: Implications of Infant and Childhood Sleeping Location for Personality Development." *Ethos* 22 (1):42–82.

Creider, Jane Tapsubei

1986 *Two Lives: My Spirit and I.* London: The Women's Press.

Creyghton, Marie-Louise

1992 "Breast-Feeding and Baraka in Northern Tunisia." Pp. 37–58 in *The Anthropology of Breast-Feeding: Natural Law or Social Construct,* ed. Vanessa Maher. Oxford, U.K.: Berg.

Crocker, J. Christopher

1985 *Vital Souls: Bororo Cosmology, Natural Symbolism, and Shamanism.* Tucson: University of Arizona Press.

Crouch, Mira, and Lenore Manderson

1993 *New Motherhood: Cultural and Personal Transitions in the 1980s.* Yverdon, Switzerland: Gordon and Breach Science Publishers.

Cummings, E. M.

1980 "Caregiver Stability and Day Care." *Developmental Psychology* 16:31–37.

Cunningham, Allan S.

1995 "Breastfeeding: Adaptive Behavior for Child Health and Longevity." Pp. 243–64 in *Breastfeeding: Biocultural Perspectives,* ed. Patricia Stuart-Macadam and Katherine A. Dettwyler. New York: Aldine de Gruyter.

Cunningham, Clark E.

1970 "Thai 'Injection Doctors': Antibiotic Mediators." *Social Science and Medicine* 4: 1–24.

D'Alisera, JoAnn

1998 "Born in the USA: Naming Ceremonies of Infants among Sierra Leoneans in the American Capital." *Anthropology Today* 14 (1):16–18.

2001 "I ♥ Islam: Popular Religious Commodities, Sites of Inscription, and Transnational Sierra Leonean Identity." *Journal of Material Culture* 6 (1):89–108.

Forthcoming *An Imagined Geography: Sierra Leonean Muslims in America.* Philadelphia: University of Pennsylvania Press.

Davin, Anna

1997 "Imperialism and Motherhood." Pp. 88–151 in *Tensions of Empire: Colonial Cultures in a Bourgeois World,* ed. Frederick Cooper and Ann Stoler. Berkeley: University of California Press.

Davis-Floyd, Robbie E.

1992 *Birth as an American Rite of Passage.* Berkeley: University of California Press.

2003 "Home Birth Emergencies in the U.S. and Mexico: The Trouble with Transport." *Social Science and Medicine* 56 (9):1911–31.

Davis-Floyd, Robbie E., Sheila Cosminsky, and Stacy Leigh Pigg, eds.

2002 *Special Issue: Daughters of Time: The Shifting Identities of Contemporary Midwives. Medical Anthropology* 20 (3).

Davis-Floyd, Robbie E., and Joe Dumit, eds.

1997 *Cyborg Babies: From Techno Tots to Techno Toys.* New York: Routledge.

Davis-Floyd, Robbie E., and Carolyn Sargent

1997 "Introduction: The Anthropology of Birth." Pp. 1–51 in *Childbirth and Authoritative Knowledge: Cross-Cultural Perspectives,* ed. Robbie E. Davis-Floyd and Carolyn Sargent. Berkeley: University of California Press.

———, eds.

1997 *Childbirth and Authoritative Knowledge: Cross-Cultural Perspectives.* Berkeley: University of California Press.

de Boysson-Bardies, Bénédicte

1999 [1996] *How Language Comes to Children: From Birth to Two Years.* Translated by M. B. DeBevoise. Cambridge: MIT Press.

Décarie, Thérèse Gouin, et al.

1974 *The Infant's Reaction to Strangers.* Translated by Joyce Diamanti. New York: International Universities Press.

Delaney, Carol

1991 *The Seed and the Soil: Gender and Cosmology in Turkish Village Society.* Berkeley: University of California Press.

1995 "Father State, Motherland, and the Birth of Modern Turkey." Pp. 177–99 in *Naturalizing Power: Essays in Feminist Cultural Analysis,* ed. Sylvia Yanagisako and Carol Delaney. New York: Routledge.

2000 "Making Babies in a Turkish Village." Pp. 117–44 in *A World of Babies: Imagined Childcare Guides for Seven Societies,* ed. Judy S. DeLoache and Alma Gottlieb. New York: Cambridge University Press.

DeLoache, Judy S.

1992 "Perspectives on Infant Development." Lecture presented to Psychology 318 class, University of Illinois at Urbana-Champaign, September 2.

DeLoache, Judy S., and Alma Gottlieb

2000 "If Dr. Spock Were Born in Bali: Raising a World of Babies." Pp. 1–27 in *A World of Babies: Imagined Childcare Guides for Seven Societies,* ed. Judy S. DeLoache and Alma Gottlieb. New York: Cambridge University Press.

———, eds.

2000 *A World of Babies: Imagined Childcare Guides for Seven Societies.* New York: Cambridge University Press.

DeLoache, Judy S., Sophia L. Pierroutsakos, David H. Uttal, Karl S. Rosengren, and Alma Gottlieb

1998 "Grasping the Nature of Pictures." *Psychological Science* 9 (3):205–10.

Demos, John

1982 *Entertaining Satan: Witchcraft and the Culture of Early New England.* New York: Oxford University Press.

Derné, Steve

1992 "Beyond Institutional and Impulsive Conceptions of Self: Family Structure and the Socially Anchored Real Self." *Ethos* 20 (3):259–88.

Dettwyler, Katherine

1994 *Dancing with Skeletons: Life and Death in West Africa.* Prospect Heights, Ill.: Waveland.

1995a "Beauty and the Breast: The Cultural Context of Breastfeeding in the United

States." Pp. 167–215 in *Breastfeeding: Biocultural Perspectives,* ed. Patricia Stuart-Macadam and Katherine A. Dettwyler. New York: Aldine de Gruyter.

1995b "A Time to Wean: The Hominid Blueprint for the Natural Age of Weaning in Modern Human Populations." Pp. 39–73 in *Breastfeeding: Biocultural Perspectives,* ed. Patricia Stuart-Macadam and Katherine A. Dettwyler. New York: Aldine de Gruyter.

Dettwyler, Katherine, and Claudia Fishman

1992 "Infant Feeding Practices and Growth." *Annual Review of Anthropology* 21:171–204.

Diener, Marissa

2000 "Gift from the Gods: A Balinese Guide to Early Child Rearing." Pp. 91–116 in *A World of Babies: Imagined Childcare Guides for Seven Societies,* ed. Judy DeLoache and Alma Gottlieb. New York: Cambridge University Press.

Dietz, V., A. Galazka, F. van Loon, and S. Cochi

1997 "Factors Affecting the Immunogenicity and Potency of Tetanus Toxoid: Implications for the Elimination of Neonatal and Non-Neonatal Tetanus as Public Health Problems." *Bulletin of the World Health Organization* 75 (1):81–93.

Dirks, Nicholas, Geoffrey Eley, and Sherry Ortner, eds.

1993 *Culture, Power, History.* Princeton, N.J.: Princeton University Press.

Douglas, Mary

1966 *Purity and Danger.* New York: Praeger.

1970 *Natural Symbols: Explorations in Cosmology.* New York: Pantheon.

1975a [1972] "Deciphering a Meal." Pp. 249–75 in *Implicit Meanings: Essays in Anthropology,* by Mary Douglas. London: Routledge and Kegan Paul.

1975b [1970] "Self-Evidence." Pp. 276–318 in *Implicit Meanings: Essays in Anthropology,* by Mary Douglas. London: Routledge and Kegan Paul.

1984 *Food in the Social Order: Studies of Food and Festivities in Three American Communities.* New York: Russell Sage Foundation.

1985 *Risk Acceptability according to the Social Sciences.* New York: Russell Sage Foundation.

1992 *Risk and Blame: Essays in Cultural Theory.* London: Routledge.

———, ed.

1970 *Witchcraft Accusations and Confessions.* London: Tavistock.

1987 *Constructive Drinking: Perspectives on Drink from Anthropology.* Cambridge: Cambridge University Press.

Douglas, Mary, and Aaron Wildavsky

1982 *Risk and Culture: An Essay on the Selection of Technological and Environmental Dangers.* Berkeley: University of California Press.

Dragadze, Tamara

n.d. "Sex Roles and State Roles in Soviet Georgia: Two Styles of Infant Socialisation." Pp. 288–306 in *Acquiring Culture: Cross Cultural Studies in Child Development,* ed. Gustav Jahoda and I. M. Lewis. London: Croom Helm.

Draper, H. H.

1977 "Biological, Cultural, and Social Determinants of Nutritional Status." Pp. 189–209 in *Culture and Infancy: Variations in the Human Experience,* ed. P. Herbert Leiderman, Steven R. Tulkin, and Anne Rosenfeld. New York: Academic Press.

Du, Shanshan
  2002 *"Chopsticks Always Work in Pairs": Gender Unity and Gender Equality.* New York: Columbia University Press.
Duncan, David Ewing
  1998 *Calendar: Humanity's Epic Struggle to Determine a True and Accurate Year.* New York: Avon Books.
Dussart, Françoise
  1984 Les aléas d'une politique militaire integrative: Le cas de Samori. *Cultures et Développement* 16 (3/4):611–28.
Dwyer, Kevin
  1982 *Moroccan Dialogues: Anthropology in Question.* Baltimore: Johns Hopkins University Press.
Dyhouse, Carol
  1978 "Working-Class Mothers and Infant Mortality in England, 1895–1914." *Journal of Social History* 12 (2):248–67.
Easterbrooks, M. Ann, and Wendy Goldberg
  1990 "Security of Toddler-Parent Attachment: Relation to Children's Sociopersonality Functioning during Kindergarten." Pp. 221–44 in *Attachment in the Preschool Years: Theory, Research, and Intervention,* ed. Mark T. Greenberg, Dante Cicchetti, and E. Mark Cummings. Chicago: University of Chicago Press.
Egeland, B.
  1993 "A History of Abuse Is a Major Risk Factor for Abusing the Next Generation." Pp. 197–208 in *Current Controversies on Family Violence,* ed. R. J. Gelles and D. R. Loseke. Newbury Park, Calif.: Sage.
Einarsdóttir, Jónína
  Forthcoming *"Tired of Weeping": Child Death and Mourning among Papel Mothers in Guinea-Bissau.* Madison: University of Wisconsin Press.
Ellison, Peter T.
  1995 "Breastfeeding, Fertility, and Maternal Condition." Pp. 305–345 in *Breastfeeding: Biocultural Perspectives,* ed. Patricia Stuart-Macadam and Katherine A. Dettwyler. New York: Aldine de Gruyter.
  2001 "The Elixir of Life." Pp. 81–126 in *On Fertile Ground: A Natural History of Human Reproduction,* by Peter Ellison. Cambridge: Harvard University Press.
Elman, J., E. Bates, M. H. Johnson, A. Karmiloff-Smith, D. Parisi, and K. Plunkett
  1996 *Rethinking Innateness: A Connectionist Perspective on Development.* Cambridge, Mass.: M.I.T. Press.
'Elota
  1983 *'Elota's Story: The Life and Times of a Solomon Islands Big Man,* ed. Roger M. Keesing. New York: Holt, Rinehart, and Winston.
Engle, Patrice L., et al.
  1996 "Growth Consequences of Low-Income Nicaraguan Mothers' Theories about Feeding One-Year-Olds." Pp. 428–46 in *Parents' Cultural Belief Systems: Their Origins, Expressions, and Consequences,* ed. Sara Harkness and Charles M. Super. New York: Guilford.
Enloe, Cynthia H.
  2000 [1989] *Bananas, Beaches, and Bases: Making Feminist Sense of International Politics,* rev. ed. Berkeley: University of California Press.

Ephirim-Donkor, Anthony

1997 "Childhood Spirituality." Pp. 81–89 in *African Spirituality: On Becoming Ancestors,* by Anthony Ephirim-Donkor. Trenton, N.J.: Africa World Press.

Erny, Pierre

1988 *Les premiers pas dans la vie de l'enfant d'Afrique noire: Naissance et première enfance.* Paris: L'Harmattan.

Escobar, Arturo

1995 *Encountering Development: The Making and Unmaking of the Third World.* Princeton, N.J.: Princeton University Press.

Etienne, Mona

1979 "The Case for Social Maternity: Adoption of Children by Urban Baule Women." *Dialectical Anthropology* 4:237–42.

Europa Publications

1999 "Major Commodities of Africa." Pp. 28–63 in *Africa South of the Sahara 2000.* London: Europa Publications/Taylor and Francis.

2000 "Côte d'Ivoire." Pp. 414–38 in *Africa South of the Sahara 2001,* 30th ed. London: Europa Publications/Taylor and Francis.

Evans-Pritchard, E. E.

1937 *Witchcraft, Oracles and Magic among the Azande.* Oxford: Clarendon.

1940 *The Nuer.* Oxford: Oxford University Press.

Eyer, Diane E.

1992 *Mother-Infant Bonding: A Scientific Fiction.* New Haven: Yale University Press.

Fajans, Jane

1997 *They Make Themselves: Work and Play among the Baining of Papua New Guinea.* Chicago: University of Chicago Press.

Falkner, Frank, ed.

1991 *Infant and Child Nutrition Worldwide: Issues and Perspectives.* Boca Raton, Fla.: CRC Press.

Falola, Toyin, and O. B. Lawuyi

1990 "Not Just a Currency: The Cowrie in Nigerian Culture." Pp. 29–36 in *West African Economic and Social History: Studies in Memory of Marion Johnson,* ed. David Henige and T. C. McCaskie. Madison: African Studies Center, University of Wisconsin Press.

Farmer, Paul

1999 "Pathologies of Power: Rethinking Health and Human Rights." *American Journal of Public Health* 89 (10):1486–96.

Farnell, Brenda

1994 "Ethno-graphics and the Moving Body." *Man* 29 (4):929–74.

1995 *Do You See What I Mean? Plains Indian Sign Talk and the Embodiment of Action.* Austin: University of Texas Press.

1999 "Moving Bodies, Acting Selves." *Annual Review of Anthropology* 28:341–73.

———, ed.

1995 *Human Action Signs in Cultural Context: The Visible and the Invisible in Movement and Dance.* Metuchen, N.J.: Scarecrow Press.

Farvacque-Vitkovic, Catherine

1998 *The Future of African Cities: Challenges and Priorities for Urban Development.* Washington, D.C.: World Bank.

Fawcett, Nancy P., and Dina K. Varon
1999 "Teething." In *Griffith's 5-Minute Clinical Consult,* ed. Mark R. Dambro and Jo A. Griffith. Philadelphia: Lippincott Williams & Wilkins. Available online with a free trial subscription at <http://home.mdconsult.com/das/book/body/8220419/846/528.html>.

Faÿ-Sallois, Fanny
1980 *Les nourrices à Paris au XIXᵉ siècle.* Paris: Payot.

Feeley-Harnik, Gillian
1991 "Finding Memories in Madagascar." Pp. 121–40 in *Images of Memory: On Remembering and Representation,* ed. Susanne Küchler and Walter Melion. Washington, D.C.: Smithsonian Institution Press.

Feldman-Savelsberg, Pamela
1999 *Plundered Kitchens, Empty Wombs: Threatened Reproduction and Identity in the Cameroon.* Ann Arbor: University of Michigan Press.

Feldman-Savelsberg, Pamela, Flavien T. Ndonko, and Bergis Schmidt-Ehry
2000 "Sterilizing Vaccines or the Politics of the Womb: Retrospective Study of a Rumor in Cameroon." *Medical Anthropology Quarterly* 14 (2):159–79.

Ferber, Richard
1985 *Solve Your Child's Sleep Problems.* New York: Simon and Schuster.

Ferguson, Charles A.
1977 "Baby Talk as a Simplified Register." Pp. 209–35 in *Talking to Children: Language Input and Acquisition,* ed. Catherine Snow and Charles A. Ferguson. New York: Cambridge University Press.

Ferguson, James
1994 [1990] *The Anti-Politics Machine: "Development," Depoliticization, and Bureaucratic Power in Lesotho.* Minneapolis: University of Minnesota Press.

Fermé, Mariane C.
2001 *The Underneath of Things: Violence, History, and the Everyday in Sierra Leone.* Berkeley: University of California Press.

Fernandez, James W.
1986 [1980] "Some Reflections on Looking into Mirrors." Pp. 157–71 in *Persuasions and Performances: The Play of Tropes in Culture.* Bloomington: Indiana University Press.

Fernandez, Renate Lellap
1979 "The Decline of Breastfeeding: Interplay of Images and Policies." Pp. 67–74 in *Breastfeeding and Food Policy in a Hungry World,* ed. Dana Raphael. New York: Academic Press.

Fernandez, Renate Lellap, and David Sutton, eds.
1998 *Special Issue: In the Field and at Home: Families and Anthropology. Anthropology and Humanism* 23 (2).

Ferreira, Mariana Kawall Leal
1997 "When 1 + 1 ≠ 2: Making Mathematics in Central Brazil." *American Ethnologist* 24 (1):132–47.

Fildes, Valerie A.
1995 "The Culture and Biology of Breastfeeding: An Historical Review of Western Europe." Pp. 101–26 in *Breastfeeding: Biocultural Perspectives,* ed. Patricia Stuart-Macadam and Katherine A. Dettwyler. New York: Aldine de Gruyter.

Filho, Gisálio Cerqueira, and Gizlene Neder

2001 "Social and Historical Approaches regarding Street Children in Rio de Janeiro (Brazil) in the Context of the Transition to Democracy." *Childhood* 8 (1):11–30.

Fine, Gary Alan

1988 *Knowing Children: Participant Observation with Minors.* Newbury Park, Calif.: Sage.

Fischer, Michael, and Mehdi Abedi

1990 *Debating Muslims: Cultural Dialogues in Postmodernity and Traditions.* Madison: University of Wisconsin Press.

Flinn, Juliana, Leslie Marshall, and Jocelyn Armstrong, eds.

1998 *Fieldwork and Families: Constructing New Models for Ethnographic Research.* Honolulu: University of Hawai'i Press.

Fofana, Ibrahima Khalil

1998 *L'Almami Samori Touré, Empereur: Récit historique.* Paris: Présence Africaine.

Fogel, Alan

1993 *Developing through Relationships: Origins of Communication, Self, and Culture.* Chicago: University of Chicago Press.

Food and Agricultural Organization

n.d. "FAOSTAT Agriculture Data. Food and Agricultural Organization." UNICEF. Available online at <http://apps.fao.org/cgi-bin/nph-db.pl?subset=agriculture>.

Fortes, Meyer

1987 *Religion, Morality, and the Person: Essays on Tallensi Religion.* Edited by Jack Goody. Cambridge: Cambridge University Press.

Foucault, Michel

1977 *Language, Counter-Memory, Practice: Selected Essays and Interviews.* Ithaca: Cornell University Press.

Franklin, Sarah

2001 "Sheepwatching." *Anthropology Today* 17 (3):3–9.

Franklin, Sarah, and Helena Ragoné, eds.

1998 *Reproducing Reproduction: Kinship, Power, and Technological Innovation.* Philadelphia: University of Pennsylvania Press.

Friedl, Erika

1997 *Children of Del Koh: Young Life in an Iranian Village.* Syracuse: Syracuse University Press.

Friedlander, Eva

1995 "Inclusive Boundaries, Exclusive Ideologies: Hindu Fundamentalism and Gender in India Today." Pp. 51–56 in *Feminism, Nationalism, and Militarism,* ed. Constance R. Sutton. Arlington, Va.: Association for Feminist Anthropology/American Anthropological Association.

Frydman, Gloria

1987 *Mature-Age Mothers.* Ringwood, Victoria, Australia: Penguin.

Gable, Eric

1995 "The Decolonization of Consciousness: Local Skeptics and the 'Will to be Modern' in a West African Village." *American Ethnologist* 22 (2):242–57.

2000 "The Culture Development Club: Youth, Neo-Tradition, and the Construction of Society in Guinea-Bissau." *Anthropological Quarterly* 73 (4):195–203.

Gaskin, Ina Mae

1987 *Babies, Breastfeeding, and Bonding.* South Hadley, Mass.: Bergin & Garvey.

Geber, M., and R. F. Dean
1967 "Precocious Development of Newborn African Infants." Pp. 120–26 in *Behavior in Infancy and Early Childhood*, ed. Y. Brackbill and G. G. Thompson. New York: Free Press.

Geertz, Clifford
1973a [1966] "Religion as a Cultural System." Pp. 87–125 in *The Interpretation of Cultures*, by Clifford Geertz. New York: Basic Books.
1973b "Thick Description: Toward an Interpretive Theory of Culture." Pp. 3–20 in *The Interpretation of Cultures*, by Clifford Geertz. New York: Basic Books.
1983 [1975] "Common Sense as a Cultural System." Pp. 73–93 in *Local Knowledge: Further Essays in Interpretive Anthropology*, by Clifford Geertz. New York: Basic Books.
1995 *After the Fact: Two Countries, Four Decades, One Anthropologist*. Cambridge: Harvard University Press.

Georges, Kodjo Niamkey
1991 *Côte d'Ivoire, 1894–1895: La Ville de Kong et Samori d'après le journal inédit du Français Georges Bailly*. Paris: L'Harmattan.

Geschiere, Peter
1997 [1995] *The Modernity of Witchcraft: Politics and the Occult in Postcolonial Africa*. Translated by Peter Geschiere and Janet Roitman. Charlottesville: University Press of Virginia.

Geurts, Kathryn
2001 "Childbirth and Pragmatic Midwifery in Rural Ghana." *Medical Anthropology* 20: 1–35.
2002 "Sensory Symbolism in Birth and Infant Care Practices." In *Culture and the Senses: Embodiment, Identity, and Well-Being in an African Community*, by Kathryn Geurts. Berkeley: University of California Press.

Giddens, Anthony
1984 *The Constitution of Society: Outline of the Theory of Structuration*. Berkeley, Calif.: University of California Press.

Ginsburg, Faye
1989 *Contested Lives: The Abortion Debate in an American Community*. Berkeley: University of California Press.

Ginsburg, Faye, and Rayna Rapp
1991 "The Politics of Reproduction." *Annual Review of Anthropology* 20: 311–43.
———, eds.
1995 *Conceiving the New World Order: The Global Politics of Reproduction*. Berkeley: University of California Press.

Ginzburg, Carlo
1983 [1966] *The Night Battles: Witchcraft and Agrarian Cults in the Sixteenth and Seventeenth Centuries*. Translated by John and Anne Tedeschi. Baltimore: Johns Hopkins University Press.

Glenn, Evelyn Nakano, Grace Chang, and Linda Rennie Forcey, eds.
1994 *Mothering: Ideology, Experience, and Agency*. New York: Routledge.

Goldberg, Susan
1977 "Ethics, Politics, and Multi-Cultural Research." Pp. 587–98 in *Culture and Infancy: Variations in the Human Experience*, ed. P. Herbert Leiderman, Steven R. Tulkin, and Anne Rosenfeld. New York: Academic Press.

Golde, Peggy, ed.

1986 *Women in the Field: Anthropological Experiences,* 2nd ed. Berkeley: University of California Press.

Goldschmidt, Walter

1975 "Absent Eyes and Idle Hands: Socialization for Low Affect among the Sebei." *Ethos* 3:157–63.

Goodwin, Marjorie Harness

1990 *He-Said-She-Said: Talk as Social Organization among Black Children.* Bloomington: Indiana University Press.

1997 "Children's Linguistic and Social Worlds." *Anthropology Newsletter* 38 (4):1, 4–5.

Goody, Esther, ed.

1982 *Parenthood and Social Reproduction: Fostering and Occupational Roles in West Africa.* Cambridge: Cambridge University Press.

Goody, Jack

1982 *Cooking, Cuisine, and Class: A Study in Comparative Sociology.* Cambridge: Cambridge University Press.

1998 *Food and Love: A Cultural History of East and West.* London: Verso.

Gopnik, Alison, Andrew N. Meltzoff, and Patricia K. Kuhl

1999 *The Scientist in the Crib: What Early Learning Tells Us about the Mind.* New York: William Morrow.

Gottlieb, Alma

1986a "Cousin Marriage, Birth Order, and Gender: Alliance Models among the Beng of Ivory Coast." *Man* 21 (4):697–722.

1986b "Dog: Ally or Traitor? Mythology, Cosmology, and Society among the Beng of Ivory Coast." *American Ethnologist* 13 (3):477–88.

1988 "Menstrual Cosmology among the Beng of Ivory Coast." Pp. 55–74 in *Blood Magic: The Anthropology of Menstruation,* ed. Thomas Buckley and Alma Gottlieb. Berkeley: University of California Press.

1989a "Hyenas and Heteroglossia: Myth and Ritual among the Beng of Côte d'Ivoire." *American Ethnologist* 16 (3):487–501.

1989b "Witches, Kings, and the Sacrifice of Identity; or, The Power of Paradox and the Paradox of Power among the Beng of Ivory Coast." Pp. 245–72 in *Creativity of Power: Cosmology and Action in African Societies,* ed. W. Arens and Ivan Karp. Washington, D.C.: Smithsonian Institution Press.

1990 "Rethinking Female Pollution: The Beng Case (Côte d'Ivoire)." Pp. 113–38 in *Beyond the Second Sex: New Directions in the Anthropology of Gender,* ed. Peggy Reeves Sanday and Ruth Gallagher Goodenough. Philadelphia: University of Pennsylvania Press.

1992 "Passion and Putrefaction: Beng Funerals in Disarray." Paper presented at the annual meeting of the Satterthwaite Colloquium on African Ritual and Religion, Satterthwaite, U.K., April.

1995a "The Anthropologist as Mother: Reflections on Childbirth Observed and Childbirth Experienced." *Anthropology Today* 11 (3):10–14.

1995b "Of Cowries and Crying: A Beng Guide to Managing Colic." *Anthropology* and Humanism 20 (1):20–28.

1996a "The Social Construction of Motherhood: The Beng of Côte d'Ivoire." Paper presented at the annual meeting of the American Anthropological Association, San Francisco, November.

1996b [1992] *Under the Kapok Tree: Identity and Difference in Beng Thought.* Chicago: University of Chicago Press.

1998 "Do Infants Have Religion? The Spiritual Lives of Beng Babies." *American Anthropologist* 100 (1):122–35.

2000a "Luring Your Child into This Life: A Beng Path for Infant Care (Côte d'Ivoire)." Pp. 55–89 in *A World of Babies: Imagined Childcare Guides for Seven Societies,* ed. Judy S. DeLoache and Alma Gottlieb. New York: Cambridge University Press.

2000b "Où sont partis tous les bébés? Pour une anthropologie du nourisson" ["Where Have All the Babies Gone? Toward an Anthropology of Infants"]. Pp. 367–85 in *En substances: Systèmes, pratiques et symboliques—textes pour Françoise Héritier,* ed. Emmanuel Terray, Jean-Luc Jamard, and Margarita Xanthakou; trans. Filip Sicard. Paris: Fayard.

2000c "Where Have All the Babies Gone? Toward an Anthropology of Infants (and Their Caretakers)." *Anthropological Quarterly* 73 (3):121–32.

2002a "Deconstructing the Notion of 'Education': A View from West Africa." Pp. 83–101 in *Research in International Education: Experience, Theory, and Practice,* ed. Liora Bresler and Alexandre Ardichvili. New York: Peter Lang.

2002b "New Developments in the Anthropology of Childcare." *Anthropology News* 43 (7):13.

n.d.a "Religions of West Africa." Unpublished manuscript.

n.d.b "Stranger Anxiety or Stranger Love? Sociable Beng Babies (Côte d'Ivoire)." In *The Stranger, the Strange, and Estrangement,* ed. Peter Frietzsche and Mark Steinberg. Forthcoming.

Gottlieb, Alma, and Philip Graham
1994 [1993] *Parallel Worlds: An Anthropologist and a Writer Encounter Africa.* Chicago: University of Chicago Press.

1999 "Revising the Text, Revisioning the Field: Reciprocity over the Long Term." *Anthropology and Humanism* 24 (2):117–28.

Gottlieb, Alma, Philip Graham, and Nathaniel Gottlieb-Graham
1998 "Infants, Ancestors, and the Afterlife: Fieldwork's Family Values." *Anthropology and Humanism* 23 (2):121–26.

Gottlieb, Alma, and M. Lynne Murphy
1995 *Beng-English Dictionary.* Bloomington: Indiana University Linguistics Club.

Gottschang, Suzanne K.
2000 "A Baby-Friendly Hospital and the Science of Infant Feeding." Pp. 160–84 in *Feeding China's Little Emperors: Food, Children, and Social Change.* Stanford, Calif.: Stanford University Press.

Gould, Stephen Jay
1996 "Triumph of the Root-Heads: We Undervalue an Organism—and Misread Evolution—When We Consider Only Adult Anatomy." *Natural History* (January):10–17.

Graham, Philip
n.d. *The Invisible Country: A Novel.* Unpublished manuscript.

Granju, Katie Allison, and Betsy Kennedy
1999 *Attachment Parenting: Instinctive Care for Your Baby and Young Child.* New York: Pocket Books.

Greenhouse, Steven
2002 "World Briefing/Africa: Ivory Coast: Cocoa Exports Questioned." *New York Times,* May 31.

Gregory, James
    1984 "The Myth of the Male Ethnographer and the Woman's World." *American Anthropologist* 86 (2):316–27.
Grimes, Ronald
    1995 *Marrying and Burying: Rites of Passage in a Man's Life*. Boulder: Westview.
Gross, Daniel R.
    1984 "Time Allocation: A Tool for the Study of Cultural Behavior." *Annual Review of Anthropology* 13:519–58.
Gudeman, Stephen, and Alberto Rivera
    1990 *Conversations in Colombia: The Domestic Economy in Life and Text*. Cambridge: Cambridge University Press.
Guldan, Georgia S.
    2000 "Paradoxes of Plenty: China's Infant- and Child-Feeding Transition." Pp. 27–47 in *Feeding China's Little Emperors: Food, Children, and Social Change*. Stanford, Calif.: Stanford University Press.
Gunnlaugsson, Geir and Jónína Einarsdóttir
    1993 "Colostrum and Ideas about Bad Milk: A Case Study from Guinea-Bissau." *Social Science and Medicine* 36 (3):283–88.
Gupta, Akhil
    2002 "Reliving Childhood? The Temporality of Childhood and Narratives of Reincarnation." *Ethnos* 67 (1):33–56.
Gupta, Akhil, and James Ferguson, eds.
    1997a *Anthropological Locations: Boundaries and Grounds of a Field Science*. Berkeley: University of California Press.
    1997b *Culture, Power, Place: Explorations in Critical Anthropology*. Durham, N.C.: Duke University Press.
Guy, Hervé, Claude Masset, and Charles-Albert Baud
    1997 "Infant Taphonomy." *International Journal of Osteoarchaeology* 7 (3):221–29.
Guyer, Jane, ed.
    1995 *Money Matters: Instability, Values, and Social Payments in the Modern History of West African Communities*. Portsmouth, N.H.: Heinemann.
Halbwachs, Maurice
    1992 [1941] *On Collective Memory*. Translated by Lewis A. Coser. Chicago: University of Chicago Press.
Hallen, Barry
    2000 *The Good, the Bad, and the Beautiful: Discourse about Values in Yoruba Culture*. Bloomington: Indiana University Press.
Hamilton, Annette
    1981 *Nature and Nurture: Aboriginal Child-Rearing in North-Central Arnhem Land*. Canberra: Australian Institute of Aboriginal Studies.
Hanks, W. F.
    1989 "Texts and Textuality." *Annual Review of Anthropology* 18:95–127.
Hannerz, Ulf
    1996 *Transnational Connections: Culture, People, Places*. New York: Routledge.
Hansson, Gurli
    1996 "Mwana Ndi Mai: Toward an Understanding of Preparation for Motherhood and Child Care in the Transitional Mberengwa District, Zimbabwe." Ph.D. diss. Uppsala

University, Uppsala, Sweden: Studia Missionalia Upsaliensia 65/Swedish Institute of Missionary Research.

Hardman, Charlotte

2001 "Can There Be an Anthropology of Children?" *Childhood* 8 (4):501–17.

Harkness, Sarah, and Charles M. Super

1983 "The Cultural Construction of Child Development: A Framework for the Socialization of Affect." *Ethos* 11 (4):221–32.

1987 "Fertility Change, Child Survival, and Child Development: Observations on a Rural Kenyan Community." Pp. 59–70 in *Child Survival: Anthropological Perspectives on the Treatment and Maltreatment of Children,* ed. Nancy Scheper-Hughes. Boston: D. Reidel.

1992 "The Cultural Foundations of Fathers' Roles: Evidence from Kenya and the United States." Pp. 191–211 in *Father-Child Relations: Cultural and Biosocial Contexts,* ed. Barry S. Hewlett. New York: Aldine de Gruyter.

———, eds.

1996 *Parents' Cultural Belief Systems: Their Origins, Expressions, and Consequences.* New York: Guilford Press.

Harris, Mark

2000 "The Child in Anthropology." Pp. 46–53 in *The Child in the City: A Case Study in Experimental Anthropology.* Manchester, U.K.: Prickly Pear Pamphlets.

Harris, Mark, et al.

2000 *The Child in the City: A Case Study in Experimental Anthropology.* Manchester, U.K.: Prickly Pear Pamphlets.

Harris, Olivia

1980 "The Power of Signs: Gender, Culture, and the Wild in the Bolivian Andes." Pp. 70–94 in *Nature, Culture, and Gender,* ed. Carol MacCormack and Marilyn Strathern. Cambridge: Cambridge University Press.

Harrison, Paul

1996 [1987] *The Greening of Africa: Breaking through in the Battle for Land and Food.* Nairobi: Academy Science Publishers/Friends-of-the-Book Foundation.

Hart, Keith

1982 *The Political Economy of West African Agriculture.* Cambridge: Cambridge University Press.

Harwood, Robin L.

1992 "The Influence of Culturally Derived Values on Anglo and Puerto Rican Mothers' Perceptions of Attachment Behavior." *Child Development* 63:822–39.

Harwood, Robin L., Joan G. Miller, and Nydia Lucca Irizarry

1995 *Culture and Attachment: Perceptions of the Child in Context.* New York: Guilford.

Hastrup, Kirsten

1994 "Anthropological Knowledge Incorporated: Discussion." Pp. 224–40 in *Social Experience and Anthropological Knowledge,* ed. Kirsten Hastrup and Peter Hervik. London: Routledge.

Heath, Shirley Brice

1983 *Ways with Words: Language, Life, and Work in Communities and Classrooms.* Cambridge: Cambridge University Press.

Henly, Susan J., et al.

1995 "Anemia and Insufficient Milk in First-Time Mothers." *Birth* 22 (2):87–92.

Héritier, Françoise

1994 *Les deux soeurs et leur mère*. Paris: Editions Odile Jacob.

1996 *Masculin/féminin: La pensée de la différence*. Paris: Editions Odile Jacob.

Hewlett, Barry

1991 *Intimate Fathers: The Nature and Context of Aka Pygmy Paternal Infant Care*. Ann Arbor: University of Michigan Press.

———, ed.

1992 *Father-Child Relations: Cultural and Biosocial Contexts*. New York: Aldine de Gruyter.

Hirschfeld, Lawrence A.

2002 "Why Don't Anthropologists Like Children?" *American Anthropologist* 104 (2): 611–27.

Hodgkinson, Edith

1999 "Côte d'Ivoire. Economy." Pp. 402–405 in *Africa South of the Sahara 2000*. London: Europa Publications/Taylor and Francis.

Hogendorn, Jan, and Marion Johnson

1986 *The Shell Money of the Slave Trade*. Cambridge: Cambridge University Press.

Hollos, Marida, and Philip E. Leis

1989 *Becoming Nigerian in Ijo Society*. New Brunswick, N.J.: Rutgers University Press.

Holloway, Susan D., and Masahiko Minami

1996 "Production and Reproduction of Culture: The Dynamic Role of Mothers and Children in Early Socialization." Pp. 164–76 in *Japanese Childrearing: Two Generations of Scholarship*, ed. David W. Shwalb and Barbara J. Shwalb. New York: Guilford.

Hopkins, Anthony G.

1970 "The Creation of a Colonial Monetary System: The Origins of the West African Currency Board." *African Historical Studies* 3:101–32.

1973 *An Economic History of West Africa*. New York: Columbia University Press.

Hoskins, Janet, ed.

2002 "Blood Mysteries: Beyond Menstruation as Pollution." Special issue, *Ethnology* 41 (4).

Howes, David

1991 *The Varieties of Sensory Experience*. Toronto: University of Toronto Press.

Hughes, Richard

1999 [1929] *A High Wind in Jamaica*. New York: New York Review of Books.

Hulit, Lloyd M., and Merle R. Howard

1997 *Born to Talk: An Introduction to Speech and Language Development*, 2nd ed. Needham Heights, Mass.: Allyn and Bacon.

Hull, Valerie

1985 "Breastfeeding, Birth Spacing, and Social Change in Rural Java." Pp. 73–108 in *Breastfeeding, Child Health, and Child Spacing: Cross-Cultural Perspectives*, ed. Valerie Hull and Mayling Simpson. London: Croom Helm.

Hull, Valerie, and Mayling Simpson, eds.

1985 *Breastfeeding, Child Health, and Child Spacing: Cross-Cultural Perspectives*. London: Croom Helm.

Hunt, Nancy Rose

1997 "'Le Bébé en Brousse': European Women, African Birth Spacing, and Colonial Intervention in Breast Feeding in the Belgian Congo." Pp. 187–321 in *Tensions of*

Empire: Colonial Cultures in a Bourgeois World, ed. Frederick Cooper and Ann Stoler. Berkeley: University of California Press.

1999 *A Colonial Lexicon of Birth Ritual, Medicalization, and Mobility in the Congo.* Durham, N.C.: Duke University Press.

Hunziker, Urs A., and Ronald G. Barr

1986 "Increased Carrying Reduces Infant Crying: A Randomized Controlled Trial." *Pediatrics* 77:641–48.

Hutchinson, Sharon

2001 "The Nuer Diaspora and the Rise of 'Segmentary Christianity.'" Paper presented at the annual meeting of the African Studies Association, Houston, November.

Hyatt, Susan

1997 "Outlaw Mothers: Poor Women's Activism and the Regimes of 'the Social.'" Paper presented at the annual meeting of the American Ethnological Society, Seattle, Wash., 7 March.

Hyman, Irwin A.

1997 *The Case against Spanking: How to Discipline Your Child without Hitting.* San Francisco: Jossey-Bass.

Iliffe, John

1995 *Africans: The History of a Continent.* Cambridge: Cambridge University Press.

Inhorn, Marcia

1994 *Quest for Conception: Gender, Infertility, and Egyptian Medical Traditions.* Philadelphia. University of Pennsylvania Press.

1995 *Missing Motherhood: Infertility, Patriarchy, and the Politics of Gender in Egypt.* Philadelphia: University of Pennsylvania Press.

Ireland, Mardy S.

1993 *Reconceiving Women: Separating Motherhood from Female Identity.* New York: Guilford.

Isbell, Billie Jean and Lauris McKee

1980 "Society's Cradle: The Socialisation of Cognition." In *Developmental Psychology and Society,* ed. John Sants. London: Macmillan, pp. 327–364.

Jackson, Deborah

1999 *Three in a Bed: The Benefits of Sharing Your Bed with Your Baby.* London: Bloomsbury Publications.

Jackson, Michael, and Ivan Karp, eds.

1990 *Personhood and Agency: The Experience of Self and Other in African Cultures.* Washington, D.C.: Smithsonian Institution Press.

James, Allison

1998 "From the Child's Point of View: Issues in the Social Construction of Childhood." Pp. 45–65 in *Biosocial Perspectives on Children,* ed. Catherine Panter-Brick. Cambridge: Cambridge University Press.

James, Allison, Chris Jenks, and Alan Prout

1998 *Theorizing Childhood.* Cambridge: Polity Press.

James, Allison, and Alan Prout

1990 "Introduction." Pp. 2–6 in *Constructing and Reconstructing Childhood: Contemporary Issues in the Sociological Study of Childhood,* ed. Allison James and Alan Prout. London: Falmer Press.

James, Wendy

1979 *'Kwanim Pa: The Making of the Uduk People: An Ethnographic Study of Survival in the Sudan-Ethiopian Borderlands.* Oxford: Clarendon/Oxford University Press.

Jansen, Jan

1996 "The Younger Brother and the Stranger in Mande Status Discourse." Pp. 8–34 in *The Younger Brother in Mande: Kinship and Politics in West Africa*, ed. Jan Jansen and Clemens Zobel. Leiden: Research School, Center for Non-Western Studies.

Jedrychowski, Joseph R.

1982 "Anesthesia, Analgesia, and Oral Surgery." Pp. 63–100 in *Pediatric Dentistry*, ed. Thomas K. Berber and Larry S. Luke. Postgraduate Dental Handbook Series, vol. 17. Boston: J. Wright.

Jenkins, Carol, and Peter Heywood

1985 "Ethnopediatrics and Fertility among the Amele of Lowland Papua New Guinea." Pp. 11–34 in *Breastfeeding, Child Health, and Child Spacing: Cross-Cultural Perspectives*, ed. Valerie Hull and Mayling Simpson. London: Croom Helm.

Jing, Jun, ed.

2000 *Feeding China's Little Emperors: Food, Children, and Social Change*. Stanford, Calif.: Stanford University Press.

Johnsen, David C.

1996 "Development and Anomalies of the Teeth." In *Nelson Textbook of Pediatrics*, 15th edition, ed. Richard E. Behrman, Robert M. Kliegman, and Ann M. Arvin. Philadelphia: W. B. Saunders. Available online with a free trial subscription at <http://home.mdconsult.com/das/bookbody/8220419/222/10000.html>.

Johnson, Michelle

2000a "A Passport to *Alijana* (the Next World): Raising Mandinga Children in Lisbon, Portugal." Paper presented at the conference on Mothering in the African Diaspora (Association for Research on Mothering), Toronto, February.

2000b "The View from the Wuro: A Guide to Child Rearing for Fulani Parents." Pp. 171–98 in *A World of Babies: Imagined Childcare Guides for Seven Societies*, ed. Judy DeLoache and Alma Gottlieb. New York: Cambridge University Press.

2001 "On the Road to *Alijana*: Reconfiguring Islam and 'Mandinga-ness' in the 'New' African Diaspora." Paper presented at the annual meeting of the African Studies Association, Houston, Texas (November 15–18).

2002 "Being Mandinga, Being Muslim: Transnational Debates on Personhood and Religious Identity in Guinea-Bissau and Portugal." Ph.D. diss. Department of Anthropology, University of Illinois at Urbana-Champaign.

n.d. "Making Persons or Making Muslims? Transnational Debates on Female Genital Cutting, Mandinga Personhood, and Islam." In *Female "Circumcision" in the World: Constructing and Contesting Transnational Bodies*, ed. Ylva Hernlund, Fuambai Ahmadu, and Bettina Shell-Duncan. Berkeley: University of California Press. Forthcoming.

Jordan, Brigitte

1993 [1978] *Birth in Four Cultures: A Cross-Cultural Investigation of Childbirth in Yucatan, Holland, Sweden, and the United States*, 4th ed. Edited by Robbie Davis-Floyd. Prospect Heights, Ill.: Waveland.

1997 "Authoritative Knowledge and Its Construction." Pp. 55–79 in *Childbirth and Authoritative Knowledge: Cross-Cultural Perspectives*, ed. Robbie E. Davis-Floyd and Carolyn F. Sargent. Berkeley: University of California Press.

Jorgensen, Dan, ed.

1983 *Special Issue: Concepts of Conception: Procreation Ideologies in Papua New Guinea. Mankind* 14 (1).

Journal des Africanistes
2002 *Special Issue: L'Enfant dans le Bassin du Lac Tchad. Journal des Africanistes* 72 (1).

July, Robert W.
1975 *Precolonial Africa: An Economic and Social History.* New York: Charles Scribner's Sons.

Kakar, Sudhir
1981 [1978] *The Inner World: A Psycho-Analytic Study of Childhood and Society in India,* 2nd edition. New York: Oxford University Press.

Karen, Robert
1998 [1994] *Becoming Attached: First Relationships and How They Shape Our Capacity to Love.* Oxford: Oxford University Press.

Kaspin, Deborah
1996 "A Chewa Cosmology of the Body." *American Ethnologist* 23 (3):561–78.

Kearsley, R. B., P. R. Zelazo, Jerome Kagan, and R. Hartmann
1975 "Separation Protest in Day-Care and Home-Reared Infants." *Pediatrics* 55 (2): 171–75.

Kelly, Kenneth G.
1997 "Trade and Commerce: Western African and Western Saharan Trade." Pp. 529–31 in *The Encyclopedia of Precolonial Africa,* ed. Joseph O. Vogel. Lanham, Md.: Altamira, pp. 529–531.

Khare, Ravindra S.
1979 *The Hindu Hearth and Home.* New Delhi: Vikas Publishing House.
———, ed.
1992 *The Eternal Food: Gastronomic Ideas and Experiences of Hindus and Buddhists.* Albany: SUNY Press.

Kilbride, Janet E.
1969 "The Motor Development of Rural Baganda Infants." M.A. thesis. Pennsylvania State University, Division of Individual and Family Studies.

Kilbride, Janet, and Philip L. Kilbride
1975 "Sitting and Smiling Behavior of Baganda Infants: The Influence of Culturally Constituted Experience." *Journal of Cross-Cultural Psychology* 6 (1):88–107.

Kilbride, Philip L.
1980 "Sensorimotor Behavior of Baganda and Samia Infants: A Controlled Comparison." *Journal of Cross-Cultural Psychology* 11 (2):131–52.

Kilbride, Philip L., and Janet E. Kilbride
1983 "Socialization for High Positive Affect between Mother and Infant among the Baganda of Uganda." *Ethos* 11 (4):232–45.
1990 *Changing Family Life in East Africa: Women and Children at Risk.* State College: Pennsylvania State University Press.

Kilbride, Philip L., Collette Suda, and Enos Njeru
2000 *Street Children in Kenya: Voices of Children in Search of a Childhood.* Westport, Conn.: Bergin and Garvey.

Kinney, Anne Behnke, ed.
1995 *Chinese Views of Childhood.* Honolulu: University of Hawai'i Press.

Kirshenblatt-Gimblett, Barbara
1982 "The Cut that Binds: The Western Ashkenazic Torah Binder as Nexus between Circumcision and Torah." Pp. 136–46 in *Celebration: Studies in Festivity and Ritual,* ed. Victor Turner. Washington, D.C.: Smithsonian Institution Press.

Kitzinger, Sheila
1995 "Commentary: Breastfeeding: Biocultural Perspectives." Pp. 385–94 in *Breastfeeding: Biocultural Perspectives,* ed. Patricia Stuart-Macadam and Katherine A. Dettwyler. New York: Aldine de Gruyter.

Klapisch-Zuber, Christiane
1985 [1983] "Blood Parents and Milk Parents: Wet-Nursing in Florence, 1300–1530." Pp. 132–64 in *Women, Family, and Ritual in Renaissance Italy.* Chicago: University of Chicago Press.

Klein, Robert E., M. H. Irwin, P. L. Engle, and Charles Yarbrough
1976 "Malnutrition and Mental Development in Rural Guatemala: An Applied Cross-Cultural Research Study." Pp. 91–119 in *Advances in Cross-Cultural Psychology,* ed. Neil Warren. New York: Academic Press.

Klein, Robert E., Robert E. Lasky, Charles Yarbrough, Jean-Pierre Habicht, and Martha Julia Sellers
1977 "Relationship of Infant/Caretaker Interaction, Social Class, and Nutritional Status to Developmental Test Performance among Guatemalan Infants." Pp. 385–403 in *Culture and Infancy: Variations in the Human Experience,* ed. P. Herbert Leiderman, Steven R. Tulkin, and Anne Rosenfeld. New York: Academic Press.

Klepinger, Linda
1997 "What Happens to the Body? Lessons from Forensic Anthropology." Talk presented to the Department of Anthropology, University of Illinois at Urbana-Champaign, October 10.

Koenig, Michael
1992 *Mortality Reductions from Measles and Tetanus Immunization: A Review of the Evidence.* Washington, D.C.: The World Bank, Policy Research Working Papers, Department of Population and Human Nutrition.

Konner, Melvin
1977a "Evolution of Human Behavior Development." Pp. 69–109 in *Culture and Infancy: Variations in the Human Experience,* ed. P. Herbert Leiderman, Steven R. Tulkin, and Anne Rosenfeld. New York: Academic Press.
1977b "Infancy among the Kalahari Desert San." Pp. 287–328 in *Culture and Infancy: Variations in the Human Experience,* ed. P. Herbert Leiderman, Steven R. Tulkin, and Anne Rosenfeld. New York: Academic Press.

Konner, Melvin, and Carol Worthman
1980 "Nursing Frequency, Gonadal Function, and Birth Spacing among !Kung Hunter-Gatherers." *Science* 207:788–91.

Konno, Mutsuko, et al.
2000 "Iron-Deficiency Anemia Associated with *Helicobacter pylori* Gastritis." *Journal of Pediatric Gastroenterology and Nutrition* 31 (1):52–56.

Korbin, Jill E.
1989 "Fatal Maltreatment by Mothers: A Proposed Framework." *Child Abuse and Neglect* 13 (4):481–89.
1991 "Cross-Cultural Perspectives and Research Directions for the Twenty-First Century." *Child Abuse and Neglect* 15 (Suppl. 1):67–77.

Kostovic, Ivica, et al., eds.
1992 *Neurodevelopment, Aging, and Cognition.* Boston: Birkhüser.

Koubi, Jeannine, and Josiane Massard-Vincent, eds.
1994 *Enfants et sociétés d'Asie du Sud-Est.* Paris: L'Harmattan.

Koven, Seth, and Sonya Michel, eds.

1993 *Mothers of a New World: Maternalist Politics and the Origins of Welfare States.* New York: Routledge.

Kozulin, Alex

1990 *Vygotsky's Psychology: A Biography of Ideas.* Cambridge: Harvard University Press.

Küchler, Susanne, and Walter Melion, eds.

1991 *Images of Memory: On Remembering and Representation.* Washington, D.C.: Smithsonian Institution Press.

La Fontaine, J. S.

1985 *Initiation: Ritual Drama and Secret Knowledge across the World.* Harmondsworth, U.K.: Penguin.

Lakshmi, C. S.

1999 "Bodies Called Women: Some Thoughts on Gender, Ethnicity, and Nation." Pp. 53–88 in *Women, Narration, and Nation,* ed. Selvy Thiruchandran. New Delhi: Vikas Publishing House.

La Leche League International

1981 [1958] *The Womanly Art of Breastfeeding,* 3rd ed. New York: New American Library.

Lallemand, Suzanne

1993 *La circulation de l'enfant en société traditionelle: Prêt, don, échange.* Paris: L'Harmattan.

2002 "Esquisse de la courte histoire de l'anthropologie de l'enfance." *Journal des Africanistes* 71 (1):9–18.

———, ed.

1991 *Grossesse et petite enfance en Afrique de l'Ouest et à Madagascar.* Paris: L'Harmattan.

Lallemand, Suzanne, and Guy LeMoal

1981 "Un petit sujet." *Journal des Africanistes* 51 (1–2):5–21.

———, eds.

1981 [Special issue on childhood]. *Journal des Africanistes* 51 (1–2).

Lamb, Michael E.

1999 "Nonparental Child Care." Pp. 39–55 in *Parenting and Child Development in "Nontraditional" Families,* ed. Michael E. Lamb. Mahwah, N.J.: Lawrence Erlbaum.

———, ed.

1987 *The Father's Role: Cross-Cultural Perspectives.* Hillsdale, N.J.: Lawrence Erlbaum.

1997 *The Role of the Father in Child Development,* 3rd ed. New York: Wiley.

1999 *Parenting and Child Development in "Nontraditional" Families.* Mahwah, N.J.: Lawrence Erlbaum.

Lamb, Michael E., Carl-Philip Hwang, R. D. Ketterlinus, and M. P. Fracasso

1999 "Parent-Child Relationships: Development in the Context of the Family." Pp. 411–450 in *Developmental Psychology: An Advanced Textbook,* 4th edition, ed. Marc H. Bornstein and Michael E. Lamb. Mahwah, N.J.: Lawrence Erlbaum.

Lamb, Michael E., Kathleen J. Sternberg, Carl-Philip Hwang, and Anders G. Broberg, eds.

1992 *Child Care in Context: Cross-Cultural Perspectives.* Hillsdale, N.J.: Lawrence Erlbaum.

Lambert, Bernd

1964 "Fosterage in the Northern Gilbert Islands." *Ethnology* 3:232–58.

1970 "Adoption, Guardianship, and Social Stratification in the Northern Gilbert Islands." Pp. 261–91 in *Adoption in Eastern Oceania,* ed. Vern Carroll. Honolulu: University of Hawaii Press. Monograph of the Association for Social Anthropology in Oceania.

Lambert, Michael

1999 "The Middle Passage, 1999." *Anthropology News* 40 (9):7–8.

Lancaster, Roger N., and Micaela di Leonardo, eds.

1997 *The Gender/Sexuality Reader: Culture, History, Political Economy.* New York: Routledge, 1997.

Lancy, David

1996 *Playing on the Mother-Ground: Cultural Routines for Children's Development.* New York: Guilford.

Langness, Lewis L.

1975 "Margaret Mead and the Study of Socialization." *Ethos* 3 (2):97–112.

Langness, Lewis L., and Gelya Frank

1981 *Lives: An Anthropological Approach to Biography.* Novato, Cal.: Chandler & Sharp Publishers.

Larrain, Jorge

1989 *Theories of Development: Capitalism, Colonialism, and Dependency.* Cambridge, U.K.: Polity Press.

Laye, Camara

1955 [1953] *The Dark Child.* Translated by James Kirkup and Ernest Jones. New York: Farrar, Strauss & Giroux.

Le, Huynh-Nhu

2000 "Never Leave Your Little One Alone: Raising an Ifaluk Child." Pp. 199–220 in *A World of Babies: Imagined Childcare Guides for Seven Societies,* ed. Judy S. De-Loache and Alma Gottlieb. New York: Cambridge University Press.

Leach, Penelope

1983 *Babyhood,* 2nd ed. New York: Knopf.

Leiderman, P. Herbert

1974 "Mothers at Risk: A Potential Consequence of the Hospital Care of the Premature Infant." In *The Child in His Family.* Vol. 3: *Children at Psychiatric Risk,* ed. E. James Anthony and Cyrille Koupernik. International Yearbook for Child Psychiatry and Allied Disciplines. Huntington, N.Y.: R. E. Krieger.

Leiderman, P. Herbert, B. Babu, J. Kagia, H. C. Kraemer, and Gloria F. Leiderman

1973 "African Infant Precocity and Some Social Influences during the First Year." *Nature* 242:247–49.

Leis, Nancy

1982 "The Not-So-Supernatural Power of Ijaw Children." Pp. 151–69 in *African Religious Groups and Beliefs: Papers in Honor of William R. Bascom,* ed. Simon Ottenberg. Berkeley: Folklore Institute.

LeMoal, Guy

1981 "Les activités religieuses des jeunes enfants chez les Bobo." *Journal des Africanistes* 5 (1/2):235–50.

Leopold, Robert S.

1983 "The Shaping of Men and the Making of Metaphors: The Meaning of White Clay in Poro and Sande Initiation Society Rituals." *Anthropology* 7 (2):21–42.

Lepowsky, Maria

1985 "Food Taboos, Malaria, and Dietary Change: Infant Feeding and Cultural Adaptation on a Papua New Guinea Island." *Ecology of Food and Nutrition* 16 (2):105–26.

LeVine, Robert

1973 "Patterns of Personality in Africa." *Ethos* 1:123–52.

1977 "Child Rearing as Cultural Adaptation." Pp. 15–27 in *Culture and Infancy: Variations in the Human Experience,* ed. P. Herbert Leiderman, Steven R. Tulkin, and Anne Rosenfeld. New York: Academic Press.

1984 "Maternal Behavior and Child Development in High-Fertility Populations." *Fertility Determinants Research Notes* 2 (September):1–9.

1987 "Women's Schooling, Patterns of Fertility, and Child Survival." *Educational Researcher* 16 (9):21–27.

1998 "Child Psychology and Anthropology: An Environmental View." Pp. 102–30 in *Biosocial Perspectives on Children,* ed. Catherine Panter-Brick. Cambridge: Cambridge University Press.

LeVine, Robert, et al.

1994 *Child Care and Culture: Lessons from Africa.* New York: Cambridge University Press.

LeVine, Robert A., Patrice M. Miller, and Mary Maxwell West, eds.

1988 *Parental Behavior in Diverse Societies.* San Francisco: Jossey-Bass.

Lévi-Strauss, Claude

1966 [1962] *The Savage Mind.* Chicago: University of Chicago Press.

1997 [1968] "The Culinary Triangle." Pp. 28–35 in *Food and Culture: A Reader,* ed. Carole Counihan and Penny Van Esterik. New York: Routledge.

Lévy-Bruhl, Lucien

1985 [1926] *How Natives Think,* translated by Lilian A. Clare. Princeton, N.J.: Princeton University Press.

Lewin, Ellen

1993 *Lesbian Mothers: Accounts of Gender in American Culture.* Ithaca: Cornell University Press.

Lewin, Ellen, and William Leap, eds.

1996 *Out in the Field: Reflections of Lesbian and Gay Anthropologists.* Urbana: University of Illinois Press.

Lewis, Berwyn

1986 *No Children by Choice.* Ringwood, Victoria, Australia: Penguin.

Lewis, Jane

1980 *The Politics of Motherhood: Child and Maternal Welfare in England, 1900–1939.* Montreal: McGill-Queens University Press.

Lewis, L. A., and L. Berry

1988 *African Environments and Resources.* Boston: Unwin Hyman.

Lewis, Michael, and Leonard A. Rosenblum, eds.

1974 *The Effect of the Infant on Its Caregiver.* New York: John Wiley.

Lewontin, Richard C.

2000 *It Ain't Necessarily So: The Dream of the Human Genome and Other Illusions.* New York: New York Review of Books.

Leys, Colin

1996 *The Rise and Fall of Development Theory.* Bloomington: Indiana University Press.

Lightfoot, Cynthia

1997 *The Culture of Adolescent Risk-Taking.* New York: Guilford.

Litt, C.

1981 "Children's Attachment to Transitional Objects: A Study of Two Pediatric Populations." *American Journal of Orthopsychiatry* 51:131–39.

Little, J., and Bryan, E.
1986 "Congenital Anomalies in Twins." *Seminars in Perinatology* 10 (1):50–64.

Litzinger, Ralph
1995 *The Work of Culture and Memory in Contemporary China.* Durham, N.C.: Asian/ Pacific Studies Institute, Duke University.

Lock, Margaret
1993 "Cultivating the Body: Anthropology and Epistemologies of Bodily Practice and Knowledge." *Annual Review of Anthropology* 22:133–55.

Lowenthal, David
1985 *The Past Is a Foreign Country.* Cambridge: Cambridge University Press.

Lowinsky, Naomi Ruth
1992 *The Motherline: Every Woman's Journey to Find Her Female Roots.* New York: Jeremy P. Tarcher.

Lozoff, B., E. Jimenez, and A. W. Wolf
1991 "Long-Term Developmental Outcome of Infants with Iron Deficiency." *New England Journal of Medicine* 325 (10):687–94.

Lozoff, B., A. W. Wolf, and N. S. Davis
1984 "Cosleeping in Urban Families with Young Children in the United States." *Pediatrics* 74:171–82.

Lugo, Alejandro, and Bill Maurer, eds.
2000 *Gender Matters: Rereading Michelle Z. Rosaldo.* Ann Arbor: University of Michigan Press.

Luhrmann, Tanya M.
1989 *Persuasions of the Witch's Craft: Ritual Magic and Witchcraft in Present-Day England.* Oxford: Basil Blackwell.

Lutz, Catherine
1988 *Unnatural Emotions: Everyday Sentiments on a Micronesian Atoll and Their Challenge to Western Theory.* Chicago: University of Chicago Press.

Lutz, Catherine, and Geoffrey M. White
1986 "The Anthropology of Emotions." *Annual Review of Anthropology* 15:405–36.

MacCormack, Carol
1979 "Sande: The Public Face of a Secret Society." Pp. 27–37 in *The New Religions of Africa,* ed. Bennetta Jules-Rosette. Norwood, N.J.: Ablex.

MacCormack, Carol, and Marilyn Strathern, eds.
1980 *Nature, Culture, and Gender.* Cambridge: Cambridge University Press.

MacGaffey, Wyatt
1986 *Religion and Society in Central Africa: The BaKongo of Lower Zaire.* Chicago: University of Chicago Press.

Maher, Vanessa
1992a "Breast-Feeding and Maternal Depletion: Natural Law or Cultural Arrangements?" Pp. 151–80 in *The Anthropology of Breast-Feeding: Natural Law or Social Construct,* ed. Vanessa Maher. Oxford, U.K.: Berg.

1992b "Breast-Feeding in Cross-Cultural Perspective: Paradoxes and Proposals." Pp. 1–36 in *The Anthropology of Breast-Feeding: Natural Law or Social Construct,* ed. Vanessa Maher. Oxford, U.K.: Berg.

———, ed.
1992 *The Anthropology of Breast-Feeding: Natural Law or Social Construct.* Oxford, U.K.: Berg.

Maiden, Anne Hubbel, and Edie Farwell
  1997 *The Tibetan Art of Parenting: From before Conception through Early Childhood.* Boston: Wisdom Publications.

Malina, Robert M.
  1980 "Biosocial Correlates of Motor Development during Infancy and Early Childhood." Pp. 143–71 in *Social and Biological Predictors of Nutritional Status, Physical Growth, and Neurological Development,* ed. L. S. Greene and F. E. Johnston. New York: Academic Press.

Manalansan, Martin F.
  2003 *Global Divas: Filipino Gay Men in the Diaspora.* Durham: Duke University Press.

Mande Studies
  2001 "The Centenary of Samori Touré." Special section of *Mande Studies* 3.

Manderson, Lenore
  1982 "Bottle Feeding and Ideology in Colonial Malaya: The Production of Change." *International Journal of Health Services* 12 (4):597–616.
  1984 "'These Are Modern Times': Infant Feeding Practices in Peninsular Malaysia." *Social Science and Medicine* 18 (1):47–57.

Mandler, Jean M.
  1998 "Representation." Pp. 225–308 in *Handbook of Child Psychology.* Vol. 2: *Cognition, Perception, and Language,* 5th edition, ed. Deanna Kuhn and Robert S. Siegler. New York: J. Wiley.

Mangelsdorf, Sarah
  1992 "Developmental Changes in Infant-Stranger Interaction." *Infant Behavior and Development* 15:191–208.

Mani, Lata
  1998 *Contentious Traditions: The Debate on Sati in Colonial India.* Berkeley: University of California Press.

Mann, Janet, Thomas Ten Have, James W. Plunkett, and Samuel J. Meisels
  1991 "Time Sampling: A Methodological Critique." *Child Development* 62:227–41.

Manning, Patrick
  1998 *Francophone Sub-Saharan Africa, 1880–1995,* 2nd ed. Cambridge: Cambridge University Press.

Marcus, George E., ed.
  1999 *Critical Anthropology Now: Unexpected Contexts, Shifting Constituencies, Changing Agendas.* Santa Fe, N.M.: School of American Research Press.

Marcus, George E., and Michael M. J. Fischer
  1986 *Anthropology as Cultural Critique: An Experimental Moment in the Human Sciences.* Chicago: University of Chicago Press.

Marsh, Margaret S., and Wanda Ronner
  1996 *The Empty Cradle: Infertility in America from Colonial Times to the Present.* Baltimore: Johns Hopkins University Press.

Marshall, Leslie B.
  1985 *Infant Care and Feeding in the South Pacific.* New York: Gordon and Breach.

Martin, Emily
  1999 "Flexible Survivors." *Anthropology News* 40 (6):5–6.

Marwick, Max
  1968 "Notes on Some Cewa Rituals." *African Studies* 27 (1):3–14.

Masquelier, Adeline

2001 *Prayer Has Spoiled Everything: Possession, Power, and Identity in an Islamic Town of Niger*. Durham, N.C.: Duke University Press.

Mathabane, Mark

1986 *Kaffir Boy: The True Story of a Black Youth's Coming of Age in Apartheid South Africa*. New York: NAL/Dutton.

Mauss, Marcel

1973 [1938] "Techniques of the Body." Translated by Ben Brewster. *Economy and Society* 2 (1):70–87.

1990 [1925] *The Gift: The Form and Reason for Exchange in Archaic Societies*. Translated by W. D. Halls. London: Routledge.

Maust, Marcia Good, Miguel Gumez Pieda, and Robbie Davis-Floyd, eds.

Forthcoming *Midwives in Mexico: Continuity, Controversy, and Change*. Austin: University of Texas Press.

May, Elaine Tyler

1988 *Homeward Bound: American Families and the Cold War*. New York: Basic Books.

McGrew, Roderick E.

1985 "Tetanus, Lockjaw." Pp. 335–36 in *Encyclopedia of Medical History*. New York: McGraw-Hill.

McKenna, James J.

2000 "Cultural Influences on Infant and Childhood Sleep Biology and the Science that Studies It." Pp. 99–130 in *Sleep and Breathing in Children: A Developmental Approach*, ed. Gerald M. Loughlin, John L. Carroll, and Carole L. Marcus. New York: Marcel Dekker.

2001 "Why We Never Ask 'Is It Safe for Infants to Sleep Alone?' Historical Origins of Scientific Bias in the Bedsharing SIDS/SUDI 'Debate.'" *Academy of Breast Feeding Medicine* 7 (4):32, 38.

McKenna, James J., and Nicole J. Bernshaw

1995 "Breastfeeding and Infant-Parent Co-Sleeping as Adaptive Strategies: Are They Protective against SIDS?" Pp. 265–303 in *Breastfeeding: Biocultural Perspectives*, ed. Patricia Stuart-Macadam and Katherine A. Dettwyler. New York: Aldine de Gruyter.

McKenna, James J., Sarah Mosko, and Chris Richard

1999 "Breast-Feeding and Mother-Infant Cosleeping in Relation to SIDS Prevention." Pp. 53–74 in *Evolutionary Medicine*, ed. Wenda Trevathan, N. Smith, and James McKenna. Oxford: Oxford University Press.

McLaren, Dorothy

1985 "Marital Fertility and Lactation, 1570–1720." Pp. 23–53 in *Women in English Society, 1500–1800*, ed. Mary Prior. London: Methuen.

Mead, Margaret

1963 "Socialization and Enculturation." *Current Anthropology* 4 (2):184–207.

Meigs, Anna

1984 *Food, Sex, and Pollution*. New Brunswick, N.J.: Rutgers University Press.

1997 [1988] "Food as a Cultural Construction." Pp. 95–106 in *Food and Culture: A Reader*, ed. Carole Counihan and Penny Van Esterik. New York: Routledge.

Michel, Sonya

1999 *Children's Interests/Mothers' Rights: The Shaping of America's Child Care Policy*. New Haven: Yale University Press.

Mickelson, Roslyn Arlin, ed.

2000 *Children on the Streets of the Americas: Globalization, Homelessness, and Education in the United States, Brazil, and Cuba.* New York: Routledge.

Millard, A. V.

1990 "The Place of the Clock in Pediatric Advice." *Social Science and Medicine* 31 (2): 211–21.

Miller, Andrea B.

2000 "A Longitudinal Analysis of the Role of Spanking in Parenting Practices, Educational Aspirations and Child Self-Esteem." M.S. thesis. University of Arkansas.

Miller, Laura

2003 "Male Beauty Work in Japan." Pp. 37–58 in *Men and Masculinities in Contemporary Japan: Dislocating the Salaryman Doxa,* ed. James Roberson and Nobue Suzuki. New York: Routledge.

Mills, Antonia

2001 "Sacred Land and Coming Back: How Gitxsan and Witsuwit'en Reincarnation Stretches Western Boundaries." *Canadian Journal of Native Studies* 21 (2): 309–31.

Mills, Antonia, and Richard Slobodin, eds.

1994 *Amerindian Rebirth: Reincarnation Belief among North American Indians and Inuit.* Toronto: University of Toronto Press.

Minturn, L., and W. W. Lambert

1964 *Mothers of Six Cultures: Antecedents of Child Rearing.* New York: John Wiley & Sons.

Mintz, Sidney

1985 *Sweetness and Power: The Place of Sugar in Modern History.* New York: Viking.

1996 *Tasting Food, Tasting Freedom: Excursions into Eating, Culture, and the Past.* Boston: Beacon.

Mintz, Sidney, and Christine M. DuBois

2002 "The Anthropology of Food and Eating." *Annual Review of Anthropology* 31:99–119.

Moghadam, Valentine M., ed.

1994 *Gender and National Identity: Women and Politics in Muslim Societies.* London: Zed.

Morell, Carolyn M. Mackelcan

1994 *Unwomanly Conduct: The Challenges of Intentional Childlessness.* New York: Routledge.

Morelli, G. A., B. Rogoff, D. Oppenheim, and D. Goldsmith

1992 "Cultural Variations in Infants' Sleeping Arrangements: Questions of Independence." *Developmental Psychology* 28:604–13.

Morgan, David L.

1988 *Focus Groups as Qualitative Research.* Newbury Park, Calif.: Sage.

Morgan, Lynn M.

1996 "Fetal Relationality in Feminist Philosophy: An Anthropological Critique." *Hypatia* 11 (3):47–70.

1997 "Imagining the Unborn in the Ecuadoran Andes." *Feminist Studies* 23 (2): 323–50.

———, ed.

1999 *Fetal Subjects, Feminist Positions.* Philadelphia: University of Pennsylvania Press.

Morton, Helen

1996 *Becoming Tongan: An Ethnography of Childhood.* Honolulu: University of Hawai'i Press.

Mothering
2000 "The Family Bed: It Is Safe and Here's Why." Special section of *Mothering* 98 (January/February):40–54.

Muller, Mike
1982 *The Health of Nations: A North-South Investigation.* London: Faber and Faber.

Munroe, Ruth H., and Robert L. Munroe
1980 "Infant Experience and Childhood Affect among the Logoli: A Longitudinal Study." *Ethos* 8 (4):295–315.

Myerhoff, Barbara
1980 "Re-membered Lives." *Parabola* 5(1):74–77.
1992 *Remembered Lives: The Work of Ritual, Storytelling, and Growing Older.* Ann Arbor: University of Michigan Press.

Myerhoff, Barbara, and Lynne Littman
1976 *Number Our Days.* 16 mm film. The Public Broadcasting Corporation.

Needham, Rodney, ed.
1973 *Right and Left: Essays on Dual Symbolic Classification.* Chicago: University of Chicago Press.

Nefsky, Marilyn F.
1991 *Stone Houses and Iron Bridges: Tradition and the Place of Women in Contemporary Japan.* Toronto Studies in Religion, vol. 12. New York: Peter Lang.

New, Rebecca Staples
1988 "Parental Goals and Italian Infant Care." Pp. 51–63 in *New Directions for Child Development.* No. 40: *Parental Behavior in Diverse Societies,* ed. Robert A. LeVine, Patrice M. Miller, and Mary Maxwell West. San Francisco: Jossey-Bass.

New, Rebecca Staples, and Amy L. Richman
1996 "Maternal Beliefs and Infant Care Practices in Italy and the United States." Pp. 385–404 in *Parents' Cultural Belief Systems: Their Origins, Expressions, and Consequences,* ed. Sara Harkness and Charles M. Super. New York: Guilford.

Nieuwenhuys, Olga
1996 "The Paradox of Child Labor and Anthropology." *Annual Review of Anthropology* 25:237–51.

Nochlin, Linda
1980 "Léon Frédéric and 'The Stages of the Worker's Life.'" *Arts Magazine* 55 (4): 137–143.
1988 "Morisot's *Wet Nurse:* The Construction of Work and Leisure in Impressionist Painting." Pp. 37–56 in *Women, Art, and Power and Other Essays.* New York: Harper & Row.

Nourse, Jennifer W.
1999 *Conceiving Spirits: Birth Rituals and Contested Identities among Laujé of Indonesia.* Washington, D.C.: Smithsonian Institution Press.

Novack, Alvin H., Beth Mueller, and Hans Ochs
1988 "Umbilical Cord Separation in the Normal Newborn." *American Journal of Diseases of Children* 142:220–23.

Nsamenang, Bame A.
1992 "Early Childhood Care and Education in Cameroon." Pp. 419–39 in *Child Care in Context: Cross-Cultural Perspectives,* ed. Michael E. Lamb et al. Hillsdale, N.J.: Lawrence Erlbaum.

Nyong'o, Anyang'
    1977 "The Articulation of Modes of Production: The Political Economy of Coffee in the Ivory Coast, 1840–1975." Ph.D. diss. University of Chicago, Department of Political Science.

Obbo, Christine
    1979 "Village Strangers in Buganda Society." Pp. 227–241 in *Strangers in African Societies*, ed. William Shack and Elliot Skinner. Berkeley: University of California Press.

Ochs, Elinor
    1988 *Culture and Language Development: Language Acquisition and Language Socialization in a Samoan Village*. Cambridge: Cambridge University Press.

Ochs, Elinor, and Bambi B. Schieffelin
    1984 "Language Acquisition and Socialization: Three Developmental Stories and Their Implications." Pp. 276–320 in *Culture Theory: Essays on Mind, Self, and Emotion*, ed. Richard A. Shweder and Robert A. LeVine. Cambridge: Cambridge University Press.

Okely, Judith, and Helen Callaway, eds.
    1992 *Anthropology and Autobiography*. London: Routledge.

Okri, Ben
    1991 *The Famished Road*. London: Jonathan Cape.

Oloruntimehin, B. Olatunji
    1971 "Franco-Samori Relations 1886–1889: Diplomacy as War." *Journal of the Historical Society of Nigeria* 6 (1):67–92.

Oluwole, Sophie B.
    1992 "Reincarnation: An Issue in African Philosophy?" Pp. 39–54 in *Witchcraft, Reincarnation, and the God-Head*, by Sophie Oluwole. Lagos: Excel.

Ong, Aihwa
    1995 "Postcolonial Nationalism: Women and Retraditionalization in the Islamic Imaginary, Malaysia." Pp. 43–50 in *Feminism, Nationalism, and Militarism*, ed. Constance R. Sutton. Arlington, Va.: Association for Feminist Anthropology/American Anthropological Association.

Ongka, Ongka
    1979 *A Self-Account by a New Guinea Big-Man*. Translated by Andrew J. Strathern. New York: St. Martin's Press.

Orta, Andrew
    2002 "Burying the Past: Locality, Lived History and Death in an Aymara Ritual of Remembrance." *Cultural Anthropology* 17 (4):471–511.

Ortner, Sherry
    1984 "On Theory in Anthropology since the '60s." *Comparative Studies in Society and History* 26 (1):126–66.
    1989–1990 "Gender Hegemonies." *Cultural Critique* 14 (Winter):35–80.
    1996 [1976] "The Virgin and the State." Pp. 43–58 in *Making Gender: The Politics and Erotics of Culture*. Boston: Beacon.

Ortner, Sherry, and Harriet Whitehead
    1981 "Introduction: Accounting for Sexual Meanings." Pp. 1–27 in *Sexual Meanings*, ed. Sherry Ortner and Harriet Whitehead. Cambridge: Cambridge University Press.

Orubu, A. O.
    2001 "The Hereafter in African Traditional Religions." Pp. 153–66 in *African Traditional Religion*, ed. A. O. Orubu. Benin City: Institute of Education, University of Benin.

Ottenberg, Simon

1989 *Boyhood Rituals in an African Society: An Interpretation.* Seattle: University of Washington Press.

1996 *Seeing with Music: The Lives of Three Blind African Musicians.* Seattle: University of Washington Press.

Over, Mead

1984 "Cost-Effective Integration of Immunization and Basic Health Services in Developing Countries: The Problem of Joint Costs." Boston: African Studies Center, African-American Issues Center, Discussion Paper No. 1.

Panter-Brick, Catherine

1992 "Working Mothers in Rural Nepal." Pp. 133–50 in *The Anthropology of Breast-Feeding: Natural Law or Social Construct,* ed. Vanessa Maher. Oxford, U.K.: Berg.

2002 "Street Children, Human Rights, and Public Health: A Critique and Future Directions." *Annual Review of Anthropology* 31:147–71.

Parin, Paul, Fritz Morgenthaler, and Goldy Parin-Matthèy

1980 [1971] *Fear Thy Neighbor as Thyself: Psychoanalysis and Society among the Anyi of West Africa.* Translated by Patricia Klamerth. Chicago: University of Chicago Press.

Parker, Andrew, Mary Russo, Doris Sommer, and Patricia Yaeger, eds.

1992 *Nationalisms and Sexualities.* New York: Routledge.

Parkin, David

1985 "Entitling Evil: Muslim and Non-Muslim in Coastal Kenya." Pp. 224–43 in *The Anthropology of Evil,* ed. David Parkin. Oxford: Basil Blackwell.

Parry, J., and Maurice Bloch, eds.

1989 *Money and the Morality of Exchange.* Cambridge: Cambridge University Press.

Pasetti, M. F., J. Dokmetjian, M. L. Brero, P. V. Eriksson, F. Ferrero, and M. A. Manghi

1997 "Structure and Protective Capacity of Tetanus and Diphtheria Antibodies Produced during Human Pregnancy and Transferred to New-Born." *American Journal of Reproductive Immunology* 37 (3):250–56.

Pateman, Carol

1992 "Equality, Difference, Subordination: The Politics of Motherhood and Women's Citizenship." Pp. 17–31 in *Beyond Equality and Difference: Citizenship, Feminist Politics, and Female Subjectivity,* ed. Gisela Bock and Susan James. London: Routledge.

Pauketat, Timothy R.

2001 "A New Tradition in Archaeology." Pp. 1–16 in *The Archaeology of Traditions: Agency and History before and after Columbus,* ed. Timothy R. Pauketat. Gainesville: University Press of Florida.

Paul, Diane B.

1998 *The Politics of Heredity: Essays on Eugenics, Biomedicine, and the Nature-Nurture Debate.* Albany: State University of New York Press.

Peacock, James

1973 *Indonesia: An Anthropological Perspective.* Pacific Palisades, Calif.: Goodyear Publishing.

Perry, Ruth

1992 [1991] "Colonizing the Breast: Sexuality and Maternity in Eighteenth-Century England." *Eighteenth-Century Life* 16 (February):185–213. Originally published in the *Journal of the History of Sexuality* 2 (1991): 204–34.

Person, Yves
  1968 *Samori: Une révolution dyula.* Vols. 1 and 2. Dakar: L'Institut fondamental d'Afrique Noire, Mémoires de l'I.F.A.N. 80.
  1975 *Samori: Une révolution dyula.* Vol. 3. Dakar: L'Institut fondamental d'Afrique Noire, Mémoires de l'I.F.A.N. 89.
  1979 "Samori and Islam." Pp. 259–77 in *Studies in West African Islamic History,* ed. John R. Willis. London: F. Cass.

Peters, Elizabeth
  1995 "The Benefits of Teaching a Course on Infancy." *General Anthropology* 2 (1):14–15.

Philips, Ruth
  1995 *Representing Woman: Sande Masquerades of the Mende of Sierra Leone.* Los Angeles: UCLA Fowler Museum of Cultural History.

Pinker, S.
  1995 *The Language Instinct.* New York: William Morrow.

Piot, Charles
  1999 *Remotely Global: Village Modernity in West Africa.* Chicago: University of Chicago Press.

Plotkin, Susan L., and Stanley A. Plotkin
  1994 "A Short History of Vaccination." Pp. 1–11 in *Vaccines,* 2nd edition, ed. Stanley A. Plotkin and Edward A. Mortimer Jr. Philadelphia: W. B. Saunders/Harcourt Brace.

Pollitt, Ernesto
  1997 "Iron Deficiency and Cognitive Function." *Annual Review of Nutrition* 13:521–37.

Pollitt, Katha
  1993 [1992] "Are Women Morally Superior to Men? Debunking 'Difference' Feminism." *Utne Reader* (September/October):101–109.

Poole, Fitz-John Porter
  1985 "Coming into Being: Cultural Images of Infants in Bimin-Kuskusmin Folk Psychology." Pp. 183–242 in *Person, Self, and Experience,* ed. G. White and J. Kirkpatrick. Berkeley: University of California Press.

Popkin, Barry M., Tamar Lasky, Deborah Spicer, and Monica E. Yamamota
  1986 *The Infant-Feeding Triad: Infant, Mother, and Household.* New York: Gordon and Breach.

Population Concern
  1998 *The Population and Development Database.* University of Nottingham. CD-ROM.

Powers, William F., and John L. Kiely
  1994 "The Risks Confronting Twins: A National Perspective." *American Journal of Obstetrics and Gynecology* 170 (2):456–61.

Punch, Samantha
  2002 "Research with Children: The Same or Different from Research with Adults?" *Childhood* 9 (3):321–41.

Quandt, Sara A.
  1995 "Sociocultural Aspects of the Lactation Process." Pp. 127–43 in *Breastfeeding: Biocultural Perspectives,* ed. Patricia Stuart-Macadam and Katherine A. Dettwyler. New York: Aldine de Gruyter.

Radin, Paul

1957 [1927] *Primitive Man as Philosopher,* 2nd ed. New York: Dover.

Ragoné, Helena

1994 *Surrogate Motherhood: Conception in the Heart.* Boulder: Westview.

Rajadhon, Phya Anuman

1965 "Customs Connected with Birth and the Rearing of Children." Pp. 115–204 in *Southeast Asian Birth Customs: Three Studies in Human Reproduction,* by Donn V. Hart, Phya Anuman Rajadhon, and Richard J. Coughlon. New Haven, Conn.: Human Relations Area Files Press.

Rajani, Rakesh, Gillian Mann, and Andrea Ledward, eds.

2000 "Rethinking Childhood: Perspectives on Children's Rights." Special issue, *Cultural Survival Quarterly* 24 (2).

Ram, Kalpana, and Margaret Jolly

1998 *Maternities and Modernities: Colonial and Postcolonial Experiences in Asia and the Pacific.* Cambridge: Cambridge University Press.

Ransel, David L.

2001 *Village Mothers: Three Generations of Change in Russia and Tataria.* Bloomington: Indiana University Press.

Raphael, Dana, and Flora Davis

1985 *Only Mothers Know: Patterns of Infant Feeding in Traditional Cultures.* Westport, Conn.: Greenwood.

Rapp, Rayna

1999 *Testing Women, Testing the Fetus: The Social Impact of Amniocentesis in America.* New York: Routledge.

Rasmussen, Susan

1999 "Making Better 'Scents' in Anthropology: Aroma in Tuareg Sociocultural Systems and the Shaping of Ethnography." *Anthropological Quarterly* 72 (2):55–73.

Ray, Benjamin C.

1999 *African Religions: Symbol, Ritual, and Community,* 2nd ed. Englewood Cliffs, N.J.: Prentice-Hall.

Read, M.

1960 *Children of Their Fathers: Growing Up among the Ngoni of Malawi.* New Haven: Yale University Press.

Reese, Debbie

2000 "A Parenting Manual: With Words of Advice for Puritan Mothers." Pp. 29–54 in *A World of Babies: Imagined Childcare Guides for Seven Societies,* ed. Judy DeLoache and Alma Gottlieb. New York: Cambridge University Press.

Reynolds, Pamela

1996 *Traditional Healers and Childhood in Zimbabwe.* Athens: Ohio University Press.

Rheingold, Harriet L., and Carol O. Eckerman

1973 "Fear of the Stranger: A Critical Examination." Pp. 185–222 in *Advances in Child Development and Behavior,* vol. 8, ed. Hayne W. Reese. New York: Academic Press.

Rich, Adrienne

1976 *Of Woman Born: Motherhood as Experience and Institution.* New York: W. W. Norton.

Richards, Audrey

1956 *Chisungu: A Girls' Initiation Ceremony among the Bemba of Northern Rhodesia.* London: Faber and Faber.

Richards, Barry, ed.

1984 *Capitalism and Infancy: Essays on Psychoanalysis and Politics.* London: Free Association Books; Atlantic Highlands, N.J.: Humanities Press.

Richman, Amy L., Patrice M. Miller, and Margaret Johnson Solomon

1988 "The Socialization of Infants in Suburban Boston." Pp. 65–74 in *New Directions for Child Development. No. 40: Parental Behavior in Diverse Societies,* ed. Robert A. LeVine, Patrice M. Miller, and Mary Maxwell West. San Francisco: Jossey-Bass.

Ridler, Neil B.

1990 "Technological Innovation in Coffee: A Comparative Study of Colombia and Côte d'Ivoire." Pp. 165–74 in *Sustainable Agriculture in Africa.* Proceedings of the Agricultural Association of African Studies Meeting, University of Alberta, Edmonton, May 1987. Trenton, N.J.: Africa World Press.

Riesman, Paul

1977 *Freedom in Fulani Social Life.* Chicago: University of Chicago Press.

1992 *First Find Your Child a Good Mother: The Construction of Self in Two African Communities.* Edited by David L. Szanton, Lila Abu-Lughod, Sharon Hutchinson, Paul Stoller, and Carol Trosset. New Brunswick, N.J.: Rutgers University Press.

Rizzini, Irene, with Andrew Dawes

2001 "Editorial: On Cultural Diversity and Child Adversity." *Childhood* 8 (3):315–21.

Roberts, Mary Nooter, and Allen F. Roberts

1996 "Body Memory. Part I: Defining the Person." Pp. 84–91 in *Memory: Luba Art and the Making of History,* ed. Mary Nooter Roberts and Allen F. Roberts. New York: Museum for African Art.

———, eds.

1996 *Memory: Luba Art and the Making of History.* New York: The Museum for African Arts.

Rodney, Walter

1982 [1972] *How Europe Underdeveloped Africa.* Washington, D.C.: Howard University Press.

Rogers, Susan Carol

1978 "Woman's Place: A Critical Review of Anthropological Theory." *Comparative Studies in Society and History* 20 (January):123–62.

Roiphe, Anne Richardson

1996 *Fruitful: A Real Mother in the Modern World.* New York: Houghton Mifflin.

Rood, Julian I., et al., eds.

1997 *The Clostridia: Molecular Biology and Pathogenesis.* San Diego: Academic Press.

Rook, Judith Pence

1997 *Midwifery and Childbirth in America.* Philadelphia: Temple University Press.

Rosaldo, Michelle Zimbalist

1980 "The Use and Abuse of Anthropology: Reflections on Feminism and Cross-Cultural Understanding." *Signs* 5 (3):389–417.

1984 "Towards an Anthropology of Self and Feeling." Pp. 137–57 in *Culture Theory: Essays on Mind, Self, and Emotion,* ed. Richard A. Shweder and Robert A. LeVine. Cambridge: Cambridge University Press.

Rosaldo, Michelle Zimbalist, and Jane Monnig Atkinson

1975 "Man the Hunter and Woman: Metaphors for the Sexes in Ilongot Magical Spells." Pp. 43–75 in *The Interpretation of Symbolism,* ed. Roy Willis. New York: John Wiley.

Rosaldo, Renato
  1989 *Culture and Truth: The Remaking of Social Analysis.* Boston: Beacon.
Roseberry, William
  1989 *Anthropologies and Histories: Essays in Culture, History, and Political Economy.* New
    Brunswick: Rutgers University Press.
Rosenthal, Robert, and L. Jacobson
  1968 *Pygmalion in the Classroom: Teacher Expectations and Pupils' Intellectual Develop-
    ment.* New York: Holt, Rinehart and Winston.
Rothman, Barbara Katz
  1989 *Recreating Motherhood: Ideology and Technology in a Patriarchal Society.* New York:
    W. W. Norton.
Ruddick, Sara
  1989 *Maternal Thinking: Toward a Politics of Peace.* Boston: Beacon.
Ruf, François, and Thierry Ruf
  1989 "Le café et les risques de l'intensification: Cas de la Côte d'Ivoire et du Togo." In
    Le risque en agriculture, ed. Michel Eldin and Pierre Milleville. Paris: O.R.S.T.O.M.
Ruthenberg, H.
  1980 *Farming Systems in the Tropics.* Oxford: Oxford University Press.
Rwomire, Apollo, ed.
  2001 *African Women and Children: Crisis and Response.* Westport, Conn.: Greenwood.
Ryan, Alan S.
  1997a "Iron-Deficiency Anemia in Infant Development: Implications for Growth, Cogni-
    tive Development, Resistance to Infection, and Iron Supplementation." *Yearbook of
    Physical Anthropology* 40:25–62.
  1997b "The Resurgence of Breastfeeding in the United States." *Pediatrics* 99 (4). Avail-
    able online at <www.pediatrics.org/cgi/content/full/99/4/e12>.
Sahlins, Marshall
  1976 *The Use and Abuse of Biology: An Anthropological Critique of Sociobiology.* Ann
    Arbor: University of Michigan Press.
Saigol, Rubina
  1999 "Homemakers and Homebreakers: The Binary Construction of Women in Muslim
    Nationalism." Pp. 89–135 in *Women, Narration, and Nation,* ed. Selvy Thiruchan-
    dran. New Delhi: Vikas Publishing House.
Salmon, Dena K.
  1996 "Teaching Good Sleep Habits: An Age-by-Age Guide to Helping Your Child Sleep
    through the Night." *Parents* (July):37–44.
Sargent, Carolyn
  1989 *Maternity, Medicine, and Power: Reproductive Decisions in Urban Benin.* Berkeley:
    University of California Press.
Scheper-Hughes, Nancy
  1992 *Death without Weeping: The Violence of Everyday Life in Brazil.* Berkeley: University
    of California Press.
  1995 "The Primacy of the Ethical: Propositions for a Militant Anthropology." *Current
    Anthropology* 36 (3):409–40.
  2001 "Moralizing Rhetorics: The Uses of Human Rights Discourses in the Defense of
    Children." Paper presented at the annual meeting of the American Anthropological
    Association, Washington, D.C., November 30.

————, ed.

1987 *Child Survival: Anthropological Perspectives on the Treatment and Maltreatment of Children.* Boston: D. Reidel.

Scheper-Hughes, Nancy, and Margaret Lock

1987 "The Mindful Body: A Prolegomenon to Future Work in Medical Anthropology." *Medical Anthropology Quarterly* 1 (1):6–14.

Scheper-Hughes, Nancy, and Carolyn Sargent, eds.

1998 *Small Wars: The Cultural Politics of Childhood.* Berkeley: University of California Press.

Schieffelin, Bambi

1990 *The Give and Take of Everyday Life: Language Socialization of Kaluli Children.* Cambridge: Cambridge University Press.

Schieffelin, Bambi, and Elinor Ochs

1986 "Language Socialization." *Annual Review of Anthropology* 15:163–246.

————, eds.

1986 *Language Socialization across Cultures.* Cambridge: Cambridge University Press.

Schlemmer, Bernard, ed.

2000 [1996] *The Exploited Child.* Translated by Philip Dresner. London: Zed.

Schmoll, Pamela G.

1993 "Black Stomachs, Beautiful Stones: Soul-Eating among Hausa in Niger." Pp. 193–220 in *Modernity and Its Malcontents: Ritual and Power in Postcolonial Africa,* ed. Jean Comaroff and John Comaroff. Chicago: University of Chicago Press.

Schneider, David M.

1995 *Schneider on Schneider: The Conversion of the Jews and Other Anthropological Stories.* Edited by Richard Handler. Durham, N.C.: Duke University Press.

Schrijvers, Joke

1985 *Mothers for Life: Motherhood and Marginalization in the North Central Province of Sri Lanka.* Delft, Netherlands: Eburon.

1993 "Motherhood Experienced and Conceptualised: Changing Images in Sri Lanka and the Netherlands." Pp. 143–58 in *Gendered Fields: Women, Men, and Ethnography,* ed. Diane Bell, Pat Caplan, and Wazir Jahan Karim. London: Routledge.

Schütz, Alfred

1944 "The Stranger: An Essay in Social Psychology." *American Journal of Sociology* 49 (6):499–507.

Scott, Janny

2001 "Truths, Half-Truths, and the Census: In Describing Us, the Count Has Its Limits." *The New York Times,* 1 July 2001.

Senchuk, Dennis M.

1991 *Against Instinct: From Biology to Philosophical Psychology.* Philadelphia: Temple University Press.

Seremetakis, C. Nadia

1991 *The Last Word: Women, Death, and Divination in Inner Mani.* Chicago: University of Chicago Press.

Shaw, Rosalind

2002 *Memories of the Slave Trade: Ritual and the Historical Imagination in Sierra Leone.* Chicago: University of Chicago Press.

Shinn, Milicent Washburn
1985 [1900] *The Biography of a Baby*. Reading, Mass.: Addison-Wesley.
Shostak, Marjorie
1981 *Nisa: The Life and Words of a !Kung Woman*. Cambridge: Harvard University Press.
2000 *Return to Nisa*. Cambridge: Harvard University Press.
Shweder, Richard A.
1990 "Cultural Psychology: What Is It?" Pp. 1–43 in *Cultural Psychology: Essays on Comparative Human Development*, ed. J. Stigler, Richard A. Shweder, and Gilbert Herdt. New York: Cambridge University Press.
Shweder, Richard A., and Edmund J. Bourne
1984 "Does the Concept of the Person Vary Cross-Culturally?" Pp. 158–99 in *Culture Theory: Essays on Mind, Self, and Emotion*, ed. Richard A. Shweder and Robert A. LeVine. Cambridge: Cambridge University Press.
Shweder, Richard A., Lene Arnette Jensen, and William C. Goldstein
1995 "Who Sleeps by Whom Revisited: A Method for Extracting the Moral Goods Implicit in Practice." Pp. 21–39 in *Cultural Practices as Contexts for Development*, ed. Jacqueline J. Goodnow, Peggy Miller, and Frank Kessel. San Francisco: Jossey-Bass.
Siegler, Robert, Judy DeLoache, and Nancy Eisenberg
2003 *How Children Develop*. New York: Worth.
Silverman, Helaine
1998 "The Spiritual Lives of Children in the Archaeological Record of Ancient Peru." Lecture presented to the Champaign-Urbana Ministerial Association, Urbana, Ill., May 19.
Simmel, Georg
1950 [1908] "The Stranger." Pp. 402–408 in *The Sociology of Georg Simmel*, trans. Kurt Wolff. Glencoe, Ill.: Free Press.
Skinner, Elliot
1962 "Trade and Markets among the Mossi People." Pp. 237–78 in *Markets in Africa*, ed. Paul Bohannan and George Dalton. Evanston, Ill.: Northwestern University Press.
Small, Meredith
1998 *Our Babies, Ourselves: How Biology and Culture Shape the Way We Parent*. New York: Anchor.
Smiley, Patricia, and Janellen Huttenlocher
1995 "Conceptual Development and the Child's Early Words for Events, Objects, and Persons." Pp. 21–61 in *Beyond Names for Things: Young Children's Acquisition of Verbs*, ed. Michael Tomasello and William E. Merriman. Hillsdale, N.J.: Lawrence E. Erlbaum.
Smith, Linda Tuhiwai
1999 *Decolonizing Methodologies: Research and Indigenous Peoples*. London: Zed.
Smoller, Esther Strauss
1997 *I Can't Remember: Family Stories of Alzheimer's Disease*. Philadelphia: Temple University Press.
Snow, Catherine
1977 "Mothers' Speech Research: From Input to Interaction." Pp. 31–49 in *Talking to Children: Language Input and Acquisition*, ed. Catherine Snow and Charles A. Ferguson. New York: Cambridge University Press.

Snow, Catherine, Akke de Blauw, and Ghislaine van Roosmalen
1979 "Talking and Playing with Babies: The Role of Ideologies of Child-Rearing." Pp. 269–88 in *Before Speech: The Beginning of Interpersonal Communication*, ed. Margaret Bullowa. Cambridge: Cambridge University Press.

Sobo, Elisa J.
1997 [1994] "The Sweetness of Fat: Health, Procreation, and Sociability in Rural Jamaica." Pp. 256–71 in *Food and Culture: A Reader*, ed. Carole Counihan and Penny Van Esterik. New York: Routledge.

Sperber, Dan
1975 [1974] *Rethinking Symbolism*. Translated by Alice L. Morton. Cambridge: Cambridge University Press.

Spock, Benjamin, and Steven J. Parker
1998 [1945] *Dr. Spock's Baby and Child Care*. New York: Pocket Books.

Sroufe, L. Alan
1996 *Emotional Development: The Organization of Emotional Life in the Early Years*. Cambridge: Cambridge University Press.

Sroufe, L. Alan, N. Fox, and V. Pancake
1983 "Attachment and Dependency in Developmental Perspective." *Child Development* 54:1615–27.

Stack, Carol
1996 *Call to Home: African Americans Reclaim the Rural South*. New York: Basic Books.

Stack, Carol, and Linda M. Burton
1994 "Kinscripts: Reflections on Family, Generation, and Culture." Pp. 33–44 in *Mothering: Ideology, Experience, and Agency*, ed. Evelyn Nakano Glenn, Grace Chang, and Linda Rennie Forcey. New York: Routledge.

Stanfield, J. P., and A. Galazka
1984 "Neonatal Tetanus in the World Today." *Bulletin of the World Health Organization* 62:647–69.

Stanislavski, Constantin
1948 [1936] *An Actor Prepares*. Translated by Elizabeth Reynolds Hapgood. New York: Theatre Arts Books.
1977 [1938] *Building a Character*. Translated by Elizabeth Reynolds Hapgood. New York: Theatre Arts Books.

Stansbury, James P., William R. Leonard, and Kathleen M. DeWalt
2000 "Caretakers, Child Care Practices, and Growth Failure in Highland Ecuador." *Medical Anthropology Quarterly* 14 (2):224–41.

Stedman's Illustrated Medical Dictionary
1982 *Stedman's Illustrated Medical Dictionary*, 24th ed. Baltimore: Williams & Wilkins.

Steinberg, Leo
1996 [1983] *The Sexuality of Christ in Renaissance Art and in Modern Oblivion*, 2nd ed. Chicago: University of Chicago Press.

Stephens, Sharon, ed.
1995 *Children and the Politics of Culture*. Princeton, N.J.: Princeton University Press.

Stern, Daniel N.
1985 *The Interpersonal World of the Infant: A View from Psychoanalysis and Developmental Psychology*. New York: Basic Books.
1990 *Diary of a Baby*. New York: Basic Books.

Stoller, Paul

1989a [1986] "The Taste of Ethnographic Things." Pp. 15–34 in *The Taste of Ethnographic Things: The Senses in Anthropology.* Philadelphia: University of Pennsylvania Press.

1989b [1986] *The Taste of Ethnographic Things: The Senses in Anthropology.* Philadelphia: University of Pennsylvania Press.

1996 "Spaces, Places, and Fields: The Politics of West African Trading in New York City's Informal Economy." *American Anthropologist* 98 (4): 776–88.

1997 *Sensuous Scholarship.* Philadelphia: University of Pennsylvania Press.

2002 *Money Has No Smell: The Africanization of New York City.* Chicago: University of Chicago Press.

Stoller, Paul, and Cheryl Olkes

1987 *In Sorcery's Shadow: A Memoir of Apprenticeship among the Songhay of Niger.* Chicago: University of Chicago Press.

Strathern, Andrew J.

1997 *Body Thoughts.* Ann Arbor: University of Michigan Press.

Strathern, Marilyn

1992 *Reproducing the Future: Anthropology, Kinship, and the New Reproductive Technologies.* New York: Routledge.

Stuart-Macadam, Patricia

1995 "Breastfeeding in Prehistory." Pp. 75–99 in *Breastfeeding: Biocultural Perspectives,* ed. Patricia Stuart-Macadam and Katherine A. Dettwyler. New York: Aldine de Gruyter.

Super, Charles

1976 "Environmental Effects on Motor Development: The Case of 'African Infant Precocity.'" *Developmental Medicine and Child Neurology* 18: 561–67.

Super, Charles, et al.

1996 "The Three R's of Dutch Childrearing and the Socialization of Infant Arousal." Pp. 447–66 in *Parents' Cultural Belief Systems: Their Origins, Expressions, and Consequences,* ed. Sara Harkness and Charles M. Super. New York: Guilford.

Super, Charles, and Sara Harkness

1974 "Patterns of Personality in Africa: A Note from the Field." *Ethos* 2:377–81.

1982 "The Infant's Niche in Rural Kenya and Metropolitan America." Pp. 47–56 in *Cross-Cultural Research at Issue,* ed. L. L. Adler. New York: Academic Press.

1986 "The Developmental Niche: A Conceptualization at the Interface of Child and Culture." *International Journal of Behavioral Development* 9 (4):545–69.

———, eds.

1980 *Anthropological Perspectives on Child Development.* San Francisco: Jossey-Bass.

Sussman, George D.

1982 *Selling Mothers' Milk: The Wet-Nursing Business in France: 1715–1914.* Urbana: University of Illinois Press.

Sutton, Constance

1998 "'Motherhood is Powerful': Embodied Knowledge from Evolving Field-Based Experiences." *Anthropology and Humanism* 23 (2):139–45.

Sutton, David

1997 "The Vegetarian Anthropologist." *Anthropology Today* 13 (1):5–8.

2001 *Remembrance of Repasts: An Anthropology of Food and Memory.* Oxford, U.K.: Berg.

Swadener, Beth Blue, with Margaret Kabiru and Anne Njenga
　2000 *Does the Village Still Raise the Child? A Collaborative Study of Changing Child-Rearing and Early Education in Kenya.* Albany: S.U.N.Y. Press.

Swerdlow, Amy
　1993 *Women Strike for Peace: Traditional Motherhood and Radical Politics in the 1960s.* Chicago: University of Chicago Press.

Symon, Brian
　1999 *Silent Nights: Overcoming Sleep Problems in Babies and Children.* New York: Oxford University Press.

Tambiah, Stanley Jeyaraja
　1968 "The Magical Power of Words." *Man* 3 (2):175–208.
　1969 "Animals Are Good to Think and Good to Prohibit." *Ethnology* 7:423–59.

Taylor, Christopher C.
　1992 *Milk, Honey, and Money: Changing Concepts in Rwandan Healing.* Washington, D.C.: Smithsonian Institution Press.

Taylor, Janelle
　1992 "The Public Fetus and the Family Car: From Abortion Politics to a Volvo Advertisement." *Public Culture* 4 (2):67–80.

ter Kuile, Coenrad H. H.
　1987 "The Humid and Subhumid Tropics." Pp. 97–108 in *Accelerating Food Production in Sub-Saharan Africa,* ed. John W. Mellor, Christopher L. Delgado, and Malcolm J. Blackie. Baltimore: Johns Hopkins University Press.

Tetlock, Philip E., and Aaron Belkin, eds.
　1996 *Counterfactual Thought Experiments in World Politics: Logical, Methodological, and Psychological Perspectives.* Princeton, N.J.: Princeton University Press for the Social Science Research Council.

Thevenin, Tine
　1987 *The Family Bed: An Age Old Concept in Childrearing.* New York: Avery Penguin Putnam.

Thoman, Evelyn B.
　1980 "Infant Development Viewed in the Mother-Infant Relationship." Pp. 243–65 in *Fetal and Maternal Medicine,* ed. E. J. Quilligan. New York: John Wiley and Sons.

Thompson, Robert Farris
　1968 "Esthetics in Traditional Africa." *Art News* 66 (6):44–45, 63–66.

Thompson, Ross A., and Susan P. Limber
　1990 "'Social Anxiety' in Infancy: Stranger and Separation Reactions." Pp. 85–137 in *Handbook of Social and Evaluation Anxiety,* ed. Harold Leitenberg. New York: Plenum.

Todaro, Michael P.
　1997 "Urbanization, Unemployment, and Migration in Africa: Theory and Policy." Population Council: Policy Research Division, Working Paper #104. New York: The Population Council.

Tonkin, Elizabeth
　1992 *Narrating Our Pasts: The Social Construction of Oral History.* Cambridge: Cambridge University Press.

Toren, Christina
　n.d.a [1988] "Annotated Bibliography: Recent Studies of Ethnography of Childhood."

Pp. 307–33 in *Acquiring Culture: Cross Cultural Studies in Child Development,* ed. Gustav Jahoda and I. M. Lewis. London: Croom Helm.

n.d.b [1988] "Children's Perceptions of Gender and Hierarchy in Fiji." Pp. 225–70 in *Acquiring Culture: Cross Cultural Studies in Child Development,* ed. Gustav Jahoda and I. M. Lewis. London: Croom Helm.

1993 "Making History: The Significance of Childhood for a Comparative Anthropology of Mind." *Man* 28:461–78.

1999 "Why Children Should Be Central to Anthropological Research." *Etnofoor* 12 (1): 27–38.

Touré, Moriba, and Theophilus Oyeyemi Fadayomi, eds.

1992 *Migrations, Development, and Urbanization Policies in Sub-Saharan Africa.* Dakar: C.O.D.E.S.R.I.A.

Toye, John

1993 *Dilemmas of Development: Reflections of the Counter-Revolution in Development Economics,* 2nd ed. Oxford: Blackwell.

Tremayne, Soraya, ed.

2001 *Managing Reproductive Life: Cross-Cultural Theories in Fertility and Sexuality.* New York: Berghahn.

Tronick, E. Z., Gilda A. Morelli, and S. Winn

1987 "Multiple Caretaking of Efe (Pygmy) Infants." *American Anthropologist* 89 (1): 96–106.

Tsing, Anna

1993 *In the Realm of the Diamond Queen: Marginality in an Out-of-the-Way Place.* Princeton, N.J.: Princeton University Press.

Tulkin, S.

1977 "Social Class Differences in Maternal and Infant Behavior." Pp. 495–537 in *Culture and Infancy: Variations in the Human Experience,* ed. P. Herbert Leiderman, Steven R. Tulkin, and Anne Rosenfeld. New York: Academic Press.

Turner, Victor

1957 *Schism and Continuity in an African Society: A Study of Ndembu Village Life.* Manchester, U.K.: Manchester University Press.

1967 *The Forest of Symbols.* Ithaca: Cornell University Press.

1969 *The Ritual Process: Structure and Anti-Structure.* Chicago: Aldine.

1973 "Symbols in African Rituals." *Science* 179:1100–1105.

1982 [1974] "Liminal to Liminoid, in Play, Flow, Ritual: An Essay in Comparative Symbology." Pp. 20–60 in *From Ritual to Theatre: The Human Seriousness of Play,* by Victor Turner. New York: Performing Arts Journal Publications.

1985 "Conflict in Social Anthropological and Psychoanalytical Theory: Umbanda in Rio de Janeiro." Pp. 119–50 in *On the Edge of the Bush: Anthropology as Experience,* by Victor Turner. Tucson: University of Arizona Press.

Tymowski, Michal

1988 "The Ruling Group in Samori's State: Its Composition and Estimation of Its Number." *Africana Bulletin* 35:43–51.

Uchendu, Victor C.

1965 *The Igbo of Southeast Nigeria.* New York: Holt, Rinehart and Winston.

UNESCO

1988 *Famille, enfant et développement en Afrique.* Paris: UNESCO.

UNICEF
2000 *Statistical Data. Côte d'Ivoire.* New York: Division of Evaluation, Policy, and Planning, UNICEF. Available online at <www.unicef.org/statis/>.

United States Department of State
2001 *Background Notes: Côte d'Ivoire.* U.S. Department of State, Bureau of African Affairs. Available online at <www.state.gov>.

United States Consumer Product Safety Commission
1999 "CPSC Warns against Placing Babies in Adult Beds; Study Finds Sixty-Four Deaths Each Year from Suffocation and Strangulation." Washington, D.C.: Office of Information and Public Affairs. Available online at <www.cpsc.gov/cpscpub/prerel/prhtml99/99175.html>.

Van de Walle, Etienne, and Elisha P. Renne, eds.
2001 *Regulating Menstruation: Beliefs, Practices, Interpretations.* Chicago: University of Chicago Press.

van der Geest, Sjaak
1996 "Grasping the Children's Point of View? An Anthropological Reflection." Pp. 337–46 in *Children, Medicines, and Culture,* ed. Patricia J. Bush et al. New York: Haworth.

Van Esterik, Penny
1989 *Beyond the Breast-Bottle Controversy.* New Brunswick, N.J.: Rutgers University Press.
1995 "The Politics of Breastfeeding: An Advocacy Perspective." Pp. 145–65 in *Breastfeeding: Biocultural Perspectives,* ed. Patricia Stuart-Macadam and Katherine A. Dettwyler. New York: Aldine de Gruyter.
2002 "Contemporary Trends in Infant Feeding Research." *Annual Review of Anthropology* 31:257–78.

Varela, Charles R.
2003 "Biological Structure and Embodied Human in Agency: The Problem of Instinctivism." *Journal for the Theory of Social Behaviour* 33 (1):95–122.

Varela, Charles R., and Rom Harré
1996 "Conflicting Varieties of Realism: Causal Powers and the Problems of Social Structure." *Journal for the Theory of Social Behaviour* 26 (3):313–25.

Veevers, Jean E.
1980 *Childless by Choice.* Toronto: Butterworth.

Viazzi, Pier Paolo, and J. A. Corsini
1997 *The Decline of Infant and Child Mortality: The European Experience, 1750–1990.* Cambridge, Mass.: Martinus Nijhoff.

Vogel, Susan
1980 *Beauty in the Eyes of the Baule.* Philadelphia: Institute for the Study of Human Issues.

Wall, L. Lewis
1996 "The Neglected Epidemic: Maternal Health in the Developing World." *The American Oxonian* 83 (3):113–21.

Wallace, Edwin R. IV
1983 *Freud and Anthropology: A History and Reappraisal.* New York: International Universities Press.

Walter, Tomas, et al.
1989 "Iron Deficiency Anemia: Adverse Effects on Infant Psychomotor Development." *Pediatrics* 84 (1):7–17.

Warren, Carol
   1988 *Gender Issues in Fieldwork.* Beverly Hills, Calif.: Sage.
Warren, Neil, and J. Michael Parkin
   1974 "A Neurological and Behavioral Comparison of African and European Newborns in Uganda." *Child Development* 45:966–71.
Watson, James, ed.
   1997 *Golden Arches East.* Stanford, Calif.: Stanford University Press.
Webster, Wendy
   1998 *Imagining Home: Gender, "Race," and National Identity, 1945–1964.* London: UCL Press/Taylor & Francis Group.
Weiner, Annette
   1978 "The Reproductive Model in Trobriand Society." *Mankind* 11 (3):175–86.
Weiskel, Timothy
   1980 *French Colonial Rule and the Baule Peoples: Resistance and Collaboration, 1889–1911.* Oxford: Oxford University Press.
Weismantel, Mary
   1988 *Food, Gender, and Poverty in the Ecuadorean Andes.* Philadelphia: University of Pennsylvania Press.
Weisner, Thomas S., and R. Gallimore
   1977 "My Brother's Keeper: Child and Sibling Caretaking." *Current Anthropology* 18 (2):169–90.
Weiss, Brad
   1992 "Plastic Teeth Extraction: The Iconography of Haya Gastro-Sexual Affliction." *American Ethnologist* 19 (3):538–52.
   1996 *The Making and Unmaking of the Haya Lived World: Commoditization and Everyday Practice.* Durham, N.C.: Duke University Press.
Werbner, Richard
   1991 *Tears of the Dead: The Social Biography of an African Family.* Washington, D.C.: Smithsonian Institution Press.
———, ed.
   1998 *Memory and the Postcolony: African Anthropology and the Critique of Power.* London: Zed.
Werbner, Richard, and Terence Ranger, eds.
   1996 *Postcolonial Identities in Africa.* London: Zed.
Werker, Janet F.
   1989 "Becoming a Native Listener." *American Scientist* 77:54–59.
Werner, E. E.
   1972 "Infants around the World: Cross-Cultural Studies of Psychomotor Development from Birth to Two Years." *Journal of Cross-Cultural Psychology* 3 (2):111–34.
West, Elliott, and Paula Petrik, eds.
   1992 *Small Worlds: Children and Adolescents in America, 1850–1950.* Lawrence, Kans.: University Press of Kansas.
Whitaker, Elizabeth Dixon
   2000 *Measuring Mamma's Milk: Fascism and the Medicalization of Maternity in Italy.* Ann Arbor: University of Michigan Press.
Whitehead, Tony Larry, and Mary Ellen Conaway, eds.
   1986 *Self, Sex, and Gender in Cross-Cultural Fieldwork.* Urbana: University of Illinois Press.

Whiting, Beatrice, ed.

1963 *Six Cultures: Studies of Child Rearing.* New York: Wiley.

Whiting, Beatrice, and Carolyn Pope Edwards

1988 *Children of Different Worlds: The Formation of Social Behavior.* Cambridge: Harvard University Press.

Whiting, Beatrice, and John W. M. Whiting

1975 *Children of Six Cultures: A Psycho-Cultural Analysis.* Cambridge: Harvard University Press.

Whiting, John W. M.

1977 "A Model for Psychocultural Research." Pp. 29–48 in *Culture and Infancy: Variations in the Human Experience,* ed. P. Herbert Leiderman, Steven R. Tulkin, and Anne Rosenfeld. New York: Academic Press.

Whiting, John W. M., et al.

1963 *Field Guide for a Study of Socialization.* New York: John Wiley.

Whitten, Norman E., Jr., Dorothea Scott Whitten, and Alfonso Chango

1997 "Return of the Yumbo: The Indigenous Caminata from Amazonia to Andean Quito." *American Ethnologist* 24 (2):355–91.

Whyte, Susan Reynolds

1997 *Questioning Misfortune: The Pragmatics of Uncertainty in Eastern Uganda.* Cambridge: Cambridge University Press.

Williams, Bruce T.

1994 *Bambo Jordan: An Anthropological Narrative.* Prospect Heights, Ill.: Waveland.

Williams, Raymond

1981 *The Sociology of Culture.* New York: Schocken.

Williamson, Kay

1997 "Western African Languages in Historical Perspective." Pp. 171–77 in *The Encyclopedia of Precolonial Africa,* ed. Joseph O. Vogel. Lanham, Md.: Altamira.

Williamson, Kay, and Roger Blench

2000 "Niger-Congo." Pp. 11–42 in *African Languages: An Introduction,* ed. Bernd Heine and Derek Nurse. Cambridge: Cambridge University Press.

Wilson, Fred

1986 *Laws and Other Worlds: A Humean Account of Laws and Counterfactuals.* University of Western Ontario Series in Philosophy of Science, vol. 31. Boston: D. Reidel.

Winnicott, D. W.

1986 *Home Is Where We Start From: Essays by a Psychoanalyst,* by D. W. Winnicott. Edited by Clare Winnicott, Ray Shepherd, and Madeleine Davis. New York: W. W. Norton.

1987 *Babies and Their Mothers.* Reading, Mass.: Addison-Wesley.

Wolf, Abraham W., Betsy Lozoff, Sara Latz, and Robert Paludetto

1996 "Parental Theories in the Management of Young Children's Sleep in Japan, Italy, and the United States." Pp. 364–84 in *Parents' Cultural Belief Systems: Their Origins, Expressions, and Consequences,* ed. Sarah Harkness and Charles M. Super. New York: Guilford.

Wolf, Diane, ed.

1996 *Feminist Dilemmas in Fieldwork.* Boulder: Westview.

Wolf, Eric

1982 *Europe and the People without History.* Berkeley: University of California Press.

Wolf, Marjorie

1992 *A Thrice-Told Tale: Feminism, Postmodernism, and Ethnographic Responsibility.* Stanford, Calif.: Stanford University Press.

Woodhead, Martin
 1998 *Children's Perspectives on their Working Lives: A Participatory Study in Bangladesh,*
 Ethiopia, the Philippines, Guatemala, El Salvador, and Nicaragua. Stockholm: Rädda
 Barnen (Swedish Save the Children).

Woolridge, Michael W.
 1995 "Baby-Controlled Breastfeeding: Biocultural Implications." Pp. 217–42 in
 Breastfeeding: Biocultural Perspectives, ed. Patricia Stuart-Macadam and Katherine A.
 Dettwyler. New York: Aldine de Gruyter.

World Bank
 1997 *Country Assistance Review #19422: Côte d'Ivoire.* Operations Evaluation Department, The World Bank Group. Available online at <www.worldbank.org>.

World Health Organization
 1996 *Weekly Epidemiological Record* 16 (19 April): 119 (table 3).

Wray, J. D.
 1991 "Breast-Feeding: An International and Historical Review." Pp. 61–116 in *Infant*
 and Child Nutrition Worldwide: Issues and Perspectives, ed. F. Falkner. Boca Raton,
 Fla.: CRC Press.

Yabilé, Kinimoz René
 1982 "Viability of Selective Agricultural Credit Programs in the Ivory Coast." Ph.D. diss.
 University of Illinois, Department of Agricultural Economics.

Yanagisako, Sylvia, and Jane Collier, eds.
 1987 *Gender and Kinship: Essays toward a Unified Analysis.* Stanford, Calif.: Stanford
 University Press.

Young, Lorraine, and Hazel Barrett
 2001 "Issues of Access and Identity: Adapting Research Methods with Kampala Street
 Children." *Childhood* 8 (3):383–95.

Zahan, Dominique
 1979 [1970] *The Religion, Spirituality, and Thought of Traditional Africa.* Translated
 by Kate Ezra and Lawrence M. Martin. Chicago: University of Chicago Press.

Zaslavsky, Claude
 1973 *Africa Counts: Number and Pattern in African Culture.* Westport, Conn.: Lawrence Hill.

Zeitlin, Marian
 1996 "My Child Is My Crown: Yoruba Parental Theories and Practices in Early Childhood." Pp. 407–27 in *Parents' Cultural Belief Systems: Their Origins, Expressions, and*
 Consequences, ed. Sara Harkness and Charles M. Super. New York: Guilford.

Zeleza, Tiyambe
 1993 *The Modern Economic History of Africa.* Vol. 1: *The Nineteenth Century.* Dakar:
 C.O.D.E.S.R.I.A.

Zerubavel, Eviatar
 1982 "The Standardization of Time: A Sociohistorical Perspective." *American Journal*
 of Sociology 88:1–23.

Note: Italicized page numbers indicate figures.